Sixth Edition

MW01492607

THE TELLER HANDBOOK

Everything a Teller Needs to Know to Succeed

JOAN GERMAN-GRAPES

McGraw-Hill

New York   San Francisco   Washington, D.C.   Auckland   Bogotá
Caracas   Lisbon   London   Madrid   Mexico City   Milan
Montreal   New Delhi   San Juan   Singapore
Sydney   Tokyo   Toronto

Library of Congress Cataloging-in-Publication Data

German-Grapes, Joan.
   The teller's handbook: everything a teller needs to know to succeed
/ Joan German-Grapes. — 6th ed.
     p.   cm.
   New ed. of: Bank teller's handbook / Donald R. German, Joan W. German.
Rev. ed. 1970.
Includes index.
   ISBN 0-7863-1216-5
   1. Bank tellers—Handbooks, manuals, etc. I. German, Donald R. II. Joan W. German.
Bank teller's handbook. II. Title.
HG1615.7.T4G47   1997
332.1′2—dc21   97-3302
                                                       CIP

McGraw-Hill

A Division of The McGraw·Hill Companies

1 2 3 4 5 6 7 8 9 0 DOC/DOC 9 0 2 1 0 9 8 7

ISBN 0-7863-1216-5

The sponsoring editor for this book was Steven Sheehan, the managing editor was Kevin Thornton, the editing supervisor was Donna Namorato, and the production supervisor was Suzanne W. B. Rapcavage. It was set in Times Roman by Judy Brown.

Drawings by Lyle D. Farquhar.

Printed and bound by R. R. Donnelley & Sons Company.

The previous edition of this book was published under the title *The Bank Teller's Handbook,* by IRWIN Professional Publishing.

This publication is designed to provide accurate and authoritative information in regard to the subject matter covered. It is sold with the understanding that neither the author or the publisher is engaged in rendering legal, accounting, or other professional service. If legal advice or other expert assistance is required, the services of a competent professional person should be sought.

> *—From a Declaration of Principles jointly adopted by a Committee*
> *of the American Bar Association and a Committee of Publishers.*

CONTENTS

PREFACE

Your Investment in the Future

Many people think of "investments" strictly as the act of putting away cash in some form for future use. Smart investors, however, don't just put money into some venture or form of savings and forget it. To the contrary, they watch their investments carefully and try to help them grow.

In a very real sense, your career is an investment of your most important asset—your time. When you chose a career as a teller, you made a wise selection of an industry in which to invest that time because it provides many opportunities for education and advancement. What's more, you can take pride in being a teller because your financial institution is important to your community and you are important to it.

But the choice of your career field wasn't all that was involved. As a teller, you have the opportunity to help your investment increase in value every day. Whenever a customer approaches your window, you have a fresh chance to grow in your job, a job that can be as interesting and rewarding as you would like it to be.

Time, like money, can be hidden away and lost . . . or it can be nurtured into growth. The banking business provides the opportunity for growth. Regardless of how long or short a time you have been part of that business, this book is meant to help you along the way. It has been revised and expanded once again to reflect the many recent changes that have taken place as they relate to tellers.

Joan German-Grapes

INTRODUCTION

"Bankability" Still

The first edition of this book introduced a new word to the language—"bankability." It is not in any dictionary. It is a noun, derived from the adjective "bankable," which means "receivable as good at a financial institution," and from the noun "ability," which means the quality of being able to do something.

"Bankability" means being able to do something of high quality. This includes the part financial institutions have played in the past in our society and the part they play now and will play in the future. It also includes the role of each individual within his or her financial institution.

HOW IT ALL BEGAN

Banking is about money. Financial institutions safeguard it, invest it, lend it, transfer it, and otherwise handle it for the benefit of the people and businesses in a community. People need money—not just in the sense of being able to pay bills, but to make things more efficient. Everyone remembers reading about the old barter system under which a farmer, for example, traded chickens for a pair of shoes ... but what happened if the cobbler didn't like chicken? Either the farmer went barefoot or the cobbler ate chicken anyway. Money made things easier. The farmer sold his chickens and used the cash he received to pay for the shoes he needed. And the cobbler bought what he wanted.

Coins

The idea of money originated about 2,700 years ago in Lydia when someone came up with the idea of coins. A coin is a piece of metal, stamped by the authority of a government as a guarantee of its value, that is used as money. Originally, the metal used was one with a value of its own, such as gold, silver, nickel, bronze, or copper. A truly great idea! Instead of barter, a universal medium of exchange. But coins have disadvantages. For one thing, they are inconvenient to carry around. So approximately 350 years ago, paper money— or currency—was invented.

The Origins of Paper Money

Everyone knows that money is important. We use it as a medium of exchange for purchasing goods and services of every description. Few people, however, know that our modern currency got its start because the King of England was broke!

People in many parts of the world once kept their gold and silver in the vault of a "goldsmith," who charged them a fee for the safekeeping. London merchants, however, kept theirs in the Tower of London. About 1640, King Charles I found that his credit was exhausted, so in order to get funds he seized the gold in the Tower of London. This upset the merchants so much that they lent the king £40,000 to get their gold back. And when they got it back, they put it with the goldsmiths, not in the Tower! The goldsmiths were very honest, and the receipts they issued for the deposited funds began to circulate in place of the actual gold. In other words, people were *spending* the receipts while the gold itself stayed locked in the vaults.

Until recently, most of our paper money was simply receipts for gold and silver stored in government vaults, such as the one at Fort Knox. But most of our paper money today is in the form of "Federal Reserve Notes," which are issued by government authorization and backed by the assets of the Federal Reserve Banks.

The value of the enormous amount of goods and services we produce each year, which is so much greater than the amount of gold and silver that would be needed in circulation to pay for them, has caused us to devise new kinds of "money." Checks enable people to "write their own money." Loans from financial institutions are usually credited to the borrower's account and actual cash rarely changes hands. Credit cards, checks, and other devices ease the strain on our money supply.

How Banking Began

Banking actually began before the first coins were minted in Lydia. About 1,000 years before that time, an elaborate system of barter was established in ancient Egypt. And about 4,000 years ago, financial institutions, similar to modern ones, were in existence in Babylon under the supervision of priests in the religious temples. Approximately 1,500 years later, a real bank, called the Igibi, was established in Babylon. It made loans, took deposits, and paid interest on savings.

Our word "bank" is from the Italian word *banca*, which referred to the bench on which money changers counted their coins during the Middle Ages. Banking made possible the giant step from feudalism to our modern-day complex economic systems. Banking serves all types of people in every economy.

American Financial Institutions

Ask anyone where he or she has a checking or savings account or where that person goes to borrow money, and he or she is likely to reply, "I bank at . . ." or "I do my banking at . . ." Dealing with any type of financial institution is commonly referred to as "banking." And there are a variety of such institutions in the United States.

For example, there were 9,528 commercial banks and 1,924 savings institutions in the United States as of the end of December 1996. In addition, 11,392 credit unions were on the banking scene at that time. Banking in America is truly competitive.

In the United States, financial institutions offer depositors a degree of safety of funds never before available. In addition, they finance most home purchases, many automobiles, and other large-ticket expenses for individuals. And business loans make possible much of the production of goods and services that help our economy to grow.

Tellers Are Important

Tellers keep our money moving—and it must move in a viable society! Besides their most important function—that of handling banking transactions—tellers watch out for counterfeits that would dilute the value of money and they segregate mutilated money so that it can be destroyed and replaced. They sort, count, and wrap the billions of bills it takes to keep our economy going.

A teller's job is an important one, requiring honesty, integrity and careful efficiency. People work hard for their money, and it should be treated with care.

A king may never come to you to cash a check or take out a loan, but next time you look at a dollar bill, remember that it all started because a king was broke! And think how far we've come!

"BANKABILITY" AND YOU

Your financial institution, through its many resources and services, has the "bankability" to handle the financial needs of the people and businesses in your community. It is up to you to develop in yourself those skills that give you the "bankability" to be an important part of its service team. Doing so will ensure you of a challenging future in an industry that makes things happen.

Technology

Over the years, financial institutions have led the way in utilizing technological advances as they have become available. By enabling them to provide more services to more people more efficiently, that technology has had an important impact on the industry as a whole and, with it, on the teller's job. Here is a list of just some of the technological advances being used by financial institutions that have had an effect on customer service:

> *Imaging.* In some financial institutions, copies of checks rather than the actual checks are returned to customers. File-folder or document imaging also is able to replace paper files with electronic files. Equipment is even available that is capable of processing checks by capturing and sorting their electronic images.

> *Point-of-sale (POS) terminals.* Customers can use debit cards to make payments in supermarkets, retail stores, and service stations, with the amount spent deducted from their checking accounts.

> *Automated teller machines (ATMs).* Convenient automated teller machines offer customers the opportunity to perform a variety of transactions without relying on person-to-person contact.

> *Interactive video systems.* These self-service machines perform some of the tasks that ATMs do. Using touch-sensitive screens with color graphics and recorded sound, customers can transfer funds between accounts, renew certificates of deposit, order checks, place stop-payment orders, and get information about services.

Bill paying. Customers can pay bills by telephone or have the financial institution pay them automatically on a periodic basis, with the amounts involved deducted from their accounts.

Direct deposit. Instead of having paychecks and Social Security and other government checks, such as tax refunds, sent to recipients, the funds can be deposited directly in each individual's account. This eliminates lost or stolen checks, saves customers from having to make a trip to make the deposit, and gives them immediate access to the funds on the day they're electronically deposited.

Electronic filing of income taxes. Using computers, financial institutions can enable taxpayers to file their returns electronically. The advantages of this service include increased accuracy, since the computers catch omissions and math errors, and quicker receipt of tax refunds. In 1996, 12 million returns were filed electronically, and 2.8 million were filed via touch-tone telephones.

Stored-value, or "smart" cards. Automatic card dispensers issue cards in predetermined amounts. They are used to pay for inexpensive transactions, such as public telephones, public transportation, and vending machines, and for purchases from fast-food restaurants and other participating merchants. At the time of each use, a terminal deducts the amount paid and re-encodes the remaining value on the card. Merchants' daily transactions are transmitted to the financial institution and credited immediately.

Home banking. Touch-tone telephones and telephones with touch screens allow customers to pay bills, transfer money between accounts, check balances, and the like. Other services are also available, such as home-shopping and stock quotation services. In addition, technology exists that enables consumers to handle financial transactions via personal computer or via interactive television, which allows a person to perform the transactions using the TV remote control.

In spite of these and other advances, it's important to keep in mind that tellers are now and will remain an essential part of the banking industry. They will not be replaced by machines any more than nurses or phone company personnel have been replaced because of the technologies in their fields. In the future, however, job emphasis is likely to be focused more on direct customer service rather than on routine transactions, so the career opportunities for tellers will be measurably broadened. This means that a teller who is interested enough in the future to ensure it with a good banking education has a golden career opportunity.

The Human Touch

The conclusion is obvious. As technology makes financial services more and more esoteric, there will be an increasing need for friendly and understanding person-to-person service. The role of the teller will be to make that technology acceptable to customers by providing the human factors that everyone seems to need so much. The teller will be the financial adviser, the listener, the financial friend. This trend has already begun.

The teller of the future will:

- Continue to handle money, which will still be the basic medium of exchange.
- Handle the individual complicated transactions and problems that a computer can't be programmed to handle.
- Spot special customer needs.
- Sell services. Tellers will play an increasingly important role in their financial institutions' direct and personal marketing.

This much is certain—smiling, using names, and saying "thank you," while vital, are no longer enough. The role of the teller has never been as important as it is now. It requires real dedication to giving one-on-one service to others.

CONTENTS OF THIS EDITION

The first edition of *The Teller's Handbook* was published in 1970; and, over the years, it has been revised on a periodic basis as changes have taken place in the banking industry. This time, however, in addition to updating the contents of the book wherever appropriate, it has been expanded in a number of ways:

- Since tellers work in all types of financial institutions throughout the United States, the audience for which this book is intended has been expanded to include those who work in all of them—commercial banks, savings institutions, and credit unions.
- A new chapter has been added titled "How to Get Ahead" (Chapter 6), which includes, among other topics, tips for achieving job success and how to get a promotion.
- A fifth section has been added that deals with selling your institution's services. It includes these chapters:

"Selling is Part of Your Job" (Chapter 28) covers your attitude about selling services, how to make use of your institution's advertising and lobby displays, how to deal with your competition, and the importance of selling benefits.

"Cross-Selling" (Chapter 29) deals with how to spot opportunities to sell more services to your present customers; how to sell checking accounts, savings accounts, loan services, and auto loans; and the importance of the mature market.

"Your Sales Talk" (Chapter 30) explains how to ask for the business, how to close a sale, and ways in which effective teamwork can help to sell your services.

Other subjects that are also included in this expanded edition deal with:

Current regulations, including updated information about the Bank Secrecy Act and the latest CTR and SAR forms, IRA contributions and withdrawals, and changes that relate to savings bonds.

Career information for tellers, including an update on popular business attire and a discussion of casual dress for the office; more child-care information for working parents, especially in relation to home caregivers; tips for using voice mail, time-saving ideas for writing business letters, and how to write effective memos; how to handle customer complaints; and information about mergers and the teller's job.

An update of security information, including more information about driver's licenses, signature verification, security features for checks, counterfeit checks and postal money orders, and shared data among financial institutions. Also included is a description of the latest currency safeguards to prevent counterfeiting, as well as information about Federal Reserve Bank letters and numbers, more things for tellers and merchants to check involving credit cards, additional rules for ATM card security, and information about programs to protect the elderly against cons and frauds.

Information about banking services that has been added includes a section on how to handle split deposits, information about nondeposit investment products, and an update on the direct deposit of Social Security benefits.

The foregoing list is just part of the new information that has been included in this edition. And the entire book was designed for one purpose—to help you develop your "bankability," a task that involves absorbing an ever-changing and expanding body of information that relates to your important work as a teller and as a front-line representative of your financial institution.

THE TELLER'S HANDBOOK

"BANKABILITY" BASICS—
THE TELLER AS A PERSON

Financial institutions are made up of people. People who enjoy successes and suffer failures. People who try to build their businesses and personal lives into meaningful and positive experiences.

Working as a teller means working with many people— other tellers, supervisors, employees from your financial institution's various offices and departments, and, of course, customers. Building your "bankability" starts with the realization that how well you relate to those with whom you spend so much of your time largely determines just how rewarding your working life, and even your personal life, will be.

Thus, chapters in this section deal with the personal side of your job—what it means to be a teller in today's busy society; what it takes to make a success of your career; personal pointers on how to look and feel your best; how to be an effective part of the team; and how to motivate those other people with whom you're in contact every day.

CHAPTER

What Is a Teller?

The original idea on which banking was founded was *safety of funds*. And this is still the basis of our system. Today, under federal or state programs, our financial institutions offer depositor protection through insurance. Their modern vaults are built to withstand robbers, fire, and natural catastrophes. Laws protect the money in these institutions, as do federal, state, and local law enforcement agencies.

Our financial institutions have a tradition of offering safety of funds as the primary benefit to their customers. They are proud of that tradition. They ensure that it will continue by making wise investments of their depositors' money, by efficient and accurate record-keeping, and by exercising care in the handling of direct money transactions. The greatest safeguard depositors have is the caliber of people who work in the industry.

YOUR ROLE AS A TELLER

As a teller, you share the responsibility for the safety of depositors' funds. It is important to know the techniques of modern banking and to apply them to your job. You must act within your institution's policies when cashing checks, paying withdrawals, or making other transactions where funds could be lost. But helping to provide stability is only a part of your job.

As a teller, you are the employee who has the most direct contact with your customers. Some people say the word "teller" comes from the Dutch *tellen,* meaning "to count." But today tellers do more than count. Tellers must accurately perform many different functions, including paying and cashing checks; receiving, counting, strapping, storing, and shipping money; handling mutilated money; accepting deposits, including night and mail deposits; selling traveler's checks and U.S. savings bonds; accepting loan payments; giving customers access to their safe deposit boxes; and participating in automated teller machine (ATM) processing.

As the first employee to be involved in most transactions, it is your responsibility to set the stage for good record-keeping by carefully checking all details. You are responsible for keeping your cash accounted for and secure. And, when you spot a customer who has a financial need, it is also your responsibility to suggest a way in which your institution can fill that need. Finally, as its most frequent representative to your customers, you are largely responsible for your institution's image. You are the person who sets the pace for service, accuracy, efficiency, and goodwill.

HELP FOR YOUR COMMUNITY

As you work behind the window, it's easy to think of your financial institution just in terms of checks, cash, deposits, and withdrawals. Transactions. They're certainly important. But more than that is involved. The next time you go home from work, take a look at your community as you ride or walk through it. Here are just a few of the things you're likely to see:

1. *A new store,* which will employ several people and provide new shopping convenience for local residents, made possible by a construction loan from your financial institution.

2. *A new car* parked in front of someone's home, financed by an auto loan from your institution.

3. *A recent graduate* starting a career made possible by funds saved for education in your savings department.

4. *Workmen modernizing a home* for better living with the job paid for with a home improvement loan from your institution.

5. *A storefront filled with merchandise* purchased with the proceeds of a commercial loan obtained from the office where you work.

And there are even more things you can't see. You can't see the pride a young couple feels as they watch their savings grow to make dreams a reality some day. You can't see the feeling of security people get when they know that their dollars on deposit are safe and efficiently accounted for.

Your financial institution is important to the well-being of your community. In addition to performing valuable services directly for customers, the loans it makes provide jobs, build businesses, raise tax revenues, and, in general, make the area a nicer place in which to live.

Types of Financial Institutions

Ask a layperson what a bank is, and chances are the person will say, "It's an institution that accepts deposits, allows withdrawals in some form, and lends money." Although this is what most people think, it is a simplification. Our banking and financial system is more complicated than this. As a teller, you will hear about the following:

Commercial banks. Despite the word "commercial," these banks don't just deal with businesses. They offer every kind of service to all levels of businesses and individuals. Commercial banks are of two kinds, *national banks,* which are chartered by the federal government, and *state banks,* which are chartered by state governments. Once there were significant differences between these two types of banks, but time and industry regulations have made such differences negligible. Both serve government, businesses, and individuals in important ways. Commercial banks pride themselves on being "full-service banks" in that they can serve the financial needs of many people and companies.

Savings institutions. As of the end of December 1996, there were 1,017 stockholder-owned savings institutions and 907 mutual savings institutions in the United States. The word "mutual" means they have no stockholders and are "owned" by their depositors. Both types include *savings and loan associations (S&Ls), mutual savings banks,* and *cooperative banks.* Sometimes referred to as "thrift institutions," they may be chartered by a state or by the federal government and are heavily involved in making home mortgage loans as well as a full range of other services.

Credit unions. As of the end December 1996, there were 7,152 credit unions in the United States that had been chartered under federal law and 4,240 that had been chartered by a state. Each credit union offers a variety of financial services to its "members"—customers who work for a certain employer, belong to a certain association, or live within a specific geographic area.

Every financial institution has its place in our economy, and you should know a bit about those located in your community. They're your friends—and your competition.

The Financial Institution of Tomorrow

Just stop for a moment and think of the banking services offered today that weren't thought of 20 or even 10 years ago. Think of the impact automation has had on many financial institutions in providing better and more efficient service to their customers. For example, ATMs all across the country offer a variety of services quickly and accurately, even after banking hours, and point-of-sale terminals enable customers to make immediate, automatic payment for their purchases right at the store.

It takes only a little imagination to foresee the future of banking. Try to envision the ways in which our economy will change in the future. Imagine the new products and services that will be available to people. Imagine the financial needs that such economic change will create. Then you'll have an idea of the potential of the banking industry. It will be up to our financial institutions to provide the services necessary to accommodate the changes.

It's fun to speculate. A cashless society? Fly-up windows for hover-craft customers? Credit techniques as yet undreamed of? A vast expansion of financial management services? One thing you can count on is that when a service need arises, our financial institutions will find a way to satisfy it. And as technological advances are made, those institutions will use them.

Where You Fit In

As a teller, you fill an important role. When customers look for safety and efficiency, they look to you. As their savings dollars grow, they have you to thank, in part at least, for helping them. To noncustomers, your services are less directly felt, but they are there. The dollars you receive on deposit are those lent out to build the various parts of the community.

People who work in our financial institutions have a strong feeling of pride in the industry. This is largely because those institutions relate to their communities. They are local, often with local ownership. Unlike the socialized central-banking systems of some countries, they cannot be impersonal because they do business right in the communities where they are owned.

Whether you work for a large institution with community branches or for a small one, be proud of your work and of your employer!

WHAT YOUR FINANCIAL INSTITUTION MEANS TO YOU

One of the primary reasons people work, of course, is to earn money. This isn't their only reason, however; all jobs pay wages. So what makes a person choose

"I realize it's a subcompact, sir, but the bank still insists that you use the fly-up window."

one job over another? Why do some people choose to work as a teller? The reasons are good ones.

Prestige

One important factor that makes a person decide to work in a financial institution is prestige. The very fact that you're eligible for this employment shows that you're a cut above average because financial institutions only hire people who are honest, conscientious, and of good moral character. The invisible "badge of approval" worn by each of these employees gives them prestige.

Group Membership

People are gregarious—they need to be around others and to feel they are part of something important. Banking fills these needs. Your institution, after all, is made up of people. In addition, handling the money needs of the people in the community is certainly important.

Pleasant Work

Helping people financially is also interesting work. Most important of all, it's very useful. As a teller, you know that your job isn't trivial. What's more, financial institutions are clean, comfortable, attractive places in which to work; and desirable conditions help to make interesting work even more pleasant.

Your Career

A financial institution is a good place to work, not just for the time being, but for a permanent career. The salaries and fringe benefits compare favorably with most other industries in the country. So, when you are considering your future, think about making banking your career. If you have already made this career decision, review your actions and see where you stand.

A teller's job is exciting in itself, but it also exposes that individual to many other aspects of the industry. This exposure can help such a person decide what direction he or she would like his or her long-term plans to take. For example:

- A teller who becomes a branch manager has the advantage of experience in dealing with customers across the window.
- A teller who goes into personal loan work brings a fresh customer-oriented attitude into what could otherwise be a cut-and-dried formula business.
- A teller who goes into internal operations knows that that account information isn't just a list of names and numbers, but that it represents *people*.
- A teller's job is a good job to have and a good job to have had if you go into any other area of banking.

Prestige, being part of a nice group of people, pleasant work, and career opportunities are all benefits that will help you determine whether or not you are happy in your work. Every job pays in money . . . but not every job pays in the kind of personal satisfaction that banking does.

2

The Elements of Job Success

A positive, willing attitude is something every teller owes his or her financial institution. Even if only implied, it is actually part of your employment contract. When you were hired, you agreed to do a job, not just to put in time, and that job includes giving cheerful and willing service to customers, giving accurate attention to details, and having a willingness to fit in as a happy member of the office team.

A positive and cheerful attitude is essential because this is the one factor that leads to success in all aspects of personal or business life. People who have this attitude make the most rewarding friendships; they get the quickest promotions on the job; they attract the most companionable spouses; they raise the happiest children; they earn the greatest personal respect; and, in general, they are the happiest and most productive members of the community.

PERSONALITY PLUSES

Some people seem to be born with a certain charisma. However, most popular people are that way because of simple personality pluses that anyone can develop, including:

Feeling well. This means having a feeling of being alive and ready to go. Proper diet, plenty of sleep, and adequate exercise help most people achieve this feeling of physical well-being.

9

Being productive. There is immense satisfaction in knowing that you perform a necessary job in society and that you do it well. This applies both to your work at your financial institution and to outside civic or charitable activities.

Trying to have a happy home life. Think for a moment of the popular people you know. Most or all of them have a happy home life. The reason is simple. When interpersonal relationships are healthy, happiness becomes a habit that carries over from home to office to outside interests.

Understanding others. Taking the time and trouble to see what makes others tick enables you to understand why they do the things they do and to like—or forgive—people for these things.

Liking others. Feeling positive about people is a most important personality trait. People sense it and return the feeling.

Having self-confidence. Knowing who you are and where you're going is a big step in getting others to follow you. People like to associate with those who have pride in themselves.

Liking Your Job

One of the most important ingredients in being successful in your job is liking it. This will also add an enormous plus to your winning personality at work.

Often, it's considered "cool" to be blasé about almost everything by some unfortunate people and very "square" to be enthusiastic, especially about something as basic as a job. Fortunately, successful people are too busy being enthusiastic about their work to pay any attention. There are three steps to take to develop a liking for your job. The first step is to gain enthusiasm, and all this takes is forgetting the idea that there's something wrong with being enthusiastic.

The second step in developing a liking for your job is to have *respect* for it, and this comes from recognizing its importance.

The third step in developing a liking for your job is *understanding* it. If you don't know how your particular work fits into the total picture at your financial institution, it's hard to develop much enthusiasm or respect for it.

How can all of this make you more successful? Consider these benefits:

- You'll be more cheerful and optimistic, and people will enjoy being with you.
- You'll gain the respect of others.
- You'll do a better job because you'll put your best efforts into your work. In turn, this will make you like your job even more.

A Good Sense of Humor

Have you ever noticed that people who are really well liked always seem to have a good sense of humor? This is not to say that they're comedians—office comedians are rarely funny. These people are able to:

Laugh when it is appropriate. When something is funny, laughter is a healthy outlet and makes everyone more cheerful. When someone is embarrassed or humiliated, however, it isn't funny, nor is it appropriate to laugh.

Make others laugh, pleasantly. Making other people laugh takes a very special skill. It means being able to get people to laugh *with* you, not *at* you. Office wit can't be forced; the corny joke-cracking bore isn't funny despite his or her too frequent efforts.

See the humor in situations. When an office situation is funny, laughing at it can take out the sting and make the difficult more bearable.

Laugh at themselves. People who can laugh at themselves are always in control of the situation because they are able to keep it under control with a smile, a pleasant word, or a laugh.

When you have a good sense of humor, it pays dividends. Customers, co-workers, family, and friends will be more receptive to you, and, even more important, you'll like yourself better.

Patience—A Necessary Attribute for Tellers

Dealing with the public in any capacity can be a test of mental endurance. What do you do when you're faced with a person who simply doesn't understand a situation or who may insist that he or she is right when you try to explain? As a teller, having patience is a big personality plus when it comes to customers and co-workers alike. What does it mean to have patience?

Patience means not losing your temper. If you do, you'll only irritate customers, get the rest of the staff worked up, and possibly get yourself overwrought at the same time.

Patience means getting help from someone else when it's needed. Perhaps a customer who is hard to deal with has a favorite teller who can reason with him or her, or perhaps the situation calls for asking the supervisor to step in.

Patience means using tact. Don't assume, for example, that every customer has banking knowledge. Start with the basics in explaining the situation. At the same time, avoid making him or her feel ignorant. Instead, you might say, "I know this can be tricky if you don't do it every day, but . . . " This is also a good approach when explaining something to a co-worker.

Make a resolution to develop a positive, cheerful attitude and to add to your personality pluses, starting today.

ATTENDANCE

It happens to everyone. You wake up in the morning aching all over and with a fever. So, naturally you stay home. It's not part of your job to infect everyone else at work, of course, and in such a condition, you're not going to be much help anyway. On the other hand, every time you miss a day of work, it makes things a bit rough for the other people at the office. You know this from your own experience of doubling up on the work when other tellers stay out.

The problem in missing time revolves around those days when you're not really sick, but when it would be convenient for you to stay out. Perhaps a child isn't feeling well, for example—not sick, which might make it necessary for you to stay home, but just not feeling up to par. Or maybe you're just plain tired; everyone gets that way occasionally. Maybe you have some important personal errands to do, such as seeing your lawyer or going to the dentist. Or perhaps your spouse is at home sick—nothing desperate for which your presence is absolutely required, but feeling just bad enough to make it more convenient if you didn't go to work yourself.

What's the right thing to do in each of these cases? If the problem isn't something that is immediately pressing, discuss it with your supervisor and try to arrange for some time off when things are expected to be slack at the office. It may seem a little difficult to bring yourself to do this; but from your supervisor's standpoint, it beats just having you phone in "sick." On the other hand, in cases in which the decision must be up to you, such as minor family illnesses, temper your judgment with common sense. Remember, you have an obligation to be at work whenever possible. It's easy to turn over and go back to sleep, but if a couple of aspirins might put you on your feet, it's certainly worth a try.

Finally, when you simply must miss time, be sure to let the proper person know as soon as possible. Provisions can then be made to cover your duties if possible.

PUNCTUALITY

One question is bound to appear on any employee evaluation sheet, and that is, "Is he/she punctual?" It's an important question. Yes, if a person is late getting to work in the morning or after lunch, chances are the other employees will come on time and get things rolling. But what would happen, for example, if your office failed to open until 30 minutes after opening time in the morning simply because no one came to work until then?

Causes for Habitual Lateness

"The bus was slow." "I got caught in traffic." "Service was really slow at the restaurant." Excuses like these will be true for everyone once in a while, but when the same person uses them time after time, his or her supervisor is going to start looking for the real reason. Habitual lateness is often caused by:

> *Sleeping too late in the morning.* Oversleeping from staying up too late can get to be a habit. Avoiding the habit of sleeping too late usually requires making a simple adjustment in a person's schedule.
>
> *Dawdling.* The dictionary defines dawdling as a "sluggish semblance of activity." In practice, it means having a second cup of coffee or casually window-shopping on the way back to the office after lunch.
>
> *Last-minute rushing.* Deciding a dress had better be pressed this morning or finding no clean shirt and having to wash one, rushing into a business office to pay a bill so it won't be late, and buying a birthday present at the last minute are all things that could and should have been done before that can make people late for work.

Plan Ahead

Everyone has about the same morning routine: Get up, shower, dress, eat breakfast, leave for work. If you make it a habit to be punctual, you already have these things well planned. If you are frequently late for work, however, stop and take stock. Why are you late . . . really? What steps can you take to better organize your time? What routines can you eliminate in order to save time?

When you've answered these questions, put them into effect with a firm resolution to be punctual every day, even if it does mean missing the late, late show or shopping or paying your bills a little early. Remember, your lateness can make your office shorthanded, and that isn't fair to others.

ON THE JOB

Another element of job success involves the way you handle your job when it comes to dealing effectively with nonroutine situations—whether or not you use sound judgment, for example, when it comes to making a decision, solving a problem, or correcting a mistake. The following tips can help.

How to Make a Decision

As a teller, you are often expected to make decisions. Should you cash this check? How should you handle this complicated transaction? How should you answer this question from a customer? What information should you pass on to your office manager? These steps will help you to make the right decision:

Know all the pertinent facts. People often make wrong decisions by allowing facts that have no bearing on the matter at hand to influence them. When you know all the pertinent facts and carefully discard the unrelated ones, the right choice is often obvious.

Know your financial institution's policy. Sometimes there will be a stated policy that can help you to make up your mind about how to handle something. If you know of one, base your decision on it. If you suspect there may be a policy that applies to the situation, check with your supervisor. Based on laws, banking regulations, and years of experience, such policies are invaluable in guiding you when you must make up your mind.

Check back on your experience. Have you ever faced a similar situation or one that entailed roughly the same principles? If so, use this experience to guide you now.

Reflect on your training and education. What were you taught that can help you to make a decision?

What does your common sense suggest? Though impulsiveness is rarely wise, often we are intuitively guided to make the right decision in a matter. Frequently, plain common sense can help.

Ask a more experienced person for help. Never be hesitant about asking for another opinion, especially if your decision involves the assets of your financial institution.

Solving Problems

Because you are human, you are sometimes going to have personal problems. Perhaps you have had an argument with someone who is close to you. Or maybe you're worried because someone is sick. Or financial problems may arise. Or maybe you're not feeling up to par. Whatever the case, problems of this nature can affect your work by making you irritable with customers and co-workers, by making you careless, by contributing to absences or lateness, or by turning others against you because you're a chronic complainer.

The first step in solving a problem is to determine how big it really is. Just ask yourself, "If the worst possible thing happened, how bad would it be?" Often you'll find your problem isn't as big as you thought, and at this point needless worrying can end. Next, break the problem down into small segments and see if you can solve them one at a time. They are much easier to deal with this way. Finally, realize that letting your work slip will only add another problem, not help to solve the first one. Sometimes letting yourself get involved in your work can even help you to forget your troubles for a time.

If a problem gets big enough to prey on your mind at work, you should talk to your supervisor about it. If it's a personal emotional problem or an embarrassing physical one, talking about it may be difficult, but you should try to do it anyway. Chances are, he or she won't be shocked because it won't be the first time an employee has discussed such a problem. Second, you needn't go into every small detail. Just knowing you *have* a problem will let your supervisor realize that when your mind is somewhere else it's not because you've lost interest in your job. In addition, when you share your problem, you'll often find you've gained an understanding friend.

Business Ethics

The key to the success of our banking system and to yours in your job as a teller is *integrity*. In these days when political and business scandals are far too common, the old-fashioned virtue of honesty is highly desirable. And the tellers in our financial institutions are tops in honesty and integrity.

But values are elusive. Where do you draw the line between what is acceptable and what isn't? For example:

- Few employers will object to a teller making a photocopy of a document for his or her scout troop, but making 100 copies is saddling the financial institution with a significant expense.
- Most employers permit an occasional personal phone call, but making a number of toll calls is wrong.
- Accepting a small gift from a grateful customer is a friendly thing to do, but accepting a large gift that might be construed as a bribe for future favors is unethical. Of course, accepting a gift of cash, no matter how small the amount, is unacceptable.

Use your sound judgment when it comes to these types of situations involving your job.

When You Must Do an Unpleasant Job

What's *your* idea of an unpleasant job? Counting a lot of coins when lines are long and customers are impatient? Coping with a grouchy customer? Making up complicated payrolls? Filling in on a certain window? When you are faced with doing something you'd rather not do, keep these points in mind:

- Your prejudice against doing a certain thing may just be in your mind.
- People sometimes dislike doing things they don't do well. If you're assigned a task for which you lack expertise, consider it a chance to learn rather than a time to gripe.
- Even if the task is unpleasant, if you tackle it willingly and cheer- fully, the time will pass more quickly and agreeably. You'll do a bet- ter job. Then, when it *is* finished, you'll be ready to face the world with a smile instead of a tired frown.

When You Make a Mistake

Everyone makes mistakes from time to time, errors in judgment as well as errors involving transactions. People who get things done sometimes do them wrong, even experts. When you do a thing right, as you usually will, there's no problem. When you make a mistake, however, the way you correct it is what counts.

A teller once received a telephone call in which the caller, without any introductory remarks, abruptly asked, "Tell me, does your bank make mis- takes?" Without a moment's hesitation, she replied, "Why, of course. And all our pencils have erasers to prove it! But we take every precaution to avoid them, and if we do make one, we correct it as quickly as possible!" The caller, who had been told by his own financial institution that a mistake on his ac- count had to have been his because they never made any errors, closed several large accounts and transferred his funds to the one that "employed human beings."

If you make an error and someone calls it to your attention, whether he or she is another teller, your supervisor, or a customer, try to handle it like this:

Be cheerful. If you did make an error, it was unintentional, so don't act as though the world is coming to an end.

Acknowledge it. Find out what you did wrong and admit that you made a mistake.

Apologize. Gracefully and quickly. Don't make excuses or go into long explanations of why it happened. That only makes too much of a small thing.

Correct it. Take immediate steps to set things right again. Delays may only mean added mistakes or hurt feelings.

Say thank you. Letting the other person know you appreciate his or her telling you about your error makes you a big person. It also lets the other person know you haven't taken offense.

Remember it. The next time you're involved in a similar situation, remember to be extra careful not to make the same mistake again.

KEEP LEARNING

Another important element of your success on the job—and in your career advancement—is continuing to gain more knowledge about your work and about banking in general. There are two ways to do this—by learning on the job and by going back to school.

Learning on the Job

The next time you get a moment free at your window, look around you. Perhaps the office manager is taking an application for an auto loan. Another teller may be issuing traveler's checks. The assistant manager may be writing a letter about a certificate of deposit. There are all sorts of things going on that don't normally concern you, but from which you can learn.

Typically, a teller is involved with accepting deposits, paying out withdrawals, cashing checks, and performing functions associated with these routines. These are of vital importance, but the other banking functions are too. So, when you look around, resolve to learn how auto loans really work . . . not just that your institution lends people money to buy cars. Ask the manager to explain them to you when you both have a moment free. By the same token, ask others who do certain jobs to explain them to you.

This doesn't mean that you must be able to put on an auto loan or issue a certificate of deposit. It simply means that a teller who understands the broad scope of banking functions is going to be a real professional. Opportunities to learn are around you every day.

Going Back to School

The American Institute of Banking (AIB), a part of the American Bankers Association, directs the largest industry-sponsored adult education program in the world. Chapters all over America offer courses that range from basic principles of banking and bank operations to graduate courses in theory.

Financial institutions vary on policies regarding continuing education, so check with your manager. If possible, give serious thought to taking a course

"Bill, here's something that will help you to avoid making errors."

or two at AIB or some other accredited school. Advanced education not only provides valuable training, it also offers the opportunity to meet people from other financial institutions. Banking is almost unique as an industry in that, while individual institutions are very competitive, their employees are extremely friendly with each other and are most cooperative in supporting civic and industry concerns.

Look over the courses that are offered at schools and discuss their advantages with your supervisor or your human resources department. Take the most valuable ones for your own development, but don't try to take too many at once. Going back to school should be fun, not drudgery!

BE A PROFESSIONAL

The definition of a professional is the opposite of an amateur. An amateur is someone who follows a pursuit without proficiency or a professional purpose—a dabbler. Being a true professional requires caring about your work and trying to advance at your job. Here is what it takes:

Know your job. In addition to being accurate and efficient, you should be vitally interested in serving the people who come to you each day. In order to do this, you must learn what your services are and how they can fill the needs of your customers. Then you can give your customers the benefit of your knowledge by helping them use these services whenever the opportunity arises.

Join your team. Because you don't work alone, you can't grow as an individual unless you cooperate with your fellow employees. Getting along pleasantly with others will help get routine work done better and faster, and your personal reputation can only be enhanced when you're known for pitching in and helping others.

Learn more about banking. When the chance for special training comes up, try to become involved with it. A real professional doesn't shy away from studying his or her field. On the contrary, he or she actually enjoys learning more about it.

Treat the customers properly. Courtesy alone isn't enough. The thing that makes a person really stand out is his or her willingness to give *extra* service. This is the mark of the true professional!

JOB LOYALTY

When you applied for your job, you made a commitment to be loyal to your financial institution. Besides having integrity and being honest, this means taking pride in your job and in your institution and developing a sense of belonging. Such loyalty is not old-fashioned or degrading, nor does it mean that you have to be a doormat or a bootlicker.

Showing Your Loyalty

What does being loyal to your financial institution require of you? As stated earlier, it means that you should be at work on time, be ready to do your job, and have a cheerful, positive attitude. In addition, you should:

- Avoid disparaging the institution, its policies, or your fellow employees to a customer. If you have a complaint, tell your supervisor, who can at least address the problem.
- Present the institution, its policies, and your fellow employees in a favorable light or, if in some instances you can't do so in good conscience, don't discuss them at all.

- Be a booster. Don't just *say* nice things; make things that way by correcting areas within your responsibility that need correction.
- Give new ideas and policies a chance without negatively prejudging them.
- Refuse to pass on rumors. If you hear something that disturbs you, question it at once by going directly to someone who will know the answer.

What Will You Get in Return?

Loyalty is something we need as individuals, as much if not more than those to whom we give it. Your employer owes you loyalty as well, including:

- A competitive salary and benefits commensurate with your job and responsibilities.
- A pleasant place in which to work and the tools with which to do your job.
- Necessary information. If, for example, a change will affect you or your work in any way, you should be told about it in time to assimilate that information into your routine.
- Support when you have problems. This may mean a supervisor offering help when you're faced with illness, a death in the family, or some other personal difficulty.

What's more, by having loyalty for your financial institution, you will also get:

- A stronger sense of belonging to an important part of your community.
- The trust and respect of your co-workers and superiors.
- Increased job satisfaction and thus increased self-satisfaction.
- A better chance for promotion or advancement.
- A happier life with a more pleasant outlook.

Compare your place of employment to a professional sports team. Its players may come from all over, yet when they sign up to play for that team, they're expected to work for and support it. The same is true for you when it comes to your financial institution.

3
CHAPTER

Personal Pointers

Successful tellers convey an image of integrity and authority to their customers and are respected by their fellow employees. At the same time, because banking is a prestigious industry, tellers enjoy dealing with nice people on a close person-to-person basis every day. Achieving this positive image and maintaining favorable personal contacts make effective grooming an important part of every teller's job.

FEELING WELL

In order to actually *be* successful, a person must *feel* that way. An important part of that feeling comes from having a sense of physical well-being, which helps the successful person to be lively, cheerful, and pleasant to be around. In other words, he or she is glad to be alive and shows it. The following pointers can help.

Your Morning Diet

Nowadays many people are weight conscious. And for good reason. As various health experts have testified, being overweight is a serious problem. The answer to weight control, however, is not to have a skimpy breakfast, perhaps followed by no lunch at all. Whether you're trying to watch your weight or are just in too much of a hurry to eat, such a diet will sooner or later make you sick. Even in the short run, if you try to exist on such fare, you will become irritable and tired and will soon cease to be an asset to your financial institution. As a matter of fact, according to the Advertising Council, people who come to work without having had a good breakfast aren't very efficient in their jobs, yet its findings show that almost half the work force in this country goes to the shop or office with an inadequate breakfast.

A donut and coffee are not a good breakfast. Eating too much sugar can actually overactivate your insulin and make your blood sugar drop. For an energy-filled breakfast, a combination of protein and complex carbohydrates is needed. Thus, every good breakfast should include protein food, such as low-fat cottage cheese or yogurt, balanced with fruit or juice and cereal or whole wheat toast or muffins. If you haven't been eating a get-up-and-go meal in the mornings, you'll find that a solid breakfast will make you feel better all day long. If you stick to a reasonable number of calories, such a meal can help you to lose weight, because if you fast during the day, you may be tempted to give in at night and eat fattening food before bedtime, when the pounds really go on.

Exercise Each Day

Just as many people eat too little protein and too much fattening food, so do most people get too little healthful exercise. Bowling is fun, but a once-a-week stint isn't the kind of exercise a person needs to keep in shape. A good daily exercise program is needed to stay toned and to feel well.

Your diet and exercise programs should start with a trip to your family doctor, just to be sure that it's okay to do what you have in mind. In addition, there are many good books on exercise and nutrition available in paperback editions. Following the advice of experts and the doctor who knows you is the best way to achieve success when exercising.

Here are a few general observations about exercise:

- Jogging, rope-skipping, or other vigorous exercise should not be attempted without a go-ahead from a physician.
- Isometrics are easy to do and produce good results but do not exercise the cardiovascular system.
- Taking a long daily walk is an excellent foundation for any exercise program. Along with isometrics, walking makes up a good keep-in-shape program. Leaving 15 minutes earlier for work and walking part way to the office is an easy way to work a daily walk into your routine. Chances are, if you do this, you'll arrive at work in a good humor and feeling better, too.

Feeling well because you're in good condition—thanks to proper diet, healthful exercise, and a good night's rest before starting your workday— should be part of your personal program for feeling and looking successful at work, at home, and anywhere you go.

GROOMING FOR THE OFFICE

In the marketing industry, *packaging* has become very important in the success of a product. A package serves to protect and to advertise the product. Manufacturers pay a great deal for packaging to encourage customers to buy their wares.

Like it or not, you, too, are offering a product—*yourself.* Those on whom you rely for acceptance of that package are your supervisors, your fellow employees, and your customers—everyone you know or deal with at work. And, like a smart manufacturer, you should do your best to package your product as effectively as possible, which means getting right down to the nitty-gritty in grooming. How should you dress to present yourself and your financial institution in the best way possible?

What to Wear

Obviously, you should wear clothes that are neat, clean, pressed, and in good condition, as well as those that bring out your best points and play down your weak ones. Those are the basics, which, once noted, can be taken for granted. In addition, there are guidelines that successful people follow to be sure they get the most mileage out of what they wear. Both men and women should follow these tips:

Remember where you work. You handle people's money. People expect you to look responsible.

Consider the situation in which a bank president passed a young clerk in the hall and blanched. She was wearing a T-shirt with the slogan, "I'm a virgin," near the top—and printed near the bottom were the words, "This is an old T-shirt." The bank president had the girl fired at once. He may have overreacted, but the clerk certainly should at least have been told that an office is a place to work, not play, a place where customers will judge your financial institution by how you dress, as well as by how you act. Among other things, this means not wearing jeans or skirts made of faded denim, avoiding the no-bra look and see-through blouses, and wearing something more appropriate than a T-shirt, slogan or no slogan.

Dress for your geographical area. Local customs vary, so what is sometimes considered proper dress in Honolulu might not be acceptable in Boston. Customs in the southwest tend to be more relaxed than in the northeast.

Be sure your clothes fit properly. Although you don't need a large expensive wardrobe for work, you should try to avoid cheapening an outfit through poor fit.

Wear clothes that keep a fresh look. Try to look as well-groomed at 3 P.M. as you did at 9 A.M. Permanent-press shirts, blouses, and dresses tend to stay wrinkle-free and can easily be washed and tumble-dried as often as necessary.

Don't be overly stylish. If most women dressed like high-fashion models or men like their male counterparts, they would have problems of acceptance. However, the latest color schemes are desirable if they're not too extreme. A good general rule of thumb is to take the more conservative approach if you are in doubt about what to wear to work. At the same time, try not to wear clothes that are out of style. In most places, men can now wear loafers and brighter colors than they once could. Long hair is not appropriate for men, but neat beards and moustaches are generally accepted.

Dress one job up. If you expect to climb the career ladder, show it in your clothing. Dress the way your boss dresses . . . or the way he or she ought to dress.

Don't look too casual on dress-down days. Some financial institutions allow their employees to wear casual clothing to the office on a periodic basis. If and when you do this, be sure to maintain a fresh, neat appearance and to avoid appearing overly casual or untidy.

Special Tips for Men

You can't go wrong with a white shirt and tie, but be sure that the cut of both is up-to-date.

The big questions are: Should you wear a suit or will a pair of slacks with a jacket do? Is wearing a shirt without a jacket or tie all right, and should sleeves be long or short? The answers depend on local custom. Watch and note what successful men on the way up wear, not just those who work where you do, but those in other businesses as well.

Lean toward the conservative when it comes to colors. Charcoal grey, navy blue, and other subdued colors work well and form a good basic background for a variety of shirts and ties. Leave the colorful plaids for recreational use. It's also best to avoid wearing chains or other such jewelry to work as well as strong aftershave or cologne.

Special Tips for Women

According to surveys, the most acceptable blouse for women in business to wear is a tailored white one. Pastel colors are also appropriate. Although brighter colors are more acceptable for business than they once were, it's best to avoid extremes, such as loud colors and bold prints.

Should you wear slacks or a skirt? A suit or a dress? Current fashion for successful businesswomen tends to favor either a suit with a skirt or a blazer with a contrasting skirt. However, an increasing number of businesswomen are now wearing trousers to the office instead of skirts. Dressy, tailored pants and jackets are popular, especially among younger women. Of course, your institution's dress code will determine what is acceptable. If your dress code is very strict, you might consider wearing tailored dresses, especially shirtdresses or those with matching jackets. The latter will give you some flexibility in working comfort because the jacket can be removed as needed. The best colors for both suits and dresses are greys and blues. Bright prints, especially florals, are not considered appropriate for the banking industry.

Women should avoid extremes in jewelry, and it's usually best to skip perfume or, at least, to keep it subtle.

The idea for both men and women in business is to look attractive, businesslike, and efficient—but not especially sexy.

Special Tips for Hot and Cold Weather

Financial institutions and other businesses all over the country are trying to cut down on energy costs. Thermostats are being set lower during the cold months and higher during the hot ones, only essential lights are being used, and office machines are being turned off when not in use.

The cooler winter temperature inside your office shouldn't be a problem for customers who come in dressed for the outdoors, but it could be uncomfortable for the employees if they don't dress suitably. Here are some suggestions for dressing more warmly in the wintertime:

- Wear heavier materials. Wool and heavy-weight, washable synthetics in tweeds and knits are both warm and durable.
- Wear long sleeves. There is an endless variety of fashions of this type on the market.

- If you're a woman, avoid very short skirts. In fact, you might consider wearing pantsuits or slacks. You will have to check on whether they are acceptable where you work. Slacks are undoubtedly warmer than skirts, and they are comfortable. Of course, some trousers, such as jeans, would be completely out of place. However, pantsuits or blazers and slacks look very much like dresses from the waist up, and, ranging in sizes to fit all figures, they need not be budget-breakers any more than skirts and sweaters.
- Dress in layers that can be added to or removed as the temperature dictates. Clothes of this type include vests, tunics, sweaters, and jackets worn over shirts or blouses.
- Wear warmer underthings. Scanty underwear invites chills.
- Wear warm shoes. If your feet are cold, you feel cold all over. Women's sandals or mesh shoes are definitely inappropriate for drafty floors.

Here are some suggestions for dressing more comfortably during the hot months:

- Wear lightweight materials for both underwear and outer clothing.
- Wear light colors. Dark colors absorb the heat and only make you feel and look hotter.
- Wear short sleeves. This should present no problem for women, but men are sometimes overheated in mandatory suit jackets or long-sleeved shirts. If so, perhaps your financial institution would consider a change in its dress code during the hot weather. One large metropolitan bank, for example, specified that ties could be removed on hot days and that short-sleeved shirts could be worn with no more than the top two buttons open and no T-shirt showing.
- Wear comfortable shoes that let your feet "breathe" instead of sweat. Leather is cooler than vinyl, and open heels and toes are cooler for women than closed pumps.

Whatever you decide to wear during the hot or cold months, keep your financial institution's preferences in mind as well as your personal comfort.

A Personal Daily Checklist

The following is a list of basic things you are no doubt doing each day in preparation for that close personal contact you have with others at work. It is a reminder of simple necessities that should need mentioning only once. To be ready for a productive and pleasant day, remember:

- A daily bath or shower is the basis of all personal grooming.
- Everyone should use a deodorant every day.
- Teeth should be brushed morning and night and after each meal if possible.
- Hair should be neat and clean.
- Underthings and socks or hosiery should be fresh daily.
- Clothing should be neat, clean, and pressed.
- Shoes should be clean and polished.
- Women should wear natural-looking makeup, and men should be freshly shaved each day.
- Fingernails should be clean and neatly trimmed.

See Yourself as Others See You

Every morning before you leave for work, you probably look in the mirror one last time to make sure you approve of your appearance. This is a good thing to do; it's essential to a self-confident businessperson that he or she approve of his or her own image. The next time you take that last-minute look, try seeing yourself as others see you. Imagine how you will look to your customers, your fellow employees, your supervisor. And when you do, keep the following points in mind:

- For women, *heavy makeup is in poor taste.* It's not how many cosmetics you use but how you use them that counts. Makeup should be soft and natural looking and used not to mask your face but to emphasize your best features. Choose shades that are the most complimentary for your eyes, hair, and complexion, and apply them under the type of lights that are used in your office. Fluorescent light, for example, changes the color of makeup and can create undesirable effects.
- A person's hair is very important in determining how nice he or she looks. Simply stated, healthy hair is best for business. When you choose a style, remember that your figure, height, and the shape of your face are important considerations. A professional haircut will help to keep your hair's shape. Daily brushing and scalp massage and washing whenever necessary with the proper shampoo for your hair type are important for healthy hair. Women should avoid hairspray buildup that makes hair too stiff; a fine mist of water to renew the spray when the hair is recombed will help.
- People see more of you from the waist up than from the waist down, so shirts, blouses, sweaters, and jackets are important. Shirts and

blouses should be worn tucked in, and, needless to say, see-throughs are inappropriate.

- Jewelry should be tasteful. Big, clanky costume jewelry is sometimes fun, but it's out of place at the teller's window.

YOU AND YOUR EYES

A teller's eyesight is extremely important. At the same time, it's a fact that bright, clear, wide-awake-looking eyes set the tone of a person's face. Unfortunately, however, eyes are often neglected or misused, and some people grope around blindly because they refuse to wear glasses. Sight is far too valuable to risk because of false vanity. Fashionable frames can be very flattering, and many people can easily tolerate contact lenses.

The minimum in eye care from a health standpoint should include:

- An annual eye examination by a qualified eye doctor.
- Wearing glasses as the doctor directs.
- Wearing sunglasses to protect your eyes from excessive glare. If you have prescription glasses, consider prescription sunglasses. At least, wear good quality clip-ons. Cheap sunglasses can distort vision and be harmful.
- Using proper lighting and good posture for reading and all close work.
- Resting your eyes by looking off into space for a few moments. The change of focus will relax them.

Eye Makeup

In order to use eye makeup properly, keep its purpose in mind: The function of eye makeup is to enhance the appearance of a woman's eyes. Human eyes are attractive by themselves, so elaborate or excessive eye makeup is not only harmful, it detracts from their natural beauty.

What any woman uses is an individual matter, depending on her eyebrows, lashes, the color of her eyes, and the distance between them. As a general rule, mascara is the minimum in eye makeup and is often enough for brown-eyed brunettes. Blue-eyed blondes may need more makeup to provide a contrast. Look at a very attractive person with your coloring and analyze what she has done. It's a good place to start.

Finally, use moderation when it comes to false eyelashes and when tweezing eyebrows. False eyelashes are rarely necessary, especially for daytime wear, and over-plucked brows detract rather than enhance.

As a person who deals with the public, you should take good care of your eyes . . . they're noticed by a great many people and are constantly involved in close paperwork.

YOU AND YOUR HANDS

As a teller, your hands are seen just as much as your face; however, unlike your face, they take a beating. Coins and bills are dirty, and office supplies, such as rubber stamps and carbon paper, add to the grime. To protect your hands while you keep them looking their best:

- Always wear gloves out of doors in cold weather; put them on indoors where it's warm.
- Wear protective gloves while doing any chores that require you to put your hands into hot soapy water or that are likely to cause dirt to become imbedded under nails or in the skin. If you frequently wash dishes and dislike wearing rubber gloves for this chore, try using a long-handled dishmop or sponge.
- Never use your fingernails instead of a tool to do a job. Staple removers, scissors, and tack hammers are certainly much stronger than fragile fingernails.
- Use soothing hand cream or lotion both at home and at the office whenever you get the chance. Frequent washings to remove irritating dirt followed by a good lotion will help keep your hands looking and feeling smooth.
- Give yourself a manicure at least once a week. This doesn't mean you have to wear nail polish. A manicure, for both men and women, can be strictly for protective purposes. Cuticles should be kept trimmed and soft in order to prevent hangnails, and nails should be neatly filed so that they won't have rough edges.
- Keep nails at a reasonable length. Extremely long nails are awkward and can be broken or torn. On the other hand, nails that are bitten down to the quick are unattractive.
- Consider keeping these supplies at the office for away-from-home hand care: a hand brush, mild hand soap, hand cream or lotion, emery board, fingernail clippers, and, if you use nail polish, a bottle to match your shade for emergency repairs to unsightly chipped polish.

Like your face, your hands reflect your personality. With a little preventive care, they can be just as attractive as the rest of you.

YOU AND YOUR FEET

Believe it or not, standing up to work has advantages over sitting at a desk all day. For example, research has shown that employees can think better on their feet. They understand complex facts better and make quicker decisions when they're standing. Productivity is increased when standing up to work. And, when speaking, even on the telephone, standing up increases lung and breathing capacity.

In order to experience these advantages, however, tellers and others who stand up to work need to wear shoes that won't cause them to be distracted by foot discomfort and pain. When your feet hurt, your face shows it. Tired feet, especially when you're on them much of the time, can make you unhappy and show in your expression and in the way you treat other people.

If you have foot problems, see a podiatrist. Otherwise, foot care is actually quite easy. Here are a few tips on what to do:

Bathing the feet. Because your feet are closed up all day inside of shoes and socks or hosiery, they are likely to perspire more than other parts of the body. Unpleasant odors and rough skin can be the result. To prevent these, during your daily bath, scrub your feet, especially the soles and between the toes, with a brush and warm soapy water. An old toothbrush is good for this. Next, rinse and rub any rough areas with a pumice stone while your feet are still wet. Then dry your feet thoroughly . . . athlete's foot fungus likes warm, moist skin. Finally, massage your feet with hand lotion and dust them with talcum powder.

Exercising the feet. Foot-strengthening exercises can help to make feet and ankles stronger and will improve the blood circulation. The stronger your feet become, the less likely they are to get tired and sore. Some foot exercises that you can do right at work during slack moments are:

1. Stand with your feet parallel, rise up on your toes and slowly sink down again.
2. Alternately stand on your toes with your heels off the floor, then stand on your heels with your toes off the floor.
3. Sit down, raise one of your legs, and revolve your extended foot clockwise then counterclockwise 20 times. Repeat with your other foot.
4. Wiggle your toes around inside your shoes.

Selecting shoes. If you're a man, you probably wear comfortable shoes. However, if you're a woman, you may be among the 90 percent that studies have found wear shoes that are too small, or the 80 percent who admit that their shoes hurt, or the 70 percent who have foot deformities, nine out of ten of which are caused by shoes that are too tight. Here are some tips for buying shoes that are comfortable:

1. Shop for shoes late in the day when your feet are more likely to be swollen. Shoes that fit in the morning may pinch by the end of the workday.

2. For proper fit, buy shoes that, when you're standing, are half an inch longer than the longest toe on the bigger of your two feet. The widest part should be the same width as your foot. The heel and instep should fit snugly. Hosiery and socks should be large enough to allow your feet to move freely.

3. Make sure the heels are no higher than 2 1/4 inches and are as wide as possible.

Preventing problems. Some people ignore their feet until they have a problem; then they want instant relief. It's far better to prevent the problem while you can. The following can help:

1. Always clip your toenails straight across to avoid ingrown toenails. This painful condition can also be caused by tight shoes or hosiery.

2. Avoid constant pressure and friction, which can cause corns and calluses. If corns and calluses do develop, nonmedicated padding and shielding can give temporary relief, and a podiatrist can remove them. If the pressure and friction are caused by ill-fitting shoes, a change to shoes that fit properly could solve the problem. Corrective shoe inserts might also help by redistributing your weight.

3. The pain and aches caused by fallen arches can be relieved by using supports that a specialist has fitted to your feet.

4. If you use public showers or locker rooms, be especially careful not to contract athlete's foot, which you can get by walking around in bare feet. If you do get this fungal infection, it should be treated promptly by a professional, and you should take measures to prevent a recurrence, such as keeping your feet dry and dusting them occasionally with powder that contains zinc.

Relieving tired feet. Even if you do not have foot problems, your feet occasionally will get tired, especially after standing all day. During a workbreak, relieve your feet by massaging them and propping them up on a stool or chair for 10 minutes, making sure that they're higher than your hips. Once you are home, soak them in a warm-water solution of either salt, baking soda, boric acid, or Epsom salts for a couple of minutes, then switch to cool water and repeat several times.

The condition of your feet has a lot to do with the rest of you. Proper care is well worth the time.

YOU AND COMPUTERS

At many financial institutions, tellers use electronic automation equipment that enables them to perform a number of functions that were formerly accomplished manually or with adding machines or other mechanical devices. Such equipment not only helps tellers to operate more efficiently, it can also give them access to information about customers, which leads to better customer service. In addition, it can help to improve security by providing branch-to-branch information about such things as account activity, balances, and stop payments. It can also help to reduce overs and shorts through the proficient handling of complex transactions.

Automation technology at tellers' windows may consist of video display terminals (VDTs), keyboards, and printers as well as card readers and PIN pads. Card readers provide an automatic means for accurately picking up a customer's account number. The customer is provided with a plastic card that has a magnetic strip across the back. He or she slides the card through the reader before making a transaction. PIN pads, on which the person enters his or her personal identification number, are a means for identifying the customer.

VDT Safety

VDTs, or computer screens, are the source of the greatest concern to people who work with computers because of the possible risks that are associated with long-term exposure to electromagnetic radiation, such as headaches, miscarriages or birth defects, and other health problems.

A study reported in 1991, conducted by researchers at the National Institute of Occupational Safety and Health (NIOSH), showed that there is no risk of miscarriages for pregnant women who are exposed to the low level of radiation emitted by VDTs. However, various studies of the effects of VDT emissions that have been conducted over the years have yielded conflicting results, although they do indicate that any risk is statistically small.

Experts suggest that it's best to work a minimum of 28 inches from the screen, or about an arm's length away, in order to minimize any possible health risk from electromagnetic emissions. In addition, since the emissions are usually stronger at the back and sides of computers, they suggest working approximately four feet from any co-worker's monitor. Laser copiers and printers should be kept five feet away. They also advise turning off a VDT when it's not in use.

People who have trouble reading the screen from a distance of 28 inches are advised to enlarge the size of the type that is displayed, get a large-type program or a magnifying screen, or wear eyeglasses that allow the wearer to focus from that distance. You can rest your eyes by looking away from your screen for a moment and by blinking or briefly closing them. It has also been found that it's best to use black letters against a white computer screen, with the screen set to be as bright as the lighting in the office. Also, you should avoid the reflection of glare on your monitor. Place it perpendicular to any window, use blinds or curtains to help control the light, and consider attaching an antiglare screen.

Repetitive Strain Injuries

Repetitive strain injuries (RSIs) are not likely to be a problem for tellers, who are not required to sit and type at a computer keyboard for long hours. Some, but certainly not all, of those who do so may experience pain in their arms and shoulders or may even develop a condition known as carpal tunnel syndrome, a swelling of the tendons inside a narrow tunnel in the wrist with an accompanying painful compression of the median nerve that passes through the tunnel. Repeatedly performing stressful motions of the hand and holding the hand in a static position for long periods of time can lead to this disorder.

The American Physical Therapy Association, a professional organization representing 50,000 physical therapists, assistants, and students, makes the following recommendations for the prevention of carpal tunnel syndrome. If you ever find it necessary to spend a great deal of time at a keyboard, they will help to keep you more comfortable:

- Keep your wrists relaxed and straight. Elbows should rest at your sides or be supported by special arm rests now available on some office chairs. Shoulders should be relaxed and level.
- Your typing table should be slightly higher than your elbows when your arms are held relaxed by your sides. Keep your wrists straight. Use only finger movement to strike the keys; do not move your wrists.
- Press the keys with the minimum pressure necessary. Make sure your keyboard is clean and in good working order to minimize resistance.

- Move your entire hand to press hard-to-reach keys rather than forcing the hand into awkward positions. Use two hands if necessary to execute combination keystrokes such as shifting to upper case.
- Break up typing tasks with other activities such as proofreading, filing, or telephone work to give fatigued muscle groups a rest.

Here are some additional guidelines that can help you to avoid RSIs if you must spend a long time working at a keyboard:

- Decrease the strain on your neck and shoulders by sitting up straight. Be careful to avoid hunching your head forward. It's best to position your screen so that, when you look straight ahead, it's just a little below your line of sight.
- Use a comfortable, adjustable chair that supports your back to maintain proper posture. The height of the chair should allow your elbows to be bent at a 90-degree angle while you're typing.
- During an occasional break, practice relaxing your back, neck, shoulders, and hands.

Consider Your Career

Like it or not, computers are in, so the teller who is concerned with career development would do well to do the following:

- Learn how to work your computer terminal to the best of your ability.
- Try to acquire some understanding of word processing. This electronic technique has made typewriters all but obsolete except for the most routine functions. With a word processor, everyone can be an expert "typist." The result is that tellers can add a marketable skill to their other knowledge.
- If possible, take a basic course in computer science at a local college or business school. This will help you to develop your skills by providing you with an understanding of the whys and hows of this important equipment.

Common sense dictates, if we're in the age of the computer, the person who understands how to use them will be a step ahead of his or her peers.

HOW TO RELAX AND OVERCOME TENSION

In today's fast-paced world, it is easy to get uptight—from an overcrowded bus where we get pushed and stepped on; from driving in stop-and-start traffic during the morning rush; from living costs that rise higher every day; from customers with problems who take out their frustrations on us; from having tired, aching muscles during a long hard day at work. What can be done about this? Consider the following suggestions.

Mental First Aid

When things go wrong, you have these choices:

1. You can become uptight and show it. This might annoy those around you, who might then react and make you even more uptight, which could lead to high blood pressure, difficulty in sleeping, indigestion, and all of the other physical and mental ills that afflict people when they're tense and irritable.
2. You can let life simply defeat you. You've probably met people who have done this; they're whipped. Except for performing basic biological functions, they've quit living.
3. Or . . . you can relax.

What do you do when a grumpy customer gets you down while you're standing at the window? Or when a co-worker puts unfair pressure on you? Or when a phone call brings the news that one of your kids has the mumps?

Some people may take an occasional tranquilizer, but taking pills is not the answer.

Yoga and other stress-relieving exercises, meditation that involves positive visualization, and time-management techniques have become increasingly popular as more and more people seek ways to relax. Some financial institutions even provide regular stress-management seminars for their employees. If you're trained in any of these techniques for overcoming tension, use them when necessary. Otherwise, try one or more of the following:

- If at all possible, leave your window for a few minutes. Go to the rest room or some place where it is quiet.
- If you can lie down, fine. If not, sit comfortably. And then deliberately relax. Some people find that in order to do this it helps to take several deep breaths that they inhale slowly, hold for a few seconds, then exhale slowly. Others find they can unwind by thinking of each part of the body relaxing in turn.
- Consciously realize that a grumpy customer or an irritable co-worker isn't all there is to your day. The whole world isn't against you, and, by and large, life is pretty good. Try thinking positive, happy thoughts.

- Most important of all, when you face your next customer or see your co-worker again, do it with a smile and a relaxed and friendly attitude. Even if you don't feel like doing this, it will help.

Being mentally relaxed is a habit, and so is being uptight. If you can learn to relax, you won't need pills or other mental first aid. What's more, you'll make more friends, have greater job success, and find life more enjoyable.

Personal Worries

If both partners in your family have a job, you are a member of what is now the typical family, in which two incomes have become a necessity. You have special concerns, especially if you are a woman. These concerns can nag at you and make you worry, which can make you less than effective at work. If you are preoccupied, you might be short with customers and other employees.

Areas that involve potential personal worries for women tellers are:

Children. In spite of the fact that fathers now play a more active role in child rearing, the daily welfare of young children rests more heavily on mothers. It is she who is more likely to miss work if they are ill, she who will be called from work if a child is injured, and she who usually must attend teachers' conferences. In order to minimize problems with children that can interfere with work:

1. Plan ahead. Arrange for competent supervision during working hours, and give this supervisor detailed instructions on how to cope with special situations. A section on child-care programs for financial institution employees' children follows.
2. Know in advance what to do if a child is ill. Ask your doctor what symptoms require that the child stay home from school and under what circumstances the child can go to school. Have a plan for unexpected illnesses.
3. Avoid feeling guilty about being a working parent. According to psychologists, working mothers often have a better relationship with their children than mothers who stay at home.
4. Get your spouse into the act. It shouldn't *always* be your turn to go to a teacher's conference or to tend a sore throat.

Household chores. Many husbands now spend more time doing housework than their fathers did, yet their wives, even those who work outside the home, are still responsible for more than half of it. No matter how you look at it, this isn't equitable, and it's bound to affect the working wife's efficiency on the job. If you have this problem:

1. **Talk it out.** Split up chores into reasonable tasks that ensure free evenings for both partners.
2. **Plan for efficiency.** Make your home easy to care for and meals easy to prepare.
3. **Put the kids to work.** Even small children can help in small ways.

Family and peer pressures. Some family members may resent a working wife and pressure her to quit. This is not a morale builder, and there is only one way to cope with such a situation. Make it clear, right from the beginning and in the firmest way possible, that this is *your* life, your chosen way of living it, and that, while you value the love and friendship of the other person, you do not intend to change. Reasonable people will back off at once, especially in light of the fact that the typical family *needs* two incomes.

Home security is another area that could cause you concern. It's hard to concentrate on a job if you're worried about burglars or other criminals jeopardizing your home. Ease your mind by doing the following:

- Install the best locks and other security devices on all doors and windows.
- Consider getting a dog, preferably one that will discourage prowlers. Dogs can be trained to guard a home while you work. Ask a reputable breeder for instructions.
- Don't advertise the fact that you're away all day. Use a timer switch to turn lights on early on winter evenings. Have a mail slot that conceals the fact that your mail hasn't been picked up all day. Ask people who make deliveries to leave packages at another house. If you use an answering machine, make sure that your recorded message does not reveal the fact that no one is home.

You will find that if you can relieve your mind of personal worries and relax mentally, you'll be happier in your job and better at your work.

Child-Care Programs

As stated earlier, mothers are still primarily responsible for the care of the children in the family. Therefore, when you consider the fact that close to 10 million U.S. preschoolers have working mothers and that almost three-fourths of the people employed by financial institutions are women, it's no surprise that child-care programs are of vital interest to both the institutions and their employees. As a result, many of these employers offer child-care programs, and an increasing number are interested in developing them.

Benefits to financial institutions. Employer-sponsored child-care programs, which come in many varieties, don't just provide valuable benefits for working parents; they offer advantages to the sponsor as well. Studies show that these advantages include improved employee morale, reduced turnover, fewer absences, and an increase in quality applicants for jobs.

Kinds of programs. The following are some of the types of employer-sponsored day-care programs that are currently available:

- Some financial institutions offer referral programs, supplying information about local child-care centers to interested employees in regard to such things as the facilities' licenses, available openings, the age of eligible children, fees, and transportation.

- Financial institutions may help to pay for child care at outside facilities. Or they may establish nearby or on-site centers of their own for their employees or participate in one that is shared with other area employers.

- Dependent care reimbursement programs are commonly offered by financial institutions. They allow employees to put a certain portion of their salaries into pretax accounts to be used to pay for child care, thus decreasing their overall taxable income.

- Some financial institutions even fund emergency-care programs for employees' sick children. Thus, if it were essential for an employee to go to work who had a child who was too sick to go to a day-care center, a trained sitter would be sent to the person's home to care for the child, and the employer would pay part or all of the cost. An annual limit is usually imposed on the number of hours that an employee can make use of the program.

- Flextime and job-sharing programs allow employees to care for their children and to meet other personal needs. They involve flexible work hours, which allow employees to vary their schedules, or having two employees share one job, a practice that is less common in financial institutions.

- Another innovative program for parents who wish to work as well as have the time to take care of school-age children allows employees to work from 10:00 A.M. to 2:00 P.M., Monday through Friday, from September through June. This is an ideal schedule for those who'd like to see their children off to school and be there when they come home, and it is designed to strengthen the teller work force during peak customer hours.

In-Home Child Care

If, instead of using an outside day-care center, you plan to hire someone to take care of your child at home, you should be able to answer these 10 questions:

1. How much experience does the person have? An inexperienced teenager, for example, may not even know how to lift and hold a baby or change a diaper.

2. Does the person like children? Would the caregiver strike your child if he or she were unruly, or frighten the youngster with threats or scary stories?

3. Is the caregiver responsible? Will the person be careless and leave doors unlocked, admit strangers, or spend too much time talking on the telephone?

4. How would he or she react in an emergency? For example, would the caregiver know what to do about your child's safety in case of a fire? Would he or she know who to contact for help in case of an accident or injury?

5. How is the person's health? If the caregiver is an older person, can he or she see and hear well? Is the individual subject to a sudden illness or likely to fall asleep when the child should be watched? Does he or she have a contagious disease or act neurotic or eccentric?

6. Is the caregiver a clean person? Someone whose own appearance is sloppy and dirty isn't likely to care whether your child comes in contact with germs or filth.

7. Does the person have references? If an applicant has had any child-care experience at all, he or she should be willing to give you references. Be sure to check them.

8. Will the person be available when needed? This is important because your work schedule is involved.

9. How much does the caregiver charge? Be sure to find out in advance so there won't be any unpleasant disagreements later.

10. Does the person need transportation? Will he or she need taxi or bus fare or does the person own a car?

Other important information can be revealed through a background check that includes a review of the person's driving and possible criminal records, the accuracy of his or her Social Security number, and a credit check. Private background services exist that can be hired to investigate these matters.

It is vital for all working parents to enjoy peace of mind about the care of their children. Carefully checking caregivers in advance will help to ensure it.

Physical Tension

In the often-demanding job of a teller, the combination of long lines of customers and the need for concentration to avoid mistakes can result in fatiguing muscle tension or headaches. Here are a few simple exercises you can do during a break to help relieve that tension and to make you more relaxed and alert. Try doing them without straining yourself and *only if you have no physical problems that would make you prone to injury.*

- To relieve the muscle tension in your neck, rotate your head in a full circle, first in one direction, then in the other, loosely and gently dropping it as far forward and back and to the left and right as you comfortably can. Repeat several times.
- To relieve the muscle tension in your back and shoulders, place your hands at your sides and rotate your shoulders in a circle, forward then up, backward then down. Repeat several times.
- To stretch tired muscles and get more blood to your brain, bend forward from the waist, with your arms dangling in front of you, getting your head down toward the floor as far as you comfortably can.
- To help get more oxygen to your brain, stand up straight and take several deep, slow breaths. Inhale deep into the diaphragm and exhale slowly.
- To relieve tension in your ankles and feet, alternately stand flat on your feet and rise up on your toes several times.
- To help get rid of a headache, lie on your back on a carpeted floor. Concentrate on one group of muscles at a time, tensing, then relaxing them. Start with your toes and work right up to your scalp. Then relax totally for a few minutes and get up slowly. This method for relief often works and just takes a little time in a quiet conference room.

Build your personal image and make a hit with the people at your financial institution by sincerely trying to look and feel successful, and you will be. All it takes is caring enough about yourself to want to succeed!

4

CHAPTER

Getting Along with Your Co-Workers

Teamwork is a word you hear a lot, but it's often misused. All it really means is working together toward a common goal. At your financial institution, you and your co-workers share several common goals relating to job efficiency, your institution's growth, and making your work pleasant and enjoyable.

Here is a simple list of rules for teamwork that, if practiced, can lead to harmony on the job and to the successful achievement of those goals. They're easy to remember because the first letter of each one combines to spell the word "teamwork." Try to remember these principles and to put them to work at your office every day:

*T*ake time . . . to consider other people's feelings.
*E*arn friendship . . . by being cheerful and courteous.
*A*im to please . . . by lending a helping hand.
*M*eet others halfway . . . by being cooperative.
*W*atch for opportunities . . . to praise others.
*O*bey the rules . . . your institution's policies apply to everyone.
*R*espect the rights of others.
*K*eep trying . . . to improve your own job performance.

Everyone Is a Salesperson

Some years ago, an extremely successful salesperson stopped in to call on a bank officer whose institution was a good customer. The bank was bedlam!

Through an oversight, someone had forgotten that certain legal notices had to be mailed to the bank's thousands of stockholders, and everyone from the senior vice president on down was busy stuffing envelopes in an effort to meet the legal deadline.

Most salespeople would have taken one look at this scene and said, "I see I've caught you at a bad time. I'll call back next week." But this salesperson didn't. Instead, she said, "It looks as though the best way I can help you right now is to stuff envelopes. We can discuss our other business later." And she rolled up her sleeves and spent the afternoon stuffing envelopes. You can imagine the size of the order she got the following week!

This story illustrates two important points about human relationships:

1. If you want to be successful, you must "sell" yourself to others before you even attempt to sell a product, service, or idea; and

2. One of the best ways to help sell yourself is to pitch in and help the team, especially when there are problems, rather than always being a loner.

How does this affect you as a teller? After all, you're not a salesperson . . . or are you? Consider:

- Wanting to be well liked by other people is nothing more or less than trying to sell them an idea—the idea that you're a nice person.

- Hoping for a raise or more responsibility involves selling your supervisor on your ability.

- Finally, as a teller, part of your job is to sell your financial institution's services; and nothing makes a better impression on a potential customer than a well-coordinated team.

Everyone is a salesperson every day. Doing your best to get along with your co-workers will make you a better one.

Pulling Together—Two Examples

Consider the following situations and the people involved:

- Mary and Sue, both tellers, have an afternoon off coming to them, which they had planned to take on Tuesday. Tuesday arrives . . . but so do problems. It is just one of those days, so Mary says, "I'll stick around and help out and take my half-day later." Sue, on the other hand, says, "Boy, I'm gonna get out of this madhouse. See you later!"

Both tellers had a chance to sell themselves to their fellow employees and to their supervisors, and both did. Sue sold the idea that she is not a member of the team and that she is not willing to go the extra mile to help her fellow employees. Mary sold the idea that she's very conscientious, and is willing to help out when she is needed.

- Bill and Bob work at adjacent windows. Ann, a very attractive young woman, works next to Bob. When Ann doesn't settle, Bill stays and helps her, but when Bob doesn't settle, Bill goes home. Ann and Bob, on the other hand, usually stay to help either one if the occasion arises.

Obviously, it's more fun for Bill to help a pretty female teller than good old Bob. But by choosing to stay for his favorite, Bill is acting in his own best interests, not his institution's. He isn't really working for the team. What's more, his fellow employees know it.

Teamwork pays off! First of all, it makes any office a nicer place to work. It also creates better service for the public because a team is more efficient than a group of loners. However, the biggest rewards are to the individuals involved. Being part of a good team gives them a sense of belonging and pride. So sell *yourself* to your boss, your public, and your fellow employees by joining and supporting your co-workers, especially when problems arise. That's when a really good employee has the chance to be noticed.

MALE-FEMALE WORK RELATIONSHIPS

The office relationship between men and women differs from any school or social relationship because people in an office form a working team, striving for a common goal. The responsibility of each person to do his or her share to reach that goal is in no way predicated on sexual differences. While the female cheerleader and the muscular football player would have vastly different roles in a school football situation, their responsibilities may be exactly the same in a financial institution, where they very likely work side by side.

The following are some suggestions for harmonious relationships with people you encounter at work who are of the opposite sex. In spite of the fact that you share common goals and responsibilities, the fact that you are different sexually can sometimes lead to potential problems.

Tips for Women

Consider these Dos and Don'ts when it comes to getting along with men at the office:

Don't flirt. Even though a little innocent flirting can sometimes be fun, it's out of place at the office. For one thing, the other women are likely to resent it. For another, the man or men involved may be embarrassed. Finally, male customers, whether they enjoy the flirting or not, will have a poor impression about your ability to handle their financial affairs. Besides, becoming too familiar with customers, particularly attractive ones of the opposite sex, could set you up for the wise guy. Adding an occasional wink to your smile, grabbing his hand with a "Listen! I've got to tell you . . ." or simply telling a story that invites a smart reply could place you in an embarrassing situation. It's best to keep your attitude and relationship strictly businesslike.

Don't take advantage of the men. Male co-workers should not be allowed to treat female co-workers to lunch or dinner on a regular basis. When fellow employees eat together, they're not on a date. Allowing him to pay could force him to avoid the women in the office at times when there is an opportunity for co-workers to get to know each other better. If he should offer, just say with a smile, "Thanks anyway, but I'm a working woman, and this is a business lunch." He'll appreciate your friendly help out of a touchy situation.

Not taking advantage also means not expecting the men at the office to be packhorses. They shouldn't have to perform your tasks just because they may be physically stronger.

Do be understanding. This rule works both ways, but the fact is, in the typical financial institution, women usually outnumber the men. Plan office activities, whenever possible, that appeal to both sexes. Don't make the men in your office feel like outsiders. For example, in planning an office outing, most men would not enjoy attending a women's fashion show, but everyone, regardless of sex, would probably enjoy going to a stage play. You won't go wrong in dealings with your male counterparts if you simply try to see things from their viewpoint.

Do be prepared to cope with sexual harassment, if it should arise. Studies show that about 90 percent of all sexual harassment cases involve men harassing women; the other 10 percent involve women harassing men or men harassing men. Because sexual harassment is illegal in the workplace, businesses have tightened their policies regarding it, and some are providing their employees with workshops and educational films on the subject.

People who work in financial institutions have all the psychological pluses and minuses that everyone has. Thus, the man who feels insecure in his social or marital relationships may seek self-assurance by making passes at women, or the woman who has problems may interpret every friendly gesture from a male as suggestive.

Any office situation in which people work together is bound to include a certain amount of kidding. Except for the supersensitive, it is usually no problem. A problem does arise when fun in acceptable taste ceases and harassment begins.

As a female teller, how can you avoid or solve problems of this type?

1. Start by defining the problem. Are you part of it? Do you encourage advances you later regret? Or is the man strictly at fault?

2. Dress and act your part. In other words, don't invite advances by deliberately wearing inappropriate clothing or by making suggestive remarks to male customers and co-workers.

3. Have a career attitude. Be good at your job. And, while every job should be enjoyable, don't allow kidding around to interfere with your work or the work of those around you.

4. If the man is strictly at fault and the problem is serious, take him aside and, in a friendly way, tell him to stop. It's tough to do this and stay on a pleasant basis, but you should try. For example, you might say, "Look, Bill (or Mr. _____, if he is a customer), if I did or said something that gave you the wrong idea, I'm sorry, but let's keep our relationship on a business basis." Be friendly and try to ease the situation by helping him to save face in suggesting that he may have had the wrong idea about you.

5. If the direct approach fails, talk privately to your supervisor. If the person involved *is* the supervisor, go the next step up the ladder.

6. If that fails, you should talk to your personnel officer. Usually, though, the problem won't get this far. Most people who are at fault in this type of situation will get the message right away.

Tips for Men

Consider these Dos and Don'ts when it comes to getting along with the women at the office:

Don't flirt. In financial institutions all over the country, it is not uncommon to see situations where female employees outnumber males two or three to one, or even where there is only one man in an otherwise all-female office. At first thought, this may sound great, but problems can arise. So, be friendly, but don't flirt—with female co-workers or customers. It just isn't businesslike, and it may very well be resented. It could also be construed as sexual harassment.

Don't take advantage of the women. Carry your share of the work. Women may tend to pamper an outnumbered man, which could lead to the man losing some of the responsibilities of his job. Say "thanks, but no thanks" when offers of help are made that wouldn't ordinarily be made to another employee.

On the other hand, don't try to railroad the women by flaunting your masculinity. That might work in a situation dependent on physical strength, but not in banking.

> *Don't become a packhorse.* Yes, you can be a good guy and give the women a hand when it comes to moving equipment or such, but don't let the women make you do all of the office heavy work. That just isn't fair or professional.
>
> *Do give women the respect they deserve.* In other words, don't act like a male chauvinist. Banking is an industry dependent on skills that are simply unrelated to sexual attributes. Therefore, financial institutions employ men and women in equal jobs, and many women are quite properly promoted to supervisory and management positions. They deserve the same respect and courtesy you would give to another man.
>
> *Do share in the women's interests.* This means being an active member of the office team. Thus, for example, even though you might decline attending a shower if a female co-worker is getting married, you should certainly contribute, along with the others in the office, toward the purchase of her gift.

BRIDGING THE GENERATION GAP

When more than one generation is put together in an office, conflict can arise from either side. With a little patience, however, each can discover that the differences they perceive between the two generations are mostly superficial and that they can work together in harmony.

Tips for Younger Employees

Before you label the older people with whom you work as old-fashioned folks who think that the ideas and styles of today's young people are outlandish, remember that their elders probably felt the same way about them when they were your age. Try to be tolerant; the older generation can be a great source of information to you. Especially:

> *Be careful of what you say.* Older people sometimes get upset when they hear younger ones, particularly younger women, use certain words or expressions. You may feel it's silly, but why rock the boat?

Go easy on the styles. Tight pants and skirts and other such styles have no place in a business office anyway.

Don't make the older generation feel old. They realize they have years on you, and some may feel a little sorry not to be your age again. So don't rub it in.

Don't resent their advice. They've had a lot more experience than you have and can help you to do a better job.

Tips for Older Employees

Relax. The younger employees at the office are just like you were—no better, no worse. Perhaps they look and talk a little differently, but that doesn't mean their ways are wrong. So:

Don't be uptight about language or styles. The fact that something seems to be in poor taste doesn't make the person who displays it guilty of anything more serious than bad taste.

Be a friend. Younger people are still a little scared—just as you were. They may show it in strange ways, just as you did, but they still need understanding and a kind word or two.

Offer advice gently. Yes, you've had more experience and, through actual practice, have learned more efficient ways to do certain jobs. But if you try to force your ideas on a younger person in a dictatorial manner, you'll probably be wasting your time, because you'll be resented. So easy does it, and don't forget to use large measures of tactfulness.

The generation gap is really just an artificial barrier created largely by advertising and fictitious stories. Why not knock it down at your office?

OFFICE SOCIALIZING

"All work and no play . . ." You know how the saying goes. No one wants to have to stick to business 100 percent of the time. On the other hand, in order to avoid excessive office socializing, certain guidelines should be followed. Consider the following suggestions.

Parties

Every employee knows several stories about people whose reputations or careers were ruined, or, if not ruined, at least badly damaged, at office parties. Therefore, people sometimes face an office social, whether it be a holiday party, autumn picnic, or annual dinner dance, with a certain amount of apprehension.

On the other hand, people who work together often come to like each other and thus enjoy occasional social affairs. What leads to the occasional trouble that mars the idea of an office party? Among other things:

Excessive drinking. For some reason, people who would never think of overindulging under other circumstances get carried away at office parties. So if you're hosting one, limit the drinks by providing a shot glass for accurate measurement (even professional bartenders use a measure) and by refusing to serve anyone who you think has had enough. If you're attending a party, set a reasonable limit and stick to it.

An irresistible romance. Suddenly, a man and woman discover, after working together quietly day after day, that the other person is absolutely irresistible. And does John feel silly in the morning! Not to speak of Jane! Don't flirt or make passes at a party. Many social occasions include husbands, wives, or escorts from outside the office, which goes a long way toward turning off a would-be budding romance.

Telling off a super. Everyone has heard of people who have taken advantage of the relaxed atmosphere at parties to tell their superiors exactly what they think of them. Mr. or Ms. Doe becomes Bill or Sally for the evening, but he or she can't help remembering what was said when the next day rolls around. Have fun, but remember you work with these people every day. Don't do anything you'll be ashamed of or regret later.

Gifts from Customers

Local customs vary widely, as do financial institution policies, regarding the acceptance of gifts by tellers from their customers. If you're in doubt about what to do, ask you supervisor. These general rules can help to guide you:

Don't accept any gift that is forbidden by your institution's policy. No matter how much the customer swears that "no one will ever know," what happens three months later when that same customer wants an illegal favor such as holding some checks in your cash drawer or backdating a certain document?

Don't accept any gift that would make you feel personally unduly obligated to the customer. If you feel "bought," then you are. This includes gifts of money, no matter how small the amount.

Do accept sincere tokens of appreciation. A box of candy, a bottle of wine, a token gourmet food item, or something of that sort can be accepted graciously.

Some years ago, a bank president advised his staff: "If a customer offers me a bottle of Scotch, I take it and thank him. No one can buy me for a bottle of Scotch. But if he offers me a case, I refuse it. He can't buy me for that either; but he may think he can, and I wouldn't want that to happen." This is a good rule of thumb for any employee.

Gifts to Each Other

Every financial institution faces the problem of what to do about gifts for employees on special occasions. This can be a problem, unless management has simply discouraged the practice altogether. What happens if Sue is popular and Bob is not, and the amount contributed toward each person's gift is vastly unequal? And should gifts be given to employees who quit and will never return, when those who stay are not so favored? Here are a few ideas to consider:

Set fixed amounts to be spent. This eliminates any discrepancies in the size of gifts. A popular employee should not get more than someone who is less well liked.

Define the occasions and the gifts to honor them. It's unfair, for example, to honor one teller's engagement with a quick lunch, and another's with a lavish dinner, and then disregard a third teller's engagement altogether.

Be sure everyone is included. Appoint an individual or, in a large office, a small committee to coordinate gift giving. This should include collecting funds. Then make it a rule that everyone contributes an equal amount. This removes the burden from some people who feel constrained to outdo others. Tell each person just what amount is expected.

Don't let the amounts collected be too large. Donations for gifts should not impose a burden on anyone.

Make sure everyone agrees. Establish gift-giving policies that suit everyone in the office. If this doesn't work, consider dropping them entirely. Office harmony is too important to risk over this issue. The important reason for even having such remembrances is to make friendship a part of working together, so conflict over the subject would have just the opposite effect.

Office Dating

It happens. A fellow employee, the office manager, or even a customer starts
to date a single teller. More than one happy marriage has resulted from such
relationships. After all, men and women *do* get married, and it is possible to
meet someone through work, either a customer or a co-worker.

Unfortunately, dating at the office can also create problems, including:

Office jealousies. It may be resented, for example, that Henry is dating
an attractive loan interviewer, especially by any other single male employees who have their eyes on her.

Office gossip. True or not, tales may spread, and they may damage reputations and morale.

Uncomfortable relationships. John and Mary, who are dating, may
spend too much time together at the water cooler. Their lunching together may be resented. And, if they break up, they may try to avoid
each other to the detriment of their work.

Policy problems. If a teller is dating a customer, it may be hard for him
or her to insist on strict adherence to the institution's policy when it
comes to such matters as cashing checks, for example.

Supervisory problems. If a teller is dating his or her supervisor, the
teller may be tempted to take advantage of this position when it comes
to such things as tardiness or long lunch periods. It puts the supervisor
on the spot with the other employees and makes the employees resent
the teller.

Problems aside, dating at the office can and does happen. If your institution has a policy on this, follow it, as it is based on local experience. Whatever
the case may be, don't date through the office lightly. Be sure you have a
sincere interest in the other person and that he or she is not trying to take
advantage of your position. In the case of a customer, insist that that person go
to another teller for banking transactions. If you're dating a supervisor, again,
be sure there is a sincere interest on both your parts. A broken relationship can
be uncomfortable and usually isn't worth the risk.

Dating in the office can bring people with mutual interests together, but
it can also lead to problems. Handle with care!

Gambling at the Office

Where can you find football pools; place bets on the World Series by team and
inning; buy a raffle ticket on a new car to benefit a local charity; get involved
in a "pyramid" or "chain-letter" get-rich-quick scheme; take a chance to bene-

fit a social club; or even, in some rare cases, play penny-ante gin or pinochle during lunch breaks? At many financial institution offices. Of course, this can create definite problems:

- Often, the people who set up and run such things as World Series pools exert a lot of pressure on others in the office to take part, as a certain number of participants are necessary to make such things work. The result can be hurt feelings or, still worse, forced participation by people who really can't afford to lose the money. *Never* force or even pressure anyone to gamble against his or her will. Others will resent you, and your friendships will suffer. By the same token, don't be pressured against your will. Saying "no" the first few times may be difficult, but soon you won't be asked again. You don't have to be nasty; just be firm.
- Sensible people who see the utter hopelessness of such things as "pyramid" or "chain-letter" schemes may find themselves put down hard—and quite wrongly—by those who desperately want to win and who refuse to see how illogical such things are. But the odds are against you in any gambling. Heavily. In a World Series inning pool, for example, the odds are 18 to 1, and they're about the best you can get! When playing a football pool— or even a state lottery—the odds against you are astronomical. Beware of token winnings that keep you coming back.
- Some few people, in dire need of money, will waste innumerable hours and dollars hoping to collect a bonanza and get out of a financial pit. When they don't—and they almost never do—they become upset because their problems have only worsened with lost money and wasted time. If you must gamble, never bet more than you can afford to lose with a smile.

Gambling at the office isn't a good idea, even though it's been going on for a long time and will undoubtedly continue.

Fun Ideas for the Office

One of the nice things about financial institution offices is that the work atmosphere is usually very friendly. As long as the main purpose of the office is customer service and not socializing, a friendly atmosphere is a good thing. It's certainly nice to be able to work in a pleasant place among friends.

Here are a few ideas for projects that take little time but that can help to make an office a more pleasant place. If any of them appeal to you, check with your supervisor about trying them.

The book exchange. Almost everyone reads paperback books, but buying current books can become expensive. So why not start a paperback swap shelf or table in the employees' lounge? Keep the rules simple. Just have everyone bring in books they've finished reading and invite others to help themselves from the shelf and return them when they're through. It's a real money-saver, and reading the same books stimulates conversation.

Cooperative meals. Most financial institutions have better-than-average facilities for their employees. Rest areas, lounges, and kitchens are usually well equipped and comfortable. Because of this and because it is often inconvenient to leave the office unattended at mealtime, many tellers stay there. This is especially true during the winter months when bad weather makes going out unpleasant.

Traditionally, in the absence of employee cafeterias, office workers who eat in carry individual lunches to work each day. After a while, these can become rather dull and unappetizing. Therefore, tellers who have the facilities to do so sometimes set up systems for sharing lunch or dinner preparation. The best way to do this is to choose a time that is not likely to be busy and assign people to bring simple foods. Perhaps these might include sandwich and salad ingredients and dessert, or even a casserole or two if there are facilities for keeping the food fresh and hot. A microwave oven can heat a wide variety of foods in minutes. Some tellers prepare soups, broth, and other hot beverages on an electric hot plate to add interest to a sandwich from home. Others take turns bringing in cakes, pies, cookies, or breakfast cakes to share during coffee breaks. Other nice snacks are cheese and crackers, assorted seeds and nuts, and fresh fruit. Good cooks abound among both men and women, so put out a sign-up sheet for people to bring in their favorite dishes.

Outings. An office outing can be fun and can help to create a more friendly team. Here are a few tips to help make an outing a success:

1. Choose a good place to go. The best place is the one that has universal appeal. An amusement park with available picnic grounds, a state or city park with beach and bathing facilities, or a local tourist attraction are all good places to go. Whatever is chosen, be sure that it is a place that is accessible and offers fun for everyone.

2. Invite the families. Office outings can be good ways for employees' families to get to know the people with whom their relatives work.

3. Be prepared for problems. At any outing, some child is bound to scrape his knee, and bugs will appear, invited or not. So have some-

one take along a small first-aid kit and insect repellent. Try to anticipate other problems that may arise as well.

4. Don't pack food that may spoil. The idea is for people to have fun,
not get sick. So avoid mayonnaise, potato salad, tuna or chicken
salad, deviled eggs, and other perishable foods, or at least be prepared to keep them cold.

5. Don't force people to play games or swim if they don't want to.
Some people are bashful and would be embarrassed in a three-
legged race, for example. Others are just plain terrible at sports and
would prefer to avoid them.

6. Don't overindulge in alcoholic beverages.

7. Don't plan overstrenuous activities for sedentary people. Nothing
cramps the style of an office outing like someone becoming ill.

Office socializing—within limits, of course—provides a good way for
employees to get to know the other people on their team. But fun times rarely
just happen. They're planned by people who take the time to think of pleasant
things to do and ways to do them.

PREPARING TO GO ON VACATION

The summer months are popular times for taking a well-earned rest from work.
For tellers, this means a respite from long lines of customers and the problems
of settling. Just as there is a need to plan ahead for any vacation trip you may
be taking, there is also a need to plan ahead for the job during your absence.
While you're away from the office, you're sure to be missed.

Consider Your Co-Workers

In addition to the things you can do to make sure you have a good time, there
are things you should do at the office before leaving on vacation to make it
easier for those who fill in for you. For example:

- Be sure your vacation doesn't overlap with that of a key employee who knows your work. The person who is responsible for
  scheduling vacations may have made a mistake in this, so it
  pays to check.
- If summer help will be filling in for you, be sure to brief them on
  any special situations that might arise.

- Leave a list telling where things can be found. Keys, office stamps, nonroutine supplies, and any items that relate to special duties you perform should be on it.
- Leave a memo explaining any procedures that should be followed that may be unfamiliar to others in the office or that cover situations you think could arise. Include an explanation of the idiosyncrasies of any equipment that you use.
- Make sure your work is up-to-date and that everything at your workstation is neat and orderly before you leave.

Consider Security

Financial institutions require people who handle assets to take minimum vacations at regular intervals as a basic internal security procedure. To put it bluntly, people usually can't cover up an embezzlement when they're on vacation. Here are a few security tips to follow before you go on vacation:

- Transfer out as much cash as you can before you leave.
- Have your remaining cash audited by whoever is designated to do this. Get a signed audit slip or other proof that you have settled out.
- Lock up any remaining cash according to your institution's policy.

It's also good to remember that when someone else goes on vacation and you're still on the job, you should never keep any records for him or her or handle any transactions that are not strictly open and aboveboard and in keeping with regular policy. Innocent tellers have been victimized by unwittingly covering up for dishonest co-workers.

Consider Your Customers

Your customers are sure to miss you while you're gone, especially those for whom you often do a little extra. Therefore, it's a good idea to tell anyone who relies on you for help that you're going to be away. Then take a moment to introduce that customer to another teller and to reassure the customer that the other teller can fill his or her special needs during your absence. This applies especially to the elderly or to anyone who is timid or unsure of how to handle business dealings.

If you handle any complicated customer transactions, such as special payroll situations, be sure to brief another teller before you leave. In this case, written instructions are helpful.

ON-THE-JOB TRAINING

Being trained isn't always a barrel of fun. For one thing, learning is hard work. For another, gearing your schedule and habits to the person who is training you isn't always easy. But training is something everyone has to go through occasionally. As a trainee, you have two possible courses. You can learn *only* what your institution insists you learn, that is, the minimum to get you by, hoping to add to your knowledge from practical experience as time passes, or you can learn as much as you can. This is the path chosen by those who sincerely want a successful banking career. It's also the path taken by those who will eventually be successful in *any* endeavor. The point here is obvious. When you are being trained, develop the attitude, "How much can I learn?" rather than "How little can I get by with?"

Here are some tips for making your training time easier:

Don't be embarrassed. The only people who never need training are those who have stopped learning and growing in the job. Be proud you were chosen for training!

"Where did you say our new training director used to work?"

Help your instructor by asking questions. Whenever you're not sure of something, ask. Don't make your instructor guess the areas in which you need help.

Fit in with the new routine. This means overlooking the fact that you always lunch with certain people at certain times, and it means trusting the person who's filling in where you regularly work. For the time being, your training is your job.

Relax. Training may not always be fun, but you'll be better off for it and you'll be a more valuable employee.

How to Be a Good Teacher

Every time you help to train a new teller or explain your job to a summer replacement, you're acting as a teacher, even if you're merely describing one phase of your work to another teller who will be rotating chores with you. If you're a good teacher, the job will get done faster, your trainee will like you and your financial institution better, and you'll add to your own prestige as an efficient and knowledgeable person.

The following techniques will help:

Be sure you are prepared to teach the right thing. No matter how well you think you know your job, review each procedure you plan to teach. Be *sure* you're not teaching the other person how to do something wrong—even a "little bit" wrong.

Choose the right time. Don't try to teach during rush hours when there's a long line waiting at your window. It is a good time, though, to have your trainee watch you. Ask him or her to stand beside you and quietly observe. He or she is bound to pick up a few things even without an explanation from you. Then, during slack periods, give the person your full attention.

Avoid being a show-off. It's human nature to take pleasure in knowing more than someone else. However, before too long, especially if you're a good teacher, your trainee will know almost as much as you do, and with experience, he or she will catch up. Besides, if you're cocky about how much you know, you're bound to be resented.

Keep it simple. Break the job down into simple sections that can be taught one at a time, and try not to overlook important details as you go along; backtracking can be very confusing. Start the training at the logical beginning and follow through in steps. Make an outline before you start just as a professional schoolteacher would do. If you check off each item in your "lesson plan" as you proceed, you'll keep your instruction simple enough to be understood and you'll avoid omitting vital facts.

Be patient. You may have to repeat an explanation more than once. Just remember, what seems very routine to you is brand new to your trainee. Above all, don't embarrass him or her by acting exasperated if something isn't understood right away. Try explaining the point from a different angle; sometimes a new slant will make the issue entirely clear. If your trainee hesitates to ask for a repetition but you can see that you weren't fully understood, politely cover the same ground again right on the spot.

Use plain English. Every line of work has its own catchphrases, words, and abbreviations, but there isn't one that can't be put into simple, everyday English. Save the confusing banking terms until later when your trainee has learned the job.

Be enthusiastic. If you're sincere and show genuine enthusiasm for your work, it's bound to rub off. If you give the impression that you simply don't care about the job, your teaching will be dull and your words will mean little or nothing to your listener. Good humor is contagious, so make the hours you have to spend with your trainee pleasant ones for both of you.

MAKE THE NEWCOMER FEEL AT HOME

As business expands and replacements are needed, newcomers are bound to come to work at your office. When this happens, it's up to you and your fellow employees to make them feel at home. If a new person is happy with his or her job, he or she will be more pleasant to get along with, more cooperative to work with, and more likely to stay. First impressions are important, so make the newcomer feel comfortable and part of your team right from the beginning. Suppose, for example, that a new person starts working at the next window. Here is a list of dos and don'ts that will help both of you to start off on the right foot:

Don't be too pushy. Take it easy at first in trying to make friends. Overenthusiasm can be frightening to a newcomer who has a great deal to get used to all at once.

Don't expect too much. In the beginning you shouldn't be disappointed if the newcomer's strangeness and preoccupation with learning the job makes him or her seem standoffish. This person will soon relax.

Don't tell a new employee office rumors or gossip. This is never good policy, but it's especially poor when it comes to newcomers.

Don't make the newcomer join anything at first. He or she has enough to think about. Later the person may be sorry and feel that he or she joined just to make a good impression on you. Or you may be sorry you asked the new employee yourself.

Don't pry into his or her personal life. For example, the reason that the newcomer left his or her previous job is none of your business. Asking too many questions will only make the new employee feel uncomfortable.

Do introduce him or her to your co-workers and to the customers. Their friendliness will help to put the newcomer at ease.

Do explain your institution's policies carefully. If you do, the new employee will know exactly what is expected of him or her, and this will give the individual a feeling of security.

Do help the newcomer with his or her work. Staying a few minutes to help a new teller settle in the beginning will go a long way toward making him or her feel welcome. Chances are, he or she will return the favor someday.

Do invite the newcomer to join you and your friends for lunch and coffee breaks.

Do be enthusiastic about your work and your financial institution. Enthusiasm is catching and will do more than anything else to make your new co-worker like you and his or her job.

DEALING WITH DIFFICULT CO-WORKERS

Annoyances

There are things that most people would never do deliberately because they know that it would make them unpopular. However, some employees do annoying things without even thinking, making it less than pleasant for those with whom they work. For example, co-workers may:

- Borrow equipment and fail to return it. Even worse, they may not ask to borrow it but just take it.
- Wait until it's good and late to call in sick.
- Ask questions, but fail to listen or give the other person a chance to answer.

- Interrupt repeatedly.
- Make unsolicited comments about overheard private conversations.
- Shout across the office.
- Hum, sing, and whistle interminably.
- Constantly drum their fingers or a pencil on the desk.
- Noisily chew gum or crunch hard candy.
- Smoke carelessly, puffing away, filling the employee lounge or other smoking area with clouds of smoke or blowing it into other people's faces.

Working closely with other people requires consideration. If someone in your office has any of these or other annoying habits, you might have a confidential talk with the office manager and suggest that he or she speak to your co-worker, tactfully asking the person to try to stop the annoying habit.

Problem People

People are human and subject to human failings, and everyone has a bad day occasionally. Unfortunately, there are some people, though they are rare, whose irritating ways can affect the efficiency of an entire office and the morale of co-workers and customers alike. Here are a few typical problem people and tips for dealing with them:

The perfectionist. This person wants everything "just so," not only for himself but for the whole office. He watches the way others work and interferes if they don't do things the way he thinks they should be done. This person has probably had years of experience and may actually be able to give valuable advice. His need for perfection may be due to a lack of self-confidence. Seeking his advice occasionally and asking his opinion could make him feel needed and appreciated. Friendliness rather than resentment could help him to relax.

The time-passer. This person fills in the day by coming to work. It is an inconvenient interlude while she waits for off-duty time and the more important hours of her social life. Or perhaps she's waiting for a job opening somewhere else. She's not interested in the welfare of the institution or her co-workers and acts annoyed with those who are. A few tactful hints might help in this case. For instance, if the time-passer happens to be a woman who expects to leave her job in the near future, learning to do it well now could be of great benefit to her in her new position. Regardless of the person's age or sex, trying to be an effective part of the team will be a valuable career-building experience.

The complainer. This person distracts everyone with his problems, constantly complaining about outside personal difficulties and knocking everything at work. He just can't find any good in anything. If his problems are real, talking them out with him may help. If they're not, kindly but firmly refusing to listen could turn off the complaints. This person obviously wants an audience—and the more sympathy he gets, the more he'll complain.

The crisis creator. This person is a negative soul who exaggerates problems, turning every head cold into pneumonia or imagining that the world is coming to an end—quickly and painfully. For example, she turns a minor error into a major offense: "We'll never get this to settle! You'll probably get fired for this mistake!" Customers expect their tellers to be calm, courteous, and efficient, but it's hard to display those traits when you always expect the worst. Working with such a person also becomes an ordeal. If you know someone who constantly creates an air of crisis, set a good example by staying calm yourself and trying to rationalize with this person.

The back-stabber. This person likes to gossip and is an expert at expanding half-truths that make another person look bad. He can also be a master of the snide or sarcastic remark and often enjoys taking public snipes at fellow employees. When it comes to dealing with this individual, it's best to try to be friendly while refusing to listen to his gossip and putdowns. If you're on the receiving end of the remarks, however, it's important to let the person know you won't be intimidated or made to look foolish. Offer to discuss the situation privately. Chances are, this will make the back-stabber back off.

The office politician. This person believes that success isn't achieved by doing a good job but by cutting down the opposition and talking about, rather than doing, successful things. The person may think that wheeling and dealing is fun or may even use office politics to cover up personal incompetence. Office politicians come in a variety of forms:

1. Those who make promises that make them look good but who never deliver.
2. Those who make speeches, especially at meetings, and brag about what they've done.

3. Those who believe that their best chance to shine comes from knowing what their peers are doing, which causes them to snoop for information.

4. Those who are convinced that the road to success is through apple polishing.

The best way to deal with an office politician is to refuse to listen to rumors, gripes, and half-truths, thus letting the person know that you recognize his or her immaturity.

The flirt. This person specializes in cozy conversations, laughter, and too-cute remarks to the opposite sex whenever the chance arises. There may be little that co-workers can do in this situation other than to set a good example with their own proper office behavior. A confidential talk with the supervisor may be necessary, however, if customers are being driven away.

Whatever the problem, understanding and friendship are more likely to help than any other approach.

MAKING POINTS WITH YOUR SUPERVISOR

There are two common approaches to dealing with the supervisor, and both of them are wrong. The first is to avoid him or her as much as possible—be inconspicuous, don't volunteer, do just enough work to get by. The second approach is the old apple-polishing routine—flatter the person, do little favors, build his or her ego. This overlooks an important fact—the supervisor is human, too, and, like anyone else, will be embarrassed when praised or fawned over for little reason.

Your supervisor or office manager or an officer at your institution is a special person just because he or she is the boss and has certain authority and discretionary powers. It's necessary to make relations with this person an important part of your efforts for effective teamwork. Ask yourself a few basic questions:

- What are this person's physical characteristics? Young or not-so-young? Male or female?
- What is his or her personality like? Outgoing? Shy?
- What is his or her experience? Is the job of supervising people an old one or a new assignment?
- What does he or she consider important in the work? Is he or she a stickler for certain things?

Answers to these few questions should provide a start toward building a good relationship between you and your supervisor. For example, an older man may prefer to be called "Mister." A woman wants and is entitled to just as much respect as a male supervisor. A shy person will appreciate being left alone when concentrating on some jobs, and an outgoing individual will respond to more personal involvement in activities. The new supervisor will be feeling his or her way and will appreciate help from experienced employees if that help is given in a friendly manner without condescension. The old hand can spare more time to help out the staff. Either way, whatever the person's experience, personality, or physical makeup, he or she will respond more favorably to the employee who gives what is expected.

Requirements will vary, of course, but anyone in a supervisory position will expect at least these minimum things:

1. Accuracy;
2. Punctuality;
3. Courtesy with customers;
4. Cooperation with co-workers;
5. Loyalty to the financial institution;
6. Loyalty to himself or herself; and
7. Completion of a fair share of the work.

Beyond this, certain supervisors will have pet things on which they place emphasis. Try to cooperate in these things even if they seem unimportant. He or she may have reasons that you don't understand.

It's foolish to think of having a good relationship with a superior in grammar school terms. Your entire institution is a team, and the boss is a leader of part of it. In the business world, respect and cooperation at all levels are vital. Someday, if you're in that person's shoes, you'll expect the same from your staff.

Plan to be a good team member and help make your office a more efficient, more pleasant place to spend your working hours. It's easy to do, and it will make a good impression on everyone around you—your fellow employees, your supervisor, and your customers—every day.

5

CHAPTER

Effective Communications—
The Key to Motivating Others

The ability to communicate effectively not only makes other people think well of you, it can open doors in your business and social life. This is particularly valuable for you as a teller because you deal with the public every day. Try to apply the following principles to help improve your skills in person-to-person communications.

BE A GOOD LISTENER

In late October 1938, millions of Americans left their homes and hysterically tried to escape death. The Martians were after them. Orson Welles, as part of a regular series of radio dramas, was presenting the famous science fiction story, *War of the Worlds*. Obviously, it was well done. Just as obviously, many people weren't really listening, for not once, not twice, but *four* times the announcement was made that the show was just a play, a work of fiction. People were hearing only what they wanted to hear; they were not listening to what was being said.

As a teller, it is important for you to develop the skill of listening as part of the art of effective communications because you are in a position to hear a great deal of important information and to influence others by taking intelligent action on what you hear. Customer feedback, via reputable employees, is important to management. In this way, future policies can be based on more facts and less guesswork.

You Benefit as a Listener

People who listen do a better job. Not only can they act as reporters for their superiors, but they are more efficient. If you are told how to handle a new procedure, and you listen, you'll probably do it right the first time. If you don't listen, you'll waste both your time and the effort involved in finding out how to correct your error. When you consistently do things right, especially the first time, management notices.

Listeners wield more influence over others than the average person. Most people don't listen. They just wait impatiently for their turn to talk. This insults those who are speaking to them. Their actions say, "I don't respect *your* ideas, so be quiet and listen to how bright *I* am!" When you listen carefully, on the other hand, you say, "I respect your ideas. . . ." And when your turn comes to speak, the other person is likely to return the courtesy, especially if you ask intelligent questions such as, "Why do you think this happened, Mrs. Smith?" "How can we improve our service, Mr. Jones?" "How can we help put over this new service, John?"

Using Information Gained by Listening

Obviously, one reason for developing the listening habit is to get useful information. Another reason is to use that information in a constructive way. For example:

Mrs. Smith has a complaint. Your financial institution, in her mind, has wronged her. Your experience tells you at once where the problem is. You have two options. One, you can interrupt Mrs. Smith, assure her that this is just a misunderstanding and that you know more about it than she does, or you can listen to her. Let her tell her side completely. Ask a few questions to be sure that she has said it all. *Then* thank her for calling it to your attention. *Then* explain that misunderstandings do arise and why this one did. If you choose the first option, you may clear up the problem, but you won't constructively create the relationship that careful listening can help you to build.

BE A GOOD CONVERSATIONALIST

Conversation consists of two parts—listening and talking. It isn't possible to do both at the same time, so, as suggested earlier, be a good listener. Then, when it's your turn to speak, try to develop a "you" rather than a "me" attitude.

Instead of talking about yourself and your interests all the time, get in the habit of doing the following:

Compliment the other person. Make your compliment sincere. Flattery is usually obvious and can do more harm than good.

Ask for advice or information. Without sounding like it, this is truly a compliment. You're telling the other person that you value his or her opinion and knowledge.

In addition, when you speak:

Be aware of your voice. You might even want to listen to a tape recording of it so you can hear the way you sound to other people. Do you sometimes speak with a whine, through your nose, or with an irritating pitch? Do you slur or mispronounce words? When you're aware of such things, you often can work to correct them.

Arm yourself with a good supply of things to talk about, not just banking. To do this, read a newspaper or listen to a news broadcast every day. Try to find time to read books as well as a weekly general-interest magazine. While you read, make it a point to remember facts to relate to particular people, knowing they'll appreciate your interest.

Use proper grammar. This is discussed later in this chapter.

Avoid relating unnecessary, tedious details. Try to condense what you have to say so you won't monopolize the conversation or become boring.

Get your point across with persuasion rather than argument.

Have a good sense of humor. Try to keep your conversations cheerful, seeing the bright or funny side of the situation at hand whenever possible.

Avoid telling offensive or off-color stories. Jokes that rely on putting people down simply aren't funny; they're insulting. And telling jokes that are off-color, even if they're funny, can lead to embarrassing situations and is simply inappropriate for a business office.

Have confidence when you talk. If you feel self-conscious about starting a conversation, try using one of the following topics to get you started: a new service, a piece of your institution's literature, or even the weather.

Emphasize the proper word. When you talk, try to avoid putting undue emphasis on words that might affect their intended meaning. For example, read the sentence, "He always says I look nice," putting emphasis on the word in italics in each case. Like this:

He always says I look nice. (No one else tells me this, only that person.)
He *always* says I look nice. (This is what he tells me every time he
talks to me.)
He always *says* I look nice. (This is what he tells me, but maybe he
doesn't really mean it.)
He always says *I* look nice. (I do, even though other people don't.)
He always says I *look* nice. (But maybe he doesn't think I act that way.)
He always says I look *nice*. (There's no mistake about it—I don't look
any other way, just nice!)

In every case, the emphasis changed the meaning of the sentence.

Good conversation is good business. It's a skill that can create a positive,
friendly image both for you and for your financial institution.

"JARGONESE"—A COMMUNICATIONS BARRIER

Jargon is defined as "the technical or secret vocabulary of a science, art,
trade, sect, profession, or other special group." In defense of jargon, realize
that it serves two needs, one physical and one psychological. Physically, it
saves time and avoids errors. Someone in the trade knows precisely what
the other person is talking about. For example, which is more readily understandable to you?

"Charlie, I have a customer coming in today who would like to make a
savings-type deposit for a period of six months for $5,000. What inter-
est will we pay her?" or
"Charlie, what rate can I quote on a six-month CD for $5,000?"

Less than half the words and much clearer, the second phrasing is preferred for internal communications.

The psychological benefit of having jargon is that it automatically identifies people with a group that has professional or skill status. All of us need to
feel that we are part of an important group, and every group, including the
banking industry, has its own language to set it off.

What's Wrong with Jargon?

If using jargon saves time, decreases errors, and gives people self-satisfaction,
what's wrong with using it? The answer is *nothing*—when it's used at the right
time. However, using jargon when speaking to a customer is not the right time.
Picture these situations:

(Timid Elderly Customer at Office Manager's Desk)

Manager: Yes, I see you've got problems, but the reason you can't reconcile your statement is that you didn't deduct two DMs. One for your service charge and the other for an OD you had on the 7th.

(Young Depositor at Teller's Window)

Teller: If you ever want to check your balance, just call bookkeeping and give them your MICR number and the date and amount of your last deposit.

(Couple at Loan Officer's Desk)

Loan Officer: Well, I wouldn't count on getting a mortgage too easily. Fannie Mae said yesterday that money is going to get even tighter.

Put yourself in the customer's place. Fannie Mae sounds like someone's good-natured graying aunt! And she's handing out predictions about *tight* (what does that mean?) money? MICR? OD? DM? CD? EFTS? If the alphabet soup doesn't chase customers down the street, esoteric terms such as *points, compensating balance, hypothecation, floor-planning, commercial paper,* and *truncation* will. Stop and consider how many times a day a customer could be made to feel inept when he or she didn't understand the language because an employee at your institution carelessly used confusing words.

Use Simple Terms

Don't talk down to a customer, but remember to avoid jargon. People just starting out in banking who have learned a few technical terms are sometimes eager to show them off, but customers don't want to know about the fine points of banking. They just want to get good financial service and to understand the terms of that service in plain English.

Communications with customers are the essence of good service and courtesy. While jargon is an asset in internal communications, it is a barrier to customer communications. Try to keep the two separated.

USE CORRECT GRAMMAR

No matter how well you do your job as a teller, no matter how much others like you or how much new business you bring in for your financial institution, your chances for getting to the top are lessened if you lack the ability to speak and write well. Unfair as it may seem to the person who possesses all the other necessary qualities for advancement, poor grammar leads to the assumption that that person lacks sufficient education, has not had a "proper" upbringing, or is less than intelligent.

Successful mastering of just a few rules can often mean the difference between doubt and confusion in expressing yourself and the self-confidence that comes from the certainty that you are using correct grammar. To train yourself to avoid common errors and to correct any other small mistakes of your own, form the following habits:

- Read good books, magazine articles, and newspapers. As you read, notice how words and phrases are put together. Proper usage is bound to rub off simply through repeated exposure, thereby improving your grammar in addition to making you well informed.
- Listen to people talk—people who are experienced in expressing themselves effectively. TV and radio commentators, with few exceptions, use correct grammar all the time.
- Care about how you impress others. Every time you have the chance to express yourself, be aware of how you come across.

The Common Mistakes

The following sentences give a few examples of mistakes that are most often made:

Pronouns. Are you going with my wife and (I) (me)? The choice is between you and (he) (him).

Singular and plural verbs. The cost of supplies (are) (is) rising. There (was) (were) a hat and coat in the office. Each of your answers (are) (is) right.

Confusing words. How does this (effect) (affect) you? He is the (principle) (principal) speaker. What is his working (capitol) (capital)?

In each of the examples above, the second answer is the correct one. Watch out for these and other tricky choices.

TELEPHONE TECHNIQUES

Did you ever have a conversation that sounded like the one that follows? Try to recall your reactions as you read it.

You place a call to a business firm. The telephone rings, and a voice at the other end answers.

Voice: Hello.

You: Hello? Is this the XYZ Company?

Voice: Yes it is.
You: I'm interested in buying a washing machine.
Voice: Yes?
You: Well, do you sell them?
Voice: Yes.
You: Well, may I speak to someone who handles them?
Voice: Oh, I guess you want Mr. Smith . . .

When this happens, don't you feel like taking your business elsewhere? Yet it's easy for a busy teller to answer the telephone carelessly and put a caller through just such a routine. Tellers are geared for person-to-person business dealings, and telephones can be an annoying interruption. Therefore, it pays to develop good techniques that will let you handle calls efficiently so that you can get back to your customers' transactions as soon as possible while still maintaining the goodwill of the person you are talking to on the telephone.

Tips for Answering the Phone

Here are some basic rules to follow when you're on the receiving end of a business telephone call:

- Answer the phone immediately.
- If a switchboard operator hasn't done so, answer with the name of your financial institution. This usually applies to direct calls only.
- Identify yourself and your office or department.
- If the call is for someone else, get that person promptly or offer to have him or her return the call. Don't keep the caller waiting.
- If the call is for you about a matter that is your responsibility, be sure you understand exactly what the caller wants and what action, if any, is necessary. Take notes if it will help, and ask questions that will clarify the situation.
- When the conversation is over, politely end it. "Good-bye" or "Good-bye and thanks for calling" are always appropriate.

Here are a few things to avoid:

- Don't answer the phone with cute phrases such as "Happy New Year!"
- If your financial institution has a long name, shorten it to the one commonly used by local businesspeople. "First National," for example, beats "First National Bank and Trust Company of Crooked Creek, Massachusetts."

- Don't pass the buck. If you can't handle the matter, tell the caller and promise to have the proper person return the call promptly— then do it.
- Don't carry over a busy or angry attitude to a phone call. Answer each call in a positive and cheerful manner.
- If a person being called isn't available, say "I'm sorry, she isn't here right now. I expect her in an hour. May she call you then?" Don't say, "I'm sorry, Sally is still out to lunch," or "Sally is in the ladies' room."

Tips on Making Calls

When it comes to making business calls, try these tips:

- Choose a convenient time to call. Don't telephone a restaurant owner, for example, during lunch hour.
- Know what you're going to say. If necessary, make a list of points to cover.
- Identify yourself and your institution immediately.
- Briefly state the basic purpose of the call right away, before you get into details. Don't let the person you're calling get upset; people do take a call from a financial institution seriously.
- Avoid discussing financial matters with anyone other than the person you are trying to reach. Give the person the same confidential service you'd give him or her in person.

General Tips

Whether you receive or initiate the telephone call:

- Be friendly. A smile *does* show over the phone.
- Get to the point.
- Be clear in what you are saying.
- Speak directly into the phone, enunciating and talking slowly enough to be understood.
- Don't drop the phone, sigh loudly, or otherwise rattle the person on the other end.
- Don't carry on a conversation with someone in the office while you're on the phone. This is inconsiderate to both people.

- Hang up gently. Bashing down the receiver is a sure way to change a pleasant call into an unpleasant one.
- If the call warrants it, make a brief note about the date, time, and purpose of the call along with a synopsis of what was said. If needed, file this for future reference just as you would a letter.

Answering Machines

Having a machine answer the telephone and using voice mail for recording messages is becoming standard business practice. But sometimes it can be frustrating for the caller. In spite of the fact that most financial institutions would rather have real people answering their telephones, personnel shortages often create the need for this alternative. In this case, the best thing to do is to keep the customer in mind.

If you're ever involved with creating a recorded telephone message, be certain that your voice is warm and friendly. Try listening to yourself after you record the message. Then, if you sound overly cold and businesslike, record it again and smile while you speak. You're sure to be pleased with the difference.

Proper phone usage is an important part of a skilled teller's effective communications techniques.

WHEN YOU WRITE A LETTER

The average teller writes few business letters, but occasionally a supervisor may say, "Will you write to this customer for me?" Such a letter may be prepared for the supervisor's signature or for the teller's. In either case, the letter is of great importance to its receiver. It represents both the teller and the financial institution.

The style in which you write business letters is very important. Just as the telephone reflects a smile or magnifies any discourtesy, so a business letter communicates an exaggeration of what you are trying to say. Trying to lend a humorous note to a serious subject may be misinterpreted as sarcasm. Making light of a problem in order to ease its burden may be misinterpreted as lack of concern.

Here are three simple rules of style to follow when you write a business letter:

1. *Write as you would speak*. Say what you have to say in a friendly, direct, and forthright manner.
2. *Cut out unnecessary words*. You'll be amazed at how much better your letters will sound if you simply stop using extra words.

3. *Avoid cliches.* Trite sayings should not be in your letters; they're an undesirable characteristic of any writing.

Steps in Writing a Business Letter

Five steps are involved in writing a business letter. Note that the first letter of each, when put together, spells the word *P-R-O-S-E*. Remember this word and the rules that go with it, and you'll write good prose:

1. *P*lan what you're going to say. This prevents rambling, disjointed letters and avoids misunderstandings. Write and edit a draft before the final typing.
2. *R*elate to the reader. Gear your letter to *that person.* How will what you have to say benefit or affect him or her?
3. *O*btain the reader's attention and hold his or her interest. This rule relates to the second and can be accomplished by keeping the letter reader-oriented.
4. *S*tate the facts clearly. Make sure the reader will understand what you are trying to say.
5. *E*nglish should be plain and proper.

Typing Tips

Business letters should not be written in longhand. They should be typed, using a typewriter, computer, or word processor. No one expects you to be an expert typist, of course. If you're not familiar with the correct format for preparing a business letter or memo, check a secretary's handbook for a guide. Your financial institution's image is reflected in this work just as it is in the work you do at your window. If a customer gets a poorly typed or sloppy letter, he or she will get the impression that your employees simply don't care what customers think of them.

The important thing to do when it comes to preparing business correspondence, as in other areas of your work, is to develop a routine that minimizes the chance for errors. These tips can help if you do not have access to a computer or word processor:

- Make sure your typewriter type is clean and that the ribbon is in good condition.
- Follow your institution's rules for format or use those described in a current secretary's handbook.

- If you use a manual typewriter, try to have an even touch on the keys. Light and dark letters are a giveaway that the typist is inexperienced.
- Correct mistakes neatly or retype the letter.
- After you have finished typing the letter, proofread it carefully before taking it out of the typewriter. This makes it easier to correct mistakes. Do the same with the envelope—remember, it makes the first impression.

If you do have access to a word processor or a computer with a word processor program, be sure to:

- Learn the proper format commands for writing business letters and memos so that they'll be printed properly.
- Carefully check each letter or memo on the display screen and make any necessary corrections before giving the command to print.
- Save what you've written on a disk if it's your institution's policy to do so, and/or make a copy of the printed piece of correspondence.
- Use any form letters that your institution provides on disk whenever it's appropriate. These not only save time, but they will most likely be well written. Form letters can be personalized with the name and address of the recipient.

Time-Saving Ideas

Here is a way to make letter-writing easier and less time-consuming:

- Save copies of good letters that you've written and use them again for similar situations. For example, if you write to a customer to ask that a certain form be signed and you know the letter is a good one, save it and use it each time you need to contact a customer with the same request. Ask your co-workers to swap effective letters with you. That way, you can help each other.
- Collect copies of letters your financial institution receives from other business sources that impress you as being well written and adapt them to your situation.

By using these sources, you can save a lot of letter-writing time. Equally important, you can make your letters more effective because each one will have been carefully worded to be highly readable and to motivate the recipient.

In fact, think of how convenient it would be if you followed the foregoing suggestions and set up a neatly indexed file, classified by subject, that contained examples of prewritten letters covering a number of common situations. If such a file were available and the need for a letter arose, the appropriate one could be duplicated—producing an original, of course—and personalized with the addressee's name. A word processor is particularly useful for this purpose. The file could be kept up-to-date by adding new letters and replacing any that had become overused or inappropriate.

Your letters are a reflection of your abilities, your personality, and your financial institution. Take the time to make them your best.

WHEN YOU WRITE A MEMO

From time to time, it may be necessary for you to write an internal memo. For example, you may need to report customer feedback, describe what took place during an office meeting, explain a change in procedures to other tellers, explain why you exceeded your daily cash limit, or request vacation time or days off.

Whatever the purpose of a memo, well-written internal communications require careful thought and planning. Here are four reasons why it's useful to convey important information to co-workers in writing:

1. The person who receives a written memo can't say he or she wasn't given the information.
2. If the words are clear, putting something in writing can help to avoid misunderstandings.
3. Written communications are more likely to be remembered than oral ones. They provide a tangible way to get attention and recognition.
4. A memo can serve as the basis for more productive person-to-person contacts.

Memo-Writing Tips

To make your memos effective, it's best to summarize your main points, detail those points, then conclude with another summary. In addition:

- Before you begin, make an outline of what you need to say. It may help to write a draft of your memo before its final typing so that you can read and edit it.
- Be brief and cover only one or two subjects. Extraneous material can be confusing.

- Break down your ideas into short paragraphs. This is a convenient, concise way to cover all of the pertinent points.
- Start with a To-From-Subject-Date heading. And be accurate in relation to the names and titles of the recipients.
- Avoid big or ambiguous words. Even if you know their exact meaning, someone else might misunderstand them.
- Avoid unnecessary words and don't be vague or let your thoughts wander. Just stick to the nuts and bolts.
- As with business letters, use correct grammar, spelling, and punctuation. If you're a bit rusty in this area, refer to a good book on the subject.
- Try to write in a light, interesting style. Above all, be friendly and optimistic.
- Be polite. Words such as "please" and "thank you" are just as important for internal communications as they are for letters to customers and other outsiders.
- Never write your memos in longhand. Instead, use a typewriter or word processor just as you do when preparing other correspondence.
- Keep a copy of what you write as well as any memos you receive. For easy reference, file them according to subject matter rather than the dates they were sent or received.

When clarity really counts, don't try to put across the facts in person; report them in easy-to-understand written form.

GOSSIP AND RUMORS

A rumor is defined as "unverified information of uncertain origin." And gossip is simply a rumor that concerns people. Often, rumors start with some issue with a factual basis that becomes distorted. For example, the board of directors may be considering the possibility of revising vacation policy. That is the fact. Someone hears this, but he or she misses the words "considering the possibility." Repeated, the "fact" is that the board *is* going to change vacation policy. "How? Well, maybe by . . . " and repeated by a totally uninformed person, the maybe becomes "fact." Add many repetitions, misunderstandings, and maybes, and you have a full-scale rumor:

"Did you hear? No vacations next year! But the year after next, one full month for everybody! In Florida! With double pay!"

Silly? Sure, but rumors always are. And when rumors become gossip, they can seriously damage the reputation of a person, just as a rumor can adversely influence the intentions of management.

Who Spreads Rumors and Gossip?

Invariably, people who spread stories have personal problems. Consider the following examples (as well as those described in the section on difficult co-workers in Chapter 4):

Malicious Mary is convinced that life dealt her a bad hand. She deserved to be born rich, beautiful, and pampered. Since she wasn't, she pampers her ego by cutting others down to her size. Taking half-truths and expanding them to make another person look bad, she is often afraid to tackle someone with a really strong personality, so she specializes in sniping at less forceful people who can't or won't hurt her in return.

Jealous Jenny thinks she should be a vice-president. Since her financial institution has overlooked her obvious talents, she'll get even by starting rumors that are carefully designed to hurt morale by making the staff dissatisfied.

Bored Bob loves to talk but hasn't had an original thought in years. So he passes on every bit of gossip he hears or imagines he hears just to have something to do. He's lonely for friendship but doesn't realize that his tongue is scaring away anyone who might try to like him.

Dull Donald is uptight about anything modern, so he does his part to put it down by spreading rumors about anyone or anything that doesn't happen to fit into his narrow viewpoint. His targets include his institution's policies, the customers, and his fellow employees.

Sulky Sue is scared of people, so she makes sure they leave her alone by making them afraid of what she might say about them. Though she has an inferiority complex, she covers it up by acting superior and aloof, spending her time showing how inferior others are by telling stories that point out their supposed deficiencies.

Notice that all of the people just described are dissatisfied with themselves, are angry or afraid of other people, and are very much in need of the understanding and affection of those around them. It's not easy to be nice to someone who has hurt you with a malicious story, nor is it easy for management to treat a person who starts destructive rumors as part of the staff team. This is worth a try, though, because if these people can be convinced to change, working with them will be more pleasant for everyone involved.

You can help by refusing to listen to gossip or rumors and by not repeating them yourself. In addition, try to be friendly to the person who spread them, and maybe he or she will get the point. If not, ask the person to stop, then offer your friendship again. If your co-worker still doesn't get the point, at least avoid his or her tongue. Rumors and gossip can destroy the effective communications necessary for an efficient, pleasant office atmosphere.

COMMUNICATING WITH MANAGEMENT

Keeping Management Informed

As a teller, you have closer contact with the public than anyone else in your financial institution. You get a better indication of people's needs, likes, and dislikes than your office manager does—or than higher management does. It's part of your job to pass on information about customer reactions. Top management can't tell if changes are needed unless it gets on-the-spot reactions.

It would be foolish to run to your supervisor with every single comment, but you should pass on the following:

- Similar comments that have been made by a number of people.
- Significant comments made by a person who is knowledgeable or is important in the community.
- A significant *lack* of expected comments. Often, people are expected to react in a certain way and they don't. For example, years ago when a large eastern bank put its savings accounts on computer and did away with passbooks, top management expected real trouble. Tellers and managers were taught how to answer questions, but few questions came. The lack of complaints was important.

Keeping management informed is an important part of your job of building effective communications.

How to Make a Suggestion

Occasionally, everyone gets an idea about how a job could be done better, more effectively, or with less effort. Unfortunately, many of these ideas never have a chance to be evaluated because they aren't passed on to the people who could do something about them. If you ever get such an idea, here's the way to make a suggestion and be sure it receives proper consideration:

Think it out. Really consider the idea from every angle. If it would save work in one place, might it create more somewhere else? What are its benefits? Who will it affect and how will it affect them?

Put it in writing. First, explain briefly how things are done now. Then, concisely and step by step, explain the new idea. List the benefits.

Answer possible objections. Finally, type it so it is easy to read, and include your name as the person suggesting the new idea.

Send it to the right person. And don't bypass your supervisor! Show it to him or her first. Often, the supervisor may do the passing on, perhaps after adding some comments, or he or she may suggest you forward the suggestion directly to a specific person.

Next time you get a good idea, pass it on. If you do so in the proper way, it may be accepted.

HOW TO MAKE A COMPLAINT

If you work for your financial institution for any length of time, you will occasionally disagree with someone who is in a supervisory position. In some cases, this may happen because you haven't understood a certain situation. Perhaps the other person has information or experience that you don't have. Either way, good communications can provide the answer. Find out what's going on, even if you have to ask.

On the other hand, the two of you may disagree because the other person doesn't understand the situation. It happens. When you're working at a certain level, it's possible to lose touch with the other levels. It's up to you to help keep management informed by providing valid feedback on customers at all times, not just when new ideas are being tested. This doesn't mean just passing on complaints; it means letting management know how things are with your customers whenever there's anything significant to report.

Perhaps you and your supervisor or someone in management will disagree because you have an honest difference of opinion. This happens, too. And when it does, there's only one answer. The other person has the prerogative of trying things his or her way, and it's your job to be supportive to the best of your ability.

When you disagree with your supervisor or management for any reason, keep these points in mind:

- *Never* voice your complaints to your customers. You may get a sympathetic ear because your customers know you better than they know anyone else who works in your office, but that doesn't prove anything—it only makes a poor impression on your customers.

- Don't get angry with the person with whom you disagree. Ask for an explanation of the situation. As an employee, you should be kept reasonably well informed in order to do your best job. So get the facts.

- Don't have gripe sessions with other employees. Sniping at someone in management won't solve anything, and gripe sessions can become an obsession that makes working something to be dreaded.
- Be sure that the situation is serious enough to warrant a complaint. Don't misinterpret an unintentional slight. Perhaps your supervisor was a little gruff or short because he or she had personal problems or because of a headache. Supervisors are human, too, and their feelings show in their work situations.
- If you decide the situation is serious enough to warrant a complaint, state your feelings to your supervisor honestly, intelligently, and without emotion or anger. Then listen to his or her side of things in the same way. If either of you is wrong, perhaps changes can be made right away. If you still disagree, say so, but give your supervisor the loyal support he or she needs.

Handled in the proper way, a complaint may clear the air and make for a mature relationship between you and your supervisor. It will go a long way toward insuring that your team is not hurt by misunderstandings.

How to Take Criticism

Everyone in the working world is going to receive some criticism sooner or later. They'll make stupid mistakes. Or they'll blow great opportunities. Or they'll let their emotions speak instead of their intellects. When this happens, they'll be criticized. As a teller, it is important to know how to take criticism when it comes. Start with these thoughts:

Criticism does not mean the end of the world. At the time that you're under fire, you may think all is lost, but it isn't.

Let the supervisor have his or her say. There's good psychology behind this. He or she is upset about two things: the thing that was wrong and having to call you to task—an unpleasant part of the supervisory job. You'll find that letting the person get everything out in the open will have a calming effect. If he or she was in error to start with, this could also become apparent during the conversation.

Consider the other person's viewpoint. It is important to do your job independently, but don't have an unreasonable attitude as a result. Sometimes the attitude is, "I have less experience than you, I have less training than you, my judgment is not as mature as yours; but my opinions are just as good as yours, so I'll do as I please!" Maybe he or she is right and you're wrong. Consider the possibility anyway.

Don't get emotional. Don't cry or lose your temper. Chances are the situation is as unpleasant for your supervisor as it is embarrassing for you. So keep cool and get it over with.

When the other person is finished, state your side. If you still feel that he or she is wrong, say so, calmly. Be rational. Explain your position carefully and don't get personal; just stick to the facts. If you're wrong, admit it and suggest corrective action if it's appropriate. This probably means just saying, "I'm sorry. I'll try to be more careful."

Don't make excuses or pass the buck. If you make a mistake and are told about it, accept it and let it go. The most important thing about mistakes is to learn from them and thus avoid repeating them. Making an issue out of criticism makes the criticism more important than the error itself, and that does more harm than good.

When it's over, forget it. Don't forget the situation that prompted the criticism, but do forget any anger or resentment you may feel. Get the office and your place in it on an even keel as quickly as possible. It's not easy to do, but it pays off in a more pleasant work relationship all around.

Everyone on your staff will benefit if communications are given careful attention. Do your best to motivate others by practicing the principles that lead to effective communications skills.

TIPS FOR ATTENDING MEETINGS

A List of Dos and Don'ts

If you're required to attend staff meetings, you'll want to do your best to participate effectively. Here are some tips for doing so:

Do your homework. If you know the subject of the meeting in advance, go to it prepared. If you have something you'd like to say, be ready to back up your ideas with facts. This way, you won't leave yourself open to criticism from others.

Do participate. Doodling on a scratch pad or mentally planning the next day's work is unfair to yourself and to the others at the meeting. Share constructive thoughts and be sure you understand what is happening and why. Don't be afraid to ask questions.

Do listen. Instead of sitting and thinking of what to say next while someone else is talking, give him or her your attention. In addition, avoid disrupting the speaker with whispered comments to the person sitting next to you.

Don't talk too soon. Think your ideas through. Then, choose the right words for expressing what you want to say. Be brief. A well-known speaker once summed up the secret of his success in just eight words— "When I get to the end, I stop."

Do keep an open mind. The mark of a truly sharp person is his or her ability to change an opinion when the logic of another's arguments becomes clear. On the other hand, you shouldn't just sway with the tide once you become convinced of a sound position. In that case, stand by your ideas.

Don't make jokes. Banking is a serious business, and getting laughs or making light of a meeting topic could hurt you, your financial institution, or your co-workers' feelings.

Don't be defensive. If someone criticizes your ideas, try not to take it personally. Try to accept criticism as constructive feedback. This attitude might even be contagious.

Do support the group. When a conclusion is reached, even if it differs from your ideas, be ready to support the group. This means letting your ideas become group ideas as well; once you've presented a good idea at a meeting, it belongs to everyone there. This helps to sell your idea as well as to insure action on it.

How to Sell Your Ideas

After taking your time and thinking it through carefully, if you're sure you have an important idea to contribute at a meeting, add a few principles of good salesmanship to help get your idea accepted:

Start out with an ally. If your idea ties in with something said previously at the meeting, start by saying, "Something John said a little while ago has given me an idea that might work . . . " or words to that effect. John is now potentially on your side. He has received some credit for sparking your idea.

Be friendly. Smile and be cooperative. A belligerent salesperson never sold an idea.

Be enthusiastic. Letting others at the meeting know that you sincerely mean what you say will help to get your idea accepted.

Be willing to help out if action is required. Few people like ideas that involve extra duties for other people but not for the originator.

Finally, be ready to accept the possibility that your idea may not be the end-all, and try not to take it as a personal affront if it isn't accepted. If someone else's idea is adopted, get behind it and be as willing to work for it as you would want the originator to have been for your idea.

Meetings can be a waste of time or they can be quite productive. They can give employees a chance to air their views, thus improving office morale. Meetings often produce a positive result, and they provide an important channel for effective communications.

6

How to Get Ahead

We all have "stars" whom we respect and admire. But these successful people didn't start out as stars. They worked long and hard to develop their skills. They made a career plan and stuck to it. As a teller, you can, too. If you'd like to remain a teller, you can be a star teller. If you'd like to have a supervisory position, then keep in mind that it's rarely easy to find a really skilled person for a higher-level job. When your financial institution is looking for such a person, make sure you're ready to step up and fill the position.

TIPS FOR JOB SUCCESS

Did you ever stop to ask yourself how effective you are in your job? You should, because it's something your supervisors are always doing. It's important to them to know for purposes of making salary or promotion recommendations. It's important to you for the same reasons.

If you will accept one single idea, you'll be a success in this or any job you ever hold: *The person who puts more into his or her work than he or she is getting paid for is bound to succeed.* This doesn't mean you have to go to ridiculous extremes; it just means sincerely trying to give a job your best.

To do this, start with a self-analysis. Pick out your strong points and use them to advantage. For example, if you're gregarious, try to develop customer goodwill and to sell your institution's services. Then pick out your weak points and try to eliminate them. The following tips will help you to succeed:

- Take on responsibilities without being asked. Remove the words "can't" and "won't" from your vocabulary. Say, "Oh, I can't do that" and you won't be asked again.
- Don't be afraid of change. Instead, look for and accept challenges.
- Don't be afraid of making a mistake. If you are, it will prevent you from trying anything new. See your mistakes as learning experiences rather than as failures.
- Be dependable. As a teller, handle your transactions carefully and do your best to establish a near-perfect balancing record.
- Sell your financial institution's services. This will be discussed in detail in the final section of this book.
- Make friends for your institution by giving the kind of service that is "above and beyond the call of duty." You'll create goodwill for yourself at the same time.
- Get recognition for your efforts. Every time you ask for and get a new account, be sure to make a note of it and pass it along to your supervisor or office manager. Keep a written list of practical things customers say about your institution and give a typewritten copy of it to your supervisor on a periodic basis. Clip newspaper articles about things that will interest management, such as the announcement of a new business that is coming to the area or the death of an important customer.

All of these positive efforts are applicable to anyone, no matter what his or her position or profession might be.

GETTING A PROMOTION

From time to time, your manager will be asked to make a recommendation for promotion from among the tellers at your office. A supervisory position may need to be filled where you presently work, or an opening that a teller from your office could fill may occur elsewhere in your financial institution. In either case, each candidate for the job will be evaluated to determine whether that person is capable of doing it well.

Desirable Traits

If you're ever considered for a promotion, the following positive traits will count in your favor:

Experience. Do you have the necessary knowledge to fill the job in question? Without this, all of your other positive traits may not be enough.

Dependability. Do you come to work every day and on time? When you're given a job to do, do you do it well?

Perseverance. When there's work to be done, do you follow it through to its conclusion?

Initiative. Do you start things on your own or do you wait to be told what to do next?

Imagination. Are you able to tackle jobs and solve problems creatively?

Sales ability. Can you sell yourself, your ideas, and your services?

Ambition. Do you really want a promotion and increased responsibilities?

In addition, you should be:

Observant. Are you alert and able to evaluate various situations and apply what you see to your work?

Well-organized. Are you neat and efficient? Do you know where to find things and how to perform your various duties without wasting time?

Decisive. Do you generally exercise good judgment and have the courage to use it?

Loyal. Do you have a sense of pride in your financial institution?

Likable. Do you have the ability to get along with other people and earn their respect?

If you possess most of the foregoing traits, you have an excellent chance of being chosen for the position you'd like to have.

IF YOU'RE ALREADY A SUPERVISOR

If you are currently filling a supervisory position, here are some qualities that can make you successful in that job. Consider them and rate yourself. Do you possess all of them to a high degree? Are there some traits that you could stand to improve?

Good supervisors:

Are objective. It is sometimes easier to see the forest than the trees or vice versa, but good supervisors know that both count. They are objective in outlook and do not allow personal prejudices to stand in the way of proper actions.

Are fair. Good supervisors are interested in all of their employees, even if some are better trained or motivated than others. They give credit where it is due and expect the best from everyone.

Are available. Nothing is quite as frustrating to an employee as having a serious problem that requires a supervisor's attention and discovering that he or she is not available. Good supervisors are there to provide help when it's needed.

Keep the staff informed. Employees don't like surprises. Even bad news is easier to take if it comes with preparation, and half the fun of good news is anticipation. Wise supervisors tell the employees what is going on at work.

Know their strengths and weaknesses. Good supervisors know the areas in which they excel and where their weaknesses lie. What's more, such people are willing to admit it when they make a mistake and act unwaveringly when they are right.

Are effective. Good supervisors get their own job done and see to it that the staff members do their work accurately and on time.

Are patient. Good supervisors are aware that employees are human, so they are patient with their efforts while encouraging positive results.

Have a good sense of humor. Good supervisors are always ready to see the cheerful or amusing side of life and are fun to work with, not because they are funny, but because they are understanding.

If you work in such a position, try to see yourself as others see you in relation to the foregoing qualities.

THE ROLE OF THE HEAD TELLER

The duties and responsibilities of various personnel vary from one financial institution to another. This is certainly true of head tellers. In some cases, the job is that of senior teller. In others, the head teller is in fact an assistant to the office manager. However, certain tasks are often delegated to head tellers. They include:

- Supervising the operations and administrative details of the tellers' department, including checking machines for proper operation each morning, inspecting date stamps for the current date, maintaining proper supplies, and other routine functions.
- Ensuring that the inventory of coin and currency is adequate for anticipated needs but not in excess of the amount set forth in the bank's security policy.
- Supervising the balancing of the automated teller machine.

- Training and cross-training personnel in the tellers' section to ensure that adequate numbers of experienced personnel are always available.
- Supervising routine personnel functions within the tellers' section, such as keeping time records and vacation schedules.
- Informing tellers of operating procedures and changes in those procedures.
- Participating in tellers' salary reviews.
- Ensuring compliance with security regulations, such as proper placement and banding of bait money, control to avoid excess drawer cash, and enforcement of correct cash-handling procedures.
- Ensuring compliance with federal regulations, such as issuing currency transaction reports (CTRs).

In addition to any operational functions that head tellers may perform, they hold the number-one public relations spot in the tellers' section. As such, head tellers may be given the responsibility for checking on grooming and keeping an eye on general customer relations actions. What's more, their attitude and disposition influence the behavior of the other tellers. If the head teller gets along well with customers, the other tellers are likely to do the same. If he or she tends to be unfriendly, they may act that way, too. Thus, head tellers act as sales managers of the tellers' section. They may even be involved in the institution's marketing plans and promotions and certainly are expected to support them.

GETTING ALONG AT A NEW OFFICE

Starting a new job is never easy, especially if you must work in an office or department where you don't know everyone. Therefore, if you should get a promotion that requires a move to another office, or if you're simply transferred to a different location within your financial institution, it's a good idea to keep the following suggestions in mind:

- Get acquainted with your fellow employees as quickly as possible. The sooner you all know one another, the sooner you can be comfortable working together.
- Be friendly. An old saying suggests that the way you start something is what counts. So do start off on the right foot.
- Encourage others to show you the way they're used to doing things. Ask them to explain office procedures so that the work can continue to flow smoothly.

- Stick to the rules. Learn all you can about the regulations that apply to your new job and do your best to follow them.
- Learn where to find things. Nothing can hold up customers and shorten tempers more than lost forms or misplaced supplies.
- Don't rely on your memory. Write things down. Until everything becomes completely familiar, make a habit of taking notes and using them. This will help you to avoid wasting time by requiring repeated explanations.
- Try to meet your regular customers. They're curious about you, too, and will be pleased when they get to know you and when you can identify them by name.
- Never make unfavorable comparisons between your new office and the one in which you previously worked. You owe loyalty to your new co-workers, and they'll resent anything less.
- Finally, relax and try not to worry. Anyone who really cares about making a good impression on new co-workers and customers is bound to work out well. Sincere efforts are always appreciated.

Your job as a teller or as a supervisor, either now or in the future, is vitally important, both to you and to your financial institution. If you can do it better, now is a good time to start.

7

CHAPTER

After Working Hours

How much responsibility do you have to your financial institution after working hours? At one time, being seen in a bar or at the races meant automatic dismissal from some institutions. However, now, as a modern employee, you have much more freedom; but you still have to keep one fact in mind: *As a teller, you are in a position of trust. Therefore, you owe it to your employer to avoid putting yourself in situations where your trustworthiness can be questioned.*

Obviously, this means different things to different people. Once, at a discussion group attended by a dozen teller-trainees and three officers, the question was posed, "Is it all right for an officer who works at a financial institution to belong to a local key club?" The 12 young teller-trainees unanimously voted that it was decidedly *not* all right, and the three officers voted just as unanimously that it was perfectly okay. The 12 younger people saw the club as something pretty daring, but the officers saw it as a place with good food and drinks in a pleasant atmosphere.

Of course, there are obvious places that no degree of sophistication can excuse, and a teller who wants to retain community respect will stay away from them. By the same token, there are certain actions that a prudent teller will avoid—such as taking drugs, becoming intoxicated, gambling excessively, and the like. Assuming a position of trust demands that a proper image be maintained both in and out of the office. The days of acting ultraconservative and prudish are long gone and happily have been replaced by a commonsense approach to the standards of conduct that being an employee at a financial institution imposes. The rule of thumb is simple: Just avoid places, situations, and actions that could cast doubt on your integrity.

GIVING ADVICE

"You know all about banking. Tell me how to balance my budget!" "What stocks should I buy?" "What's the best way to finance my new car?" People who work in financial institutions hear these questions every time they go out socially. There's nothing wrong with giving advice if you are careful to follow two simple rules:

1. Really know what you're talking about and
2. Make it clear that you're not speaking for your employer.

These rules are important. No one likes to say, "I don't know," but it's far better than having the other person get hurt with bad advice. When someone asks for advice because he or she knows where you work, the best thing to do is to put it on business terms. Just say, "Automobile financing isn't my job, but I'll be glad to get the information for you. Better yet, why not come to my office and let me introduce you to Mr. Brown? He can really help you."

When you *do* feel qualified to advise someone on your own, avoid putting yourself in the position of speaking "officially" for your institution. In the first place, you could create some sticky situations. In the second place, speaking officially is a function reserved for corporate officers, unless specific authorization is given to the contrary. If friend Marge asks for help with the family budget, for example, help her as a friend, not as a teller.

On-the-job financial tips for customers are discussed in detail in Chapter 27. Such subjects as tax advantages for average people and special tips for checking account customers are covered.

Making Referrals

As an insider in the banking business, you will often see situations in which your financial institution could help your friends and acquaintances. This is not to suggest that you be a 24-hour-a-day salesperson—on the contrary, you would only succeed in alienating your friends. But you can take some opportunities to refer these people to those in your institution who can help them. This is simply being a friend and it is good public relations.

HANDLING CONFIDENTIAL INFORMATION

Every teller will, at some point, have a friend say something such as, "How much dough does that old miser, Smith, have? People say he socks it away like he expected to take it with him . . ."

The temptation is great to be a big deal and tell the friend, in confidence, of course, all about Mr. Smith. Sooner or later, though, the friend will realize that a teller who couldn't keep quiet about Mr. Smith won't keep quiet about him or her either. So the answer should be, "You know I can't answer that. If the boss found out I told you, I'd be in real trouble. Even more important, I want *you* to trust me, and you won't if I prove I can't keep my mouth shut."

Handling confidential information is a full-time part of your job. It's an easy part if you simply follow the rules of common sense and treat information about your customers as you would like similar information about yourself to be treated.

Topics That Should Not Be Discussed

Your financial institution is proud of the fact that its staff can keep secrets, and some things definitely should be kept secret. A customer's balance, for instance, or the answers to personal questions on a loan application should not be discussed. But how about not-so-obvious things? It is an important part of your job to be able to distinguish between items that are of interest and can be shared publicly and those that are confidential—although they may be of some interest! For example:

You are going to night school. This is a fact that will interest your friends. It is not confidential information.

A customer is getting divorced. This is strictly private, even if he or she happened to tell you at work, shouting it out so everyone in the lobby could hear. It's not your job to spread gossip.

A customer is getting married. Tell anyone you want, unless there is some unusual circumstance that would indicate silence.

A customer is late with a loan payment. That's strictly his or her business and that of the loan officer. You shouldn't even comment on it to the customer. He or she may have made private arrangements or you might be overheard.

A customer is taking a trip. This may or may not be confidential, depending on the circumstances. If he or she has saved for years to go to Europe and is proudly telling everyone about the coming trip, public

"These savings ledgers are fascinating! Next week, can you come to my party and bring the payroll printout for the Jones Company?"

congratulations may be in order. On the other hand, crooks love to know who will be out of town and when.

A fellow employee had a hangover. That's unfortunate, but it's the individual's and his or her supervisor's problem, not yours.

A customer made a large withdrawal. You should have told your supervisor in case he or she wanted to find out why. Other than that, it's privileged information.

A fellow employee got a promotion. Tell the world if you like! Everyone enjoys hearing good news about someone else. What's more, no one minds such news being told.

A fellow employee got a raise. That's confidential. People, generally speaking, like to keep financial matters under their own hats.

A new alarm system was just installed at your office. The security system of your financial institution should *never* be discussed with anyone! Someone may overhear you talking, and the information could come to the attention of a potential robber.

Discussing confidential information with other employees isn't even a good idea. Picture the following situation. Two tellers are having lunch together in a booth at a restaurant near their office. One speaks:

"I should've checked Mrs. Smith's balance before I cashed her check this morning. Now I'm in real trouble with John (the branch manager). But he never remembers his mistakes! Why, look at the time he put on a bad loan for that deadbeat, Bill Jones, or the time he okayed a check for Sue Doe. He didn't check her balance because he was too busy looking at her big blue eyes!"

Suppose that friends, neighbors, or casual or business acquaintances of the parties being discussed were nearby and overheard. They might tell the person about the incident and really cause trouble. Chances are they wouldn't because they'd be embarrassed. There are two things they are likely to do, though. If they're not good friends of the people involved, they might repeat what they heard to someone else: "Did you hear that Mrs. Smith writes bum checks?" "I hear that the manager at Last National is really easy to get favors from . . . if you're a pretty blonde!" "Yeah. And Bill Jones is a real deadbeat; he didn't pay back the money he borrowed." Thus, the people who overhear might repeat the gossip with the possibility of injuring an innocent party.

The other thing they are bound to do is lose confidence in your institution. After all, what would the employees say about *them*? And who might overhear? Discussing work, personalities, or problems in a restaurant or other public place is never wise. Some people delight in eavesdropping on supposedly private conversations and further delight in repeating to others what they have heard.

Here are five simple rules for handling confidential information:

1. Know what *should* be confidential. At the least, this will include anything that might embarrass a customer.
2. Keep all information confidential that was given to your financial institution in confidence.
3. Keep all transactions or current or past account status confidential.
4. Keep all information of a personal nature confidential. Don't gossip.
5. Keep all information pertaining to security confidential for your own safety and the safety of your fellow employees and customers.

Confidentiality should not be taken lightly. It's an attitude of concern that should be exhibited by everyone who works in a financial institution, regardless of his or her job. What's more, each time you show respect for your customer's privacy, he or she is bound to appreciate it and to recognize your professionalism.

BUILD YOUR "BANKABILITY"—
TELLER OPERATIONS

Whether or not a long-term career in banking is in your future, it pays to build your "bankability." For one thing, it helps you to do a better job as long as you continue to work in a financial institution. Another reason to build your "bankability" involves self-confidence. It is a wonderful boost to the human ego to know how to do something important and to be able to do it well.

The chapters in this section deal with the things you should do and know in order to build your "bankability." The emphasis is on the practical aspects of being a teller. Such subjects as the arithmetic associated with a teller's job, how the bookkeeping works, how to handle money and how to settle, developing efficient work habits, opening new accounts, and being audited painlessly are important.

Some of these things directly affect you as a teller. Others affect you only indirectly. The important thing to remember is that you and your fellow tellers are on a highly trained team that serves the businesses and individuals in your community. As a teller, you are in the forefront because you deal directly with the customer, but the bookkeeper who maintains records and files checks, the loan clerk who computes rates and posts payments, the transit clerk, the loan officer, the vault attendant—these and others are on the team as well. To build your "bankability," learn something about their jobs, too. After all, directly or indirectly, you're all involved in providing good service to your public.

8

CHAPTER

The Mathematics of Banking

As a teller, you are involved in performing mental arithmetic and written computations every day. In order to do your work competently, you must, of course, be able to handle figures efficiently and accurately.

To achieve this skill, certain good work habits are necessary:

- Always make your figures legible.
- Write them in straight, vertical columns, being especially careful to line up the decimal points.
- If you copied the numbers, check them before doing anything else.
- Concentrate while you work and be very accurate.
- Check your final results, doing the computation by a different method than you used the first time, if possible.

For much of your work, you probably use a calculator or a computer. This equipment may not always be convenient, though, so make sure that you are skillful when it comes to doing basic addition, subtraction, multiplication, and division without a machine. The more practice you get, the more capable you'll become.

PERCENTAGES

A percentage is a way of expressing a fractional part of a quantity on the basis of so many parts out of 100. Financial institution employees work with percentages every day. Interest paid by customers on loans and interest paid to customers on savings deposits is expressed in percentages. To find a percentage of a number, simply multiply that number by the percentage rate expressed as a decimal.

For example, $5\frac{1}{2}\%$ of $250 is

$$
\begin{array}{r}
\$250 \\
\times.055 \\
\hline
1250 \\
1250 \\
\hline
13.750 \text{ or } \$13.75
\end{array}
$$

For practice, figure out the amount of interest in these examples:

(a) 4% of $3,000
(b) $5\frac{1}{2}\%$ of $488.65
(c) $6\frac{3}{4}\%$ of $825
(d) 7% of $1,200
(e) 10.65% of $14,500

Here are the answers: (a) $120 (b) $26.88 (nearest penny) (c) $55.69 (nearest penny) (d) $84 (e) $1,544.25.

Turning the Problem Around

It is conceivable that you may, from time to time, be asked what percent one number is of another. In other words, if someone asked what percent $25 is of $200, you would divide the percentage by the base amount and reduce the resulting fraction to a decimal, which would then be expressed as a percent. Using the problem given . . .

$$
\frac{25}{200} = \frac{1}{8} = .125 \text{ or } 12\frac{1}{2}\%
$$

Try these examples:

(a) What percent of $200 is $60?
(b) What percent of $350 is $26.25?
(c) What percent of $28.50 is $3.42?

Answers: (a) 30% (b) $7\frac{1}{2}\%$ (c) 12%

The following table shows a list of common fractions and their equivalent percents. It provides a convenient way to quickly convert from one numerical expression to the other.

$\frac{1}{2} = 50\%$	$\frac{1}{5} = 20\%$	$\frac{5}{6} = 83\frac{1}{3}\%$
$\frac{1}{4} = 25\%$	$\frac{2}{5} = 40\%$	$\frac{1}{8} = 12\frac{1}{2}\%$
$\frac{3}{4} = 75\%$	$\frac{3}{5} = 60\%$	$\frac{3}{8} = 37\frac{1}{2}\%$
$\frac{1}{3} = 33\frac{1}{3}\%$	$\frac{4}{5} = 80\%$	$\frac{5}{8} = 62\frac{1}{2}\%$
$\frac{2}{3} = 66\frac{2}{3}\%$	$\frac{1}{6} = 16\frac{2}{3}\%$	$\frac{7}{8} = 87\frac{1}{2}\%$

USING AN ADDING MACHINE

A basic computation tool for anyone who deals in figures is the adding machine. Although these machines are used less frequently in financial institutions than they used to be, they can be handy because they are easy to use and they provide a tape you can check in the event of an error.

There are two common types of adding machines. One is the 10-key machine, on which the keyboard looks something like this:

$$7 \ 8 \ 9 \ \oplus$$
$$\otimes 4 \ 5 \ 6 \ \ominus$$
$$1 \ 2 \ 3 \ \text{\textcircled{T}}$$
$$0$$

The other is the square-keyboard type, which looks like this:

```
9999999999
8888888888 (NA)
7777777777 (+)
6666666666 (−)
5555555555 (ST)
4444444444 (T)
3333333333
2222222222
1111111111
(R) 0000000000
```

In each type, there may be either a nonadd key or the total key may give you a nonadd print.

Functions

Addition with either type of adding machine is easy. You simply punch the numbers to be added into the machine and punch the add key or motor bar after each. With the 10-key type, subtracting is also easy; you perform functions the same as for addition except that you use the subtract key.

You can also subtract with the square-keyboard machine. The technique is simple, though it sounds complicated. All you do is *add* in a number that will cause the total being carried to exceed the number to be subtracted by the number of total digits in the machine. For example:

If you have erroneously put $20 into your figures and wish to subtract it, before you hit a total, throw this figure into the machine:

$$9999998000$$

You make the *digit not a zero* furthest to the right add up to 10 with the number you wish to subtract, then make all of the digits all the way to the left add up to 9. Thus, to subtract $11,723.92, you would add in 99988276.08. Try it; it works. The best technique for error correction is to completely subtract the incorrect figure, circle the incorrect figure *and* the correction, then add in the correct figure.

Multiplication is also easy with either machine. Simply realize that multiplication is just a fast way to add numbers. Thus $123 \times 456 = 56{,}088$ is really the same as:

$$
\begin{array}{r}
12300 \\
12300 \\
12300 \\
12300 \\
1230 \\
1230 \\
1230 \\
1230 \\
1230 \\
123 \\
123 \\
123 \\
123 \\
123 \\
+\ \ 123 \\
\hline
56088
\end{array}
$$

Within the calculation 123 × 456, you are really saying 123 × 400 or 12,300 × 4; 123 × 50 or 1,230 × 5; and 123 × 6. Thus, in order to multiply on the adding machine, key in the base number—in this case, the 123—then follow with zeroes as digits up to the number of zeroes that would be in the highest number in the multiplier—in this case, two zeroes because 456 is *hundreds*. Add in this figure the number of times indicated in the digit in the multiplier—in this case, four times. Then key in the digits again, but use one *less* zero—in this case, take it to the *tens* column—and add it in the number of times indicated by the digit. Continue to follow this procedure until you finish the *units* column.

With the 10-key machine, it is easier to do this process in *reverse*. Thus, in this example, you would key in 123, press the *repeat* key, and enter the figure *six* times; add a zero and, with the repeat key still depressed, enter the figure *five* times; add another zero, enter the figure *four* times; then total.

Here are a couple of other things you can do with your machine:

- Run a tape sequence beginning with 1 and ending with 100. Like this:

  1
  2
  3
  4
  5 and so on

You have made a figure counter to use in determining whether or not you have omitted any figures when proving a tape. Just lay your "yardstick tape" beside the one you are proving, and you'll get a quick and accurate count. For accuracy, be sure you always use the same or a similar machine, of course.

- Throw in a nonadd number as an identifier when it comes in handy. Thus, if you want to remember the account number proved on a tape, throw in the last four digits on nonadd, or list the transit numbers of checks.

Adding machines may be less technologically advanced than other machines, but they can be very useful.

CALCULATORS ARE HANDY

Calculators can be handy for tellers. When buying or using a calculator, keep these tips in mind:

- Choose a model with an easy-to-read display.
- Select a portable model with a dual-powered solar battery.
- Make sure it's a business calculator with adequate financial functions, avoiding a model with a fixed decimal.
- Don't use a nonprinting calculator when you should be running a tape.
- Don't trust important figures you've run only once—prove yourself.

Basic Math

Addition, subtraction, multiplication, and division are easily done on any calculator. Calculators are also useful for converting fractions to decimals and percentages. To go to a decimal, just divide the top number by the bottom number. The result is the decimal. Thus, $\frac{3}{4}$ becomes 3 divided by 4; the decimal is .75.

To convert to a percent, go one step further. Here, it's top number divided by bottom number times 100 equals percent. Thus, with $\frac{1}{8}$, 1 is divided by 8 and this number is multiplied by 100, which is the same as moving the decimal point two places to the right; the percentage is 12.5. These calculations come in handy when determining the value of securities as collateral and in other basic situations.

Savings Math

If you ever have a customer who wants to know just how much his or her dollars will grow, your calculator can provide the answer. You'll need some basic symbols and formulas:

FV equals the future value of the account.
P equals the present value of a deposit.
i equals the interest rate per payment period as a decimal.

Thus, 5 percent compounded monthly would be .05 divided by 12 or .0041666.

n is the number of interest payments or deposit periods.
PMT is the amount of periodic deposits.

Formula One:

$$FV = P \times (1 + i)^n$$

That tells you the future value of a savings account with a fixed starting figure and no additional deposits. Thus, $500 left in a savings account at 5 percent interest compounded quarterly for two years would grow to $552.24. Here are the steps:

$$FV = P \times (1 + i)^n$$

$$FV = \$500 \times (1 + .0125)^8$$

$$FV = \$500 \times 1.0125^8$$

$$FV = \$500 \times 1.1044858$$

$$FV = \$552.24$$

Formula Two:

$$FV = \frac{PMT}{i} \times [(1 + i)^{n + 1} - (1 + i)]$$

This formula tells how regular deposits to a savings account will grow, at compounded interest. Thus, a deposit in a savings account of $25 per month for one year at 5 percent interest compounded monthly would grow to $308.25. Here are the steps:

$$FV = \frac{PMT}{i} \times [(1 + i)^{n + 1} - (1 + i)]$$

$$FV = \frac{\$25}{.0041666} \times [(1 + .0041666)^{12+1} - (1 + .0041666)]$$

$$FV = \frac{\$25}{.0041666} \times (1.0041666^{13} - 1.0041666)$$

$$FV = \frac{\$25}{.0041666} \times (1.05554 - 1.0041666)$$

$$FV = \$6000.096 \times .0513734$$

$$FV = \$308.25$$

The difficult part in each case is multiplying by the exponent. If the formula says $(1 + i)^n$, remember that the exponent, in this case n, means to multiply the quantity $(1 + i)$ times *itself* the number of times n indicates.

Now determine how much money a customer would have to deposit today in order to have a certain amount in the future. In this formula, P equals the principal amount:

$$P = \frac{FV}{(1+i)^n}$$

For example, if a depositor wished to have a total of $50,000 10 years from now, here's how to determine the amount he or she would have to deposit today in order to reach that goal at an interest rate of 5 percent compounded annually:

$$P = \frac{FV}{(1+i)^n}$$

$$P = \frac{\$50,000}{(1+.05)^{10}}$$

$$P = \frac{\$50,000}{1.05^{10}}$$

$$P = \frac{\$50,000}{1.6288942}$$

$$P = \$30,695.67$$

Here's the formula for figuring out the amount that would have to be deposited on a regular basis in order to reach a specified goal in the future:

$$PMT = FV\frac{i}{(1+i)^{n+1} - (1+i)}$$

Assume that the same customer would like to have $50,000 in 10 years and wants to make yearly deposits. How much would those deposits have to be?

$$PMT = FV\frac{i}{(1+i)^{n+1} - (1+i)}$$

$$PMT = \$50,000 \times \frac{.05}{(1+.05)^{10+1} - (1+.05)}$$

$$PMT = \$50,000 \times \frac{.05}{1.05^{11} - 1.05}$$

$$PMT = \$50,000 \times \frac{.05}{1.7103389 - 1.05}$$

$$PMT = \$50,000 \times \frac{.05}{.6603389}$$

$$PMT = \$50,000 \times .0757186$$

$$PMT = \$3,785.93$$

The Math of Lending

When it comes to doing loan computations, nothing beats a good payment table for accuracy and ease of operations. (See Figure 1 for an example of a payment table.) However, for a situation in which such a table is not available, you can figure out fairly accurate answers to the following questions with your calculator:

- What is my true annual interest rate?
- How much would my note have to be to get the amount of money I need?
- About how much a month will I have to pay? Or . . . What would my mortgage payments be?

Consider each of these questions in turn:

True Annual Interest Rate. Most people have little interest in exactly how much loans cost. Their concern is with how much they must repay each month. Nevertheless, the Truth-in-Lending law has made people aware of true annual interest. Here's the way to determine it:

$$\text{TRUE ANNUAL INTEREST RATE} = \frac{\text{COST OF LOAN}}{\text{DOLLARS LOANED} \times \text{TERM IN YEARS}}$$

Thus a $2,000 loan for six months with interest of $120 would be:

$$\text{TRUE ANNUAL INTEREST RATE} = \frac{\$120}{\$2,000 \times (\,^{6}/_{12}\,)}$$

$$\text{TRUE ANNUAL INTEREST RATE} = \frac{\$120}{\$2,000 \times .5}$$

$$\text{TRUE ANNUAL INTEREST RATE} = \frac{\$120}{\$1,000}$$

TRUE ANNUAL INTEREST RATE = .12 or 12 percent

Discounted loans. Most commercial loans are discounted for short terms. Here's the way to tell what a customer must borrow to end up with a desired amount as net proceeds:

$$\$ \text{ TO LEND} \times \frac{\text{PROCEEDS DESIRED}}{1 - (\text{ANNUAL INTEREST RATE} \times \text{FRACTION OF YEAR})}$$

Thus, to get proceeds of $2,000 for a six-month loan at 12 percent annual interest, the discounted note should be for $2,127.66. Here's why:

$$\$ \text{ TO LEND} = \frac{\$2,000}{1 - [.12 \times (\frac{6}{12})]}$$

$$\$ \text{ TO LEND} = \frac{\$2,000}{1 - (.12 \times .5)}$$

$$\$ \text{ TO LEND} = \frac{\$2,000}{1 - .06}$$

$$\$ \text{ TO LEND} = \frac{\$2,000}{.94}$$

$$\$ \text{ TO LEND} = \$2,127.66$$

Installment Loans. Installment loans can be complicated. Interest discounted in advance, add-on charges, insurance fees, and other factors can make them difficult to work out without special tables. For a simple installment loan, though, here is the formula to find out what customers most want to know—the amount of the monthly payment.

In this formula, *PMT* is the monthly payment, *P* is the principal, *n* is the number of payments, and *i* is the interest rate expressed as a decimal fraction. An annual interest rate of $13\frac{1}{2}$ percent is .01125 per month.

A loan of $1,500 for a year and a half at an annual rate of $13\frac{1}{2}$ percent would have monthly payments of $92.51. Here's the formula:

$$PMT = \frac{P \times i \times (1+i)^n}{(1+i)^n - 1}$$

$$PMT = \frac{\$1,500 \times .01125 \times (1+.01125)^{18}}{(1+.01125)^{18} - 1}$$

$$PMT = \frac{\$1,500 \times .01125 \times 1.2231}{1.2231 - 1}$$

$$PMT = \frac{20.639812}{.2231}$$

$$PMT = \$92.51$$

If you have access to a payment table, you can use it to determine monthly loan payments as calculated here. With regard to this example, use the payment table shown in Figure 1 and find 13.5 percent in the left-hand column. Then scan across to the monthly payment figure in the 18 months column. The figure is 6.168113 per $100. Multiply this figure by 15 (for the amount of the loan, which is $1,500). The answer is $92.521695.

F I G U R E 8–1

Sample Payment Table

INSTALLMENT LOAN PAYMENTS

MONTHLY PAYMENTS

Description: This table shows the monthly payment, the finance charge, and the add on rate for an installment loan of $100 written at an Annual Percentage Rate.

Example: The monthly payment for an installment loan of $1,000 at a 4.00% APR for 18 months is $ 57.33. The finance charge is $ 31.97.

	12 MONTHS			15 MONTHS			18 MONTHS		
ANNUAL PERCENTAGE RATE	ADD ON RATE	FINANCE CHARGE	MONTHLY PAYMENT	ADD ON RATE	FINANCE CHARGE	MONTHLY PAYMENT	ADD ON RATE	FINANCE CHARGE	MONTHLY PAYMENT
4.00	2.18	2.179885	8.514990	2.15	2.687372	6.845825	2.13	3.196523	5.733140
4.25	2.32	2.317004	8.526417	2.29	2.856705	6.857114	2.27	3.398284	5.744349
4.50	2.45	2.454226	8.537852	2.42	3.026200	6.868413	2.40	3.600278	5.755571
4.75	2.59	2.591551	8.549296	2.56	3.195855	6.879724	2.54	3.802504	5.766806
5.00	2.73	2.728978	8.560748	2.69	3.365671	6.891045	2.67	4.004982	5.778053
5.25	2.87	2.866508	8.572209	2.83	3.535649	6.902377	2.81	4.207653	5.789314
5.50	3.00	3.004141	8.583678	2.96	3.705787	6.913719	2.94	4.410575	5.800587
5.75	3.14	3.141877	8.595156	3.10	3.876086	6.925072	3.08	4.613729	5.811874
6.00	3.28	3.279716	8.606643	3.24	4.046546	6.936436	3.21	4.817115	5.823173
6.25	3.42	3.417657	8.618138	3.37	4.217167	6.947811	3.35	5.020733	5.834485
6.50	3.56	3.555700	8.629642	3.51	4.387948	6.959197	3.48	5.224582	5.845810
6.75	3.69	3.693847	8.641154	3.65	4.558890	6.970593	3.62	5.428663	5.857148
7.00	3.83	3.832095	8.652675	3.78	4.729993	6.982000	3.76	5.632975	5.868499
7.25	3.97	3.970447	8.664204	3.92	4.901256	6.993417	3.89	5.837519	5.879862
7.50	4.11	4.108900	8.675742	4.06	5.072679	7.004845	4.03	6.042294	5.891239
7.75	4.25	4.247456	8.687288	4.20	5.244263	7.016284	4.16	6.247300	5.902628
8.00	4.39	4.386115	8.698843	4.33	5.416007	7.027734	4.30	6.452537	5.914030
8.25	4.52	4.524876	8.710406	4.47	5.587912	7.039194	4.44	6.658006	5.925445
8.50	4.66	4.663739	8.721978	4.61	5.759976	7.050665	4.58	6.863705	5.936872
8.75	4.80	4.802704	8.733559	4.75	5.932201	7.062147	4.71	7.069635	5.948313
9.00	4.94	4.941772	8.745148	4.88	6.104586	7.073639	4.85	7.275796	5.959766
9.25	5.08	5.080942	8.756745	5.02	6.277131	7.085142	4.99	7.482187	5.971233
9.50	5.22	5.220214	8.768351	5.16	6.449836	7.096656	5.13	7.688809	5.982712
9.75	5.36	5.359588	8.779966	5.30	6.622701	7.108180	5.26	7.895661	5.994203
10.00	5.50	5.499065	8.791589	5.44	6.795726	7.119715	5.40	8.102744	6.005708
10.25	5.64	5.638643	8.803220	5.58	6.968910	7.131261	5.54	8.310057	6.017225
10.50	5.78	5.778323	8.814860	5.71	7.142254	7.142817	5.68	8.517600	6.028756
10.75	5.92	5.918106	8.826509	5.85	7.315758	7.154384	5.82	8.725373	6.040299
11.00	6.06	6.057990	8.838166	5.99	7.489422	7.165961	5.96	8.933378	6.051854
11.25	6.20	6.197976	8.849831	6.13	7.663245	7.177550	6.09	9.141609	6.063423
11.50	6.34	6.338065	8.861505	6.27	7.837227	7.189148	6.23	9.350072	6.075004
11.75	6.48	6.478255	8.873188	6.41	8.011369	7.200758	6.37	9.558764	6.086598
12.00	6.62	6.618546	8.884879	6.55	8.185670	7.212378	6.51	9.767686	6.098205
12.25	6.76	6.758940	8.896578	6.69	8.360131	7.224009	6.65	9.976838	6.109824
12.50	6.90	6.899435	8.908286	6.83	8.534751	7.235650	6.79	10.186218	6.121457
12.75	7.04	7.040032	8.920003	6.97	8.709529	7.247302	6.93	10.395828	6.133102
13.00	7.18	7.180731	8.931728	7.11	8.884467	7.258964	7.07	10.605667	6.144759
13.25	7.32	7.321531	8.943461	7.25	9.059564	7.270638	7.21	10.815736	6.156430
13.50	7.46	7.462433	8.955203	7.39	9.234820	7.282321	7.35	11.026033	6.168113
13.75	7.60	7.603436	8.966953	7.53	9.410235	7.294016	7.49	11.236559	6.179809
14.00	7.74	7.744541	8.978712	7.67	9.585809	7.305721	7.63	11.447313	6.191517
14.25	7.89	7.885747	8.990479	7.81	9.761541	7.317436	7.77	11.658297	6.203239
14.50	8.03	8.027055	9.002255	7.95	9.937432	7.329162	7.91	11.869508	6.214973
14.75	8.17	8.168464	9.014039	8.09	10.113482	7.340899	8.05	12.080949	6.226719
15.00	8.31	8.309975	9.025831	8.23	10.289690	7.352646	8.20	12.292617	6.238479
15.25	8.45	8.451587	9.037632	8.37	10.466057	7.364404	8.34	12.504514	6.250251
15.50	8.59	8.593300	9.049442	8.51	10.642583	7.376172	8.48	12.716639	6.262035
15.75	8.74	8.735114	9.061259	8.66	10.819266	7.387951	8.62	12.928991	6.273833
16.00	8.88	8.877029	9.073086	8.80	10.996108	7.399741	8.76	13.141572	6.285643
16.25	9.02	9.019046	9.084921	8.94	11.173108	7.411541	8.90	13.354380	6.297466
16.50	9.16	9.161164	9.096764	9.08	11.350266	7.423351	9.04	13.567416	6.309301
16.75	9.30	9.303383	9.108615	9.22	11.527583	7.435172	9.19	13.780680	6.321149
17.00	9.45	9.445702	9.120475	9.36	11.705057	7.447004	9.33	13.994171	6.333010
17.25	9.59	9.588123	9.132344	9.51	11.882689	7.458846	9.47	14.207889	6.344883
17.50	9.73	9.730645	9.144220	9.65	12.060480	7.470699	9.61	14.421835	6.356769
17.75	9.87	9.873268	9.156106	9.79	12.238428	7.482562	9.76	14.636008	6.368667
18.00	10.02	10.015991	9.167999	9.93	12.416533	7.494436	9.90	14.850407	6.380578
18.25	10.16	10.158816	9.179901	10.08	12.594797	7.506320	10.04	15.065034	6.392502
18.50	10.30	10.301741	9.191812	10.22	12.773218	7.518215	10.19	15.279887	6.404438
18.75	10.44	10.444767	9.203731	10.36	12.951797	7.530120	10.33	15.494967	6.416387
19.00	10.59	10.587894	9.215658	10.50	13.130533	7.542036	10.47	15.710273	6.428348
19.25	10.73	10.731121	9.227593	10.65	13.309426	7.553962	10.62	15.925806	6.440323
19.50	10.87	10.874449	9.239537	10.79	13.488477	7.565898	10.76	16.141565	6.452309
19.75	11.02	11.017878	9.251490	10.93	13.667685	7.577846	10.91	16.357550	6.464308
20.00	11.16	11.161407	9.263451	11.08	13.847050	7.589803	11.05	16.573761	6.476320
20.25	11.31	11.305037	9.275420	11.22	14.026572	7.601771	11.19	16.790198	6.488344
20.50	11.45	11.448767	9.287397	11.37	14.206251	7.613750	11.34	17.006861	6.500381
20.75	11.59	11.592598	9.299383	11.51	14.386088	7.625739	11.48	17.223750	6.512431

ACCURACY

Most of the time, the mathematics you will be required to perform in conjunction with your job will be fairly basic. But to a teller, getting 80 percent of the problems right means that one answer out of every five is *wrong*, which is far too many.

Because you deal with people's hard-earned money, there isn't any room for mistakes. This means checking and, when necessary, rechecking. Follow the rules for good work habits given at the beginning of this chapter. Be as careful in doing calculations for your customers as you would be for yourself.

9

The Bookkeeping of Banking

Asset. Liability. Journal. Ledger. Register. Credit. Debit. Charge. Float. General ledger. Bookkeeping. Statement of condition. These are the terms of the bookkeeping of banking. It is important to know what they mean and how they fit together. First, some definitions:

Asset. An asset is a thing of value owned by the person or business involved. The money in a savings account is an asset to the *saver*. Cash in the vault is an asset to the financial institution.

Liability. A liability is an obligation. The savings account is a liability to the financial institution because it owes the money to the saver. It is the saver's asset but the institution's liability.

Debit. A debit is an increase in assets. When an individual gets paid, if he or she were to *keep books like a business does*, the person would *debit* his or her cash account. As shown before, what is an asset to one party is a liability to the other. When a financial institution deducts money from a customer's account, it *debits* it, and the customer records a *credit* entry in his or her checkbook.

Credit. A credit is a decrease in assets. When a person buys a chair, he or she, in effect, *debits* his or her "furniture account" because of the increase in this aspect of personal assets and *credits* the "cash account" because some of this asset has been used up to buy the chair.

General ledger. The financial institution keeps two kinds of records: records of the customers' accounts and records of the institution's own accounts. The place in which records of the institution's accounts are kept is called the "general ledger." Included are the assets, liabilities, income, expense, surplus, capital, and reserves of the financial institution. When customers make deposits to checking accounts, they increase their own cash assets, and this reflects in a higher balance in the account. The general ledger, on the other hand, shows that the financial institution has increased its liabilities because it now owes the customer those funds.

Ledger. A ledger is a place where records are kept. You could draw the idea of a ledger and it would look like this:

Cash Account		Income Account		Clothing Account	
Debit	Credit	Debit	Credit	Debit	Credit

Housing Account		Auto Account		Medical Account	
Debit	Credit	Debit	Credit	Debit	Credit

Grooming Account		Misc. Account	
Debit	Credit	Debit	Credit

This is a personal ledger. Consider the following example. When Mary gets paid, she:

Debits her CASH account because she is increasing that asset; and

Credits her INCOME account. (An increase in income is always a credit, just as an increase in assets is always a debit. This way it is possible for every debit to be offset by a credit.)

Then Mary buys a new dress. She:

Debits her CLOTHING ACCOUNT because she has increased that asset; and

Credits her CASH account because she has decreased that asset.

If Mary made a payment on her car or home, she could make similar entries. If she paid the hairdresser or dentist, the entries would be similar but the reason different. An increase in expense is always a debit in some category. Again, this makes it possible to balance the books; if you remember that every increase in an asset is a debit, it makes sense anyway.

Journal. A journal is a book of original entry, or a place where you write down what you are going to record in a ledger. A loan register is a kind of journal. So are the tapes on your teller's machine and in your transit department's proof machine. A journal is kept so that the original transaction can be referred to if necessary.

Float. Float is money you've been promised but haven't yet received. If a customer deposits a check drawn on an out-of-town financial institution for $200, your institution will have a "float" for that amount until the out-of-town institution pays the check. The total of all such amounts is the "float" for your financial institution at any given time. Obviously, it can't lend or invest the money because it doesn't have it. Nor can the customer draw on it because it is "uncollected." Therefore, it is desirable to collect such items as quickly as possible; check-clearing procedures are always being reviewed by a financial institution's finance department with this end in mind.

Bookkeeping. Traditionally, this refers to the keeping of customers' accounts, especially checking accounts. Deposits increase the account, and checks drawn by the customer or charges issued by the financial institution decrease it. In many institutions, such charges are called, properly, *debits*, because they increase its assets in the general ledger.

YOUR STATEMENT OF CONDITION

Each year, your financial institution gathers together figures from every activity in which it engages and issues an *annual report* or *statement of condition*. Credit unions prepare a regulatory report that is sent to the appropriate governing agency. They also post a monthly balance sheet and income statement in their lobbies for members (their customers) to see. There are various reasons for doing these things:

- Directors, trustees, and stockholders want a clear, concise picture of the financial status of the institution during the past year.
- Certain customers and members of the business community may wish to compare your institution's activities and profit picture with those of others.
- If yours is a large financial institution whose stock is actively traded, investors will find an annual report invaluable.

These are the people who will most use your statement of condition. Actually, however, you and every officer and employee of your financial institution should read and understand it as well, because it shows several things that should interest you:

- It shows the profitability of your efforts. This is an important consideration for potential or present investors and for every member of the staff.
- It reflects the involvement of your institution in the community it serves.
- When compared with prior statements, it shows areas in which your institution is growing.

The problem with many statements of condition is that they are confusing and a bit complicated to the uninitiated. As a teller, you should study yours and be able to explain the basics to any customer who might ask a question. The guidelines in the following sections will help you understand the statement.

Assets

Assets are things of value. Money is an obvious asset. So are the buildings a financial institution owns. Under the statement heading "assets," you will find listed "cash and due from banks," which includes money on hand and that on deposit with other institutions. And you will find "premises and equipment" or words to that effect.

The largest entry under assets will be "loans." In a short statement, the word may just be "loans" with no breakdown. In a longer report, the figure may be split according to the type of loan. Either way, this reflects the involvement of your financial institution in the community. That figure represents the people of the community and their pride in their homes. The education of their children. The business that supplies a neighborhood with food or clothing. Autos that people drive, medical bills that have been paid, vacations that have been enjoyed. And since the money is owed to your institution, each loan is an asset or thing of value and is so shown on the statement.

LIABILITIES

Liabilities are what your financial institution owes. In this column, you will find some items that are confusing to nonaccountants, such as deposits. If money is an asset, why isn't a deposit an asset? It is to the depositor, as was mentioned before. The money is due him or her just as the money from a loan customer is due the financial institution. The institution has an obligation to return the depositor's money at his or her request, so while it has the advantage of using the money when it is on deposit, it still must show the deposit as a liability.

Demand deposits are checking accounts. They are the funds of people and firms in your community who rely on your financial institution to safeguard their cash and to pay them as directed. Again, they represent community involvement.

Savings deposits are also shown as liabilities, but they are real assets to the depositors. For many financial institutions, they represent the most basic kind of interaction with people in the area. They are retirement funds, vacation plans, college for the kids, or a safeguard against a rainy day.

"Other liabilities" include expenses incurred but not yet due for payment, such as some taxes.

Reserves for possible loan losses may be included under liabilities or added on beneath the total. Either way, these are funds a prudent management sets aside to take care of loans that may go bad for whatever reasons.

Stockholders' Equity

The entry under "stock" will show the par value of the stock multiplied by the number of shares issued. Normally, this will be much less than the market value of the stock, but it is accurate because it is the amount originally and actually invested in the financial institution.

"Surplus" and "undivided profits" are the last two entries. These represent the excess of the assets over the liabilities. The undivided profits may be paid to the stockholders. The surplus, along with the reserves, contribute to the financial stability of the financial institution. Some experts believe that in order for an institution to be in a secure financial position, its "net worth" (the sum of the surplus, undivided profits, and reserves for contingencies) should equal 6 percent or more of its total assets. When that ratio falls below 3 percent, the institution may be in trouble.

Read your employer's statement when it comes out. See not only dollars but the importance of your financial institution's place in the community.

INVESTMENTS

A financial institution's funds on deposit do not sit idle. Most are put to work earning interest in loans. Typically, loans are an investment, but when an employee who works at a financial institution uses the word "investment," he or she usually means the security-type assets owned and held by the institution. They include government bonds, corporation bonds, and any required stock in the Federal Reserve district bank. Bonds and corporate stocks, where allowed, are purchased by the financial institution on the open market from a bond or security house or a wholesaler or government bond dealer just as an individual would buy them.

In order to qualify as an investment, a property, security, or other thing of value must:

Be of long-term duration. Also, investments are made with well-spaced maturity dates so that there will be a more or less constant rate of return.

Be extremely safe. Unlike a speculation that is likely to produce a larger profit at a greater risk of loss, an investment yields a lower rate of profit at very low risk.

Have stability of income and a satisfactory rate of return. Slow and steady is the goal, though, because financial institutions have the obligation to protect their depositors' funds.

Have marketability. The investment should be convertible to cash with little or no loss in principal.

Financial institutions also want diversification when it comes to making investments. They are careful not to overpurchase the bonds of any one corporation. Also, there are banking laws that specify limits on bond buying and that restrict the purchase of stocks.

The Financial Institution's Portfolio

The selection of bonds or other assets makes up a financial institution's investment portfolio. The largest percentage of institutions' bond portfolios is made up of federal government securities. This is because they are practically free of risk and have high marketability. The institutions also purchase state, municipal, corporate, and public utility bonds.

Large institutions have investment departments with trained personnel who are experts in security research and analysis. The investments of smaller institutions are usually handled by an officer who may rely on the advice of investment services or larger correspondents.

When a financial institution, no matter what its size, carefully invests the dollars it takes in, it is helping our national economy as well as its local economy.

10

CHAPTER

Knowing and Handling Money

As a teller, your business is serving people and your inventory is money. You accept money in deposits, pay out money in withdrawals, accept money for loan payments, and cash checks. How you handle money is important. You are responsible for large sums that represent the savings and capital of many people. Therefore, you must be efficient and you must be accurate.

ABOUT OUR CURRENCY

Originally, English, French, and Spanish money circulated in America. Even before the American Revolution, paper currency was printed by authority of the Continental Congress. Counterfeiting and lack of faith in the colonial government made its value so little that the phrase "not worth a Continental" commonly meant "worthless."

Following the Revolution, paper money was issued by banks under federal laws. Again, counterfeiting was so rampant that some experts estimate that at the time of the outbreak of the Civil War one note in every three was phony.

Through a process of trial and error, and by applying technologies as they developed, the United States today has the best currency in the world. The paper is manufactured under a special permit by one firm exclusively for the government. It is engraved on machines designed just for that purpose by expert engravers whose work has won awards at world fairs and exhibitions since 1872.

It is your job to keep our country's money moving. This chapter focuses on our currency and coins and your responsibility in handling them.

Currency Paper

The paper used for U.S. currency is manufactured by Crane & Company, located in Dalton, Massachusetts. This high-quality rag paper was first produced in 1844 by the firm's founder, Zenas Crane, and is based on ancient Chinese papermaking methods.

Crane's first customer was a bank in Northampton, Massachusetts, and soon many others followed suit. The American Bank Note Company began purchasing Crane paper during the 1850s and has been doing so ever since. This company uses the paper for stocks, bonds, traveler's checks, and other security items, as well as for the currency for many foreign countries. During the 1870s, U.S. Secretary of the Treasury John Sherman began buying currency paper on a competitive basis. Thus, Crane & Company got its first government contract in 1879.

Tight security is an important aspect of the manufacture of currency paper. At Crane, strict inventory of the paper is constantly maintained, and all waste is shredded and repulped into fresh paper. A person found to have unauthorized possession of scraps of currency paper is subject to prosecution on a felony charge.

Kinds of Currency

The only common type of currency in circulation today is the Federal Reserve Note, which is issued in denominations of $1, $2, $5, $10, $20, $50, and $100. The $2 bill, which was last printed in 1979 and is still in circulation, was produced again in 1996 when 153 million were printed. Occasionally you will still see a Silver Certificate or United States Note, even though these are no longer being printed and are gradually being withdrawn.

Bills are packaged by financial institutions in these amounts:

Bill	Amount in Strap
$ 1	$ 100
$ 2	$ 100
$ 5	$ 500
$ 10	$1,000
$ 20	$2,000
$ 50	$1,000 or $2,000
$100	$1,000 or $2,000

F I G U R E 10-1

Positions of Important Features of Paper Currency

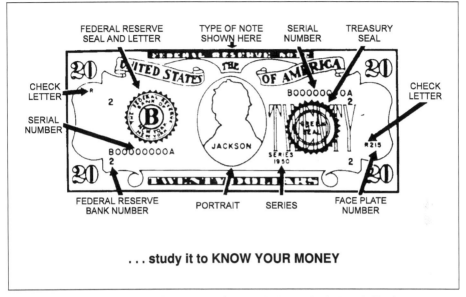

FEDERAL RESERVE
SEAL AND LETTER
TYPE OF NOTE
SHOWN HERE
SERIAL
NUMBER
TREASURY
SEAL

CHECK
LETTER
CHECK
LETTER

SERIAL
NUMBER

JACKSON

FEDERAL RESERVE
BANK NUMBER
PORTRAIT
SERIES
FACE PLATE
NUMBER

. . . study it to KNOW YOUR MONEY

Courtesy of U.S. Secret Service. The security features in the newly designed bills, first printed in 1996, are discussed in Chapter 19.

Portraits

In order to get your picture on U.S. currency, you have to be famous—and dead. But it was not always so. At the time of the Civil War, 500,000 five-cent notes were issued by the National Currency Division of the U.S. Treasury (now the Bureau of Engraving and Printing) bearing the picture of a man named Spencer M. Clark. Mr. Clark was not a war hero or a past president, but the chief clerk of the National Currency Division, the agency that issued the notes. Congress was furious, so it became law that a person had to be dead to be so honored.

Current portraits on bills are:

$ 1 — George Washington
$ 2 — Thomas Jefferson
$ 5 — Abraham Lincoln
$ 10 — Alexander Hamilton
$ 20 — Andrew Jackson
$ 50 — Ulysses S. Grant
$100 — Benjamin Franklin

Mutilated and Damaged Currency

As currency wears out or is mutilated, it is destroyed and replaced by the Federal Reserve Banks. It is your job as a teller to help in this effort. If you get a worn or mutilated bill, hold it aside and check with your supervisor on the procedure for handling it. There should be a procedure for accumulating these bills and forwarding them to your Federal Reserve Bank.

Damaged money is still good, at least in part. If a bill is *partly* burned or otherwise destroyed or mutilated, and if more than one half of the bill is clearly still intact, the nearest Federal Reserve Bank will redeem it for full face value.

If the money is more severely burned, destroyed, or mutilated, a claim may be filed by sending the bill or fragments, along with supporting evidence as to why the bill was damaged (fire reports, etc.) to the Department of the Treasury in Washington, D.C.

COINS

You deal with small, smooth, round coins that can be stacked neatly and handled easily. Your job would be much more difficult if, instead of our orderly, uniform coins, you had to handle deposits and withdrawals using primitive objects.

Clam shells, teeth, pearls, strings of beads made from shells or shark bones, seal tusks, fish hooks, ostrich egg shells, and even slabs of limestone anywhere from 10 inches to 10 feet in diameter have been used as money by people in various parts of the world.

The neat, easy-to-handle coins you deal with are packaged by financial institutions as follows:

Coin	Amount in a Roll
Pennies	$ .50
Nickels	2.00
Dimes	5.00
Quarters	10.00
Half dollars	10.00
Anthony dollars	25.00

Gresham's Law

In 1560, Sir Thomas Gresham, an observant English businessman, stated a basic law of economics. This law may be summarized as follows: "When two coins of equal legal value but of unequal real value are in circulation at the same time, the coin of lower real value will tend to drive the coin of higher real value out of circulation." People will begin to hoard the coins of higher real value and spend the coins of lower real value. This is happening today with certain of our coins. It is becoming more and more unusual to see a half dollar, quarter, or dime dated before 1965. Nickels from 1942 to 1945 are also becoming rarer. The reason is simple. These coins contain more valuable metals than coins of other dates but of equal legal value. Therefore, people are saving them and creating a scarcity.

Prior to 1965, dimes, quarters, and halves were made of a metal composed of 90 percent silver and 10 percent copper. Halves minted for general circulation from 1965 through 1969 had a silver content of 40 percent. Enormous demands created by increased use of vending machines and increased buying in general forced the government to change the formula for its coinage. The "clad" coins of today are nickel and copper with no silver content, except for special mintings made for collectors at premium prices. Thus, applying Gresham's Law, along with real silver dollars, the "pure" (actually, 90 percent silver) dimes, quarters, and halves of 1964 and before are worth the greatest premium and are used very infrequently; the less "real-value" halves of 1965 through 1969 are worth a lower premium, while the current coins are worth no premium at all. To a teller, however, the important thing is keeping money in circulation efficiently. Only the legal value of coins counts.

Numismatics

The teller who decides to collect coins is in an enviable position. After all, thousands of coins pass through his or her hands every day. If you are interested in numismatics, there are certain basic rules that you should follow. *Never* let collecting interfere with banking business. *Never* collect coins against your institution's policy. Do not hoard unopened bags of coin, for example. In other words, a teller who collects coins should be a *numismatist*, that is, a person who studies and collects coins, not a coin dealer.

There are two ways to start a coin collection. One is to buy an inexpensive folder or two and concentrate on getting a complete set of dates for certain coins. You might wish to start with pennies, then go on to nickels and so on. Another way to collect coins is to watch for interesting coins and "buy" them for yourself. Soon they'll mount up, and when they do, you'll find you have the beginning of a nice collection. In either case, finding your own coins is more exciting, more fun, and much less expensive than buying them from a dealer.

$1 Coins

The earliest dollars in the United States were coins authorized by the Coinage Act of 1792. One, based on the Spanish milled dollar then in common circulation, was made of silver and similar in size to the current Eisenhower dollar coin, which, of course, is made of clad metal and contains no silver. The other authorized dollar was made of gold; it was tiny, much smaller than a dime.

Over the years, there have been many changes in design, size, and precious-metal content. However, in general, the silver dollar was too unwieldy to carry and the gold dollar was so small that it was too easily lost.

Paper dollars were first issued as bank notes; that is, issuing banks promised to redeem them for gold or silver dollars if they were presented at the bank. The first bills to bear the likeness of George Washington were issued in 1800 by the Washington Bank (now The Washington Trust Company) of Westerly, Rhode Island. They were $3 bills, and they read, "The President, Directors and Company of Washington Bank in Westerly, promise to pay to _____ or Bearer on Demand Three Dollars." The bills were signed and dated by the president and cashier of the bank.

The Westerly bank's dollars were as good as the gold that backed them, but many bank-issued notes fluctuated in value and often depreciated relative to the gold or silver standards.

In 1863, Congress authorized national banks to issue bank notes backed by government bonds, and a tax on state bank notes gave national banks a control of bank note issuance. Federally issued silver certificates, first printed in 1878, and gold certificates, issued in 1900, have long been replaced in current usage by Federal Reserve Notes, backed by collateral held by the issuing Federal Reserve Banks. The tiny gold dollar and the silver "cartwheel" have been replaced with the large Eisenhower dollar, which itself is used on an infrequent basis.

On July 2, 1979, the first Susan B. Anthony $1 coins were placed into circulation in Adams, Massachusetts, the town where Ms. Anthony was born in 1820. Smaller than a half dollar and only slightly larger than a quarter, the coins were felt to be desirable for the following reasons as stipulated by the Treasury Department at the time of their inception:

1. They would cost less than three cents to mint compared to eight cents for an Eisenhower dollar coin.
2. They would be easier to carry compared to the large dollar coin, and they could fit into adapted vending machines.
3. They would have a lifetime of around 15 years compared to 18 months for a paper dollar.

Moreover, if the Susan B. Anthonys could replace just half of the paper $1 bills in circulation at the time the coins were first minted, the expected immediate savings to taxpayers would be $20 million in addition to saving the Bureau of Engraving and Printing from having to undergo a $100 million expansion.

Regardless of the desires of the government, however, the coins met with strong public resistance, just as the $2 bills had earlier. After the coin had been in circulation for one year, financial institution employees generally had these observations to make about it:

- From the coin's inception, the public disliked it because it resembles a quarter. This caused a great deal of confusion between the two, with many people paying out too much money or receiving too little when using the Anthony dollars to buy goods or services. Thus, the coin was often rejected by individuals and businesses alike. In addition, people believed it would lead to higher prices, especially for goods dispensed from vending machines.

- In spite of the fact that the coin has an eleven-sided blocking of the inner border that is designed to benefit blind people, it is still difficult for people who are visually handicapped to distinguish it from a quarter, which is only nine percent smaller in size.

- Having a third type of dollar in circulation created handling problems for merchants and financial institution employees. Tellers, for example, complained because the coins didn't fit in their coin racks.

The Anthony dollar coin is not the first experimental money to be rejected by the public. The steel and zinc pennies, issued in 1943 to save wartime copper, were rejected because people got them mixed up with dimes. The silver three-cent piece went out of circulation because a nickel three-cent piece was put into circulation. Likewise, in 1866, the new nickel five-cent pieces forced the silver half-dimes out of circulation.

Another coin that was not accepted was the twenty-cent piece. When it was issued from 1875 to 1878, people didn't accept it because it was very similar in *both size and design* to the quarter. The difference in size was almost exactly the same as the difference between the quarter and the Anthony dollar, except that the twenty-cent piece was smaller than a quarter instead of larger.

From 1979 to 1981, 857 million Susan B. Anthony dollars were minted. Even though, at the time, more than half of the coins were sitting idle at the U.S. Mint and Federal Reserve Banks, legislation, titled the United States Coinage Reform Act of 1989, was introduced that would have provided for the minting and circulation of an entirely new $1 coin. Designed to commemorate the 500th anniversary of the discovery of the New World by Christopher Columbus, the coin was planned to be *the same size as the Anthony dollar*, but would be gold colored and made of at least 90 percent copper.

The bill also included the provision that paper dollars be taken out of circulation no later than 18 months after the coin was placed in circulation, and it directed a study of the advisability of phasing out production of the penny and half dollar and of rounding cash sales to the nearest five cents.

In 1995, the proposal to replace $1 bills with coins was no longer considered by the Senate and House banking committees. The legislation was dropped because the savings that were anticipated by producing coins instead of bills were thought to be exaggerated, and because consumers were strongly opposed to the idea. A national poll showed that 65 percent were against eliminating the bills, and 88 percent said they think $1 bills are easier to use than coins.

Historically, our coinage has changed many times, and it may again. However, with coin vending machines and mechanical counters so widely used, it is a safe bet that any major change will meet with massive resistance.

TIPS FOR HANDLING MONEY

The most important part of a teller's job is the safe and accurate handling of cash. A difference caused by improperly entering a check is not hard to trace and correct. On the other hand, a real cash shortage is usually impossible to either pinpoint or recover. When handling money, always adhere to the procedures prescribed at your financial institution; this will also help to avoid differences. But in cases where no specific rules exist, these tips will be helpful:

1. Above all, have a routine. Always count money in the same way.
2. When receiving currency in a deposit, start by sorting it into denominations, then arrange it neatly and face up. Count the largest denominations first, noting each amount as you count it. Also, count coin in the same way—largest coins first, noting totals. Prove it before putting it away.
3. When paying out cash, ask the customer how he or she wants the bills. Then count and recount the coin first, the currency second, again largest denominations first. Pay out the coin, then the currency, recounting to the customer.
4. Prove cash-in as soon as you receive it.
5. Get in the habit of looking at the total face of a bill. This helps spot counterfeits and altered bills and helps avoid differences.

6. Sort out mutilated bills as you get them.

7. When you cash a check, look at both the figures and the amount written in words. Count the money yourself, then prove it by re-counting it to the customer.

8. When taking a deposit, prove the cash portion before proceeding with the transaction. If your count doesn't agree with the amount on the ticket, ask the customer to verify it. If he or she recounts the money, recount it yourself before putting it away.

9. Don't allow money to be mixed with other items. Put deposit tick-ets, withdrawal slips, checks, and other papers where they belong immediately and put money where it belongs.

10. Never, never allow anyone access to your cash drawer unless he or she is authorized and you are there.

11. Don't leave cash on top of your counter.

12. Never keep excess cash that is beyond your limit in your drawer. Turn it over to the head teller or otherwise transfer it to vault cash as soon as it builds up.

13. Don't leave your window during a cash transaction. If you must use the phone, don't turn your back to the customer. When you do leave your window, lock your drawer.

14. Don't keep packaged currency in with your working cash.

15. When noting cash totals or counts, always recheck your math, even if you use a computer, calculator, or adding machine.

Avoiding Potential Problems

It is sad but true that:

- Many people who receive too much cash from a teller will simply not return it. They think that the institution can afford the loss. They fail to consider the problems they may cause the teller and the fact that the loss will eventually be made up in higher interest rates or in-surance premiums; or if they do consider these problems, they ignore them.

- Historically, tellers have been innocently involved in embezzlement schemes by trusting others. Make safe cash-handling routines just that—routine. There is no need for other tellers to feel slighted be-cause you won't let them have free access to your cash. It's good banking practice, and so is dual control.

- Tellers who become distracted can easily make mistakes in counting or in paying out. It's part of your job to be friendly and to build good customer relations, but while you're counting money, don't let anything or anyone distract you. If it does, start over. If necessary, say to a friendly, chatting customer, "Excuse me for a minute while I count this."

Concentrate. Stick to a routine. Keep neat records. You won't eliminate all differences, but you'll cut down on them, and you'll make it easy to find most of the few that still happen.

A Final Tip on Handling Money

Two Kentucky medical doctors once cultured various coins and bills of small denomination that they had borrowed at random from a varied group of people. The results showed that 13 percent of the coins and 42 percent of the bills contained potentially disease-causing germs. Most often contaminated were pennies, nickels, and small bills due to their rapid turnover and frequent exchange from person to person.

According to the Treasury Department, however, paper money is relatively germ-free. The paper contains fungicidal and germicidal agents, and the ink contains bacterial inhibitors. This is comforting to know, but it is still sensible to wash you hands thoroughly after leaving your window, especially before handling food.

11

How to Settle

The process of making a settlement varies from one financial institution to another. Types of teller's machines differ, as does the use of even similar machines. So the details of settlement differ. Whatever method your institution uses, be sure to learn it and to do it properly.

In another sense, however, all financial institution settlements are alike. In essence, all a teller's settlement really shows is:

- The cash balance as of the preceding business day, plus—
- Incoming deposits and other cash-in items for the current day, minus—
- Checks paid and other cash-out items for the current day, which should equal—
- The cash-on-hand balance for the end of the current day.

In other words, your cash plus your cash-in items less your cash-out items should give you a cash balance. If that cash balance in figures totals the cash actually on hand, you settle. Even though settlement sheets are a lot more complicated than that because they have to take special transactions into consideration, essentially that's all there is to it.

Whatever system your institution uses, stick to it. Following it will help you to avoid errors.

DEALING WITH OVERS AND SHORTS

Differences are the primary problem faced by most tellers. Their cost in time is staggering. Every financial institution is concerned with a potentially serious shortage in dollars. In addition, because accuracy is one of the most important features offered by any institution, errors always make a poor impression on customers.

There are two types of differences:

An error in written figures. The error may be on the part of the customer and may not be detected by the teller or it may be a teller error. In any case, eventually it will be picked up by the proof department. This is not to say that such errors should not be taken seriously. They waste many hours and cause much concern.

An error in cash. Again, this may be on the part of the customer or the teller. However, it will not be corrected by the proof department. A shortage or overage is not traceable to any specific account. Tellers faced with a cash difference may try to recreate the day's transactions, sometimes successfully. Occasionally, a customer may spot a cash difference and report it. Usually, however, the customer, not wishing to appear distrustful, accepts the verification of cash by the teller without question. He or she does not count again after leaving the window, and if the teller calls later and says, "I think there may have been a mistake," the customer, who has mixed the money with the cash that he or she already had, usually can't be of much help. Therefore, it makes sense for tellers to encourage their customers to count their cash while still at the window.

Avoiding Differences

Carelessness causes differences, and everyone is guilty of carelessness sometimes. Developing a routine can help, though. Go over the tips for handling money as outlined in Chapter 10. Specifically, remember to:

1. Concentrate when you are counting money. Do not be distracted by customers or other tellers. Never hurry to the point of distraction.
2. Count and recount money taken in or to be given out. Adopt a routine for counting and always use this routine.
3. Be accurate in your math. Use a computer, calculator, or adding machine.

"Well, Miss Roberts, you failed to balance again . . . you're short three keychains, two fondue forks, and one dog bank!"

4. Be alert during transactions. Finish the transaction, *then* chat with the customer.

5. Look at each item you are paying at least three times: once when you get it, again as you count out the cash, and one last time as you hand the money to the customer.

6. Always pay coin first, currency second. Making this a habit prevents paying out one or the other twice.

7. Carefully check to see that the amount deposited agrees with the amount on the deposit slip. This is the easiest way for a teller to make a mistake.

8. Keep your counter clear at all times. This way you will not mix cash with scrap paper or confuse two transactions. Put cash away as it comes in and put deposit slips, checks, withdrawal slips, and other papers in their proper places.

9. Never leave your window or cash unattended.

10. Avoid split deposits (except for well-known, established customers). Unless your financial institution's policy is otherwise, have the customer deposit the whole check and then cash his or her check drawn against a prior balance. For a savings account, check and recheck the accuracy of the transaction before accepting a split deposit.

11. Carefully check your opening cash figure.

12. Never allow anyone but a supervisor or auditor to have access to your cash drawer; then, for the protection of both of you, watch him or her. Be sure to prove vault cash received.

These tips will help to prevent overs and shorts if you follow them carefully. Exercising the proper procedures should become habitual so that overs and shorts will occur much less frequently.

Finding a Difference—A Settlement Checklist

An over or short isn't recorded until it is determined that the difference simply can't be found. If you exercise preventive steps and still have a difference, chances are it's not because you gave a customer too much or too little cash or accepted too much or too little in a deposit. These are differences that usually can't be traced. The following differences *can* be traced:

- The cash-forwarded total from the previous day improperly recorded on the settlement sheet.
- Cash from the vault during the day improperly recorded.
- Cash-paid items not properly listed.
- Cash-in not properly listed.
- Errors in math on the settlement sheet and on any papers with totals that go forward to the settlement sheet.
- Loose coin or currency improperly counted or recorded.
- Coin or currency rolled or wrapped today improperly counted.
- Mutilated money improperly counted.
- New money improperly counted.
- Cash or papers necessary for proper settlement accidentally misplaced in the trash basket, cash drawer, or cash box.
- Corrections from the proof or transit department not properly made.

When a difference occurs, check each of these items yourself. If the difference still exists, call your supervisor to help recheck everything.

Here are a few quick solutions for common outages:

- If the difference is 10¢, 15¢, 25¢, or 50¢, look over check or money order fees.
- If you are out 25¢, 50¢, $1, $5, $10, or $20, recount coin rolled or currency banded that day.
- With a difference in any even dollar amount, check mutilated money.
- For a difference of $50, $100, $500, or $1,000, check cash received from or paid into vault cash.
- If you have a difference divisible by 2, make the division, then take your answer and see if you have a debit or credit for that amount in the wrong place. Here's the way it works: If you listed $5 as a debit when it should be a credit, you will have a difference of $10. So if you should have a difference of $10, divide by 2, then check all your debit and credit entries for $5 items to see that they are correctly entered.
- If the amount of the difference is divisible by 9, check for a transposition. (See the information that follows regarding transpositions.)

Don't Use a Kitty

A "kitty" is a reserve of money for some special purpose. Although financial institution policies strictly prohibit kitties, some tellers still use them for minor overs and shorts. It's tempting to toss in an "extra" dollar or two or make up a small shortage by using money from the kitty.

Taking the easy way out leads to carelessness—which leads to large and important differences. The best way to fix overs and shorts is to be more careful so that you avoid them entirely.

FIND TRANSPOSITIONS FAST

Transpositions occur when number sequences get out of order. For example, you may throw an 18 into a machine instead of 81. The digits are correct, but the sequence is wrong.

It is easy to spot a transposition. Adding up the digits in the difference will produce a number divisible by 9 if a transposition has taken place. Here's how it works. If you punch 276 into your machine instead of 627, the difference will be 351. Adding the digits, $3 + 5 + 1 = 9$, indicates that a transposition has taken place.

The simplest and most common transpositions occur between adjacent digits. The handy table that follows is a quick guide, showing what numbers to look for when a transposition occurs. If a difference is 90 instead of 9, simply add a zero to the number you are looking for. If you have a difference of $810, for example, it is likely that you punched in 900 instead of 90.

Difference	9	18	27	36	45	54	63
Check these	10—01	20—02	30—03	40—04	50—05	60—06	70—07
numbers	21—12	31—13	41—14	51—15	61—16	71—17	81—18
	32—23	42—24	52—25	62—26	72—27	82—28	92—29
	43—34	53—35	63—36	73—37	83—38	93—39	
	54—45	64—46	74—47	84—48	94—49		
	65—56	75—57	85—58	95—59			
	76—67	86—68	96—69				
	87—78	97—79					
	98—89						

Difference	72	81
Check these	80—08	90—09
numbers	91—19	

Ed Everts, senior vice president, operations/retail banking, Dubuque Bank & Trust Company, Dubuque, Iowa, is a former math teacher who designed a more detailed transposition chart, which follows. He explains that it "deals with any transposition of two numbers. Three numbers or more would not be quite as simple to deal with, but that is much less likely to happen than the two-number transposition." Try working with the chart a few times by deliberately transposing two digits in your examples, and you'll find it easy and accurate to use.

As mentioned previously, if you divide the amount you are off by 9 and get a whole number, the problem could be a transposition. (However, not every number divisible by 9 is due to a transposition. In fact, very few are. For example, 108 when divided by 9 is 12, not a transposition, and 414 when divided by 9 is 46, not a transposition.) Here's the way to use the chart:

1. After you have divided the amount you are off by 9, check to see if your answer is any of the values in the following table.
2. After you locate the number on the chart that represents your difference divided by 9, look across to the right-hand column to find where the transposition lies.
3. Next, look down in the corresponding vertical column to find the actual numbers that may be responsible for the transposition.

WHERE THE TRANSPOSITION LIES

→ Between 1's & 10's digits
→ Between 10's & 100's digits
→ Between 1's & 100's digits
→ Between 10's & 1000's digits
→ Between 1's & 1000's digits

YOUR DIFFERENCE DIVIDED BY 9

1's & 10's	10's & 100's	1's & 100's	10's & 1000's	1's & 1000's	
9	90	99	990	999	→ Indicates numbers are 9 apart (0 & 9 only)
8	80	88	880	888	→ Indicates numbers are 8 apart (0 & 8, 1 & 9)
7	70	77	770	777	→ Indicates numbers are 7 apart (0 & 7, 1 & 8, 2 & 9)
6	60	66	660	666	→ Indicates numbers are 6 apart (0 & 6, 1 & 7, 2 & 8, 3 & 9)
5	50	55	550	555	→ Indicates numbers are 5 apart (0 & 5, 1 & 6, 2 & 7, 3 & 8, 4 & 9)
4	40	44	440	444	→ Indicates numbers are 4 apart (0 & 4, 1 & 5, 2 & 6, 3 & 7, 4 & 8, 5 & 9)
3	30	33	330	333	→ Indicates numbers are 3 apart (0 & 3, 1 & 4, 2 & 5, 3 & 6, 4 & 7, 5 & 8, 6 & 9)
2	20	22	220	222	→ Indicates numbers are 2 apart (0 & 2, 1 & 3, 2 & 4, 3 & 5, 4 & 6, 5 & 7, 6 & 8, 7 & 9)
1	10	11	110	111	→ Indicates numbers are 1 apart (0 & 1, 1 & 2, 2 & 3, 3 & 4, 4 & 5, 5 & 6, 6 & 7, 7 & 8, 8 & 9)

Slide Differences

In the past, all adding machines had a big square keyboard. The operator threw numbers into the units, tens, hundreds, thousands—and so forth—columns by pressing down keys in those columns. Computers, calculators, and most adding machines require the operator to put in zeros to move a digit into higher columns. Thus, to become a 10, a 1 must have a zero added. When a hurried operator fails to add the zeros, he or she creates a special form of transposition called a *slide*.

A slide difference, which usually won't conform to the rules in the transposition chart, is easier to pinpoint than most transpositions. Suppose, for example, that you entered $7.35 instead of $735.00. In this instance, you dropped two zeros, the most common error. The amount of the imbalance, $727.65, is not only divisible by 99, but the answer that you get by making this division *is the number that has been incorrectly entered*. That is, $727.65 divided by 99 equals $7.35, and adding two zeros makes it $735.00. These are the two numbers that were responsible for the imbalance.

The following guidelines will help you to find slide differences:

- If one zero has been dropped, dividing the difference by 9 will give you the number responsible for the error. For example, if the difference is $486, dividing by 9 indicates that you have entered $54 instead of $540.

- If two zeros were dropped, dividing the amount of the imbalance by 99 will give you the number responsible for the error. For example, if the difference is $618.75, dividing by 99 indicates that you have entered $6.25 instead of $625.

- If three zeros were dropped, dividing the difference by 999 will give you the number responsible for the error. Thus, if the difference is $11,988, dividing by 999 indicates that you have entered $12 instead of $12,000.

This method will work for any number of zeros dropped as long as you continue to add another 9 to the divisor for each zero dropped.

It's easier to search through a tape with an indication of a number to look for than to simply guess and grope.*

DEVELOP A ROUTINE

Mistakes sometimes happen because people are careless, but more often, mistakes happen because people are inefficient. This is especially true where routine matters are concerned. The teller who *always* counts out cash in the same way will make fewer mistakes than the teller who varies his or her routine. The transit clerk who *always* handles checks in a certain way will make fewer mistakes than the clerk who skips around in his or her work.

Every step of every routine operational job should be considered and a system worked out for each, whether it is accepting a deposit, cashing a check, or issuing an official check drawn by the institution on itself. Make your routine operations *really* routine.

---

*   The transposition and slide charts shown in this chapter are now available in PC software form as a spreadsheet template—available for EXCEL, 1-2-3, and Quatro Pro spreadsheet software. Created by Ed Everts of Dubuque Bank & Trust Co., the "Teller Balancing" software sells for $49.95. It licenses up to five PC installations and allows up to five concurrent users on a network installation. If you would like to order the software, send a check to Ed Everts, 1105 Richards Road, Dubuque, IA 52003. Requests for more information should also be sent to him at that address.

12
CHAPTER

Develop Efficient Work Habits

You may feel at times that there just aren't enough hours in the day to finish all of your work. While lines at your window seem endless and less-than-patient customers put pressure on you to hurry each transaction, other duties may be mounting. You may, for example, be required to participate in ATM processing, make up complicated payrolls, count large quantities of coin, file signature cards, or handle night deposit bags or mail deposits.

Rushing can cause mistakes, and while you can't stop time or eliminate all errors, it is possible to make your available time more productive and your work more accurate through the development of efficient work habits.

INCREASE YOUR PRODUCTIVITY

In order to get more work done more quickly, follow these helpful suggestions:

- Get rid of waste paper at or near your window. Important papers often get mixed in with worthless ones. This not only slows you down, but it can also cause errors.
- Keep necessary supplies at hand.
- Have an adequate assortment of forms in an easy-to-locate arrangement near your workstation.
- Don't try to commit everything to memory. Take notes.

- Have a calendar and use it. Before you finish the day's work, spend a few moments with your calendar. Turn the page to the next day and list the tasks you need to accomplish. The following day, tackle the most important jobs first. When you finish one task, cross it off. At the end of the day, place any unfinished tasks on the next day's list.
- Be sure of the objectives of each job before you tackle it. If you understand what has to be done, you can save time that might be wasted on false starts.
- Try dividing big jobs into smaller, more manageable ones with easier-to-meet deadlines.
- Look for easier ways to get things done. Use practical tools such as a computer or calculator to give you extra time.
- Avoid procrastination.

The extra pressure of busy times calls for extra organization. If you succeed in developing more efficient work habits, you'll be amazed at how much more you can accomplish.

RULES FOR SYSTEMIZING FILES

Research has shown that people in offices spend an amazing 20 to 30 percent of their time each day just looking for information. This can create both wasted work hours and negative customer relations for your financial institution.

Setting up a good filing system is an essential part of developing efficient work habits. Although you, as a busy teller, might not want to concern yourself with the filing system, you might have to do so. For example, what do you do if you can't find the records for an important account? Or if an essential document is missing? Although these things will probably turn up eventually, you do not have time to waste looking while a customer is waiting at your window.

Here is a list of basic rules that can help you to systemize the files at your office. If the files can be improved, suggest that these guidelines be followed on a uniform basis throughout the office:

1. File in alphabetical order by last name.
2. In joint accounts, file under the name of the first person listed on the account on a consistent basis.
3. Cross-file wherever you may need to make future references. This is especially important in cases in which business and personal accounts involve the same people.

4. Don't file under the word "The" unless it is an unusually important part of the company name.

5. File company names by the first initial or word, except where companies use given names. For example, "Jane Doe Company" would be filed "Doe, Jane Company."

6. Treat hyphenated words as single words.

7. Don't file under titles such as Doctor, Mr., Mrs., Ms., Lieutenant, and so forth.

8. "Mac" and "Mc" should be filed in their place as spelled, not in separate sections.

9. Where there are identical names, use a system to differentiate, such as the customers' addresses or, in the case of businesses, the product or service involved. For example, the folders for two individuals named John Smith might be labeled "Smith, John (Main Street)" and "Smith, John (Oak Lane)."

10. Treat abbreviations and numbers as though they were spelled out. Thus, "50th Ward Republican Club" would be filed under "F" for "Fiftieth."

11. Even if "Saint" is spelled "St.," file it as though it were spelled out.

12. Keep file headings as simple as possible.

13. Make sure that file labels are neatly typewritten so that they are completely legible.

14. Place a label on the outside of each drawer to describe the drawer's contents. For example, use the range of dates or the range of the alphabet that is included in the drawer.

15. Don't overfill file folders. If a folder gets filled, start another with the same title, indicating the number of folders being used on each label, such as "Jones & Company—Folder 1 of 2" and "Jones & Company—Folder 2 of 2."

16. Don't overcrowd file drawers. Leave a few inches of extra space in each for easy access to folders.

17. Put the most recent document toward the front of each folder.

18. If a paper is to be filed later, be sure to write the correct file heading on it before putting it aside.

Files are an important part of banking, but they are useful only if you can find the things you need when you need them without wasting time.

13 CHAPTER

Opening New Accounts

The way you treat a brand new customer is an important part of your operational function as well as a chance to exercise good public relations. Getting started on the right foot can have a far-reaching effect on the future relationship between that person and your financial institution.

WHEN YOU OPEN A CUSTOMER ACCOUNT

This is the ideal situation involving a new customer. When you open his or her account, you have the opportunity to make a good first impression and, at the same time, to make sure the customer understands the account he or she is opening. Follow these steps:

Offer the customer privacy if it is required. If any embarrassing questions or confidential information are involved, talk to the customer where you can't be overheard.

Take care of details as simply as possible. Use plain language, not technical banking terms. Be quick and efficient.

Brief the customer on the details of the service. Especially:

- Tell a savings customer the current rate of interest that applies to his or her account.

- Tell a savings customer how interest is compounded and when it is added.
- Explain any rules concerning deposits and withdrawals.
- Explain to a new checking-account customer the minimum-balance requirements, interest earned, if any, and any applicable service charges.
- Show a checking-account customer how to use the check stubs or register.
- Explain how to reconcile a statement, using a sample blank statement form or the first statement that the customer receives, and encourage the person to make a habit of doing so each time a statement is received.
- Explain why checks cannot be drawn on uncollected funds, then tell the customer how long a deposited check takes to be collected.
- Explain what happens if a check is drawn on insufficient or uncollected funds. Be courteous, and don't give the customer an excuse to say later, "But no one ever told me!" Some financial institution employees report that they actually have had customers argue that they can't be overdrawn because there are still checks left in their checkbooks! Take time to explain, but do so tactfully, without talking down to the customer.
- Explain to customers who are about to use direct deposit for the first time how the service works.
- Tell new ATM customers how to operate the machines, the transactions for which the machines can be used, and how to protect their cards.
- When opening a safe deposit account, explain the entry requirements and the amount and due date of the rent.
- When selling traveler's checks, tell the customer what to do if the checks are lost or stolen and how to handle unused checks when he or she returns from the trip.
- Explain bank-by-mail to all deposit customers. Give the customer a starter envelope and any necessary forms.
- Explain any home-banking service that your financial institution provides, describing what it enables the customer to do and any equipment that is required in order to use it.

Be sure to introduce the new customer to your manager or other supervisor. Let the customer know that if he or she needs a loan or any other banking service, you have a well-trained team ready and willing to be of assistance.

Follow your financial institution's rules and procedures for opening new accounts.

The Importance of Following the Proper Procedures

As indicated earlier, opening a new account is more than just getting a few basic facts and choosing the style and color of a new checking-account customer's checks. It means following your financial institution's rules and regulations to the letter. Here's an example of the kind of thing that can happen if you fail to do so:

A financial institution had a manual that specifically described how to open new accounts. Nevertheless, when an estate account was opened, the person handling the details did so on the signature of *one* co-executor and sent a signature card to the other co-executor.

While both co-executors should have been required to sign checks, the account was not so flagged. In fact, the two-signature requirement was not even discussed.

Statements were sent to the one person who was signing the checks.

Unfortunately, this person drew on the account for his own use to the tune of over a quarter of a million dollars. The heirs of the estate sued the financial institution and won. One reason was the failure to follow procedures set out in its own operations manual.

Never skip basic rules or take shortcuts. You could create many problems for your financial institution and for yourself.

The Almost-New Customer

If another employee opened a new account and you are involved in a first or early transaction, you still have an opportunity to help establish a good relationship with the customer. Specifically, you can:

- Be sure the person opening the account made the appropriate explanations. If he or she did not or if the customer is a bit confused, take a moment to straighten things out. Be tactful, but fill in any gaps.
- Make an effort to learn the customer's name.
- Make the customer feel welcome. Start with a smile and make introductions that are appropriate.
- Look for additional banking needs that the customer may have. New customers can often use other services.

14

How to Be Audited Painlessly

People who work in financial institutions usually dread an audit, not because they're doing something dishonest and fear being found out, but for these reasons:

1. It is common for a person in a position of trust to have a little nagging fear that he or she has made an unintentional error.
2. It's hard not to feel that an audit implies distrust.
3. It is uncomfortable to have anyone, especially strangers, inserting themselves into your work situation.
4. Auditors and examiners do disrupt your daily schedule and inconvenience you.

Nevertheless, the law requires both examinations and internal audits, so tellers and other employees must learn to deal with them effectively. Remember, being audited is a part of your job, and the auditors or examiners are only doing their jobs.

Audit versus Examination

There are a few differences between an audit and an examination. An examination is held to determine an institution's financial condition. It is conducted by an outside agency or government, such as the FDIC, Federal Reserve, or a state banking department. At credit unions, it is conducted by the National Credit Union Association (NCUA) or by the Credit Union Commission. Examiners are not specifically looking for employees who are embezzling, although if an employee is doing this, it will probably be uncovered. Basically, they are checking to see that the financial institution keeps proper records, safeguards its assets, and, in general, follows good banking practice in the handling of money, negotiable collateral, and other valuables.

An audit is conducted on behalf of the bank directors or the credit union supervisory committee to determine that assets and liabilities are properly stated, that operations are safely conducted, that expenses are legitimate, and that income is accounted for. Auditors are employed by the institution, though in the case of outside accounting firms, they are not employees of the institution. The auditor is the officer designated to supervise the auditing of the institution's affairs. Normally, he or she reports directly to the board or supervisory committee in order to be independent and impartial.

The main function of an audit is verification, and there are two main ways to achieve it. One is to check the accounting records of the financial institution. Tellers are often familiar with auditors who do this on the local office level by proving the savings and safe deposit records. Accounting records routinely checked also include loan registers and, the one tellers are the most familiar with, the proving of teller's cash against the cash balance records. The other way auditors check records is to contact customers and ask them if their figures agree with those the institution has on file. This is usually done by mail with a return reply requested.

In short, an examination basically determines whether or not a financial institution is being properly run at the management level, while an audit is concerned with internal operations. Of course, there is a certain amount of overlapping in the two.

What to Expect During an Audit and What to Do

In order to cause minimal inconvenience and to have as many tellers' windows open as possible, it is usual for auditors (and examiners) to make a sudden unannounced appearance either at the very beginning or the very end of a workday.

The first act auditors perform is to individually go to preassigned stations and instantly "seal" certain things. They do this by taping forms, which they have initialed or signed, over access to things they wish to examine. Thus, they may place a seal over a teller's drawer or a collateral file in the vault.

After sealing the institution, the next thing the auditors do is verify teller's cash so that customer service may proceed as soon as possible. The

"I hate to tell you this during an audit, Mr. Stephens,
but your account is overdrawn."

cash audit is the one that makes tellers the most nervous, but it shouldn't if you follow these rules:

- Never keep any extra cash in a cash drawer. This includes everything from personal funds, to a kitty, to cash for the office coffee fund.
- Be sure your cash is really correct when you settle each evening.
- Never, ever, cash a check for anyone and hold it.

The tedious part of an audit follows the cash audit. This is when auditors check records and ask questions relating to the assets, liabilities, income, or expenses of the financial institution, such as traveler's checks, safe deposit rental records, loan registers, vault cash, and so on. These tips may help you:

- Realize that to be effective auditors and examiners *must* have control. Therefore, the first and most basic rule is: NEVER, NEVER BREAK A SEAL! If you do, the examination of your work is invalidated, and that's bound to have a bad reflection on you. If you need something, ask. The auditor will break the seal and get it, making a record as he or she does so, and then replace the seal.

- Be friendly and helpful. The auditors or examiners aren't there to harass you. They'd like to finish quickly just as much as you would. In the meantime, try to provide a pleasant atmosphere in which to work for both of you.
- Accept the audit as part of your job. Examinations and internal audits are required by law for very good reason. While they're not part of the daily routine, they are part of banking.
- Learn from the examination. Examiners and auditors can often pass on valuable tips. Listen to their suggestions.
- During the examination, follow the procedures set up by the examiners or auditors even if they differ from your regular routine. If there is a conflict on security matters or your institution's basic policy, check with your supervisor.
- Answer any questions honestly and simply. Most audit exceptions are minor procedural matters that can be simply explained. On the other hand, don't offer advice or help unless you are asked. Examiners are required to follow certain procedures, and your comments only take time.
- Don't gossip about others who work at your institution or try to point out faults to the examiners or auditors. They know what they're looking for and how to find it.

HOW TO AUDIT YOURSELF

As a teller, you are subject to examination because you are responsible for part of your institution's cash. Therefore, it's a good idea for you to audit yourself from time to time just to be sure you're taking that responsibility seriously. The checklist that follows covers many items for which auditors or examiners look. Some items may not apply to all financial institutions, but most do. Disregard any items that do not apply, and, in all other cases, check to be sure your procedures are right. Follow your institution's policies, of course, should they differ from anything stated here.

A Self-Auditing Checklist

1. Do you lock up your cash at all times when you are away from your window?
2. If you have an identification stamp, do you lock it up when you are away from your window?

3. If you have a teller's machine with a key, do you take the key out of the machine and keep it locked when you are away from the window?

4. Do you keep your cash out of the reach of everyone but yourself?

5. Do you keep all currency in the cash drawer and out of the sight and reach of the public?

6. Do you keep your daily cash record in ink?

7. Do you checkmark or initial deposits containing cash to show that you have verified it?

8. When you get or give coin or currency from or to another teller, do you follow your institution's policy for handling the exchange?

9. Do you avoid processing your own personal transactions, especially cashing your own checks?

10. Is the signature card file current?

11. If you work on mail deposits or night deposit bags, do you always do so with another person verifying your work?

12. Do you always observe your check-cashing limit, if any?

13. Do you carefully check for stop-payments?

14. Do you always keep cash in your drawer within the limit specified by your institution's policy?

15. Do you avoid holding over any cash items until the next day?

16. When you have a void transaction, do you carefully follow operating instructions?

17. Do you carefully prove any cash received from the vault?

18. Do you keep on hand a packet of "bait" or "decoy" money with the amounts, serial numbers, issuing Federal Reserve Banks, and series recorded?

19. Do you change the band on bait money at least monthly?

20. Do you insist on proper identification before cashing any check for a person unknown to you?

21. Do you verify the balance and, if necessary, hold the funds on any check that might be returned?

22. Do you check all endorsements before cashing any check or receiving it for deposit?

23. Do you always follow procedures for early opening of the office, including any set signal system between employees, even if the other person involved is a friend?

24. Do you know where all alarms and security devices are located and how to activate them?

25. If you have any responsibility for dual control on such items as the vault, unissued safe deposit keys, duplicate teller's keys, or other such items, do you always carefully exercise your responsibility and not just allow the other person access without your presence?

26. Are your settlement sheets neat, in ink, and initialed or signed by you?

27. If you use a tape, do you sign or initial it as your institution's policy requires?

28. Do you keep your work area, and especially your cash drawer, neat at all times?

29. Do you avoid using a kitty for differences?

30. Do you check your work area for any misplaced cash or checks before leaving each day?

As previously mentioned, disregard any questions that do not apply to the operating policies where you work. If you answer "no" to any of the other questions, ask yourself why. Even if a specified policy is not involved, it just makes sense to be neat and careful in handling money or the records of cash transactions.

When there is an actual audit or examination at your institution, remember that auditors and examiners don't expect to be greeted with open arms, but they do appreciate efficiency and cooperation. Make it easy for them to do their job, and they'll do the same for you.

THREE

"BANKABILITY" INVOLVES SECURITY

To a teller, effective security means many things. It means keeping the money entrusted by your customers safe from thieves and keeping yourself, your customers, and your fellow employees protected from bodily harm. To do so requires the use of alarms, surveillance cameras, and a variety of protective devices and procedures that augment the mechanical security afforded by vaults, fire- and theft-resistant files, and other standard equipment.

Most security, however, exists to keep honest people honest. This kind of security is affected by such things as accurate record-keeping, latches closing off the tellers' section, and so on. These things are so routine that they are rarely thought of as security at all and are simply taken for granted. And much routine security is internal in that it is aimed at the people who work in financial institutions. Audit procedures, for the most part, fall into this category. The fact that an unexpected audit is always possible certainly prevents many innocent "borrowings" that could turn into serious embezzlements. Such audits not only protect the employee against himself or herself, they also help to ensure that the person will not be victimized by an unscrupulous employee who has somehow gained a job at the institution.

When most people think of security at a financial institution, they think of outside criminals: the crook who confronts the teller with a gun; the forger who charms his or her way into the office manager's confidence; the kiter who rushes from one institution to another hoping that a sharp-eyed bookkeeper won't notice the telltale pattern of transactions in the account; the counterfeit passer whose funny money is another headache for the busy employee. These are the criminals who prey on financial institutions, and they do so for a simple reason: That is where the money is.

True, other businesses deal with large amounts of cash, but financial institutions must keep it more available in order to be able to serve their publics. The ready availability of cash makes these institutions attractive places for every type of con artist or crook.

The methods used by criminals against financial institutions vary from basic gunpoint robberies to complex fraudulent schemes. This means the teller must know how different types of criminals operate, how to avoid them, if possible, and how to deal with them, if necessary. Thus, real security relies on a staff in which each individual knows how to act during all possible circumstances.

Security begins with you, and you begin by being informed. The following chapters will help you to become more knowledgeable about your financial institution's security.

CHAPTER

Safeguarding Your Cash

As a teller, you are responsible for a sizable amount of cash. The following rules will help you minimize the risk of loss through carelessness or theft. Of course, your financial institution's policies should be followed if these rules conflict with them or if the rules do not conform to the physical layout of your office.

1. Lock your cash drawer at all times when you are not at your window, even if you'll only be gone for a short time.
2. Lock your identification stamp in your cash drawer at night and when you leave your window.
3. Remove the key to your teller's machine at night and when away from your window.
4. Keep cash out of the reach of customers *and* other employees.
5. Keep currency in drawers and out of sight of the public. Avoid offering temptation!
6. Keep your cash record in ink to avoid tampering.
7. If you cash your own personal check, do it at a window other than your own.
8. Keep your cash drawer neat.
9. Don't allow *anyone* else to use your cash drawer—ever.
10. Carefully check your workstation for dropped cash or checks before leaving each day.

11. Keep your cash at a minimum, following your institution's policy on amounts to have on hand. If it builds up into large sums, put the excess in the vault to reduce loss exposure.

12. Keep strapped money separate from ready cash, in a separate drawer if possible.

13. Remove the old strap from transferred cash and put your own teller-stamped strap on the money. When transferring cash, make a written transaction that is signed by both of the people who are involved.

14. Never tell outsiders how much money you keep in your drawer. Anyone may be listening, and even the most honest customer could repeat what you say to someone who is not as honest.

15. Be especially careful when you have extra cash for busy times, such as local paydays. Robbers sometimes know about company schedules.

16. Don't let anyone distract you into turning your back on your cash.

17. If you are called away to the phone, take a moment to lock up your cash. Some crooks set up fake calls to distract people from their work areas.

18. Be alert for strangers, especially suspicious looking persons. If you see one, tell your supervisor or take the action prescribed by your institution.

Responsibility for a large amount of cash need not be a source of worry. Just make security, especially cash safeguards, a routine part of your job. It's easy to make security a habit.

Rolls of Coin

Dishonest persons sometimes place flat metal objects such as washers in rolls of coin. Here are two tips on how to detect such objects quickly and easily:

- Strike the roll of coin on an inverted piece of carbon paper, and the imprint of the coins will appear on the wrapper. Dimes, quarters, halves, and Susan B. Anthony dollars are milled on the edges. This milling shows clearly after the roll has been struck.

- Pass a stud finder (an inexpensive tool found in any hardware store) along the roll of coin. If it contains iron washers, the arrow of the finder will point to them. Since the stud finder picks out all magnetically sensitive metals, it will also pick out Canadian coins, except for Canadian pennies, which are copper and not magnetically sensitive. Using this method, several rolls can be checked in just a few seconds' time without the customer even realizing it.

AVOID THE SNEAK THIEF

Picture yourself $1,000 short. You count and recount your cash, total and retotal your figures, and you're still $1,000 short. The odds against accidentally paying out that much extra are enormous. So you hope for a phone call from the proof section telling you they've picked up an error in addition on a deposit. But suppose no error turns up? Chances are you've been the victim of a sneak thief.

Dapper men with umbrellas, little old ladies with canes and shopping bags, quick-fingered young people, parents with strollers—all can quickly reach inside a teller's section and deftly snatch out a pack of bills while the teller turns his or her back to verify a balance. Canes and umbrellas help because they can be used to reach piles of money the teller may think are safely out of reach, and shopping bags and the folds of umbrellas are good places to conceal cash.

This can happen at any financial institution. Even those in "nice" or rural towns are not immune to sneak thieves.

The best way to deal with sneak thieves is to avoid them. They aren't going to pull out guns, so, if they don't see anything to steal, they'll go away. The pile of cash left out at the teller's workstation, the official check made out and waiting for the loan customer to come and get it, and the night deposit bag laid aside to be counted during a free minute are the things that attract the sneak thief. Therefore, follow the foregoing rules for safeguarding cash and especially:

- Keep all items of value, including cash, money order blanks, official check blanks, checks awaiting customers, savings bonds, and other negotiable items in their appropriate drawers at all times. When you're away from the drawers, keep them locked and take the keys.
- Keep your cash and cash drawer neat. Avoid clutter.
- Don't be distracted into turning your back on cash or negotiables.
- Be alert for suspicious strangers, especially anyone who asks unusual questions or who looks equipped to take and hide money.
- Don't put your fellow employees on the spot. Keep your cash drawer for your own use.

The sneak thief isn't as dramatic as the robber with a gun, but he or she can be just as effective. Discourage thieves by being careful.

16

CHAPTER

Cashing Checks

WHAT A CHECK IS

As defined by the Uniform Commercial Code, the laws that govern business activities in every state, a check—or, at a credit union, a share draft—is an order to pay, drawn upon a financial institution and payable on demand. A check has five distinct parts that affect its acceptance:

1. *A date.* Checks you receive in deposits or to cash are usually properly dated with a current date. When this is the case, the check is payable "on demand." But there can be problems with check dates, including:

   - *No date.* When a check has no date at all, the check is legally negotiable and, like the properly dated check, is payable "on demand." But since it is impossible to tell when a check without a date was really issued, the check could be "stale."

   - *Stale dated.* A check is normally presumed to be stale when it is presented for payment more than 30 days from the date on which it was drawn. After six months, the paying financial institution has no obligation to pay a routine check.

   - *Postdated.* A check dated in advance is good when the date on it arrives. For example, in a divorce case in Massachusetts, as part of the settlement, a father gave his son certain assets, including a check for $20,000 dated 14 years in the future. The check was held to be good and to be payable on that date.

Make it a habit to glance at the date section on every check you process. If the space is blank or if the check is either stale or postdated, refer it to a supervisor. Don't risk a legal tangle.

2. *An amount payable in money.* This appears on the check in two places: to the right of the check in figures and written in words (or with a checkwriter) on the body of the check. The two amounts should agree. If they do not, the check is said to be *informal.* In such a case, the amount written in words or with a checkwriter is the legal amount.

3. *A payee.* This is the person, business, or organization to whom the check is payable. The payee may either get the funds itself or may endorse the check to another payee or even to the bearer.

4. *A drawee.* This is the financial institution upon which the check is drawn. Eventually the check will be routed to this institution, which will then take the funds from the account of the maker and honor the check. If the maker does not have sufficient funds in the account, the institution may return the check to the one that sent it marked "not sufficient funds." It will eventually be returned to the original payee who must make it good.

5. *A maker.* This is the person who issues and signs the check. In doing so, the maker purports to have an account with sufficient collected funds at the drawee financial institution; if the maker does not, he or she is liable for the check.

Types of Checks

Among the many types of checks that may be presented to you each day are the following:

Personal and business checks. This is the most common type of check written. The maker's name and address, whether those of an individual, an organization, or a business, are usually printed on these checks. They are available in a wide variety of colors, sizes, and designs.

Certified checks. These are personal or business checks for which the drawee guarantees payment. The word "certified" is stamped on the face of each one, and a certification number and official signature are included. The amount of the check is actually withdrawn from the maker's account and held aside by the drawee until the check is presented for payment. A check may be certified at the request of either the maker or the payee, although some financial institutions require the maker's permission in the case of the latter.

Official checks or bank checks. These are drawn by a financial institution on its own cash. They are used to pay loan proceeds and to pay large withdrawals to checking or savings customers. Those issued by national institutions are called *cashier's checks*, and those issued by state institutions are called *treasurer's checks*. Some financial institutions charge a fee for issuing these checks.

Bank drafts. These checks are drawn by a financial institution on its own funds on deposit in another financial institution. The checking account in the other institution is called a *correspondent account*. Because these checks clear faster if presented for payment in the drawee's location, they are often used by businesspersons to buy merchandise in distant areas.

Traveler's checks. Traveler's checks are internationally redeemable checks, issued by centralized large financial institutions or travel companies, that can be purchased from a financial institution, an express company, or a travel agency. They are valid only when the holder's own endorsement is placed against his or her original signature on the face of each check in the presence of the person who cashes them. Typically, they come in $10, $20, $50, $100, and $500 denominations and are used to safeguard funds of people who take trips since these checks are insured against loss or theft. Traveler's checks are almost universally acceptable.

Personal money orders. These checks are purchased from a financial institution for cash. The purchaser fills in the date, the payee, and his or her own name and address. The issuing institution, which is the drawee, guarantees the payment of these checks and usually limits the maximum amount for which it will issue them. Typical charges for this service are $1 or $2 per check regardless of the amount involved.

Postal money orders. These are money orders that are sold by the U.S. Post Office and are good for two years from the date of purchase. As of this writing, the charge for issuing them is $0.85 each for any amount up to a maximum of $700.

United States Treasurer Checks. These are government checks issued and paid by the U.S. Treasury Department for which the U.S. government is both the drawee and the maker. They are used to pay government obligations.

How a Check Clears

Consider a typical transaction at your window. Mrs. Smith asks you to cash a check. The check is drawn on a financial institution that is over 1,000 miles away, but you know Mrs. Smith and you know that she has an account with your institution with sufficient funds to cover the check should it be returned. The amount of the check does not exceed your check-cashing limits and it is properly made out and endorsed, so you cash it.

At the proper time, you send the check along with your other work to your proof department. There, the check is processed, which includes being endorsed by your institution and probably being photographed. Then the check is sorted into a batch of checks that is sent to a Federal Reserve Bank, to a clearinghouse, or to a correspondent financial institution for collection.

In many cases, such a check might be sent to the Federal Reserve Bank in your district, which in turn sends it to the Federal Reserve Bank that serves the drawee. This FRB sends it to the drawee for payment. If the check is good, the Federal Reserve Bank credits your institution's account with it for the amount of the check. If for any reason the check is unacceptable, it is returned to each *holder in due course* until your office receives it and you return it to Mrs. Smith and the institution either gets the money from her, charges her account, or, on occasion, resubmits the check.

KNOW YOUR ENDORSEMENTS

Every teller should understand check endorsements because they legally involve the financial institution and its customers. Basically, any writing, typing, rubber stamp, or other words made on the back of the check make up the endorsement. The teller is responsible for verifying that every check is properly endorsed. Technically, checks drawn on your institution, referred to as "on-us" checks, that are payable to cash need no endorsement. However, it's still a good idea to ask the customer to endorse such a check because this could help its maker if it had been stolen or fraudulently obtained.

Kinds of Endorsements

Checks are legal instruments, and there are rules regarding their endorsements:

> *Blank endorsements.* This is the common endorsement in which the payee simply signs the back of the check. It then becomes payable to anyone who presents it. In other words, if there are sufficient funds in the account, a check endorsed in blank is as good as cash. No one

should ever endorse a check in this way unless he or she is right in the financial institution in which it will be cashed.

Restrictive endorsements. As its name implies, a restrictive endorsement restricts the transfer of the check. "For Deposit Only" followed by the name of the payee restricts the check to one purpose: It must be deposited to the account of the payee. Such restrictive endorsements should be encouraged, especially to customers who do their banking by mail or send in deposits via a third person. If a check so endorsed becomes lost or stolen, it is worthless and a new check may be issued in its place.

Special endorsements. A special endorsement makes a check payable to someone especially named. "Pay to the order of Joe Jones, /s/ John Smith" is a special endorsement. No one can use the check in any way except Joe Jones, and he may do anything with it that he might have done as the original payee. In other words, he may endorse it in blank and cash it; he may endorse it restrictively or in blank and deposit it; or he may make it payable to someone else with still another special endorsement.

Qualified endorsements. A qualified endorsement limits the liability of the endorser. "Without recourse, /s/ John Smith" is a qualified endorsement. This means that if the check is returned for any reason, no one can collect from John Smith. For obvious reasons, financial institutions do not cash checks or accept them for deposit if they have qualified endorsements.

You should always know your *endorser* when you cash a check, but you should know your *endorsements* whether you cash a check or accept it for deposit. It takes only a second to glance at the back of each check and to be sure it is endorsed properly. If it simply lacks endorsement, ask the customer to sign it. If it is irregularly endorsed, politely refer the matter to your supervisor in order to protect your customers and your institution.

Common Check-Cashing Situations

When you are handed a check to be cashed, there are four things you can do with it:

1. Cash it;
2. Refuse to cash it;
3. Accept it for deposit but refuse to cash it (of course, after it clears, the customer can then draw his or her own check on the funds); or

4. Refer the customer to an officer or supervisor to have the check approved for payment.

Keeping these four options in mind, which course of action would you take in the following situations?

- A customer, John Jones, presents an "on-us" check payable to himself that is drawn on an account with sufficient collected funds, endorsed simply "John Jones."

You may cash this check or accept it for deposit as the customer wishes.

- A stranger presents an "on-us" certified check payable to herself for $500. She offers a driver's license for identification.

Refer this one to a supervisor. The amount is too large to accept this identification without an approval.

- A check payable to John Smith is endorsed "Pay to the order of Jane Doe /s/ John Smith." It is "on us" and there are sufficient collected funds. Jane Doe, who is known to you, asks for cash.

Cash it, but have her endorse it first.

- In a deposit, a check is endorsed, "Without recourse, John Smith."

Either reject it or refer it to your supervisor, depending on your institution's policy.

- A check is presented that is endorsed "For Deposit Only, Jane Smith." Mr. Smith, who shares a joint account with his wife, wants to cash it.

Do not cash the check. Suggest that Mr. Smith deposit it and write his own check for cash.

- An "on-us" check is payable to "cash" and is presented by a stranger. There is a sufficient collected balance, but the stranger refuses to endorse the check.

Technically, the stranger may be entitled to the cash, but refer him to your supervisor anyway. A person who won't endorse a check is acting suspiciously.

- A check on an out-of-town financial institution is presented by a customer, Mary Brown, in a deposit. It is payable to John Smith. It is endorsed, "Pay to the order of Jane Doe /s/ John Smith." Then "Pay to the order of Mary Brown /s/ Jane Doe." Finally, "For Deposit Only, Mary Brown."

Accept it for deposit. That's an unusual group of endorsements, but all are perfectly legal.

When in doubt, refer a check to your supervisor. Don't take chances!

HANDLING SPLIT DEPOSITS

Split, or cash-back, deposits are those transactions in which customers wish to deposit a check, taking back part of the amount in cash. Financial institutions generally dread them because they pose dangers to tellers:

1. They create a potential cash-error situation because they involve a transaction within a transaction.
2. Errors created in a split-deposit transaction may be very difficult to trace, especially cash shortages.
3. They offer criminals an opportunity to confuse a busy teller into paying out too much cash.

Split deposits open the way to errors because it is too easy for the transaction total to fail to equal the cash back plus the amount deposited. Therefore, at a minimum, a teller should use a machine and recalculate the deposit ticket carefully, then count and recount the cash back against the proven figure, asking the customer to verify the count.

Fraud is tougher to avoid. The most common one is the simple flimflam in which the crook causes the teller to make an error by hurrying and then confusing him or her. But some crooks are more creative. One scheme involves the criminal opening an account and making a few legitimate transactions, then, after building the teller's confidence, presenting a large check drawn on a well-known company as a split deposit. The check, of course, is either phony or stolen.

The best way to handle split deposits is to avoid them. Suggest that customers deposit all checks and then write their own for the cash. This not only prevents split-deposit errors and frauds, it also avoids paying out against uncollected funds. In addition, it gives the customers better records of their own transactions.

Unless your financial institution's policy prohibits the acceptance of split deposits, you will occasionally have to accept them, especially to accommodate good customers. When that happens, be careful. Figure carefully, count carefully, and, to avoid fraud, don't pay back more than the amount of collected funds already in the account.

CUSTOMER IDENTIFICATION

What documents will help to identify a customer? This is an important question to you because, as a teller, you will frequently be called on to cash checks for people you have never seen before. Remember that you are under no legal

*"I believe you, Mr. Smith, but a driver's license
would have been enough identification."*

obligation to cash any check that is not drawn on your financial institution, and even in cases where the check is "on us," it is important that you know your endorser.

Naturally, you will always be guided by the policies of your own institution. However, you can avoid many problems if you know your endorser and if you, when in doubt, refer the customer to an officer for approval to cash the check.

The following chart may help you to evaluate types of identification.

Types of ID	*Adequate Identification*
Customer ID card	Name has been on account for six months and the signature matches that on file.
Personal identification	Identified by a known customer.
Driver's license	Permanent license at least two months old, with photo, or a nonphoto license with another photo ID.

Types of ID	*Adequate Identification*
Employer ID card	Issued by an employer known to the employee of the financial institution, with a photo or physical description and signature of the employee.
Trade license issued by local government (taxi driver, etc.)	License at least two months old, with a photo or physical description and signature, and validated by the issuing authority.
Armed forces ID card	Military Identification Form DD2 or DD2A, listing the branch of service. The active duty cards are green; reserve forces cards are red or pink; cards for retired personnel are blue or gray; and cards for dependents are tan.
U.S. passport	With photo, signature, and physical description.
Federal employee ID card or badge	With employee's photo or physical description and signature, countersigned or validated.

Unacceptable identification documents:

Social Security cards
Auto registration certificates
Birth or marriage certificates
Credit cards or charge plates
Insurance policy ID cards
Organization membership cards
Passbooks from financial institutions
Voter registration cards
Armed forces discharge certificates

A driver's license is the primary document used as identification, because most people have one and because the licenses are carefully issued by the various states. Almost every driver's license includes a photograph of the person to whom it is issued as well as the person's birth date, general description, Social Security number, and specimen signature. This information enables you to further check the individual's identity. Obviously, the person must look like the photo on the license. You should also check to see if the descriptive matter relating to sex, height, and hair and eye color match the person. In addition, you might be able to check the Social Security number against that on another ID card. If the person has a driver's license that does not include a photograph, it is best to back it up with another form of identification that does include one.

Two publications that provide quick verification of driver's licenses are the *I.D. Checking Guide* and the *International I.D. Checking Guide,* which help tellers to determine whether the person at their window has presented a forged, altered, or counterfeit license. The guides, which are updated regularly, include full-size color photos of every valid driver's license in the United States and Canada and those from more than 50 foreign countries. You can get information about these publications by writing to the Drivers License Guide Co., 1492 Oddstad Drive, Redwood City, CA 94063, or by phoning 800-227-8827.

Most credit cards do not contain a photo of the cardholder or a physical description of the person. Because such a card does contain a specimen signature, it is primarily useful as a backup to help validate a driver's license.

Membership cards can range from the elaborate to the odd. Even if the card does contain a photo, description, Social Security number, and more, it is worthless for identification purposes. Membership cards are easily stolen, are often easy to copy, and can be fakes.

In short, a document is useful in helping to identify a person if it is hard to obtain, it shows or describes the person, and it is a document the person would take pains to keep from being lost or stolen. Keep in mind, however, that people can buy identification cards of various types quite easily. So easily, in fact, that tellers should be especially alert when it comes to cashing checks. According to the American Bankers Association, phony driver's licenses are the most common type of false identification used to defraud financial institutions.

No matter what kind of identification the person offers, and no matter how honest he or she looks, KNOW YOUR ENDORSER! For example, a somewhat put-out law enforcement official who specialized in bad-check passers complained that a teller who worked in an institution where he was not known refused to cash his paycheck. "I showed her my badge and my ID and she said, 'I'm sorry, sir. I've never seen this kind of badge or ID card before, and I wouldn't know a real one from a fake one. So I'm sorry, but I can't cash your check.'" The teller was right in refusing to do so.

TRAVELER'S CHECK SECURITY

For many people, the next best thing to having an office of their financial institution nearby is to have traveler's checks. Traveler's checks are a great way for vacationers or businesspeople to safeguard travel cash. Traveler's checks are protected against loss, and, at the same time, they are just about universally accepted. This also makes them a great target for crooks.

Especially vulnerable are traveler's checks that have not yet been issued. In the hands of criminals, these are easily passed and could represent a substantial loss for the financial institution from which they were stolen. If you are involved in the issuance of traveler's checks, be sure to follow the security policies of your institution. In addition, if it is not already policy, be sure to:

- Handle traveler's checks as you would cash.
- Keep unissued checks locked up and out of sight and reach of a possible sneak thief. Use a cash drawer or other safe spot that can be locked whenever you leave the area.
- Get payment for the checks as soon as the purchaser has put his or her name, address, and signature on the application form.
- Give the purchaser the exact amount of checks for signing, and, as he or she begins to sign them, put the kit in its place of safekeeping. *Never* leave it unattended at a window or desk.
- Watch out for typical flimflam ploys: the customer who changes the amount in the middle of a transaction; the customer who tries to distract you while counting; or the customer who "needs additional checks for his or her spouse." An exception to the latter incident involves American Express Travelers Cheques *for Two,* which became available in 1992. These traveler's checks have two signature lines instead of one in the upper left-hand corner. The person who buys them signs the line labeled "Signature 1." The other authorized user does not have to be present when they are purchased; he or she simply signs the line labeled "Signature 2" as soon as possible. Later, when the checks are used, either traveler can countersign in the lower left-hand corner without the other person being present.

According to experts, most traveler's check thieves are professional criminals. This calls for extra precautions in your safekeeping techniques.

Cashing Traveler's Checks

The basic acceptance procedure for traveler's checks is simple. You watch the customer countersign the check, then you compare the countersignature with the signature already in the upper left-hand corner. If they are the same, you cash the check.

Never cash presigned checks. Some thieves will rely on you not to ask them to re-sign the checks. However, if you get a check that is already countersigned, have the customer sign it again on the back of the check while you watch.

Crooks also have several clever tricks to make you think you saw them countersign the checks. For example:

- A crook may let you watch him or her sign the *top* check, then, using that as a shield, he or she will pretend to sign the rest of the checks—which have already been carefully forged. Palming the top check, the person will present the other checks for payment. Watch the actual signing of each check.

- Another trick is to secretly re-sign the checks in the upper left-hand corner with a broad, felt-tipped pen. Then the crook can let you watch him or her countersign the checks, because the signatures will match. When you see a broad, felt-tipped signature in the upper left-hand corner, look closely for signs that another signature is underneath.

- A crook buys traveler's checks beforehand in the name he or she intends to use to pass stolen checks. You watch the person countersign the checks that were just purchased. Then the crook "drops" the checks on the floor and, as he or she picks them up, switches them for previously forged stolen checks. Naturally, the crook can cash the "good" checks later. If anyone takes the countersigned checks from your sight, have the person re-sign them on the back while you watch.

Being aware of what to watch for and carefully following the rules will go a long way in helping you to avoid cashing stolen traveler's checks.

WHEN YOU CASH GOVERNMENT CHECKS

Time Limit on Cashing Government Checks

The Department of the Treasury's Financial Management Service manages and operates most federal payment systems and, by check and direct deposit, disburses Social Security benefits, veterans benefits, IRS tax refunds, railroad retirement benefits, and payments to vendors.

The law requires that those federal government benefit checks dated October 1, 1989, and later be cashed within one year of their issue. The checks bear the legend "Void After One Year." All government checks issued any time before that date had to have been cashed no later than September 30,

1990. Prior to the passage of that law, government checks were payable without any time limitation.

The law also allows a one-year period for filing a claim concerning a lost or stolen check. In turn, the Treasury Department has 18 months to begin recovery of funds from a financial institution if a check has been negotiated over a forged or unauthorized endorsement.

Although the law sets a time limit on cashing government checks, it does not affect an individual's entitlement to payment. A bona fide holder of an expired check must contact the government agency that authorized the check, and the agency can arrange for a replacement to be issued.

Government Check Security

The federal government issues hundreds of millions of checks annually, valued at hundreds of billions of dollars. While many of these checks are issued directly to the recipient, many others are handled by direct deposit. In fact, people who have signed up to receive Social Security benefits after August 1, 1996, are required to use direct deposit. Those who don't have an account with a financial institution will still be sent checks. Then, beginning in 1998, all recipients who have such an account will receive their payments via direct deposit regardless of when they began to receive them.

In the meantime, crooks know that many government checks are mailed directly to the recipients. They also know that merchants and financial institutions often cash these checks under circumstances for which personal checks would be refused. So tens of thousands of government checks are stolen and forged each year.

A special problem exists with forged government checks that generally does not exist with forged checks drawn on financial institutions. With government checks, it takes a long time to determine that a forgery has taken place. This makes catching the crook difficult. If a crook steals a check drawn on your institution, the customer will catch it when he or she gets the statement, usually within a month. But in the case of a government check, a forgery often is first suspected when an intended recipient reports that the check did not arrive. Many people may wait several days, weeks, or possibly months before making such a report. Then an investigation must be made to see if the check ever cleared. Then it must be traced. This process could take such a long time that the teller involved may forget any details of the circumstances under which the check had been cashed.

This makes it vitally important for you, as a teller, to exercise extreme caution in cashing government checks. They are a favorite target for crooks.

To avoid problems, follow these rules and any special policies your institution might have on cashing government checks:

1. Know your endorser.

2. Demand current, valid identification. Follow your institution's policy on this issue. If there is no specific policy, make sure that whatever is used for identification is difficult for a crook to obtain. A person can get a library card in any name, but a driver's license with a photo on it is harder to come by illegally.

3. Ask yourself this: "If this check is forged, can I find the person who cashed it and recover the loss?"

4. Have all checks endorsed in your presence.

5. Initial any checks you cash and note the identification used.

6. Make sure that checks payable jointly are endorsed by both payees. If not, the check may be invalidated entirely, or at least it may cause a stop payment while an investigation is made.

7. Do not cash a government check payable to someone who has died, even when presented by the estate. Such a check must be returned to the government agency that issued it, and this agency will then give a new check for any funds due to the survivors.

Be sure to exercise caution in cashing government checks. Above all, with all checks, know your endorser!

BASIC CHECK-CASHING PROCEDURES

If you're a typical teller, you cash many checks each day. Most of the time, it's very routine. You know the customer, it's an "on-us" check, you know that there are sufficient collected funds in the account to cover it, so you simply hand over the money. But even in the simplest case, because there is an element of risk involved in check cashing if certain basic rules aren't followed, be sure to follow this checklist:

1. Make sure the check is really a check. Verify that it contains the five distinct parts outlined in the beginning of this chapter.

2. Be sure the check is current. Look at the date. If it is postdated, it should not be cashed because it is technically not yet a check but only a promissory note. If the check is stale dated, it should be referred to your manager or supervisor for approval.

3. Be sure the amount is clear. Poorly made figures cause innumerable errors in check processing. Also, be sure the amounts written in figures and words agree.

4. Make certain that the check has not been altered in any way. Study the information on this subject in Chapter 18.

5. Be sure the check is properly signed. In most cases where the casher is well known to the teller, this just means glancing at the check to make sure there is a signature. If the casher is a stranger, however, a comparison with the signature-card file may be in order. Also, in the case of a business check for a large amount, it may be necessary to ascertain whether more than one signature is required.

6. Make sure there is a sufficient collected balance in the maker's checking account to cover the check.

7. Be certain that any holds against the account do not reduce the balance below the amount of the check. Holds are notations put on an account by the financial institution that earmark a portion of the balance for other uses.

8. Make sure there is no stop payment on the check. A stop payment is an instruction to the financial institution from the maker of a check that it not be paid. If the institution cashes the check, it is then liable for any loss that is incurred.

No matter who the customer is or how honest or well known he or she may be, things can go wrong if the basics aren't followed. So before you cash any check, take care to do it properly.

17

This Is a Holdup!

Although chances are good that no one will ever lean over the counter at your workstation and say, "This is a holdup!" it pays to be prepared. It pays to know what to do both during and after a holdup. If your financial institution has a procedure that is spelled out, study it and be ready to act on it.

The most effective deterrent to robbing financial institutions is a long prison term. Alert tellers can help to see that robbers face such an outcome.

BE READY FOR A HOLDUP

Mental Preparation

It is certainly normal to be afraid if someone has a gun pointed at you. Preparation cannot ease that fear, but understanding and considering certain facts can help you to avoid panic. Realize that:

- Very few tellers are injured during holdups. The robber intends to threaten, not to harm.
- Your financial institution does not expect you to sacrifice yourself. If the robber has a gun, be ready to go along with what he (or she) wants.
- Your chances of being robbed are slim. But if you should be held up, be prepared to be calm.

Physical Preparation

Take stock of your work area and your own workstation. Particularly check to be sure that you:

- Avoid having large posters or other obstructions near your window that a criminal might use to conceal the fact that he is robbing you.
- Have a minimum amount of cash in your drawer. Keep vault cash under time lock. Robbers work fast, so a 15-minute delay for a time lock will discourage them. So will robbing financial institutions and getting only a couple of thousand dollars, which isn't worth the risk of a prison term.
- Suggest (or have your manager suggest) that people who regularly deposit large sums of cash try to vary the times at which they make their deposits.
- Have on hand at least one pack of bait money, currently banded, from which you have recorded the required information.

"I'm sorry, but you'll have to get this note approved by an officer . . ."

- Know how *and when* to activate any protective devices your institution may provide, such as alarms and cameras.

- Prepare to be a part of the office team. Know who should comfort upset customers, who should call the police or other authorities, who should notify other offices of your institution. Check with your supervisor if you don't have this information. It helps in any emergency if everyone knows in advance what he or she is supposed to do.

- Be prepared to help the police. Know how to give accurate descriptions and to preserve evidence. Perhaps the robber will touch your counter or a pen. Perhaps he'll leave a holdup note or a footprint on the floor. How would you preserve any of these things? Remember, your fingerprints could mar those of the robber, and other feet could wipe out his print.

Practice Giving Descriptions

Practice is the training that counts the most in this type of situation. You can do the following right at your own window to prepare for a possible holdup:

- When you're not too busy, notice a customer who comes to the window of another teller. Without offending the person, really look at the customer. As soon as he or she leaves, write a description: Sex. Height. Weight. Age. Hair color. Distinguishing marks. Clothing. Mannerisms. (See the Witness Questionnaire at the end of this chapter.) Practice this several times. You'll find that you will become more aware of people.

- Now expand your practice. Get another teller involved. After both of you write your own descriptions of the same person, compare them. You'll probably be surprised at how many discrepancies there are.

- Most holdups are committed with handguns as weapons. Handguns break down into two basic types: revolvers and automatic pistols. A revolver has a chamber that holds several bullets, usually six or nine. This chamber is a cylinder that revolves as the hammer of the gun is cocked or as the trigger is pulled. It gives the gun a distinctly rounded bulge just above the trigger housing. An automatic holds the bullets in a magazine, often in the butt, or handle. Thus, an automatic is flat and lacks the cylinder above the trigger. Learn to tell the difference between the two. Test yourself. If you're ever in a store that sells guns, take a minute and see if you can identify both types. It can be very helpful to the police if you can identify the type of gun that a robber used in a holdup.

- Practice describing vehicles. There are many brands and models of cars. Learn to identify the make, model, and year of the common ones. Chances are, crooks won't use a fancy model. Practice identifying cars as you drive.

The more you practice giving descriptions, the more prepared you'll be to give an accurate one in the event of an actual holdup.

BAIT MONEY

Bills, for which you keep a record, that are deliberately passed along with other money to a holdup man to aid in his apprehension are called bait money. Obviously, robbers expect to be given such bills, so precautions should be taken to make the packet of bait money look just like the other packets of bills that are turned over to the robber. This means:

- The bills should be changed occasionally so that they don't become obviously outdated.
- Bands should be changed even more frequently, especially if the band is dated, so that they will appear to be fresh.
- The money should be kept with the rest of your cash. Obviously, if you have to "fish" for a certain pack of bills, the crook is going to be suspicious.

There are four "identifiers" that help to describe a bill so that identification in a court of law is certain. These identifiers should be recorded on your bait money sheet. They are:

1. The denomination or amount. Denominations should be small, since the more bills that are distributed, the better the chance of their being traced.
2. The type of note (Federal Reserve Note, United States Note, Silver Certificate). Only Federal Reserve Notes are currently being issued, but some of the others are still around. In the case of a Federal Reserve Note, also list the issuing Federal Reserve Bank.
3. The series of the note.
4. The serial number.

A diagram of a bill appears in Chapter 10. It shows where each of these important items is found on a bill.

Your bait money sheet should look like this:

Bait Money

Name of teller _____ Date banded _____

Number	Denomination	Type	Series	Serial Number
1.	$20	FRBN-2	1985	B66480770F

The type FRBN-2 means Federal Reserve Bank Note, issued by FRB New York. The Federal Reserve Bank district numbers appear four times on each bill (see the diagram in Chapter 10).

Tear Gas/Dye Packs

A tear gas/dye pack is a security device that emits tear gas and red dye after a robber removes it from the premises. The device resembles a regular pack of strapped bills. Some packs actually consist of Treasury-approved currency. When used properly, the pack emits tear gas outside the financial institution, causing the robber to drop the money. The red or orange smoke attracts attention to the robber. The dye also stains clothing, currency, vehicles, and other material, which aids the police in gathering evidence.

Tear gas/dye packs have proven to be extremely effective in helping law enforcement agencies catch and prosecute robbers. Since financial institutions began installing these devices in the early 1960s, they have been responsible for the apprehension of many robbers and the recovery of a great deal of money. In general, institutions that use tear gas/dye packs recover about three times as much of their money as those that don't use them.

Unfortunately, the full benefits of these devices aren't being realized because employees sometimes fail to use them. Studies have shown that those tellers who have used them received intensive, formal security training, usually from security staff personnel. Of the tellers who have failed to use the packs, most received little or no security training.

If tear gas/dye packs are available at your institution, be sure you understand how they work and how to use them. Then, if you're ever robbed, you can take advantage of this effective security aid by including it with the robber's loot.

A ROBBERY AT YOUR FINANCIAL INSTITUTION

People who rob financial institutions don't just take money. They also take away the human dignity of their victims, and they often affect the work attitudes of the employees who have been robbed. Consider the following example:

Joanne works in an office that is attractive and sunny, with plants in the windows and comfortable, modern furnishings. Joanne always liked her job and her fellow employees, enjoyed her customers' friendly banter, and was proud of her office.

Then one day, three masked gunmen ran into that office.

One robber made Joanne and the other tellers lie on the floor. Another covered the branch manager and the customers, while the third jumped over the counter and scooped up the money from the cash drawers.

This was the first time Joanne had ever seen a pistol, except in the movies, on television, or in a police officer's holster. It was larger than she expected it to be, and more frightening. The floor, which she had never examined nose-to-rug before, was dusty. She studied a dropped rubber band in some detail.

Her first thought had been that the gunman who told her to lie down was rude. She became angry and gave him a sharp comment. He ordered her to lie down and shut up or he would shoot her. She did what she was told.

Though it seemed longer, the robbery took less than two minutes by the office clock, and the thieves got away with $41,000. The automatic cameras recorded only their masked faces, but an alert merchant in a nearby store got a license number. Within three days, the holdup men were caught, and the money was returned.

Although the incident is over and the robbers were apprehended, Joanne and her fellow employees know they will never feel the same. Joanne is nervous every time the office door opens. She thinks of the dusty floor and the rubber band instead of the plants and her attractive surroundings. She regrets making a foolish comment to the robber. The robber could have panicked and shot her. In short, some of the pleasure is gone from her job.

What should someone like Joanne do? For anyone who has been or may be victimized in this way, here are a few suggestions:

- After the robbery, expect to have a fear reaction. It's common and human. But don't give in to these fears. In time, the memory of the experience will be softened.
- Don't be angry with yourself for an action you may later think was foolish. Remember, robberies happen fast, and your instinctive reac-

tions may seem strange later. The best thing to do is to prepare before the occasion ever arises and try to plan what you will do.

- Expect to feel humiliated, angry, and, most of all, helpless and frustrated because you have been victimized.
- Discuss your psychological reactions with family, friends, your supervisor, and, if necessary, a professional counselor.

The Psychology of the Robber

In the past, financial institutions were usually held up by professional robbers who knew precisely what they were doing. Most robberies are now committed by:

Loners, as opposed to gangs. The loner won't try to take over the whole office, but is more likely to concentrate on just one teller.

Novices, who have only a fuzzy idea of how much money a teller might have on hand.

A *frightened person,* who, if armed, is very dangerous.

The robber may also be young. So-called youthful offender laws make penalties for youth crime so light that more and more young people seem to be trying their hands at robbery. Although financial institutions have been held up by women, in more than 90 percent of the cases, the robber is a male. He may be a drug user or emotionally disturbed. In short, the teller facing a gun should be prepared to protect his or her own life and the lives of customers and other employees by using sound psychology.

Here are some worthwhile dos and don'ts on how to deal with robbers that were outlined some years ago in the *FBI Bulletin* by Dr. Bruce L. Danto:

Assure him that he is in control. The nervous robber fears losing control. Don't challenge his orders. If you can't comply with an order, try to offer an acceptable alternative.

Address him respectfully. Don't swear, insult him, or cast doubt about his authority or his looks. Try to talk in an easy style and a well-modulated voice. Let the robber know that you're uncomfortable at having to face a gun.

Don't threaten him. Threats may cause the holdup man to focus on his anger rather than on maintaining control of himself. He may then become nervous or feel threatened from the outside (as opposed to self-imposed fears), lose control, and even fire his gun. Therefore, don't inflame a robber who may be fighting for self-control. Threats may allow deep-rooted psychological problems to surface.

Don't make any sudden movements. If you do, the robber might assume that you are reaching for an alarm or a weapon. Make your moves slowly, openly, and deliberately, so as not to upset him. Again, let him see that he is in control. Keep his trust by doing what he says and by not upsetting him.

Keep others at a safe distance. The object is to try to keep the robber from using a customer or employee as a shield or hostage. The fewer people who speak to him, the less chance that someone will upset him. And the more people who do upset him, the greater chance that he will become confused and lose control of himself.

Remember, the object in a holdup situation is to get the gunman out of the office as quickly and as peacefully as possible, with no one getting hurt. When the robber is facing you, it's too late to make up bait money, load the security camera, or review your description techniques.

Protective Devices

One of the main reasons that people use financial institutions is because they offer protection. Some of your institution's most important protective devices are so commonplace that you probably take them for granted. Your vault is an example. Faced with the impossibility of forcing its doors, crooks rarely consider looting it when no one is around. This is why they resort to armed robbery—when the vault is open and the money is available. Record-keeping systems are also protective devices. Other common protective devices are cameras, alarm systems, and fire systems.

Cameras are effective protective devices that can record robbers for tracing and identification. Some cameras are activated by employees pressing an alarm-type button or other device, and some simply take pictures continuously, recording any activity in the office. This latter type has not only trapped robbers but forgers and other criminals as well, often days or weeks after the crime.

Closed-circuit cameras in financial institutions are quite expensive. A phony camera that looks impressive—but takes no pictures—sells for a great deal less. Therefore, some institutions use such cameras to deter robbers and other crooks. Crooks know this—*but* they don't know which cameras are fake and which ones are real, so even the phony variety can act as a deterrent.

As a teller you should *never* tell *anyone* whether the cameras in your office are real or fake. Nor should you disclose the workings of an alarm system or office opening-signal systems. In short, never tell anyone anything that would help a robber. Even if you tell your husband or wife, he or she could be overhead telling someone else. Don't jeopardize your safety or that of your co-workers by discussing your financial institution's security systems.

Although there are several kinds of alarm systems, there are basically two main types: automatic and manual.

Automatic Alarms. These protect against nighttime burglary, employees being ambushed, and other situations where people are either not available to give the alarm or may be unable to do so. Such alarms may consist of electrical circuits that are activated when a window or door is opened or broken, usually setting off a signal in some off-site facility such as a police station or alarm-monitoring agency. Or they may be photoelectric devices, commonly called "electric eyes," which generate a signal if someone breaks a beam of light. There are also sensors that detect the heat of a person's body or that sense sound or motion.

Automatic devices are enabled by the person who last leaves the office and locks up and are disabled by the person who opens the office for the morning's work. Usually a signal is sent to the police or the agency where the alarm is monitored to notify them that the alarm has either been activated or deactivated.

Manual Alarms. These must be set off by an employee to alert police that a robbery is taking or has taken place. Modern alarms are silent to prevent the robber from knowing that an alarm has been triggered. Of course, no audible alarm, such as one used to test the operability of the system or the type that rings throughout the neighborhood, should ever be activated until any chance of panicking the robber has passed.

You should know the location of every alarm in your office and how to activate it. In particular, you should know the exact location and method of operation of every alarm within a 25-foot radius of your workstation. If you should ever have to use an alarm, *don't* let the criminal notice what you are doing. He knows financial institutions have alarm systems. He expects you to try to use one and will notice if you press a foot button, even if both of your hands are in full view. If you decide to press an alarm while a criminal is still on the premises, be extremely careful.

Be aware that some police departments may phone the office to learn if a robbery is really occurring or whether a false alarm has accidentally gone off. After an alarm is activated, an officer may phone the institution with a prede-termined message and, depending on the answer, decide whether or not to send someone to investigate. If your local police do this, be extra careful as the crook just may answer the phone or decide to listen in on an extension. Be sure to learn your institution's policies on how to handle such a situation.

Alarm systems and other protective devices are for your protection and for the safety of your customers and fellow employees. Learn to use them properly.

A Robbery Checklist

It is best to get the robber out of the office as quickly as possible. Don't risk lives—your own or anyone else's. In a 1990 incident, two robbers held up a branch of the National Westminster Bank located in a village south of London, England. The tellers refused to hand over any money or to come out of the sealed areas where they had taken cover, even though one of the robbers said he was going to shoot a customer in the leg and both of them fired warning shots into the ceiling. The customers begged the tellers to comply with the robbers' demands. Luckily, the robbers finally gave up and left empty-handed. Had they not done so, the consequences could have been extremely serious. Although every employee owes a certain amount of loyalty to his or her financial institution, including protecting its assets, the well-being of customers and other personnel always comes first.

Follow this checklist of things to do during a bank robbery:

1. Activate an alarm *if* you are absolutely sure you are not noticed, AND *if* you are absolutely sure it is silent, AND *if* you are absolutely sure you know what to do if the police telephone to verify the alarm.

2. Keep calm and calm your customers. This is easier said than done, but try.

3. Give the crook what he wants and let him leave. Avoid heroics.

4. Include bait money with the loot if at all possible.

5. If the robber has given you a note, try to avoid calling attention to it after you've read it. He may forget it and leave it behind.

6. Observe the robber. Note the basic facts about him in your mind, such as height, weight, race, and overall appearance. Especially note distinctive features such as scars, moles, and eye defects.

7. Also observe any weapon the crook may display, remembering what kind it is and noting anything distinctive about its appearance.

8. If the robber speaks, try to remember his voice. Note speech defects or regional accents.

9. Watch the robber as he leaves. Note his walk. If possible, try to get a look at his car and the license number. Except for a positive identification of the robber, the license number of the escape vehicle is the most useful information you can give the police.

10. Protect evidence after the criminal leaves. Don't smudge fingerprints or discard or handle a note. Don't discuss the robbery until you have been interviewed by the authorities. You may only confuse the facts. It's a good idea to make written notes about what you observed so that you'll be prepared to speak to the authorities.

The more calm and observant you are, the more you can do to help the authorities.

AFTER THE HOLDUP

If your office should be held up, it's important for you to keep calm even after the bandit has gone. Follow these tips:

- *DON'T* talk to reporters. Let your manager or security officer be the spokesman for the institution.
- *DON'T* tell anyone the amount of the loss. Just say, "They're doing an audit."
- *DON'T* give anyone your name or address or the name or address of any employee or customer.
- *DON'T* allow your picture to be taken.
- *DON'T* admit that bait money was involved, and never reveal any of the serial numbers, of course.
- *DON'T* discuss any cash the criminal overlooked. Letting the robber know what was missed may be an invitation for him to come back.
- *DON'T* discuss your security systems or procedures.
- *DON'T* discuss alarms, cameras, or other protective devices or allow unauthorized personnel to take pictures of these systems.
- *DON'T* allow the press to enter the vault or any nonpublic area.
- *DO* help the police. As mentioned previously, avoid talking to others about the holdup until you have spoken to the authorities. Others may confuse you and invalidate your evidence. Be prepared to give a description of the holdup man to the police and to give them your bait money sheet. And, if possible, give the police a description of the car used by the robber and, if you saw it, the license number.

Description of the Robber

Robbers often tend to look big, especially when they have guns. If you should ever be robbed, try to see just how big the robber really is. Few people can accurately guess height, weight, or age, yet these are three of the most basic identifiers. Try these tips:

Height. Pick out a fixed object the same height as the bandit and remember it. When the police come, you can say, "He was as tall as the top of that sign," for example. Then the police can measure the height of the object you named to determine the robber's height. Some financial institutions have a piece of colored tape pasted in a strategic place, such as an entrance, six feet from the floor. Then employees can say, "He was about two inches shorter than the tape," or whatever is appropriate.

Weight. Get the robber's weight by comparing him with someone you know. For example, "He was about the same size as our branch manager." The police can then check and get a good idea of the bandit's weight.

Age. This can be difficult to guess. Stick to generalities if you aren't sure, such as late twenties, midthirties, early fifties, and so on.

The most important thing in giving a description is to remember what *you* saw. Don't let someone else convince you that what you saw wasn't quite the way you remember it. After all, that other person could be wrong, not you.

The following Witness Questionnaire will help you to record the physical details about an individual, whether that person was actually a real armed robber or is someone you are practicing describing.

Witness Questionnaire

Name of Teller _____ Date _____

Try to remember the details of the robber's appearance and the way he acted and fill in the appropriate blanks.

Sex _____ Race _____ Height _____ Weight _____ Age _____

Who do you know in person or from TV or the movies that the robber resembles? _____

In what way do they resemble each other? _____

_____

_____

_____

Have you ever noticed this person before? If so, where? _____

_____

_____

_____

Hair

    Color:
    Length:
    Description (curly, straight):

Face

    Shape:
    Distinguishing marks (freckles, scars, pockmarks, dimples):
    Complexion (light, dark, ruddy):
    Eyes
        Color:
        Shape:
        Distance apart:
    Eyebrows
        Color:
        Type (thin, bushy):
    Nose
        Size:
        Shape (flat, pointy, wide):
        Shape of nostrils:
    Mouth
        Size:
        Color:
        Shape:
    Teeth
        Size:
        Condition (straight, crooked):
        Missing:
    Mustache
        Color:
        Shape:
        Other (beard, sideburns):

Cheeks
    Color:
    Type (pronounced, flat):
Chin
    Size:
    Type (pronounced, recessed, cleft, wide, narrow):
Ears
    Size:
    Type (protruding, flat):
Neck
    Length:
    Thickness:

Other Physical Characteristics

Shoulders
    Size:
    Type (sloping, square):
Chest
    Type (broad, hollow, flat):
Hands
    Which used (right-handed or left-handed):
    Condition (dirty, scars, shaking, calm):
    Fingers (length, straightness, thickness, missing):
    Fingernails (length, dirty, broken, polished):
Mannerisms
    Speech (manner of talking, accent):
    Words spoken:
    Voice (soft, deep):
    Walk (stride, limp):
Distinguishing marks
    Tattoos:
    Birthmarks:
    Moles:

Clothing

Hat
    Style:
    Color:
    Material:

Mask
    Style:
    Color:
    Material:
Coat
    Style:
    Color:
    Material:
Jacket
    Style:
    Color:
    Material:
Sweater
    Style:
    Color:
    Material:
Suit
    Style:
    Color:
    Material:
Dress
    Style:
    Color:
    Material:
Blouse or shirt
    Style:
    Color:
    Material:
Tie
    Style:
    Color:
    Material:
Trousers or skirt
    Style:
    Color:
    Material:
Socks or stockings
    Style:
    Color:
    Material:

Shoes
>   Style:
>   Color:
>   Material:

Gloves
>   Style:
>   Color:
>   Material:

Jewelry
>   Item:
>   Description:

Weapon

>   Type:
>   Description:

Vehicle Used

>   Before robbery:
>   After robbery:
>   Make:
>   Year:
>   Color:
>   License:
>   Person(s) in vehicle:
>   Direction taken:

No teller likes to contemplate being involved in a holdup. However, it pays to be prepared just in case the situation arises. It's up to management, of course, to purchase expensive equipment, but the branch manager and the teller do share the responsibility for the security of the office. The most important thing you can do is to be prepared. The primary objective of this preparation should be the protection of the lives of customers and staff and, of lesser but still vital importance, the conservation of the assets of your institution.

18

CHAPTER

Forged, Counterfeit, and Altered Checks

BE ALERT FOR FORGERS

Tellers should be on the lookout for forgers at any time, but especially during busy hours. Crowded financial institution offices provide just the right atmosphere for these criminals. Tellers trying to cope with long lines of customers are preoccupied with handling transactions quickly and accurately and can be victimized by those who know how to take advantage of this kind of situation.

What to Watch For

Forgers are very careful to make sure that they look believable. Invariably, financial institution employees who happen to remember them report that they were well-spoken, well-dressed, and thoroughly convincing. Time after time, they've said, "She was a forger? I don't believe it! She had such an honest face! And she was so well-dressed and friendly." And time after time, they describe the forger in terms that fit almost any successful businessperson.

Experienced forgers look average and act average. They are full of tricks that make them appear to be above suspicion. They can act as though they know their way around and can usually lie quite convincingly. Their specialty is blending in, which not only makes these criminals hard to spot in the first place but makes them even more difficult to describe when a forgery is discovered, perhaps weeks after it took place.

Forgers often try to distract busy tellers by pretending to be regular customers of the institution. A smile and a wave to the branch manager or a member of his or her staff will most likely be returned out of common courtesy and can make the forger seem to be well known when, in fact, this is not the case. Or the forger may engage in small talk that reveals a "friendship" with an important officer of the institution. "When I was having lunch with your president yesterday . . ." Of course, the president is safely out of sight at the main office, and the teller assumes that the forger is telling the truth.

Forgers also try to distract tellers by being pushy. Having tellers take time to check up on them is the last thing that they want, so they try to rush the tellers. "I'm double parked!" and "I'm late for an important appointment!" are common ploys that forgers use.

There is only one defense against this type of criminal that is sure to work: know forgers' methods and how to avoid them.

The Check Stealer

There are two types of check stealers. The first steals legitimate checks that are already issued, such as Social Security checks from mailboxes. The second steals blank checks, such as a book of payroll checks from an office drawer, and then forges them.

In the first case, the forgery involved is of the endorser's signature. There is one sure way to avoid this type of forgery: KNOW YOUR ENDORSER.

Many Social Security, welfare, or other government checks are delivered on or about the same day each month. These checks are often left unprotected in unlocked mailboxes. Crooks know this and just follow the letter carrier. Again, know your endorser. *Anyone* can be a forger.

Forgers who steal blank checks are more flexible. They are more likely to do their business in a crowded supermarket than in your financial institution, but beware of them anyway. Here are some signs that might give them away:

1. The official amount is filled in with a typewriter or ink rather than with a checkwriter. Most business firms use checkwriters, although crooks can buy their own checkwriters, which are readily available and inexpensive.

2. Even amounts appear on supposed paychecks. With taxes, Social Security, and all of the other deductions, the odds against a paycheck amount coming out even are great—one chance in a hundred, to be exact.

3. A person who is trying to cash several paychecks "for friends."

Knowing your endorser is the only sure way to avoid getting "hit" by forgers.

The Check Writer

There was a time when a person could walk into a financial institution and say, "May I have a checkbook, please?" Chances are, the customer would get one without question. Magnetic ink character recognition (MICR), in which magnetic ink is used to encode checks so they can be processed electronically, has made this more difficult. However, most institutions still give out small quantities of unimprinted checks to tide someone over who has forgotten to order a new supply. Be especially careful of the check that lacks MICR numbering. It could be phony.

When you must cash a check for a stranger, demand positive identification *that bears a signature* that can be checked. Then, even if the check is already endorsed, have the person sign it again in your presence. Check the signature carefully. If possible, deposit the check for collection.

Refer any questionable cases to a supervisor. Above all, in every case, follow your institution's check-cashing policies, and when necessary, refuse to cash checks.

What Else Can Be Forged?

The average person thinks of checks when thinking about forgeries, but crooks think further. They can also forge savings bonds, withdrawals from stolen passbooks, signatures in order to gain access to safe deposit boxes with stolen keys, and money orders.

The best defense that every person who works in a financial institution has against the potential forger is to know with whom he or she is dealing and to be certain that the person has a right to the instrument that is being presented.

Verifying Signatures

Whenever a checking account is opened, the new customer must provide the required information for a signature card, which must be signed by the account holder. In the case of joint accounts, both people must sign. This card can then be used to verify the customer's signature on checks and other documents. Likewise, a signature card must be filled in and signed when a savings account is opened. This enables the financial institution to authenticate any withdrawals the customers may make.

Special devices designed to help prevent forgery by verifying signatures are also available. Included are:

- Monitors for displaying a computer-stored master of a customer's signature for comparison with the one being written.

- Devices that enable a financial institution to check a customer's signature through a technique that scrambles a signature written on a passbook so that it can't be read by the naked eye. The signature can only be unscrambled at the teller's window. When a customer presents a withdrawal slip or other document, the teller inserts the scrambled signature into a device that removes the distortion and enables him or her to make a comparison with the signature on the document.

- The invisible signature verification system, which works on the same principle as carbon paper. The customer signs his or her name on a passbook or a statement savings account ID card, writing on special phosphor-coated paper that is placed between the pen and the passbook or card. The resulting signature is invisible and must be held under an ultraviolet lamp, called a black light, to be seen. From then on, whenever the customer signs a withdrawal slip, he or she must do so in front of a teller. A black light at the teller's window is then used to enable him or her to compare the signature on the withdrawal slip with the one on the passbook or ID card.

- Devices that measure and analyze the speed, pressure, and rhythm used as a person writes his or her usual signature. No matter how well a forger could copy a signature, that is something he or she could not hope to duplicate. A forged signature lacks the freedom of movement that characterizes a genuine one.

A special device for verifying signatures may not be available, however; and the average financial institution employee is not an expert on signatures. In addition, the teller may not have time to carefully check each signature against the customer's signature card. Therefore, the best protective device of all is still an alert teller who, as stated previously, insists on knowing the person with whom he or she is dealing.

COUNTERFEIT CHECKS

Offset printing and color copiers have made it possible for counterfeiters to copy perfectly good checks drawn on reputable firms. Money orders, payroll checks, company checks—all can be convincingly reproduced in seconds.

Therefore, firms that manufacture documents constantly endeavor to produce checks that help to prevent their being duplicated.

For example, Deluxe Corporation, the world's largest check printer and a leader in fraud prevention programs, introduced a new document in 1995 called Rub and Reveal, which is available to financial institutions on select check products. The feature, which is incorporated into the check paper itself, enables tellers to instantly verify the authenticity of a document without any special equipment. Tellers simply scratch or rub the back of a check to reveal the word "original." The Rub and Reveal feature protects against duplication and chemical altering of checks. Other document security features available from Deluxe include MicroPrinting, security screens, chemically sensitive paper, and watermarked paper.

Suppose a crook obtains some perfectly good checks drawn on the accounts of well-known companies. The crook makes excellent copies of these checks. He then obtains deposit tickets that are MICR encoded and bear the name of a valid depositor. The crook makes two checks payable to the depositor. He goes to the financial institution, deposits one large check, and cashes a smaller one.

The teller probably doesn't question the crook's identity. After all, he's just deposited a check issued by a company of high repute to his account and then cashed a smaller check also issued by a reputable company. Of course, somewhere along the line the counterfeit check will be spotted, but by then the crook will be long gone.

Again, suppose that a crook obtains checks drawn on the accounts of well-known local companies and makes copies of them. This time, however, the crook opens a savings account with a small amount of cash. Soon she comes into the financial institution and deposits a large counterfeit check that the teller would not question.

The next day, or perhaps two days later, she returns and makes another deposit, then either cashes a separate check or makes the deposit a split. Either way, the crook gets a large amount of cash, and all the financial institution can recover is the small initial cash deposit she made to open the account.

Teller error is involved here, and the error is simply paying out against uncollected funds because the big paper balance is so impressive.

Although schemes involving checking accounts or even fraudulent loan gimmicks overshadow criminal efforts in the savings account field, the scheme just described works well. It's easy for tellers to get careless in handling savings accounts because they assume that the financial institution can't lose money. Tellers know that people put checks in for collection and must have a passbook and/or a valid signature and/or good identification to make a withdrawal.

When you handle savings transactions:

1. Know with whom you are dealing whenever you pay out cash. Get good identification and follow all of your institution's policies.
2. Refer any questionable cases to a supervisor.
3. Look at all checks, even those for deposit. Especially examine large checks and watch for counterfeits.
4. Be suspicious of any inactive accounts that are suddenly reactivated unless you know the person with whom you are dealing. Finding an old passbook, making a few deposits to establish identity, and then cleaning out the account is an old trick.
5. Don't assume that all crooks work their schemes on checking accounts or that all crooks look like criminals. Some of the best con artists are innocent-looking elderly folks and well-dressed "businesspeople."

Clues for Identifying Counterfeit Checks

Here are four tests to use if you have any reason to be suspicious of a check:

1. Check to see if one edge of the check is perforated. With the exception of government, computer-card, and counter checks, most good checks are perforated on at least one edge and possibly two because they are removed from a book or from a continuous series. Counterfeit checks are often smooth on all four edges.
2. Check the reaction of light on the MICR numbers on the bottom of the check. Remember that these numbers are imprinted in magnetic ink, which doesn't reflect light. If you note shiny numbers, consult your supervisor.
3. Try to smear the ink on a clean piece of white paper. Printer's ink smears in the same color you see on the check. Checks from a color copier smear in different colors because of the chemical reaction. Or, if time permits, try one of the other methods for spotting color-copier counterfeit bills or documents as described in Chapter 19.
4. Check for the proper routing number. The first two digits of the check's nine-digit MICR number indicates the Federal Reserve District in which the issuing financial institution is located. This number also appears in the bottom portion of the fraction in the upper right-hand corner of most checks. On most phony checks, the routing number has been changed in order to route the check to the

wrong Federal Reserve so as to buy time in passing it. Therefore, it pays to know where the districts are located and to make sure that checks bear the proper one. For more information about these numbers, see the section on checking accounts that appears in Chapter 24.

Follow the basic rule about knowing your endorser. And expand that rule to be sure you've known him or her for a long enough time to be able to trust the person's honesty. If the collected balance in an account isn't sufficient to cover a check being cashed, either refer the customer to an officer or accept the check for deposit. Even an authentic-looking check drawn on a big company can be counterfeit.

Clues for Identifying Counterfeit or Altered Postal Money Orders

The U.S. Postal Service began issuing new money orders in 1991 and added improvements in 1993 that are designed to deter counterfeiting and alterations. Here are six tests to use if you have any reason to be suspicious of a postal money order:

1. Hold the money order up to the light to see if a water mark portrait of Benjamin Franklin and an imbedded security thread that runs from the top to the bottom are visible.

2. Check the background colors. To the naked eye, they appear to range from orange to blue, but close examination shows that the lines of ink are purple and yellow to produce the orange cast and purple and green to produce the blue cast. This is designed to fool color copiers.

3. Check to see if anything has been erased. If an erasure is made on the money order, the background printing will vanish.

4. See if the numbers have been altered. Specially designed numerals make them extremely difficult to change. A 1 cannot be changed to a 7, for example, or a 0 to an 8.

5. See if any portion of the money order bears a brown mark. Because of the chemical treatment of the paper, using bleach to make alterations turns the paper brown.

6. If you have access to a means of powerful magnification, use it to check the horizontal line on the back of the money order. It will reveal the words "U.S. Postal Service" printed over and over again in almost microscopic letters.

The new postal money orders were introduced in an effort to stop convicts who have been operating elaborate money order alteration schemes from prisons throughout the United States and bilking consumers of millions of dollars. If you should spot one that is a counterfeit or has been altered, report it to your supervisor, who should see that the Postal Inspection Service is notified immediately.

ALTERED CHECKS

Many times rushed tellers have cashed a check—frequently one that is "on us"—for a properly identified person only to find later that the check has been fraudulently altered. Often weeks go by before the customer gets the statement and reports the altered check. When this amount of time has gone by, it is very difficult for a teller to make a positive identification of the suspect.

Here are some rules that can help to eliminate this problem:

1. As stated before, know your endorser.
2. If the check looks at all suspicious, get your manager's approval to cash it.
3. Watch for the common types of alterations that are described in this section.
4. Be suspicious of the customer who tries to rush you or distract you with small talk.

Common Types of Alterations

As MICR and printed checks have become universal, alterations have become more common. It is simply getting harder to get blank checks to forge. It is much easier to take an already issued check and change it. The crook does this simply by using similar ink and changing words or numbers.

Here are the four common types of alterations:

Altered figures. In this case, the passer is counting on a hurried teller to read only the figure amount of the check. It would be easy to change the number 13.50 to 73.50 but next to impossible to change the word "Thirteen" to "Seventy-three." Changing figures is the most common of all types of alterations, and tellers can detect this alteration simply by developing the habit of reading the words as well as the figures.

Altered figures and words. Almost everyone reads the amount written in figures on a check first, so changing the amount written in words

FIGURE 18-1

How Checks Are Altered by Pen Changes

Forty	4 TO 40	40⁰⁰/100
Fifty	5 TO 50	50⁰⁰/100
Sixty	6 TO 60	60⁰⁰/100
Seventy	7 TO 70	70⁰⁰/100
Eighty	8 TO 80	88⁰⁰/100
Ninety	9 TO 90	90⁰⁰/100
Fifty	10 TO 50	50⁰⁰/100 50⁰⁰/100
Fourty four	14 TO 44	44⁰⁰/100
Fifty five	15 TO 55	55⁰⁰/100
Sixteen	16 TO 66	66⁰⁰/100
Seventeenen	17 TO 77	77⁰⁰/100
Eighteenght	18 TO 88	88⁰⁰/100
Nineteenine	19 TO 99	99⁰⁰/100
Twenty-five	25 TO 75	75⁰⁰/100
One Hundred	100 TO 400	400⁰⁰/100
Two Hundred	200 TO 500	500⁰⁰/100
Eight Hundred	100 TO 800	800⁰⁰/100
Nine Hundred	100 TO 900	900⁰⁰/100

F I G U R E 18–1

Continued

Crane Co	To	Chakes Cox
Wilson + Co	-	Wilson H Collier
R Turner + Co	-	Rev. Turner H Cooper
Morris + Co	-	Morris H Cohen
Edison + Co	-	Edison H Cooper
May Co	-	May Cook
Donald Inc	-	Donald Ingersol
Borden Co	-	Borden Collier
Walker + Co	-	Walker H Coleman
Burlington RR	-	Burlington R Rebelski
Borg Inc	-	Borg Ingram
Jarvis Corp	-	Jarvis Corpinski
Thomas Corp	-	Thomas Corpus

These examples of payee name pen changes illustrate what a few strokes of a pen can do.

without changing the figures would be foolish. This means that the crook must find a check in which both the amounts written in words and figures lend themselves to changing. For example, it is possible to change a $4 check into one for $84 by adding an 8 and the word "Eighty" in the appropriate places. It is very important for all check writers to be sure to start at the extreme left of the line when filling in the dollar amount in words and figures.

Altered payee. Be careful when *cashing* checks payable to companies. Businesses deposit their checks as a rule, so such a deviation should raise questions in a teller's mind. A few letters added to "Moss Co.," for example, changes the payee to "Moss Copeland." With a forged driver's license, the alterer is in business. If the alterer has stolen a whole stack of checks from the Moss Company's mail, he can have a field day. Watch for names that start with Co., Corp., and Inc.

Altered endorsement. Altering an endorsement, like altering the payee, enables the crook to cash a check on a forged driver's license or other false identification. This is the least common type of alteration because it is the most likely to be questioned. Any check with two endorsements (and an alteration requires changing the first one) is unusual enough to be questioned. But if the stakes are high enough, crooks will try this scheme. So be safe; refer all suspicious endorsements to your supervisor. And encourage your customers to avoid changed endorsements by using a special endorsement, such as "For Deposit Only."

Technology Causes Problems

No consideration of altered checks would be complete without mentioning two modern products that make the task of changing checks easier.

Correctable typewriters. These machines, which enable typists to "lift" errors without a trace, make it possible for someone to easily alter a check that has been written on such a machine. For example, if a check has been typed in an office where the crook has access to the same or a similar machine, he or she need only place the check back into the typewriter, remove the original amounts typed in words and figures and/or the name of the payee, and fill in the desired replacements. Urge your customers to avoid these machines when writing checks.

Erasable ink. Erasable-ink pens present potential problems for financial institution employees because crooks can erase the ink with any pencil eraser and thus change various items on the check. Usually, you can write with one and, for 24 hours, you can erase it just like a pencil. Then the ink sets and becomes permanent. The manufacturers of these pens may include a warning against using them on checks or legal documents, but many people don't read or ignore package warnings. Tell your customers not to use these pens for checks because they could easily be altered in amount, payee, or endorsement.

Here's an example of a fraud involving erasable ink. The crook opens a new checking account and instructs that statements be held at the financial institution, which prevents them from being returned "addressee unknown." After the funds from any checks used in opening the account have had a chance to be collected, the person writes several small checks drawn on the new account and presents them for certification. They are written in ink with an erasable pen and are payable to companies that don't accept personal checks for the purchase of high-priced items. After certification, the amounts are altered, raising a $5 check to $5,000, for example. The crook can then use the certified checks to make expensive purchases. The best way to prevent this fraud is to imprint the amount on certified checks with a checkwriter or make sure that a check to be certified has not been written in erasable ink.

Dissolving Checks

Early in 1988, chemically treated checks worth thousands of dollars were presented in the Chicago area as well as in Tennessee and Indiana. The chemicals caused the checks to disintegrate shortly after they were deposited.

The checks were burnt orange in color, many were signed in green ink, and they had a damp, oily finish. Since the checks fell apart within hours of being deposited, before they could be microfilmed, none of the information on them could be identified.

The financial crimes unit of the Chicago Police Department reported that all of the bogus checks were drawn on out-of-town banks. Most were for $2,200 to $4,800; the most typical amount was $4,000 or $4,500. All involved straight deposits to relatively new accounts.

Tellers were advised to avoid accepting any checks that felt wet or damp to the touch. They were instructed to ask the person who presented the check to allow it to dry out first, and the tellers offered a polite excuse for the delay, such as the fact that the check couldn't be processed when it was damp.

Tellers should be suspicious of any checks like those described, because it is possible that someone else may try this scheme.

SHARED DATA

To combat check fraud, some of the companies that print checks have developed systems that provide electronically shared information about lost and stolen checks. To help financial institutions and retailers to avoid losses, they have set up 24-hour hot lines to receive information about these checks. This information is reported to a data base, which is supplied to financial institutions and participating merchants, enabling them to avoid accepting the checks.

Some financial institutions are also joining regional bad-check alert networks in order to reduce the losses that result from fraudulent checks and from closed, frozen, or overdrawn checking accounts. The participating financial institutions electronically share pertinent information with each other.

PROBLEMS IN PUBLIC RELATIONS

Here's an actual comment from a teller: "Okay, so I check on every customer I don't know. One day I check on a personal friend of the president. The friend squawks to the president, who calls my boss, who tells me—and I quit checking as carefully. Then the next week I pay out on a forgery. What am I to do?"

Walking a fine line between maintaining proper security and practicing positive public relations can be difficult, but there are ways to make it easier:

- Treat each customer with courtesy, even when you are checking on him or her.
- Don't make a big deal of checking. Act as though it's routine, and the customer will probably accept it as such.
- If the customer does become angry and you cannot assuage his or her anger, refer that person to your supervisor.

Don't get discouraged or change your security practices because of an occasional gripe, regardless of its source. An officer of your institution would rather have you delay his or her friend than have you get involved in a forgery.

Security precautions pay. Just stay calm, be careful, and be courteous.

19

Counterfeit Currency

HOW TO SPOT A COUNTERFEIT

Counterfeiting requires less skill than it did years ago, when a "good" counterfeiter had to spend many hours carefully engraving a copper plate with a reproduction of our currency. Today, producing fair, though not excellent, counterfeits requires a good camera, an inexpensive offset printing press, and a reasonable eye for color matching. In addition, color copiers make counterfeiting possible, even for rank amateurs.

Counterfeit money usually comes into financial institutions through deposits made by regular customers. Counterfeiters can pass their bills much faster by going from store to store and making small purchases than they can by going from one institution to another. To a large extent, the government relies on alert tellers to spot counterfeits and to help trace them to their source. Even though any bills you may spot are likely to be in deposits, your alertness can lead trained investigators to the criminals. Counterfeit currency can hurt everyone by watering down the value of our dollars. More specifically, counterfeit money passed on to an innocent person hurts this individual because he or she must turn it over to the authorities without reimbursement. Unfortunately, people who get stuck with bad bills are often those who can least afford to lose money.

How to Spot a Nondeceptive Bill

Printing presses and crooks are found all across the country. The authorities call counterfeits produced by offset printing on regular paper *nondeceptive* notes. By this, the Secret Service means that any alert teller should be able to spot them. Here are some tips that might help you to do so:

> *Check the paper.* The paper of a phony bill looks and feels like good grade typing paper rather than the special paper on which money is printed. It is most noticeable when the bill gets slightly worn, because regular paper simply won't hold up to much handling. Look at a real bill and note the special feel. Note the tiny red and blue fibers worked into the paper, and note the off-white color. A counterfeit will probably be printed on paper that is too white.
>
> *Check the printing.* The fine lines on the portrait and in the design on the reverse of a phony bill may be blurry and fuzzy rather than being distinct. This results from the process of photographing the bill and making a plate from the negative. Every added step in the printing process causes some loss of detail. That's why real bills are of high quality; they are *engraved* by experts from original plates. In addition, a real bill feels a bit rough where the engraving plate has scratched the paper while forcing in the ink, whereas a phony bill is slick and smooth.
>
> *Check the color.* The face of a real bill is printed in black, which is not hard to duplicate. The back is green, however, and getting the exact shade is difficult, especially because of the off-white color of a real bill. Thus, a phony bill usually looks too green on the reverse.

A counterfeit bill, if rubbed vigorously on a sheet of blank paper, smears the blank paper with green ink, but a new genuine bill does the same thing. Ink on newly-printed paper smears if rubbed hard. Therefore, this common test is invalid.

> *Check the color of the Treasury seal and serial numbers.* Three types of U.S. paper currency are in circulation. The name of each appears on the upper face of the bill. The different bills are identified by the color of the Treasury seal and serial numbers:

Type	Treasury Seal & Serial Number	Denomination
Federal Reserve notes	green	$1, $2, $5, $10
		$20, $50, $100
U.S. notes	red	$2, $5, $100
Silver certificates	blue	$1, $5, $10

A counterfeiter may not use the appropriate color for the Treasury seal and serial numbers in producing a certain type of currency. Therefore, being aware of what the correct color should be can help in detecting a phony bill.

Check the denomination. The numerals may not match the portrait. Counterfeiters sometimes shave the numerals off the corners of the bill and print or paste on higher numbers.

The denomination of a counterfeit is often $10 or, more likely, $20. Makers of bogus bills produce fifties and hundreds as well, but these bills are more likely to be closely examined than those of lower denomination.

Check to see that the Federal Reserve Bank letters and numbers match. The Federal Reserve seal is on the left side of the face of the bill and bears a letter; the Federal Reserve numbers appear in the four corners. The code is simple: A-1, B-2, and so forth. Thus, bills issued for the Federal Reserve Bank of Philadelphia, for example, will show the letter "C" in the seal and a "3" in each corner. Each Federal Reserve Bank will use the same letter and corresponding number without variation. Here are the letters and numbers for the 12 Federal Reserve Banks:

A-1	Boston	G-7	Chicago
B-2	New York	H-8	St. Louis
C-3	Philadelphia	I-9	Minneapolis
D-4	Cleveland	J-10	Kansas City
E-5	Richmond	K-11	Dallas
F-6	Atlanta	L-12	San Francisco

Check the serial number. It should be different on each bill. Sometimes counterfeiters just set the type once and use the same number on every bill. A real bill that has been damaged in printing is replaced with a "star note," in which case, the serial number contains a star and will be out of sequence with the other bills in the series.

Check and double-check large cash deposits for counterfeits. Contrary to popular belief, most passers don't come into a financial institution with a single bill and ask for change, although you should watch for strangers who do. These people know that tellers are likely to spot a bogus bill. Instead, they pass the counterfeits in supermarkets with inexperienced clerks who are in a hurry or in gas stations or dimly lit bars. Thus, counterfeits are likely to be found in deposits from retail establishments.

When a few counterfeits appear, watch for more. Nondeceptive bills are usually passed in bunches. Counterfeiters want to get rid of as much bogus money as possible in as short a time as possible. This means being extra careful when the Secret Service or other authorities report an influx of counterfeits. An alert teller can help to put the authorities on the trail of the passers and to cut the supply off at the source.

Counterfeiting and Color Copiers

Color copiers have enabled many amateurs to make counterfeit bills and checks. Here are some tests to help you tell a photocopy from an original bill or document:

- Rub any suspected bill or document with a piece of white tissue. A real bill or document will smudge, but with the same color as that on the bill or document. A photocopied bill will leave a different off-color smudge.
- Touch a hot iron to a piece of blank paper over a suspected bill or document. If it is a photocopy, the blank paper will stick to the bill. If it is genuine, it will not stick.
- If you wipe a bit of cotton saturated with trichloroethylene on the suspected bill or document, it will produce a color change if it is a photocopy. However, this solvent has anesthetic properties and should be used very carefully.

The foregoing tests work only on photocopies. *Printed* phonies will pass the tests as well as the genuine articles will, so you should also rely on paper feel and close examination.

CURRENCY CHANGES

New bills were introduced late in 1991 to help foil counterfeiters who use color copiers to reproduce bills. The bills are the same size, shape, and color as traditional bills, but a metalized, clear polyester thread is imbedded in the paper that is invisible in reflected light, but visible when held up to direct light. This means it cannot be reproduced by photocopiers.

The thread was first included in some of the new $20 bills and all of the new $50 and $100 bills. Minute letters spell out "USA Twenty" on the $20 bills, "USA 50" on the $50 bills, and "USA 100" on the $100 bills. They appear between the seal and the left border on all three denominations. In addition to the thread, the words "United States of America" are printed in a border around the portraits in type so small that photocopiers can't reproduce them. Tellers using magnifying glasses, however, are able to see the words. These features were added to all new $20 bills by the end of 1992 and were added to $5 and $10 bills during 1993.

Subsequently, more major changes were planned for U.S. currency in order to combat the production of counterfeits. The $100 bill, which was the first to be redesigned because it's a favorite with overseas counterfeiters, went into circulation in 1996. Each succeeding year, a new design for another denomination is to be introduced, starting with fifties and followed by twenties, tens, and fives. New $2 and $1 bills may not include the security features, and the other denominations may not include all of those incorporated into the new $100 bills.

Here are the security features that are included in the 1996 $100 bills:

- The portrait of Benjamin Franklin has been enlarged and is more detailed, to make it more difficult to counterfeit. It has been moved slightly to the left of center to reduce wear on this important part of the design.

- A watermark of Franklin's portrait has been added, which shows when the bills are held up to the light. Color copiers and scanning equipment can't reproduce it.

- Concentric fine-line printing that is hard to reproduce appears on the background of the portrait and on the picture of Independence Hall on the back of the bill. In addition, "USA 100" is microprinted on the number 100 in the lower left-hand corner of the bill, and "United States of America" is microprinted on the lapel of Franklin's coat.

- A security thread glows red when the bill is held under an ultraviolet light. This thread is to be placed in a different position on each new denomination.

- The number 100 in the lower right-hand corner of the bill changes from green to black when it is viewed at an angle.

- New serial numbers include two prefix letters, eight numerals, and end with a single letter. The first letter of the prefix is an "A," which designates the 1996 series. Also, a new universal Federal Reserve seal represents the entire Federal Reserve system, replacing those for the individual Federal Reserve Banks.

The size, color, and portraits are to remain the same on the new bills as those used on current bills, which will continue to stay in circulation.

How to Spot a Deceptive Bill

A *deceptive* bill is one that may very likely fool someone who routinely handles money, such as a teller. It is a bill that is made very carefully to duplicate real currency as exactly as possible. Much rarer than nondeceptive bills, deceptive counterfeits are likely to be different in two major ways:

> *A deceptive bill is more likely to be engraved.* This means that the counterfeiters make printing plates in the same manner used by government currency producers. By hand or chemical means, they cut the lines that appear on the bill on a metal plate that they use in printing the bills. Counterfeiters thus get sharper lines than those obtained by plates made in a photographic manner.

> *A deceptive bill is more likely to be printed on paper that has a closer resemblance to real currency paper.* This may just be a very good grade of paper with a color that comes close to the real thing, or it may be actual $1 bills that have been bleached and painstakingly split into two full-sized sections, which are then carefully glued back to face, leaving a printing blank that looks just like real official paper because it *is* official paper. Of course, bills thus produced have the tiny red and blue fibers sprinkled through the paper.

Producing a deceptive bill is no small job. For this reason, counterfeiters don't make them in small denominations because it's simply not profitable enough. You are not likely to see a deceptive bill in the amount of $1, $5, or $10. Usually they are in the amount of $50 or $100, but occasionally very good $20 bills do appear. However, the practice of including the polyester thread in new bills helps to foil these counterfeiters as well as those who use photocopiers. Because the thread is imbedded in the currency paper, it will be missing from counterfeit bills.

If you have any reason to suspect a bill, do the following to spot a deceptive one:

- Check the back. The color might not be quite right.
- Check the hair-thin lines around the portrait and denomination numbers in the corners. Criminal engravers usually do not have the time or the skill, let alone the equipment, to do the clean, expert work of government engravers.
- Wet the bill thoroughly. Good U.S. currency holds up well. However, a bill that has been bleached, split, and glued back to front is likely to fall apart in warm water.

- Examine the denomination numbers in the corners and make sure they match the amount written in words and the portrait that should be on the bill. When you spot George Washington on a twenty, you know you have a phony!
- Look at the seals on the face of the bill. In a counterfeit, the points in either the Treasury or Federal Reserve seal may be unevenly spaced or dulled.

Bills may be designated as deceptive to indicate that they contain better workmanship than nondeceptive bills, but they eventually get spotted and usually don't really deceive anyone for too long. Alert financial institution employees can spot them and are thus the biggest allies the Secret Service has in controlling this criminal activity that threatens to weaken our currency and thus rob everyone.

Counterfeit Currency Detectors

Various mechanical devices are available for spotting counterfeit bills. They are designed to identify defects in the paper and in the inking, coloring, and printing. Small pen-size devices are now available that determine whether or not a bill is counterfeit by detecting the magnetic particles embedded on the front of all U.S. currency. Vending machines that accept bills and make change operate under the same principle and reject those bills that are phony.

While financial institution employees who have such detectors find them to be simple and easy to use, they must realize that the devices are not foolproof. The public affairs officer for the Bureau of Engraving and Printing warns, "An enterprising counterfeiter could also make ink magnetic and thereby fool such a device." For this reason, Secret Service agents rely on visual detection rather than on equipment.

WHAT TO DO IF YOU SPOT A COUNTERFEIT

In 1865, it was estimated that one bill out of every three in circulation was a counterfeit. So the United States Secret Service was formed as an arm of the Treasury Department to protect our currency. The Secret Service is our oldest federal law-enforcement agency. Since its founding, additional duties have been assigned to it, including guarding the president and vice president of the United States and their families, as well as major candidates for the presidency and others.

As far as counterfeiting is concerned, the Secret Service is charged with the responsibility of detecting and arresting persons who break the laws of the

United States with regard to its money, obligations, or securities or who commit certain offenses relating to the Federal Deposit Insurance Corporation or Federal Land Banks. It is extremely effective in carrying out these duties.

As stated before, currency isn't the only thing counterfeited by criminals. U.S. savings bonds are also subject to counterfeiting. The same rules apply to spotting and reporting them as apply to currency. They, too, are printed on official government paper from plates made by expert engravers, and their bogus counterparts have the same faults as those of counterfeit currency. The Secret Service investigates—and usually solves—cases involving bond counterfeiting as well as those involving currency.

If You Know the Passer

If you spot a counterfeit, it will be under one of three circumstances: You know the person who gave it to you, you do not know the person who gave it to you, or you spot the bill after it has been given to you, in which case you may or may not remember the person.

If you know the person, DON'T give it back to the customer. You are simply not allowed to do so no matter how good the customer is or how friendly. The law requires that a counterfeit be reported to the proper authorities at once. This can present a problem in customer relations. The average customer can't afford or doesn't want to lose $10, $20, or more. So people are often inclined to say to the teller, "Oh, just give it back to me and I'll take care of it." Loosely translated, this means, "Give it back to me, and I'll pass it on to some busy clerk in a not-too-brightly-lit place. Then I won't have to stand the loss."

First of all, this is illegal. Passing a counterfeit knowingly is quite a different thing from inadvertently passing one that was accepted innocently. Second, letting the bill circulate further deprives the authorities of a chance to track down the originator of the bogus bill and, perhaps, to stop a stream of such bills from hurting the community.

Be polite but firm and tell your supervisor or manager at once. He or she should give the customer a receipt that states that the bill is a counterfeit and should then call the police or the Secret Service. If the bill turns out to be real currency after all, the person will get his or her money back. If not, the receipt is evidence that the financial institution kept the bill to turn it over to the authorities, who will later contact the customer and try to find out where that person got the counterfeit so that they can trace the operation to its source.

DO be polite and friendly to the customer. Few people can afford to lose $50, for example, and to be told that you have just passed a counterfeit is an additional shock. Be sympathetic rather than suspicious. Leave the detective work to the authorities. You will have done your job by catching the counterfeit and comforting the customer.

If you have reason to suspect that a customer whom you know has deliberately passed a counterfeit, you will need to be extra tactful. Be sure to avoid any accusations, implied or otherwise, and politely excuse yourself so that you can talk privately to your supervisor or manager. This situation is unlikely to occur, however, because such an individual would realize that you'd have no trouble identifying him or her to the authorities.

If You Don't Know the Passer

If you are given a counterfeit by a stranger, it is always possible that he or she is working as part of a counterfeiting ring, so openly confiscating the bill might be dangerous. In this case, use your common sense, and act as the circumstances warrant. Any of the following courses of action might be appropriate:

- If you have a silent alarm and can activate it without being seen, do so.
- If possible, signal the manager or someone else to notify the police.
- Retaining the bill, say, "I'm sorry, but we're having quite a few bad bills come in, and I must ask our manager to check this one." Signal or call the manager *before* or *as* you say this.
- Take a few seconds to get a really good look at the person so that you can give a description to the police in case he or she runs from the office.
- If you are given a counterfeit and then spot it after the person has left, try to recall who gave you the bill and what the individual looked like. Try to remember the time of day, the circumstances under which the bill was given to you, and so on.

Counterfeiting is a crime that robs everyone. As an alert teller, you are the first line of defense against such criminals.

20

Defalcations

Defalcation is defined as misusing funds or embezzling. Embezzling is further defined as appropriating money to one's own use in a breach of trust. In short, embezzling is the act of stealing from a financial institution by a trusted employee. This is what defalcation usually means, but it may also include the lesser offense of simply misusing funds. Both happen occasionally even in the best-run institutions.

In addition to stealing, there are a few other activities in which financial institution personnel occasionally indulge. Covering their own checks until payday by holding or even misrouting them and "borrowing" a sum of money to tide them over until payday are two examples of such activities.

This is one reason why financial institutions have audits and why they have set policies for such things as handling cash, cashing checks, and so forth. Every employee should know the policies of his or her institution and make following them a routine matter.

NOT-QUITE-LEGAL ACTIVITIES

Sometimes people are short of cash and "borrow" some money for a few days. A teller, for example, may use a few dollars to hold him or her over until payday without anyone knowing about it. Of course, this person is risking a cash audit. If the financial institution has a policy of checking every teller's cash when the teller is absent for a day or two, the person in this position had better not get sick! A transit clerk may cash a check, watch for it to come through the department, then misroute it so that it will take several extra days to clear—until payday, for instance. Of course, this person is ignoring the possibility that the item may be missed for one reason or another.

Some financial institution employees do "favors" for customers. A teller may hold checks for a few days before putting them through, or a bookkeeper may knowingly overdraw an account when the item should be returned.

None of these activities are those of a dangerous criminal, but they are dangerous all the same. For one thing, they can become habitual. Then worse habits can develop. Many embezzlers started out by putting back a few dollars they had "borrowed" for a short time. Then they started falsifying records instead of putting the money back. A second danger is that of having to suffer the stigma of being caught doing something that impugns the person's honesty.

The Legal Alternative

Most people are short of cash now and then. When such a situation arises, the financial institution employee should apply for a loan, not "arrange" one on his or her own. Most institutions make getting a loan easy for their employees, either internally or through another institution with which they have a reciprocal agreement. For the employee who only wishes to borrow a small amount for a short time, there are always legitimate small-loan companies. In the long run, the interest that these companies charge is often high; but, for a small short-term loan that may be unavailable through the person's own institution, the few extra dollars may make little real difference.

The employee who is *always* $20 short until payday needs a budget, not a loan. "Borrowing" from his or her employer's cash supply, however, is not the way to get a loan until the budget can be set up!

Not-quite-legal practices usually don't send anyone to prison, nor do they help anyone to get ahead. The employee who uses them is usually so afraid of being found out that he or she can't concentrate properly on work. And if that person is found out, he or she is likely to be dismissed along with having to suffer the stigma of being dishonest. So it simply isn't worth it.

It's a good idea for employees to familiarize themselves with any formal written code of ethics that a financial institution may have. It helps to have an understanding of what is considered to be improper conduct as well as any disciplinary action that might be taken against offenders. Many institutions include a section in their new-employee training manual that deals solely with this subject.

EMBEZZLING

Rotten apples are found occasionally, no matter how carefully they are picked and sorted. The same is true of people. Financial institutions select employees very carefully on the basis of their competence to do a job as well as for their integrity, and their honesty is taken for granted. However, sometimes that trust is misplaced.

There are many stories about the loyal employee who never took vacations, never missed a day for illness, and was always right there when the examiners came in because he or she could answer any and all questions that they might have. Then an auditor found the clue that led to the discovery that this employee was using that "loyalty" to cover up huge sums he or she was stealing. Not just *from* the financial institution, but *at* the financial institution, because the money rarely belongs to the institution; it is usually a depositor's or a group of depositors' or is from the surplus the institution holds in reserve to protect its financial position. In any case, everyone suffers because the loss is usually made up by an insurance claim, which, together with all other claims, must be paid by financial institutions in the form of premiums—premiums that mean fewer dollars for dividends, interest, and staff salaries.

Why Do People Embezzle?

There are many theories about why people embezzle. Those who do so use money for every purpose ranging from gambling to giving it away. Indeed, some of the biggest embezzlements in history didn't benefit the embezzler one cent. These people stole to give the money away. As pointed out previously, *everyone* pays for losses by theft. Although society can't control the desire to steal, it can control the opportunity. This is why financial institutions have rigid rules governing money handling and the supervision of accounts.

Experts claim that embezzlers are not timid people who slip a dollar here and a dollar there from the till. On the contrary, many are extremely egotistical and believe themselves to be so superior that no intellectual "inferior" with whom they work could ever catch them. Why do these people steal?

- Some, because they feel they are being cheated of success by supposed inferiors who are jealous. These people may steal simply to prove their intelligence.
- Some who embezzle are competent people who don't get promoted because of a lack of openings or perhaps because of personality problems. They may become security risks if they are irrational about their future careers and thus decide to lash out at the financial institution.

Not everyone who feels superior or frustrated at work is a security risk, or course, just as not every security risk telegraphs his or her problems. However, some symptoms of potential problems may be manifested by people who:

Drink excessively. This includes employees who drink to the point of missing workdays, being sick with frequent hangovers, and coming back from lunch high from drinking.

Gamble excessively. This does not refer to employees who play bingo at church, buy lottery tickets, or indulge in a weekly poker club. Instead, this refers to those who try to borrow from fellow employees to pay large gambling debts, encourage other employees to co-finance bets, or brag about supposed winnings—or weep over losses—at the track.

Have debt problems. This includes employees who have wage garnishments or other deep financial problems.

What can you do? Don't allow yourself to become a security risk. And don't, under any circumstances, cover—even for a day—for someone who is embezzling. Keep your cash drawer to yourself. And remember that most financial institution employees are honest.

The Way It Happens

Some schemes for embezzling are simple, such as the situation in which a teller just helps himself or herself to cash. Others are elaborate, involving the switching of notes, juggling of overdrafts, or other complicated procedures. In any case, embezzling, unlike the "not-quite-legal" activities, is a serious crime carrying penalties that include stiff fines and prison sentences.

One thing is certain. Embezzlement is always discovered sooner or later. And it always ends in disgrace for someone who has enjoyed a position of trust and responsibility.

Embezzlement usually happens in a situation in which a person, who may or may not have an accomplice or two, is in a position where he or she can control part of the assets of the financial institution. This may be a teller who handles cash, a loan officer who makes fraudulent loans, a bookkeeper who juggles dormant accounts, or anyone else in a position of responsibility.

Methods of embezzlement vary widely, and there are many cases in which ingenious persons have come up with unbelievable schemes. Financial institution personnel have designed elaborate kiting plans based on using institutions that cleared through theirs so that they could control the flow of checks.

"I hear that XR-125 got $50,000 into a Swiss bank before they caught it."

Savings clerks have systematically bled inactive accounts. Loan collection personnel have falsified bad-debt collection records. Embezzlers have ranged from part-time transit clerks to financial institution presidents.

Computers have made embezzling easier. For every detected computer crime, there are a great many undetected crimes in progress. Some of these crimes are very clever, and include such things as feeding transactions into dormant accounts and capturing the fractional remainder of computed interest on savings accounts. One crook who did this skimmed off $17,000 over a four-year span in accumulated fractions of cents.

Misuse of computers can involve the following:

- Input can be altered.
- Computer programs can be altered or created.
- Data contained in auxiliary storage files can be added to, deleted from, or changed.
- Output can be altered.
- Operating systems can be modified to allow perpetrators control of the computer.
- Computer communications can be intercepted or altered.

Here is an example of a scam involving computers that might be tried in a financial institution: Tom works in the pension department, and Cliff is a programmer in the computer department. They devise a scheme for getting some of the institution's money. Whenever a pensioner dies, Tom tells the people in the computer department, so that the name of the deceased can be erased from the printout of those receiving pension payments. Sometimes, however, Tom neglects to tell the computer department about a death. Instead, he passes on the name of the deceased to Cliff, who enters an address change into the computer. The pension payments are then mailed to the new address, which is a mail drop for Tom and Cliff. They open a phony account and withdraw the funds at their leisure. As they add new names to their list, they "kill off" some of the others who have actually died so as to avoid packing the files with too many phony pensioners.

As banking becomes more and more complex, methods of embezzlement also become more complex. However, there is always someone who feels smart enough to avoid detection or who is willing to face the risk of being caught. But there are too many honest people in banking to let that person continue to get away with it.

DON'T GET INNOCENTLY INVOLVED

Innocent persons have often become involved in illegal situations because they felt sorry for other people who were doing something illegal or because they simply failed to use common sense. Anyone who is embezzling, or even indulging in "not-quite-legal" activities, may give himself or herself away by one or more of the following actions:

- Failing to take a full-term vacation. The embezzler who must cover his or her activities may not be able to take a two-week or even a one-week vacation. This person may take single days or just skip a vacation altogether because of being "so busy."
- Working overtime consistently and alone.
- Keeping records and procedures private and not allowing anyone else to really learn the job.

You Could Be an Accomplice

Embezzlers, when faced with illness or a vacation, often approach a co-worker and get that person involved. "I'll make it good as soon as I get back," the embezzler may say, "but help me cover it for a few days to protect John and the kids." Sound corny? Lots of innocent employees have fallen for it, covered the embezzler, and then became implicated as accomplices.

Don't get involved, no matter who requests it or how much sympathy you may feel. There is never any excuse for criminal activities, especially any that must be as carefully premeditated as embezzling. And don't let yourself be deceived. If someone suggests you do something in his or her absence and keep that activity secret, say "no" no matter to whom you must say it. Secret activities don't belong in a financial institution, and neither do embezzlers. Don't help to perpetuate either one.

Reporting Suspected Activities

Reporting a suspected embezzler isn't the same as reporting a suspected forger or robber. In the case of an embezzler, the person involved is within the institution. He or she is a trusted member of the staff *until proven otherwise,* and reporting the employee may damage that person's reputation even if it turns out that he or she is innocent.

This does not mean that you shouldn't report suspicious activities. But first, you must be sure that they really are suspicious. You can learn this by finding out what the person should be doing. For example, depending on the duties and nature of the job, it may be suspicious if one person consistently works late but perfectly normal if another person does.

If an activity is suspicious, you should report it to the auditor, not your supervisor. The auditor is responsible for investigating such things and, if investigation is warranted, may act without arousing suspicion or casting aspersions on the character of what may be an innocent person. By going directly to the auditor and explaining your suspicions, you can protect yourself and the reputation of the employee you suspect in case this person should prove to be innocent. Such a report is best made in person to avoid any misunderstandings.

It is never easy to point the finger at a co-worker, and employees who work at financial institutions should not feel that being a detective is part of their jobs. It isn't. But if you should be approached by someone who wishes to involve you in an illegal scheme, or if you have good reason to suspect illegal activities, you have a duty to report such things, quietly and without fuss, to the right person—the auditor. Even if you are approached by someone who works in a position that is superior to yours, who implies that you could lose your job or face other consequences if you don't cooperate, don't hesitate to report the situation to the auditor, who will see to it that you are protected.

Don't Take Shortcuts with Security

Consider the following example. A branch manager prepared to close up for the Labor Day weekend. His institution's policy called for dual control of the vault, but to speed things up, the manager had his assistant attend to other duties while he set the time locks himself. He might have gotten away with this breach in procedures except for one thing. The branch manager had made a mistake; Labor Day weekend wasn't really coming up. It was just a two-day weekend, and the vault clocks were set for three days!

On the following Monday, the office opened, but the vault didn't. Collateral-loan customers couldn't pay off their loans because their collateral was locked up. People couldn't buy traveler's checks, cashier's checks couldn't be issued, savings bonds couldn't be sold, and so on. A loan of cash from the main office opened up the tellers' windows, but they labored under handicaps because the signature-card file, checkwriter, and other necessities were also locked up.

The purpose of the dual control was thwarted. What turned out to be an unpleasant situation could have been a seriously tragic one if either the manager or his assistant had been in league with criminals. Control procedures may seem overdone and often tedious, but they are important. They are instituted to protect you, your customers, and your financial institution.

Allowing improper access to the cash of another person is the most common shortcut that tellers and branch managers take. John needs ones and, instead of "buying" them from Janet as he should, he helps himself because she is busy at the moment. Sure, they're good friends and trust each other, but how do they explain that to the FBI if there is a serious shortage?

Another common practice is taking the customer's safe deposit key and getting the box for him or her. This seems to be a courteous thing to do, because the customer can wait in the comfort of the booth. But what happens if the customer later claims that something is missing?

A shortcut that branch managers sometimes take is unfair to tellers. It involves signaling the teller to cash a check without initialing it. The manager knows the customer, but the teller doesn't. If the manager makes a mistake, who's going to remember that verbal approval or visual high sign when the check comes back days later?

Controls don't have to be arduous, but they should be kept. If they are treated as a matter of routine and not as an imposition, they will become commonplace. And they'll go far in the long run to preserve security and morale.

As an employee at a financial institution, you have a great responsibility in safeguarding its assets. Your institution has policies to help you.

Never, no matter who requests it, relax those policies. They are for your protection as well as for the cash with which you are entrusted.

21

Cons and Frauds

THE KEY WORD IS *CONFIDENCE*

It may be the old flimflam. Or passing counterfeit money as discussed in Chapter 19. Or offering a get-rich-quick scheme to a customer of a financial institution. Whatever the con game involved, the crook must first be believable.

There is no typical description of a con artist:

- The con artist may be male or female. In one New England city, police reported that in every case of the well-known pigeon-drop swindle reported during a three-year period, the crooks were female.
- The crook may be any age. Elderly con artists aren't more honest—just more experienced.
- The con artist may be dressed in any fashion. A successful con man who operated some years ago hit every financial institution in a Massachusetts town dressed as a garbage collector, complete with smelly overalls.

Above all, the con artist *inspires confidence*. Ideally, the con will work so smoothly that the crook won't even have to prove his or her honesty—it will just be taken for granted.

Two former confidence men who specialized in bilking financial institutions started a business of teaching employees of financial institutions the tricks of the confidence game. They made two interesting points:

The most difficult tellers to con are often those with the least experience. This is because the new teller has regulations and policies fresh in mind. There is a moral here for all tellers: Financial institution policies *do* work, but tellers must always follow them.

Forgers can get all kinds of identification to establish themselves with tellers as respectable people. Sometimes they will print their own material, and sometimes they use things that they find or steal.

According to these two former con artists, counterfeit Christmas Club checks were a favorite for crooks, with some forgers passing as many as $45,000 worth in the weeks between Thanksgiving and Christmas.

Using split deposits to gain confidence is an often-used con. This works two ways. In the first, as described in Chapter 16, the crook opens a small account and then, soon after, makes a split deposit with a large but bogus check. In the second method, the crook acquires a printed deposit slip or even the account number of a legitimate account. If it is a savings account, the crook may claim to have left the passbook at home. Then he or she makes a large split deposit with a phony check.

Another frequently used trick is to learn to forge the initials of an approving officer for getting a check cashed by having a legitimate check approved, then forging the initials on a phony one.

Flimflam is another favorite technique of the con artist. The person fast-talks the teller into giving him or her much more change than is due for a large bill. It works something like this . . .

The flimflam artist waits until the teller is busy. Then he or she goes to work. "May I have 10 tens for a hundred?" "I'm sorry. Could I switch that to twenties?" "Oh, I need $5 of that in change and 10 ones . . ." and so on and so on until the teller is confused. A sharp flimflam artist may palm part of a stack of bills using a small disappearing device that can be bought in a magic supply store. Or the person may be patient and just wait for the teller to make an error and short his or her cash. The flimflam artist is quick at figures and counting, is not flustered as the teller probably is, is not annoyed with the growing line behind him or her, and, finally, counts heavily on the fact that the teller tries to serve every customer with courtesy. Many tellers, after having been taken in by such an individual, will exclaim, "That nice person was a crook? I don't believe it!"

Here are some more basic ploys used by confidence persons. Be careful when dealing with strangers or you may be taken in by:

The friend of the manager. The con artist comes into the institution, goes to the office of the branch manager or some other officer, makes a big display of shaking hands, laughing, and otherwise giving those outside the office the impression that he or she is well known to the officer.

Then the con artist comes out and presents a check to a teller to be cashed. And, not wishing to offend a friend of the manager, the teller just may cash it.

Another version of this scheme was described in Chapter 18. The con artist asks for an officer he or she knows is not present, someone who's at lunch perhaps, and then engages the teller in conversation about the absent officer. By asking personal questions and making appropriate remarks, the crook gives the impression that the absent person is a longtime pal. Then out comes the check.

The official. Some con artists are so nervy that they even impersonate police officers or Treasury officers.

The crook flashes a badge at a teller and identifies himself or herself as an officer. Then the con artist informs the teller that he or she is on the track of a counterfeit-passer and asks to see the teller's twenties. Naturally, the crook spots several phonies, which he or she takes as "evidence" and for which the crook gives the teller a receipt. And that's the end of the twenties!

In another version of this scheme, the crook uses an accomplice who comes into the financial institution for a routine transaction. The con artist comes in a little later with a photo of the accomplice and asks if anyone recognizes this counterfeit-passer. Naturally, one teller does, so the "officer" goes through his or her bills and confiscates several.

The honest person. This is an old con, but it still fools some tellers. The crook comes into the institution and asks for change for a twenty. He or she walks away, counts the money, then comes back to the teller and says, "You made a mistake. Count this again." The teller does and discovers that the "customer" has $5 too much. Naturally, the teller is grateful and thanks this honest person. A conversation starts and a friendly rapport is built up. That's when the "customer" remembers he or she must cash a check. Would the teller oblige? Well, who could refuse such an honest person? The teller who doesn't bother to check the person's identification ends up being $5 over that day, and pretty embarrassed when the check comes back.

A financial institution officer who worked with tellers who had been bilked by confidence persons had this to say: "Every teller I ever talked to who had been conned gave me a description of the con artist that was so vague that it was useless. These people specialize in looking and acting like everyday people. And the teller was always shocked that such a nice, pleasant, honest person could really be a crook."

The rule is that *every stranger is not a crook, but every crook is a stranger.* In all of your transactions, follow your institution's policies to the letter, even with the friendliest stranger you've ever met!

KITING

The term "kite" refers to passing worthless checks or "paper" between financial institutions with no (or, at best, insufficient) assets behind them. The kiter does this to create a false balance on which he or she may then draw cash and leave town.

The University Dictionary of Business and Finance, published by Thomas Y. Crowell Company of New York, defines the word "kite" as follows:

> "To discharge an obligation by the expedient of incurring a fresh one. For example, a depositor in a bank may have issued a check which overdraws his account. To cover this, he makes out another check, cashes it somewhere and deposits the cash to replenish his account before the first check is presented. He must now cash still a third check to cover the second and so on."

That's one way a kite can work. But ingenious crooks can think of others. Alert financial institution personnel should know how they work and what to look for so that their schemes can be detected.

Two Typical Kiting Schemes

Knowing how kiters operate will help you to spot them and put an end to their activities. Here is one typical kiting scheme:

Bank A is in a town 10 miles from Bank B. Bank A and Bank B clear each other's checks through the Fed, which is in City C. A check deposited in Bank A drawn on Bank B takes two days to clear and vice versa. The kiter knows these facts or he or she can easily get them just by cashing checks on each financial institution in its opposite number. The kiter is ready to act.

First the kiter opens an account in each financial institution with a nominal cash deposit. Then he or she gets checkbooks. Follow these transactions:

1. July 2. Deposits check drawn on Bank A for $500 in Bank B.
2. July 3. Deposits check drawn on Bank B for $1,000 in Bank A.
3. July 6, after the weekend. Check for $500 clears Bank A. Deposits check for $1,500 on Bank A in Bank B.

4. July 7. Check for $1,000 clears Bank B. Deposits check for $2,000 on Bank B in Bank A.

5. July 8. Check for $1,500 clears Bank A. Deposits check for $2,500 on Bank A in Bank B.

6. July 9. Check for $2,000 clears Bank B. Deposits check for $3,000 on Bank B in Bank A.

7. July 10. Check for $2,500 clears Bank A. Kiter now shows $1,500 in each account. So he or she draws two checks for cash, $1,500 each, and presents them for payment at their financial institutions. Then the kiter leaves town, and the checks for $3,000 bounce because there are not sufficient funds in the accounts.

Here's another scheme:

1. Doe Company, at the moment, has a short cash position and a payroll to meet.

2. Doe Company expects $5,000 in payments to be made to it within a few days.

3. Doe Company has an account at both Bank A and Bank B. The owner cashes a check for $1,000 at Bank A, drawn on Bank B, which he or she uses to meet the payroll. The owner then deposits a check in Bank B for $1,500 drawn on Bank A.

4. Before this can clear, the owner deposits a check in Bank A for $2,000 drawn on Bank B. He or she can now cash another $1,000 check at Bank A drawn on Bank B.

5. If the payment is received in time, the owner simply deposits the $5,000 in Bank B, and no one is the wiser. In effect, he or she has arranged a short-term, unauthorized loan until the accounts receivable come in. Actually, the owner is kiting. Should the payment *not* arrive on time, he or she is in trouble! In any event, this is unauthorized use of the financial institution's money.

By mixing deposits partly with cash, partly with legitimate checks, and partly with kited items, a depositor can make it very difficult for the financial institutions to catch a kiting operation. Of course, the kiter must know the clearing and collection procedures of the institutions that are involved in some detail and be willing to spend the time to keep track of the operation and to go from one institution to another.

A kiter might go into operation to establish a reputation for credit purposes. In this case, he or she might inflate an account, keep it inflated for some time, then slowly "deflate" it without actually keeping any money for his or her own purposes. The only thing that the kiter accomplishes is having an average balance in the account that is much higher than it actually should be.

Kiters, therefore, may be criminals who intend to fleece the financial institution of substantial funds by a careful scheme of inflating false accounts, or they may be customers who are attempting to "borrow" from the institution for a short period, or they may be persons with less-than-good credit ratings who are trying to improve them by inflating their accounts. In any case, their operation is illegal; the alert financial institution employee, especially the teller and the bookkeeper, should be on the lookout for clues that a kite is taking place.

Kiting And Computers

Computers not only save time and cut down on errors, they also eliminate boring, time-consuming chores, such as posting transactions. But they can make it harder to catch kiters. This is because computers post transactions, but they cannot analyze them. Without special kiting detection software, they can't get hunches about a pattern that simply doesn't look good.

This means that catching the kiter is up to fewer employees of the financial institution. As fewer bookkeepers physically handle transactions, more alertness is demanded of tellers. In smaller institutions, proof clerks can also be alert to suspicious patterns.

Computers can be programmed, however, to detect attempts to draw checks against uncollected funds—and obviously, all kiting is done with uncollected funds. Computers can also signal unusual activity in an account. When this happens, the person to whom such activity is reported must check the actual items immediately to see if a kite is in progress.

What to Watch For

All kites have certain things in common. There is the use of uncollected funds. There are regular deposits, offset by a regular flow of checks. In short, there is a pattern. Financial institution personnel can spot this pattern. As a teller, you should:

1. Know your depositors. Watch the amounts they usually deposit and note important changes in those amounts.
2. Watch for frequent, regular deposits in even amounts with checks always drawn on the same financial institution (they may or may not be signed by the kiter—he or she may use an alias).

3. Take notice of any customer who makes frequent inquiries about an account balance or other account activity.

How to Report a Suspected Kiter

Kiting is different from some crimes against financial institutions. A holdup is obviously being committed when an armed person points a gun at a teller and says, "Give me the money." A forgery is equally obvious when the signature on a check is not that of the person who supposedly signed the item. But how can you be sure that a kite is taking place? The fact that a customer is making regular deposits under certain circumstances is no crime. Thus, the employee is in a different position when he or she suspects a kite, because there is a grave risk of embarrassing the financial institution or even subjecting it to a lawsuit.

Reporting a suspect, then, isn't as simple as pressing an alarm button. In the first place, the financial institution must make discreet inquiries to be certain that a kite is taking place. Then it should act to prevent loss from the kite—which usually means simply placing a hold on any accounts involved and, equally important, instructing all tellers not to cash checks for the suspect on any uncollected funds or without the approval of a supervisor.

If you should spot a situation that suggests that kiting is occurring, don't mention it to the customer or to anyone else. Quietly report it to your supervisor or office manager at once and let that person handle the situation. But do report it. As a teller, it's your duty to safeguard the funds entrusted to you.

CREDIT CARD SECURITY

Credit cards are increasing in numbers and in use. People like them because they are safe and convenient. Merchants like them because they reduce the risk of loss from uncollectable accounts receivable. And financial institutions like credit cards because of the fees from merchants and the interest payments from card users.

Considering the popularity and advantages of credit cards, it is obvious that criminals are going to try to profit from them. Thus, credit card security, from the financial institution's standpoint, is even more difficult to maintain than cash security.

The security process begins before the card even gets to the customer.

- Holograms, three-dimensional images on silver or gold foil that were developed with the help of laser technology, are incorporated in the design of credit cards in order to help to prevent counterfeiting.

- Credit cards that bear a photograph of the cardholder are becoming available. The card issuer is provided with the image and other personal information about the cardholder. Tampering with the photo becomes evident because of the layering process and dyes that are used to produce it.

- Another identity verification system was developed by Eastman Kodak Company. The Kodak Image Verification System (Kodak IVS) "draws" a face on a computer display—or can print it on a sales receipt—every time an identity is verified. The process requires data to be stored on the 400 bits of a credit card stripe, a 2D bar code, or an inexpensive computer chip. Kodak claims that this process addresses the weaknesses in fraud prevention techniques that are based on the use of holograms or cardholders' photographs, which can be stolen or duplicated. The cardholder can be identified while a terminal is being used to enter data and print a receipt, without disrupting the flow of the transaction and without the cardholder noticing.

- The digital scanning of a credit card customer's retina, fingerprint, or voice to see if it matches the data that is encoded on the card is another new technology that is designed to combat credit card fraud.

- The manufacturing process of the cards is closely watched, and shipment to the financial institution is carried out under strict security.

- Handling within the institution is done with as much care as handling cash.

- Cards are mailed to customers in envelopes that give no clue that one is enclosed. A pre-mailer is often sent to the person to verify the address before the card is sent. In high-crime areas, certified mail, Federal Express, United Parcel Service, or private couriers may be used for deliveries. A post-mailer may also be sent to verify that the person has received the card. And some issuers ask new cardholders to telephone and go through a verification process in order to activate their cards.

After the customer has the card, security is still a problem. The card may be lost or stolen and then used by a criminal. Or the customer may simply become incompetent to handle credit wisely and may misuse the card. Running up unrealistic credit card bills is believed to be a contributing factor in the rising number of personal bankruptcies.

Merchants can help prevent misuse of credit cards by:

- Watching for people who seem to buy almost compulsively, charging large amounts.

- Noting people who buy items that total just under the limit for which authorization must be obtained and who may seem nervous until they are sure of the total amount.
- Reporting to the issuing financial institution those people who suggest signing a sales ticket and receiving cash instead of merchandise or who try to sell their cards.

Both tellers disbursing cash advances and merchants should:

- Be alert for people whose general appearance, attitude, or actions arouse suspicion.
- Carefully check the signature plate on the card to be sure it has not been tampered with. Forgers have been known to remove signatures from credit cards by using a chemical solvent, after which they re-sign the card with an easily duplicated signature. The signature panel on some charge cards turns a muddy brown color if an ink eradicator or solvent touches it. If your institution issues credit cards, check with a supervisor to find out what happens to a card when the signature block has been tampered with. Some may turn brown, or the word "void" may appear. If it seems to have been altered in any way, don't pay out any cash advances on the card. Follow the required procedures, and, when in doubt, ask for a supervisor's approval.
- Make certain the person using a card that contains a photograph is the one who appears in the photo.
- Check the expiration date to determine whether or not the card has expired.
- Hold the card up to the light to see if the area around the name and numbers is marred.
- Check the hologram on the card to see if the image seems to move as a genuine one should.
- Check to see if the card has rounded corners; crooks may cut counterfeit cards with a paper cutter, which results in square corners.
- Urge cardholders to safeguard their cards as outlined in the following section.

Advice for Cardholders

Credit card losses to financial institutions because of fraud amount to hundreds of millions of dollars every year. Educational programs for consumers and merchants have proved helpful in teaching them what to look for and what to avoid. For example, the American Bankers Association released a video that was designed to help financial institutions educate people in their communities; and seminars for the public are given by the U.S. Secret Service and the the U.S. Postal Inspection Service.

If your institution issues credit cards, your customers, especially new cardholders, should be cautioned about the loss or theft of the card and should be apprised of how to use it in a secure manner. Encourage your customers to:

1. Sign a new card as soon as it is received. This makes the card a bit more difficult to use if it is lost or stolen because the cardholder's signature has to be forged.
2. Carry only those cards that are used most often and carry them in such a way that it is easy for the cardholder to spot a missing card.
3. Avoid leaving a card where someone else can pick it up—on a counter, in a glove compartment, or in an unattended wallet or purse.
4. Watch salesclerks while they are using the card. Be alert for undestroyed duplicate slips, and make sure that the figures are correct for charges and total amounts due. Never sign a blank sales slip.
5. Ask for and destroy charge slip carbon papers.
6. Make sure that the right card is returned immediately after it is used.
7. Promptly check each credit card statement for accuracy and notify the financial institution about anything questionable.
8. Avoid giving a credit card number over the telephone unless the cardholder initiates the call to place a charge order. (See the section that follows.)
9. Keep a written record of all credit and charge card issuers and numbers in a safe place at home.
10. Report a missing card immediately.
11. Destroy all unwanted cards so they can't be used by anyone else.

Credit Card Numbers on Checks

Some merchants may ask people who pay by check to show a driver's license and a credit card for identification purposes. The merchant then writes the number from each on the check. This means that the customer's name, address, driver's license number, and credit card number are all written on the same piece of paper. Thus, a crook could:

- Charge goods ordered from a mail order supplier and have them shipped to a different address, giving the correct one to confirm card ownership.
- Apply for a credit card in the victim's name, using that person's Social Security number if he or she is a resident of a state in which driver's license and Social Security numbers are the same.

Ironically, having the numbers is not actually useful to the merchant. If a check bounces, the merchant cannot charge the purchase to the credit card. Therefore, the printed address on the customer's check is enough information for the merchant.

Financial institutions that issue credit cards often ask customers to write their account numbers on the checks when paying their monthly credit card bills. However, some believe that even this is unnecessary if the customer returns the appropriate portion of the bill with the payment.

Information on Credit Card Slips

Some merchants may ask people who pay by credit card to write their address and phone number on the charge slip. Again, this means that the person's name, address, phone number, and credit card number are all written on the same piece of paper.

Merchants are not entitled to this information. Requiring it is illegal in some states, and it is prohibited by the major credit card issuers. Furthermore, unless the store wants the address for a mailing list, the information is useless. The financial institution that issues the card already has the address, and the institution, not the merchant, is responsible for covering any loss. A sales clerk should only verify the customer's signature and get authorization for the purchase from the credit card company.

Giving Card Numbers Over the Telephone

A crook might call a cardholder and, after verifying the cardholder's name and address, claim to be an employee at the customer's financial institution. The crook explains that the institution needs the card number and expiration date so that it will have the correct information for issuing a new card. If the cardholder reveals this information, the crook can use it to buy merchandise over the telephone and have it sent to a different address.

In a similar scam, the crook calls a cardholder to report that he or she is the winner of a valuable prize or trip and that the credit card number and expiration date are needed for verification purposes. As stated previously, it is important that credit card customers avoid giving their numbers to anyone over the telephone unless they initiate the call to place an order.

Credit cards are an important convenience. They are almost as acceptable as cash in many places of business. Therefore, their security is essential. As a teller, you can help credit card customers maintain the security of their cards by sharing the foregoing information with them. By doing so, you will also help your financial institution to avoid losses that are a result of fraud.

ATM CARD SECURITY

Customers who make cash withdrawals from automated teller machines are sometimes vulnerable to being robbed, and debit cards can be lost or stolen. Therefore, if your financial institution provides ATM services ask your customers to:

1. Always have the ATM card ready to use and always fill in and seal a deposit envelope before approaching a machine.
2. Avoid using a machine if a suspicious-looking person is nearby.
3. Choose a personal identification number (PIN) that is different from a significant number, such as a birth date, Social Security number, address, or phone number, which might be found in a wallet or purse and tried by a crook.
4. Memorize the PIN and avoid writing it on the card or on a slip of paper carried by the customer.
5. Avoid using a PIN if anyone is watching.
6. Never give the PIN to family members or friends or reveal the number to anyone over the telephone. The latter is especially important with regard to missing cards. Crooks have been known to telephone a cardholder and, claiming to be an official from a financial institution or a police officer, promise to return the card if the person can identify it by reciting the number.
7. Avoid making cash deposits or withdrawals at the same machine on a regular basis, especially after dark.
8. Report a missing card immediately.
9. Report any unauthorized withdrawals or transfers as soon as the credit card statement is received.
10. Never throw ATM transaction receipts in the trash where they can be picked up by crooks.

Like credit cards, automated teller machines are a great convenience, but people must use common sense and caution in order to avoid being robbed or swindled.

MAIL FRAUD

Some crooks will try to swindle your customers, and perhaps even your financial institution, through the mail. As a teller, you may hear about it when a customer comes in to make a withdrawal to buy a money order to send to the crooks, or even when a customer just mentions some "great deal" he or she has made through the mail.

Typical Schemes

The obituary hoax. The crook sends COD merchandise to people who recently died. The person gets the names from the obituary columns of local papers. The idea is that a grieving friend or relative will want to get and keep the item that the deceased person so recently ordered.

The free vacation. You've won a free vacation, the letter says. To a real paradise. All expenses paid. Just send a deposit that will be returned when you leave.

The retirement home. The con artist advertises "$50 down and $50 a month for your dream retirement spot." Cheap? Absolutely. So lots of people buy land sight unseen and plan for the day they'll retire and build a home on it. Sometimes the land is under water. Sometimes it is undeveloped, inaccessible desert. Or it is at the impossible-to-reach top of a mountain. Whatever the case, the buyer has been had.

False bills. There are an increasing number of schemes designed to defraud businesses, including financial institutions, in which false billings are sent for such things as advertising supplies and various services. In smaller institutions, tellers have many responsibilities, even to the point of paying some bills. If you approve bills for payment or disburse funds on behalf of your institution, check before you pay them no matter how small the amounts. It's a good idea to pass on this warning to those businesspeople who deal with you, too.

Correspondence schools. Some of these schools sell worthless training material or guarantee to find jobs for students but never do.

How-to-get-rich schemes. Send $10 for the secrets of getting wealthy.

Missing heirs. You may have inherited a fortune. Send $10 and your name to the search bureau.

If you hear a customer mention such an offer, especially someone who might seem to be easy prey for swindlers, suggest that the customer check it out with the local Better Business Bureau or the postmaster. If it's legitimate, there's no harm done. If it's not, the Postal Inspectors may want to look into it.

PROTECTING YOUR CUSTOMERS

Con men and women will go to almost any lengths to trick gullible people into handing over money. The bizarre swindles perpetrated many years ago by a Scotsman named Arthur Furguson illustrate just how gullible some victims can be.

It all started in London's Trafalgar Square in the 1920s when Furguson "sold" Nelson's Column, the famous monument erected in memory of England's Admiral Lord Nelson, to a wealthy American tourist for the bargain price of £6,000 (about $30,000). That same year, Furguson also sold Big Ben to another American for £1,000 and accepted a £2,000 down payment on Buckingham Palace from a third.

Deciding that the United States was ripe for the plucking, Furguson came to Washington, D.C. in 1925, where he managed to rent the White House to a rich cattleman for $100,000, the first year's advance rental on a 99-year lease.

He was finally caught by the police after selling the Statue of Liberty to a visiting Australian who became suspicious of him during a delay in raising the requested $100,000 deposit.

Nowadays people are more savvy, so your customers aren't likely to withdraw enormous sums to make extraordinary purchases such as these, but they could become the victims of lesser swindles that take place in your area. As a teller, you may be able to help a customer avoid being conned.

Typical Swindles

The following are brief descriptions of just some of the many cons worked against victims:

The pigeon drop, or the classic envelope drop. In this case, a con artist, after making friends with the victim, claims to have found an envelope containing a large amount of cash. The crook offers to split it with the victim, who, in order to show "good faith," has only to put up some more cash that will later be returned along with an equal share of the found money. After getting the victim's cash, the con artist says he or she is going to arrange for a split of the fortune, perhaps with an attorney. When the victim goes to the attorney's office to get his or her share, the person finds that the attorney doesn't exist and that the crook has merely split. Elderly people have been shown to be the most vulnerable targets in society for the operators of confidence games, and this trick is used often.

"Helping" the FBI. In this scheme, a person telephones a customer of a financial institution and pretends to be an FBI agent or police officer. "Hello, Mrs. Doe? This is Inspector Jones of the FBI. We need your help in investigating an embezzler! We know that you have an account with the First National Bank, and we suspect that Mr. Smith, the branch manager, is stealing money by tampering with customers' accounts. Will you help us to trap him? You will? Fine! You're certainly a good citizen, and we at the FBI appreciate it! Now here's what we want you to do. At one o'clock sharp, you go into the bank and withdraw $1,000 from your savings account. Please notice if Mr. Smith acts suspicious in any way or if anyone else does. He may have a confederate who works there! We'll meet you outside and switch the money you withdraw for $1,000 in marked bills. Then, you go back into the bank, tell them you've changed your mind, and put the money back. That way, we can get $1,000 in marked bills where we can trace them!" Of course, when Mrs. Doe opens the package of "marked bills," she finds newspaper or play money. Variations of this swindle are worked on unsuspecting financial institution customers all the time. The police and the FBI *never* use this technique to trap embezzlers.

Loan sharking. When a person is turned down for a loan, he or she may feel that the situation is desperate and go to a loan shark for the money. One victim of a loan shark, testifying before a Senate committee, related that he borrowed $1,900 and, by the end of five years, had repaid $14,000. When he tried to pay off the balance due, the shark told him he still owed $5,800. The interest charged by loan sharks is always exorbitant.

The business opportunity. Many people want to get something for nothing, especially money for little or no work. Thus, they are likely to fall for the promise of big profits from selling "hot" items that "everyone needs." The swindler makes his or her money by selling the victim the secret of earning a fortune. Any reputable company making a legitimate business offer requires a reasonable, if any, investment on the part of the "investor" and is happy to be investigated through its financial institution references, the Better Business Bureau, or other agency. Ads that promise fantastic profits to persons with no special skills or training are suspect. A big and risky investment is almost sure to be involved.

The miracle cure. Millions of dollars are elicited from people who suffer from various ills and are desperate for a cure. Nostrums that cure anything from arthritis to cancer are offered, and at high prices.

The home improvement. The average homeowner often doesn't have a great deal of knowledge about making home improvements, so he or she is in a good position to be swindled. Making their charges sound less than those of a reputable contractor, home improvement swindlers usually start with a solicitation at the door or by phone. Legitimate contractors get business through local advertising and operate out of offices where they can be reached if anything should go wrong.

The charity ploy. In one eastern city alone, almost every single financial institution was victimized within a few days' time by this scheme. A child goes door to door selling candy that he or she claims is for the benefit of a specified reputable organization. But there's a catch. The child can't accept cash. Even though the candy costs only $1, the organization insists that the children who collect may accept only checks so that they can't keep any of the money for themselves. The crooks thus get a supply of checks from local individuals, each complete with name, address, account number, and specimen signature. They then go to each institution on which a check is drawn, ask for a counter deposit slip, deposit a large company check drawn on an out-of-town institution to the real customer's account, then ask the teller for a counter check, which they write for cash for a modest sum compared to the huge check just deposited. The company check is phony, of course, and the counter check is forged. So the financial institution is stuck for the amount of the bad check. This is a clever scheme because, even if the deposited check is held until the funds clear, there may very well be enough in the legitimate customer's account to cover the forgery.

Pyramid clubs. Before it became illegal to send chain letters that requested money through the mails, a typical letter would state, "Send this letter to 10 friends and $1 to . . ." Chain-letter-type schemes that don't use the mails are called pyramid clubs. They may involve anything from money to bottles of expensive liquor to savings bonds. Only the swindlers who start these schemes get paid off. To keep a "chain" or "pyramid" going that requires each participant to enlist 10 more people would soon require the entire population of the United States! For every new name added to the list, 1,000 additional names would have to be added for a payoff, with each of these in turn requiring another 1,000, and so on.

Buying used cars. This is a fraud that is worked against private sellers of expensive used automobiles. The buyer pays with a certified check and gets the title and the license plates, which he or she promises to mail back. But then the "certified" check won't clear because the stamp and the authorized signature are as phony as the check. Customers who are planning to sell such cars should call the financial institution that is supposed to have certified the check to make sure it is valid.

The found property scheme. In this ploy, the crook calls the financial institution and claims that he or she has found some property belonging to a customer, perhaps a checkbook or a credit card. This person asks for the customer's address and phone number so that he or she can return the customer's property. After finding out where the customer lives as well as the phone number, the crook can victimize the customer in a number of ways, ranging from breaking in when the customer isn't home to having phony IDs made. A person who claims to have valuables belonging to a customer should be told to bring them to the financial institution for the institution to return. Or this person should supply his or her own name and phone number so that the customer can make the contact.

What You Can Do to Help

As a teller, what can you do to help protect your customers from being victims of fraud? You are in a position to help when it comes to their financial affairs. Keep these things in mind:

1. Watch for suspicious withdrawals, unusually large checks for cash, or remarks that might suggest a swindle. Elderly people, especially, who take out large sums deserve a friendly question. People who confide in you that they have a get-rich-quick deal going need advice, and fast.

2. Be extremely tactful! After all, the customer is acting under his or her own free will and may resent missing "the opportunity of a lifetime." And no one likes to be accused of being less than honest in joining in any confidence-type scheme. In some cases, it may be a good idea to refer the customer to your manager.

3. Don't fall for a con game yourself. At the window, this means avoiding the flimflam artist who will try to confuse you into paying out more cash than you should as well as all the other swindlers who want your money. Away from the window, it means avoiding dubious schemes of all sorts.

Those who work at financial institutions are financial advisors to many people, and this includes a moral obligation to help protect these people, no matter how much they seem to welcome the con artist. In fact, a program that is designed to protect the elderly who go to financial institutions to make large cash withdrawals is now being used throughout Wisconsin and Illinois.

Jerry E. Wiesmueller, vice president and corporate security officer for M&I Bank, Milwaukee, Wisconsin, is a former police lieutenant who often gives security seminars for senior citizens. A recipient of a U.S. Department of Justice award for public service in assisting victims and witnesses of crime, he participated in the creation of the program. In order to give potential victims time to think about what might be happening to them, tellers ask each elderly customer who comes in to make a large cash withdrawal to read and sign a special form that asks questions regarding the possibility of being swindled. If he or she answers yes to any of the questions, the customer is advised to contact the manager or security officer of the financial institution, the local police department, or his or her own attorney. The form is then dated and signed by the teller and an officer of the institution. This program has succeeded in reducing such swindles by more than 80 percent.

CUSTOMERS WHO CAUSE PROBLEMS

Sooner or later, every teller must come to terms with those customers who use the financial institution in not-quite-ethical ways to benefit themselves. What they do would not land them in jail and would be unlikely to get them even a legal reprimand. Here are a few common examples:

The chronically overdrawn. In order to stretch their money, some customers overdraw their accounts or even risk checks being returned due to insufficient funds. In most cases, the customer is making an unauthorized loan just until payday. In other cases, however, a customer may deliberately write a bad check hoping that he or she will make a big sale or win on a gamble.

Financial institutions impose stiff penalties for overdrafts or for returning checks. In addition, the customer who often bounces checks will soon suffer from an undesirable reputation.

As a teller, do *not* cash a check, regardless of how small it may be, for someone who is frequently overdrawn without first checking the overdraft sheet and without putting a hold on the account.

The angler. This individual is a bit more sophisticated than the over-drawer and, if allowed, may get a teller into trouble. The person gives the teller a hard-luck story and asks him or her to cash a check that the teller is then to hold for a short time, carrying it over from day to day in his or her cash.

The customer intends, of course, to make the check good during that time. But what happens if he or she doesn't? And, from your point of view, how do you explain a check in your cash drawer when you have an unannounced before-opening or after-closing cash audit?

Obviously, every teller should simply refuse to be a part of such schemes and should quietly report requests of this kind to his or her supervisor *and* to the institution's internal auditor. The supervisor can alert the rest of the office staff, and the auditor can quietly check out the customer's transactions to insure that no other teller is involved.

The uncollected funds user. One of the hardest things that financial in-stitution employees have to explain to a customer is why a check, de-posited by the customer but drawn on another institution, isn't good for cash immediately.

With rising costs, many people need cash as soon as they receive a check. Yet financial institutions must insist that checks clear the drawee before they pay out on the funds. When you must refuse to cash a check on uncollected funds, be tactful; don't imply that the check may not be good. State firmly that it is your institution's policy to have the check clear because it would other-wise be making a no-interest loan, and, therefore, paying on uncollected funds, which is a violation of banking practice.

Under the provisions of the Expedited Funds Availability Act of 1987, customers usually have a shorter time to wait for checks to clear than they had in the past. Financial institutions are required to clear local checks—those drawn on an institution in the same Federal Reserve check-processing region—after two business days and nonlocal checks after five business days. However, the first $100 of a deposit must be available after one business day, regardless of whether the check is local or nonlocal. Financial institutions have five business days to clear local checks that are deposited in shared automated teller machine networks ("nonproprietary" ATMs) in order to give them time to determine whether the checks are local or nonlocal items and to make sure they are backed by sufficient funds. Local checks deposited in an institution's own

ATMs must be cleared in two business days. There are also exceptions to all of these specified waiting times. Funds may be held longer if the deposit amounts to more than $5,000, if the account is less than 30 days old, if the check had been returned, if the account has been frequently overdrawn, or if the institution has reason to believe that the check may be uncollectible.

> *The gimmick user.* The use of gimmicks may range from the person who insists on using special checks that can't be photocopied or microfilmed to the person who has a little legal knowledge and tries to find loopholes to offset his or her obligations.

In the case of the former, checks have been manufactured that are printed either in a dark red color on red paper or in a shade of blue that is designed to be used with a light blue, felt-tipped pen. The purpose of both is to thwart the photocopying or microfilming of checks and thus frustrate account investigation. Use of these checks may cause a violation of the Bank Secrecy Act, which requires financial institutions to keep copies of checks exceeding statutory limits, and the American Bankers Association (ABA) has warned that they may create potential liability should institutions accept them. A depositor might claim that his or her account was charged with an on-us check that he or she did not draw. Or, should an on-us item be destroyed, the institution would have no way to reconstruct the item and charge the proper customer. Lost return and transit items could also cause a loss for the institution because misplaced or destroyed items could not be reconstructed. Be sure to consult your supervisor if you should ever receive such a check.

People who try to find legal loopholes for avoiding their obligations might, for example, involve two company officials who open a business checking account that requires both to sign checks. They then might deliberately attempt to disavow a check paid with only one signature, creating a loss for the financial institution.

When people do something to indicate that they don't trust each other—as in the case of a married couple requiring co-signatures on checks—or when the customer tries to do something that might indicate suspicious activities, financial institutions usually either refuse the account, refuse to go along with the activity, or, in some cases, simply keep a watchful eye on the customer and his or her transactions.

Customers who cause potential problems are part of every teller's day. Learning to cope with them is part of your job. Here are some general rules to follow:

1. Keep your cool. The customer who wants to do something that will cause problems probably has his or her own problems. So, while

you can't pay a check on a depleted account, you can sympathize with a customer who may need the money to buy groceries.

2. Quietly report suspicious activities to a supervisor. Don't make an issue of it, because the customer probably hasn't broken any laws. Even if he or she has, it's not your job to be a police officer.

3. Begin with the assumption that the customer doesn't understand, not that the person is a crook. Chances are good that this is exactly the situation.

Finally, realize that your definition of a customer varies considerably from that of the public. To you, a customer is a depositor, a borrower, or someone who uses a banking service. Even though it really isn't such, most people consider a financial institution to be a public institution, and they believe a customer is anyone who walks in and asks for change or wants to cash a check. Dealing successfully with problem customers means recognizing the difference, then being courteous to everyone, customer and noncustomer, and politely sticking to the rules of good banking practice at the same time.

THE BANK SECRECY ACT

The federal government has established strict regulations under the Bank Secrecy Act in an effort to stem the flow of money from the sale of drugs and other illegal activities that criminals pass through financial institutions in order to hide its true ownership, a practice known as "money laundering."

These regulations require that every financial institution currency transaction of over $10,000 be reported to the Internal Revenue Service on Form 4789, the Currency Transaction Report (CTR), within 15 days of the transaction. A copy of that form appears at the end of this chapter. Deposits, withdrawals, exchanges of currency, transfers of currency, and other payments are included, and multiple transactions are treated as a single transaction if they are made by or on behalf of the same person during one business day. Certain customers are exempt, such as other depository institutions or major retailers, which often deal in large amounts of cash.

In addition, financial institutions must keep a record of all cash transactions of between $3,000 and $10,000 involving bank checks, cashier's checks, traveler's checks, and money orders. The Internal Revenue Service may request this information. This law is designed to help suppress the practice known as "smurfing," under which criminals hire people to buy these financial instruments in order to avoid the over-$10,000 reporting requirements.

In order to help the government suppress the transfer of illicit money, the U.S. Treasury requires that financial institutions keep a detailed record of all fund transfers of $3,000 or more. Information that must be recorded includes the names and addresses of the transfer initiator and beneficiary, the amount and date of the transfer, the financial institution that originated the transfer, and information about the beneficiary's financial institution and account.

At some institutions, CTRs are completed by hand; others have computer programs that enable tellers to enter the information on terminals at their windows while the customer waits. Either way, you, as a teller, should receive periodic training in how to comply with the Bank Secrecy Act.

Furthermore, if you notice that someone seems to be making transactions designed to evade the reporting requirements or appears to be involved in some other illegal activity, you should quietly report your suspicions to your supervisor. In such a case, your institution may decide to report the information using a Suspicious Activity Report (SAR), Form FR 2230. A copy of this form appears at the end of this chapter. Suspicious activities for which a report should be filed are those that involve $5,000 or more in cases in which a suspect can be identified and those that involve $5,000 or more for which money laundering or violations of the Bank Secrecy Act may have taken place. Those that involve $25,000 or more should be reported regardless of whether or not there is a suspect. Officers and employees of financial institutions who are under suspicion involving any amount of money are also subject to being reported. SARs must be filed no later than 30 days after the detection of the suspicious activity.

Noncompliance with these regulations can result in extremely heavy penalties for the institution that is involved. Thus, it's important for you to carefully follow the instructions that you are given.

It is interesting to note that the Postal Service has also established rules to deter the use of its money orders in money laundering. Anyone who buys $3,000 or more is required to fill in certain forms. In addition, there is a limit of $10,000 on same-day purchases of postal money orders.

F I G U R E 21–1

Currency Transaction Report—Page 1

Form **4789**	**Currency Transaction Report**	
(Rev. October 1995)	▶ Use this 1995 revision effective October 1, 1995.	OMB No. 1545-0183
Department of the Treasury / Internal Revenue Service	▶ For Paperwork Reduction Act Notice, see page 3.　▶ Please type or print. *(Complete all parts that apply—See instructions)*	

1 Check all box(es) that apply:
a ☐ Amends prior report　b ☐ Multiple persons　c ☐ Multiple transactions

Part I　Person(s) Involved in Transaction(s)

Section A—Person(s) on Whose Behalf Transaction(s) Is Conducted

2 Individual's last name or Organization's name	3 First name	4 M.I.

5 Doing business as (DBA)	6 SSN or EIN

7 Address (number, street, and apt. or suite no.)	8 Date of birth　M M D D Y Y

9 City	10 State	11 ZIP code	12 Country (if not U.S.)	13 Occupation, profession, or business

14 If an individual, describe method used to verify identity:
a ☐ Driver's license/State I.D.　b ☐ Passport　c ☐ Alien registration　d ☐ Other ....
e Issued by:　f Number:

Section B—Individual(s) Conducting Transaction(s) (if other than above).
If Section B is left blank or incomplete, check the box(es) below to indicate the reason(s):

a ☐ Armored Car Service　b ☐ Mail Deposit or Shipment　c ☐ Night Deposit or Automated Teller Machine (ATM)
d ☐ Multiple Transactions　e ☐ Conducted On Own Behalf

15 Individual's last name	16 First name	17 M.I.

18 Address (number, street, and apt. or suite no.)	19 SSN

20 City	21 State	22 ZIP code	23 Country (if not U.S.)	24 Date of birth　M M D D Y Y

25 If an individual, describe method used to verify identity:
a ☐ Driver's license/State I.D.　b ☐ Passport　c ☐ Alien registration　d ☐ Other ....
e Issued by:　f Number:

Part II　Amount and Type of Transaction(s). Check all boxes that apply.

		28 Date of Transaction　M M D D Y Y
26 Cash In $ _____ .00	27 Cash Out $ _____ .00	

29 ☐ Foreign Currency _____ (Country)　30 ☐ Wire Transfer(s)　31 ☐ Negotiable Instrument(s) Purchased

32 ☐ Negotiable Instrument(s) Cashed　33 ☐ Currency Exchange(s)　34 ☐ Deposit(s)/Withdrawal(s)

35 ☐ Account Number(s) Affected (if any):　36 ☐ Other (specify)

Part III　Financial Institution Where Transaction(s) Takes Place

37 Name of financial institution	Enter Federal Regulator or BSA Examiner code number from the instructions here. ▶ [ ]

38 Address (number, street, and apt. or suite no.)	39 SSN or EIN

40 City	41 State	42 ZIP code	43 MICR No.

Sign Here ▶	44 Title of approving official	45 Signature of approving official	46 Date of signature　M M D D Y Y
	47 Type or print preparer's name	48 Type or print name of person to contact	49 Telephone number ( )

Cat. No. 42004W　　Form **4789** (Rev. 10-95)

F I G U R E 21–1

Currency Transaction Report—Page 2

Form 4789 (Rev. 10-95)   Page **2**

Multiple Persons

(Complete applicable parts below if box 1b on page 1 is checked.)

Part I   Person(s) Involved in Transaction(s)

Section A—Person(s) on Whose Behalf Transaction(s) Is Conducted

2 Individual's last name or Organization's name	3 First name	4 M.I.

5 Doing business as (DBA)	6 SSN or EIN

7 Address (number, street, and apt. or suite no.)	8 Date of birth M M D D Y Y

9 City	10 State	11 ZIP code	12 Country (if not U.S.)	13 Occupation, profession, or business

14 If an individual, describe method used to verify identity:
a ☐ Driver's license/State I.D.   b ☐ Passport   c ☐ Alien registration   d ☐ Other ....
e Issued by: f Number:

Section B—Individual(s) Conducting Transaction(s) (if other than above).

15 Individual's last name	16 First name	17 M.I.

18 Address (number, street, and apt. or suite no.)	19 SSN

20 City	21 State	22 ZIP code	23 Country (if not U.S.)	24 Date of birth M M D D Y Y

25 If an individual, describe method used to verify identity:
a ☐ Driver's license/State I.D.   b ☐ Passport   c ☐ Alien registration   d ☐ Other ....
e Issued by: f Number:

Part I   Person(s) Involved in Transaction(s)

Section A—Person(s) on Whose Behalf Transaction(s) Is Conducted

2 Individual's last name or Organization's name	3 First name	4 M.I.

5 Doing business as (DBA)	6 SSN or EIN

7 Address (number, street, and apt. or suite no.)	8 Date of birth M M D D Y Y

9 City	10 State	11 ZIP code	12 Country (if not U.S.)	13 Occupation, profession, or business

14 If an individual, describe method used to verify identity:
a ☐ Driver's license/State I.D.   b ☐ Passport   c ☐ Alien registration   d ☐ Other ....
e Issued by: f Number:

Section B—Individual(s) Conducting Transaction(s) (if other than above).

15 Individual's last name	16 First name	17 M.I.

18 Address (number, street, and apt. or suite no.)	19 SSN

20 City	21 State	22 ZIP code	23 Country (if not U.S.)	24 Date of birth M M D D Y Y

25 If an individual, describe method used to verify identity:
a ☐ Driver's license/State I.D.   b ☐ Passport   c ☐ Alien registration   d ☐ Other ....
e Issued by: f Number:

A Currency Transaction Report, used to report currency transactions in excess of $10,000 to the Internal Revenue Service. It is important for tellers to know how to fill in the form correctly and completely.

F I G U R E 21–2

Suspicious Activity Report—Page 1

<table>
<tr><td colspan="2" align="right">**1**</td></tr>
<tr>
<td rowspan="2">
<h2>Suspicious
Activity Report</h2>
</td>
<td>
FRB: FR 2230   OMB No. 7100-0212
FDIC: 6710/06   OMB No. 3064-0077
OCC: 8010-9,8010-1   OMB No. 1557-0180
OTS: 1601   OMB No. 1550-0003
NCUA: 2362   OMB No. 3133-0094
TREASURY: TD F 90-22.47   OMB No. 1506-0001
</td>
</tr>
<tr>
<td>ALWAYS COMPLETE ENTIRE REPORT</td>
<td>Expires September 30, 1998</td>
</tr>
</table>

1 Check appropriate box:
a ☐ Initial Report   b ☐ Corrected Report   c ☐ Supplemental Report

Part 1   Reporting Financial Institution Information

2 Name of Financial Institution

3 Primary Federal Regulator
a ☐ Federal Reserve   d ☐ OCC

4 Address of Financial Institution
b ☐ FDIC   e ☐ OTS
c ☐ NCUA

5 City   6 State   7 Zip Code   8 EIN or TIN

9 Address of Branch Office(s) where activity occurred   10 Asset size of financial institution $ _____ .00

11 City   12 State   13 Zip Code   14 If institution closed, date closed (MMDDYY) ___/___/___

15 Account number(s) affected, if any
a _____
b _____

16 Have any of the Institution's accounts related to this matter been closed?
a ☐ Yes   b ☐ No   If yes, identify _____

Part II   Suspect Information

17 Last Name or Name of Entity   18 First Name   19 Middle Initial

20 Address   21 SSN, TIN or EIN (as applicable)

22 City   23 State   24 Zip Code   25 Country   26 Date of Birth (MMDDYY) ___/___/___

27 Phone Number - Residence (include area code)   ( )   28 Phone Number - Work (include area code)   ( )

29 Occupation

30 Forms of Identification for Suspect:
a ☐ Driver's License   b ☐ Passport   c ☐ Alien Registration   d ☐ Other _____
e Number _____   f Issuing Authority _____

31 Relationship to Financial Institution:
a ☐ Accountant   d ☐ Attorney   g ☐ Customer   j ☐ Officer
b ☐ Agent   e ☐ Borrower   h ☐ Director   k ☐ Shareholder
c ☐ Appraiser   f ☐ Broker   i ☐ Employee   l ☐ Other _____

32 Is insider suspect still affiliated with the financial institution?
a ☐ Yes
b ☐ No   If no, Specify { c ☐ Suspended   e ☐ Resigned
d ☐ Terminated }

33 Date of Suspension, Termination, Resignation (MMDDYY) ___/___/___

34 Admission/Confession
a ☐ Yes   b ☐ No

F I G U R E 21–2

Suspicious Activity Report—Page 2

Part III	**Suspicious Activity Information**	**2**

35 Date of suspicious activity (MMDDYY)

_____ / _____ / _____

36 Dollar amount involved in known or suspicious activity

$ _____ .00

37 Summary characterization of suspicious activity

- a ☐ Bank Secrecy Act/Structuring/ Money Laundering
- b ☐ Bribery/Gratuity
- c ☐ Check Fraud
- d ☐ Check Kiting
- e ☐ Commercial Loan Fraud
- f ☐ Consumer Loan Fraud

- g ☐ Counterfeit Check
- h ☐ Counterfeit Credit/Debit Card
- i ☐ Counterfeit Instrument (other)
- j ☐ Credit Card Fraud
- k ☐ Debit Card Fraud
- l ☐ Defalcation/Embezzlement

- m ☐ False Statement
- n ☐ Misuse of Position or Self-Dealing
- o ☐ Mortgage Loan Fraud
- p ☐ Mysterious Disappearance
- q ☐ Wire Transfer Fraud

r ☐ Other _____

38 Amount of loss prior to recovery (if applicable)

$ _____ .00

39 Dollar amount of recovery (if applicable)

$ _____ .00

40 Has the suspicious activity had a material impact on or otherwise affected the financial soundness of the institution?

a ☐ Yes b ☐ No

41 Has the institution's bonding company been notified?

a ☐ Yes   b ☐ No

42 Has any law enforcement agency already been advised by telephone, written communication, or otherwise? If so, list the agency and local address.

Agency _____

43 Address

44 City

45 State

46 Zip Code

Part IV	**Witness Information**

47 Last Name

48 First Name

49 Middle Initial

50 Address

51 SSN

52 City

45 State

46 Zip Code

55 Date of Birth (MMDDYY)

_____ / _____ / _____

56 Title

57 Phone Number (include area code)

( )

58 Interviewd

a ☐ Yes b ☐ No

Part V	**Preparer Information**

59 Last Name

60 First Name

61 Middle Initial

62 Title

63 Phone Number (include area code)

( )

64 Date (MMDDYY)

Part VI	**Contact for Assistance (If different than Preparer Information in Part V)**

65 Last Name

66 First Name

67 Middle Initial

68 Title

69 Phone Number (include area code)

( )

70 Agency (if applicable)

22

CHAPTER

Security and Customer Courtesy

SECURITY, ACCURACY, SPEED, AND COURTESY

To be effective, tellers must do four things that can be difficult to accomplish simultaneously. Tellers are expected to be:

1. Security conscious;
2. Accurate;
3. Fast; and
4. Courteous.

How can you smile and be courteous while quickly and accurately handling a transaction that involves security? It's not easy, but it can be done. First, you have to set priorities. Second, you must eliminate certain preconceived ideas.

PRIORITIES

Consider the four aspects of a teller's job that were just mentioned. Some are more important than the others, and should be handled as such.

Obviously, security must come first, because in some instances human lives literally may be at stake; in any case, financial institution assets may be at risk. Therefore, in a situation in which questioning a person about the details of a transaction might seem offensive, that offense must be risked.

Accuracy follows closely after security in importance. If a customer was absolutely overwhelmed with the courtesy that was shown to him or her, would that individual allow it to override any possible annoyance because of an avoidable error involving his or her account? Not very likely.

Tellers must sometimes make a choice between courtesy and speed. Sometimes talkative customers chat with the teller while holding up a long line of annoyed people. The teller should be as courteous as possible but must get that customer to move on so that the next customer can be served. Courtesy, with all of its implications in terms of building goodwill and selling services is very important as well. Tellers must always try to provide courteous service.

Preconceived Erroneous Ideas

Consider a few old, erroneous ideas. Some people feel that:

Tending to security details requires rudeness. This is not true. Asking a stranger for identification needn't be done in a way that is offensive. If you smile and say "please," you can be courteous while also being alert. So being security-conscious doesn't mean that you have to abandon courtesy.

Being accurate means sacrificing speed. Not true. An old adage states that "There's always time to do it over, but never time to do it right." This could be the slogan of those who opt for speed at all costs—these people often have to do whatever it is over again. Go as fast as you can while being as careful as you can.

Being courteous means sacrificing speed. Also not true. Being courteous doesn't require having long chats with every customer when lines are long and tempers are short, nor does it mean rushing people out of the office. It doesn't take any time to smile at the customer as he or she steps up to the window, and it doesn't take any time to say "thank you" as the customer steps away. Nor does using the word "please" in your instructions add time to the transaction. A smile, a "please," and a "thank you" do add up to courtesy.

To be a truly effective teller, try to make security, accuracy, courtesy, and speed work together.

SECURITY, SALES, AND COURTESY

As a teller, you're expected to keep your cash to a minimum and to beware of strangers. At the same time, you're expected to sell services while you're being courteous to those who come to your window. (The teller as a seller is discussed in Part IV.) Thus, you may wonder whether you can establish a relationship of trust when you're supposed to be suspicious. The answer is yes, you can. The key is to make following security policies second nature.

The Rules

To help avoid the various types of criminals who prey on financial institutions, follow these four basic rules:

1. *Never deviate from established policy.* Endorsements should not be waived; essentials should not be bypassed. If, for example, accounts should have resolutions of one kind or another on file, be sure to get them. If signature cards should be on file, obtain them. Most important, get any identification that's called for in every case.

2. *Know with whom you are dealing.* If you really know the people with whom you are dealing, can make a positive identification, and know how those people can be reached, they're less likely to do anything illegal.

3. *Use common sense.* Make certain that money, negotiable checks, securities, and other items of value are put out of the reach of sneak thieves. Vary your routines enough to make it difficult for robbers to observe a pattern. Encourage depositors of large amounts to do the same. And never give anyone else, even a close friend, access to your cash drawers.

4. *Report your suspicions.* You may feel foolish telling your supervisor or security officer about the strange person who asks so many questions or about the individual who makes large, round-numbered, ever-growing deposits at regular, short intervals with checks drawn on the same out-of-town financial institution. Consider, though, that you might foil a holdup or stop a kiter. Anything suspicious should be reported.

Selling Services

Keeping all these rules in mind, how can you still maintain security and sell your institution's services?

Start with the assumption that people are honest until proven otherwise. Tellers who suspect every customer show it, and that's bound to offend people. Be courteous and be friendly and helpful as well. It's possible to follow security rules without acting suspicious.

Avoid telling customers that security procedures are being followed. For example, if you walk over to a cabinet, take out a card, examine it, put it back, then cash the check, the average customer will simply accept your actions as part of the check-cashing routine and won't be offended.

Suggest services to anyone who seems to be a good prospect. Each of your customers qualifies as a potential user of additional services. In fact, suggesting that a financial institution can be of further service to present customers when the need arises is the definition of "cross-selling," a subject that is discussed in Part IV. If you are courteous, friendly, and helpful while you follow your institution's security procedures, you'll not only avoid offending anyone, you'll also be able to perform another important part of your job—suggesting services to fill your customers' needs when the opportunity presents itself.

Keep in mind that most of the people with whom you deal are not criminals and that courtesy and carefulness are not antithetical.

23

CHAPTER

Handling Emergencies

Day in and day out, most of your work as a teller involves efficiently dealing with people in pleasant surroundings. Helping customers, getting along with co-workers, and calmly and quietly performing the duties of your job make for a typical day. But what do you do when the unexpected happens? What do you do when:

- A customer or fellow employee slips, falls, and gets injured in your lobby?
- Someone has a heart attack?
- A fight starts in your lobby?
- A fire breaks out in your office?
- Someone on your staff is taken hostage?
- A riot occurs in your institution's neighborhood?
- A telephone call is received reporting that a bomb has been planted in your office?

These are only a few of the emergencies that can and sometimes do happen in financial institutions. If something unexpected suddenly occurs, you, as a teller, must be prepared to cope with the emergency.

Get Ready

If you haven't done so, get ready for any conceivable emergency right now. Start by making a neat and legible list of telephone numbers to keep near your window. Include a doctor and a backup doctor, the nearest hospital, ambulance service, police, fire department, rescue squad, garage, the FBI, and people within your institution who are skilled in first aid or other emergency procedures. A form for this purpose is provided at the end of this book.

Then be prepared mentally. Think things through for yourself or, better yet, discuss them with your fellow tellers. Determine how you should handle certain situations and what the best course of action is in each situation.

What to Do

In any real emergency situation, with very few exceptions, you always have a little time to stop and think. All it takes is a few seconds of consideration to make the difference between rushing in foolishly or taking careful action. So in most emergencies, these steps will help:

1. STOP AND THINK! What is the best thing to do? What will get the fastest and best results? Who is the best person to call for help? What steps can you take personally?
2. Protect your customers, your fellow employees, yourself, and the assets of your financial institution.
3. If possible, get expert help fast. Call a doctor. Or the police. Or the fire department. Whichever is best for the situation. Unless you really know what you are doing, for example, you could waste precious seconds ministering to a heart attack victim while an ambulance could be on the way.
4. Keep cool. This can be very difficult, but remember, the customers who are present will look to you for leadership.

After the emergency is over, you can sit down and calm down. But still keep in mind that you represent your institution. Therefore, you should:

1. Notify your officials at once of what happened, the steps that you and others took, and the outcome of the situation.
2. If necessary, call any authorities.
3. Keep confidences when talking to reporters. Customers are entitled to privacy. Let an officer trained in public relations handle the press.
4. Don't say anything to customers in the excitement of the moment that you might regret later. This especially applies to sharing confidential information.

Emergencies happen in financial institutions. Heads-up tellers have saved lives, helped accident victims, and coped with fires and hurricanes. It doesn't happen often, but it's part of dealing with people. Consider the specific situations discussed in the following sections of this chapter.

HAVE A SAFE OFFICE

As safe and comfortable as financial institution surroundings are, many potential causes of accidents that can result in injuries still exist, as they do in any business office. To help safeguard yourself, your fellow employees, and your customers, take a look around your office and watch for:

Tripping hazards. Loose cords from telephones and appliances, pens, pencils, and other debris can cause people to stumble and fall. Take a moment to pick up anything that doesn't belong on the floor and route cords to areas where people won't trip on them.

Open drawers. Close the drawers on filing cabinets and desks as soon as you are finished with them. Otherwise, they are a potential source of painful bumps and cuts or damage to clothing. Also, if the heavy top drawer of a filing cabinet is left open, there is a chance that the whole cabinet will tip over.

Sharp objects. Pens, pencils, pins, and tacks that are left unguarded or mixed among drawer contents can puncture or cut hands and fingers. Have a place to put such things and keep them there.

Long hair. If you have exceptionally long hair that could get caught in fans, typewriters, or other moving equipment, consider arranging it in a style that will reduce the possibility of injury.

Paper edges. Sharp edges on paper and envelopes can cause cuts to skin, tongue, or lips. Handle them with care.

Cigarettes. A forgotten, lighted cigarette can set paper afire, especially volatile carbon paper. If you smoke anywhere in your institution, be extra careful to thoroughly extinguish your cigarettes. And don't throw the contents of a full ashtray into a paper-filled waste basket.

The best way to avoid painful accidents is to keep your work area neat and hazard-free.

IN CASE OF FIRE

Financial institutions are located where the people are. This means that many of them are located in shopping centers where they share common walls with stores or in renovated older buildings in downtown areas . . . again with common walls. These common walls increase fire hazards for financial institutions because they are exposed to their neighbors' risks as well as their own.

Modern financial institution construction is less likely to be as fire resistant as the stone buildings of several decades ago. Employee lounges with electrical and gas appliances, facilities for smoking, and the vast amount of highly flammable paper attendant to banking all increase the risk of fire. Therefore, you must be prepared for fire in your office.

During Working Hours

If a fire should break out during working hours, you and your co-workers would probably have the advantage of early detection. The following steps should be taken as quickly as possible:

1. Notify the fire department.
2. Safeguard your customers. Get them out of the office immediately.
3. Get the cash and valuable papers, such as collateral and notes, into the vault and *lock the door*. Your vault is not fireproof or theftproof with the door open.
4. Get yourself to safety.
5. Notify the police.
6. Notify the main office of your institution if you work in a branch.

Obviously, the intensity of the fire and how rapidly it is spreading will influence the steps you take and how well you take them. The key is to have a plan. Know which person is assigned to get customers out. Know who should go outside to call the fire and police departments and notify the main office. Have a plan for putting valuables away quickly, and know who should lock the vault.

After Working Hours

The main thing to do about fire after working hours is to try to prevent it. This means:

1. Safely discard cigarettes in a fireproof container. Carelessly-disposed-of cigarettes are a major cause of fires.
2. Be sure that all electrical appliances are turned off properly.
3. Point out any faulty wiring or defective appliances to your manager.

Fire prevention and fire safety are primarily the responsibility of your office manager, of course. But in an emergency and for real prevention, fire safety is everyone's responsibility.

Fire Extinguishers

As part of the emergency preparedness at your office, you and each of your co-workers should know how to operate any fire extinguishers that are available. You should also know which type of extinguisher to use on which type of fire. Not every extinguisher is safe for all fires. Here is a list of the common types of fires and the proper extinguishers to use for each:

> *Class A fires* involve ordinary combustibles, such as trash, paper, cloth, and wood. Pressurized water extinguishers or water from a pail or hose will cool the objects and stop the burning.

> *Class B fires* involve flammable liquids. Foam, dry chemical, or carbon dioxide extinguishers should be used instead of water. Burning paint, oil, and kerosene are examples of Class B fires.

> *Class C fires* involve electricity. Dry chemical, carbon dioxide, or other Class C extinguishers should be used. NEVER put out an electrical fire with water because of the danger of shock. Shut off the electricity to the appliance by unplugging it or by turning off the wall switch or the circuit breaker. Then use the proper extinguisher on the fire.

If a Class ABC extinguisher is available, it can safely be used on all three types of fires.

KIDNAPPING AND HOSTAGE SITUATIONS

Holding a financial institution officer, his or her family, or a member of the staff as hostage either for ransom or while the institution is being robbed is a rare occurrence, but it does happen. Situations of this type will be less dangerous if you are prepared for them in advance.

Tips for Avoiding Problems

Study these tips from the FBI on ways to lessen the danger of kidnapping or hostage taking as a means of robbing your institution:

1. Instruct your family and co-workers not to provide information concerning you or your family to strangers.

2. Avoid giving unnecessary personal details in response to inquiries from information collectors for use in publications such as business or community directories.

3. Review your institution's plan regarding kidnappings. Make sure that you know what to do in such a situation.

4. Establish simple, effective signal systems that, when activated, will alert your co-workers or family members that you are in danger.

5. Be alert to strangers who are on your institution's property for no apparent reason.

6. Vary your daily routine to avoid habitual patterns that kidnappers can learn. Alter your travel times and routes to and from the office.

7. Refuse to meet with strangers at secluded or unknown locations.

8. Always advise a co-worker or family member of your destination and what time you intend to return when leaving the office or home.

9. Lock the doors and roll up the windows of your car when traveling to and from work.

Here are some additional precautions that you should take:

1. *Never* pick up hitchhikers.

2. If you walk to work, make some changes in your route occasionally. If you use public transportation, avoid suspicious strangers, try to sit near the driver, and try to avoid taking the same transportation at the exact same time every day.

3. After dark, walk away from buildings or bushes where someone may be lurking. Walk in the street if necessary.

4. Carry a whistle in your hand if you are in a high-crime area, and use it if anyone tries to bother you.

5. In addition to arranging pre-opening signals to indicate that it is safe for others to enter the office in the morning, devise a signal that you can use when entering later to let those already inside know if something is wrong.

Some of these points may not apply in your situation, but some perhaps do. In any case, avoiding potential problem situations is a most effective security measure.

A Pre-Opening Security Checklist

Here's a simple checklist for you to follow in the morning before getting started on the day's work if you are the first to arrive at the office:

1. On the way into the building, check to see that there are no suspicious persons or vehicles nearby.

2. Quickly check to see that no doors or windows have been tampered with at the office.

3. After entering, follow any necessary alarm procedures and check quickly to see that no one is lurking in any unlocked rooms or behind or under large pieces of furniture.

4. Use a prearranged signal that will allow people who arrive later to know that all is safe. This signal may be turning on a certain light, adjusting a blind, moving something in the window, or the like. Change the signal occasionally so that the routine won't become obvious to would-be robbers.

5. Finally, if there *is* something suspicious outside the office, *don't go in*. Call the police and let them go in with you. Or, should you see something suspicious inside after you enter, leave at once and call the police from the nearest phone. Don't let yourself or anyone else get into a hostage situation. Remember, crooks like to surprise financial institution employees.

If a Kidnapping Occurs

What should you do if there is an actual kidnapping and someone from your office is taken hostage? If you should answer the telephone and be informed that the caller is holding a fellow employee or officer or one or more of his or her family members, follow these steps:

1. Keep calm. The call may be a hoax or a phony extortion scheme.

2. Do not upset the caller.

3. Try to get proof that the caller really has a hostage.

4. Make notes. Write down the sex of the caller, voice mannerisms, the time of the call, the exact words used, any background noise, details of the demand, and so forth.

5. If possible, try to have someone use another phone to have the police trace the call.

6. Indicate a willingness to cooperate.

7. Immediately after the call, notify the FBI, the police, and the senior management of your institution.

If a person is kidnapped at the office:

1. Notify the authorities at once.

2. Maintain secrecy to protect the kidnapped person. The FBI and other authorities involved with the situation will guide you on this.

3. Preserve any evidence, such as notes or letters. Nothing at the scene of the crime should be handled or disturbed.

4. Try to keep calm and maintain a normal routine.

5. Trust the authorities and, to the best of your ability, give them any information they want. The safety of the victim is paramount, and this is always the first concern of law enforcement agencies.

The kidnapping of people who work at financial institutions is rare, so it is not something that should prey on your mind. However, as with any security situation involving your institution, knowing what to do IF it occurs is very important.

CIVIL DISTURBANCE

Financial institutions are usually not directly related in civil demonstrations or disorders, but some offices are located in areas where such disturbances could take place. Your office will probably never be affected by a riot or similar occurrence but with the increase of such activities, it is wise to be prepared. The following list of procedures can help:

1. In the event of a riot, stay home if possible.

2. Avoid heroics.

3. Remain calm and don't become involved with rioters or demonstrators by answering barbs or taunts.

4. If necessary, get food, drink, and first aid locally during any time that it is inadvisable to go home.

5. Keep a list available of the home phone numbers and addresses of your institution's supervisors. They should be notified in case of an emergency if they are not at work.

6. Make arrangements for transportation. Police officers and representatives of armored car services may be cooperative.

7. Make sure that the police or other agencies are notified in case of this kind of disturbance.

8. Put cash or other assets into their cash boxes or other containers and place these in the vault or a locked fireproof storage area as quickly as possible in the event of disorder.

9. Make sure that the vault door is locked after the assets have been put away.

If you work in a branch that is located close to your main office, your manager might also wish to consider having on hand a set of walkie-talkies in case of a breakdown in telephone communications, as well as a supply of heavy plywood, two-by-fours, nails, and hammers to board up windows.

Chances are you will never see a riot or other civil disturbance. But a wise employee, especially one who works in an urban area, should be ready for any emergency.

BOMB THREATS

Any public place is a possible target for a bomb, including an office of a financial institution. The best way to avoid a bomb hazard is to be very sure that no one, except authorized employees, enters any area of the institution except those designated for the public. This drastically cuts down on places where a bomb might be hidden, because public areas are, or should be, relatively clear of clutter.

Employees should also be alert for suspicious-looking persons with packages. If you should spot such a person, notify your supervisor at once; in turn, he or she should watch the individual and decide whether or not to call the police.

According to authorities, most bombings never happen. They are simply threats. Often, groups that plant bombs have no intention of injuring anyone; they just want publicity for their cause. Whatever the case, bombings or bomb hoaxes are likely to be accompanied by a telephone call. The hoax won't work without some sort of notification, and the person or group responsible won't get the desired publicity without taking credit for the bomb.

If you should receive such a phone call, try to get as much information as possible. Where is the bomb planted? If it's a time bomb, when will it go off? If it's another type of bomb, what action will set it off? According to police officials, people who make such threats may reveal this information either to avoid causing personal injury or simply to show that they are clever.

The next step is to notify the police immediately. Usually they will clear the area for a safe distance and then conduct a search of the premises. They may ask for assistance from one or more employees who are familiar with the area and would quickly notice any unfamiliar object.

Your office will probably never be the object of a bombing or bomb threat. However, vigilance on the part of tellers and other employees may help to discourage potential attempts. And being prepared could prevent injuries and save lives.

"BANKABILITY" MEANS DEALING WITH CUSTOMERS EFFECTIVELY

As stated in Chapter 1, the word "teller" is said to derive from the Dutch *tellen*, or from the Old English *tellan*, meaning "to count." But tellers do a great deal more than that.

Many years ago, tellers were senior clerks who had probably been trained in both transit and bookkeeping functions. But the years have changed both tellers and the job. Many people, including some tellers themselves, aren't aware of just how encompassing their work can be. Tellers do handle routine transactions involving deposit accounts, which means that they accept deposits, pay out withdrawals, and cash checks within the policies of the financial institution. In addition, tellers may prepare payrolls and accept club account payments, loan payments, and payments of utility bills. Duties vary from institution to institution and sometimes even from branch to branch.

Tellers are also the key customer-contact employees in the financial institution. In addition to handling each transaction with accuracy and efficiency, their job is to be pleasant and courteous, to reflect the goodwill of management. The years may have changed the routines and the people, but the position is more important than ever.

Tellers are so important because they are the financial institution's direct connection to the public. It is up to tellers to put the institution's policies into practice, and it is up to them to operate in all the important areas of public contact as representatives of the institution. Tellers don't just "receive or pay out money" as one dictionary suggests. They implement policy at the most direct level in banking—person to person with the customer.

The following chapters, which tell you how to deal with your customers more effectively, should help you to become a truly first-rate front-line representative for your institution.

24

CHAPTER

Know Your Services

PRODUCT KNOWLEDGE—A TELLER'S MUST

As a teller, *you* are the person in the financial institution who is most likely to have individual contact with the customer. To the customer, you represent a degree of expertise in banking and in personal finance. You are the one who will most likely be asked to recommend a savings plan, to advise on types of checking accounts, for information about the availability of loans for various purposes, for facts about the cost and availability of safe deposit boxes, and much more.

A popular phrase in the retail industry is "product knowledge." It means knowing what products are offered, what they can do, and what each costs. As a teller, you should know these basics about the services your institution offers.

Gaining Knowledge

There are two ways in which you can learn about your services. The first is to study them by reading your financial institution's advertising and the literature it makes available; by learning on the job, especially by asking questions of other employees; by studying this handbook and reading professional journals; and by taking courses.

The second basic way in which you can gain product knowledge is from practical experience. As a teller, you are exposed to your services through your job, but as a *consumer*, you are exposed to financial services through their application to your daily life.

Practical knowledge is usually much more valuable than theoretical knowledge. When a customer asks, "Is a credit card really easy to use?" it makes a much greater impact if you say, "Yes, I use mine all the time and find that almost every merchant and restaurant in town accepts it," than if you say, "Yes, most of the people who have them seem to be very satisfied."

Thus, you should gain all of the product knowledge you can from study, and, even more importantly, by being a careful user of these services yourself. Let them benefit your own life, and then translate those benefits into useful terms for others.

Using Product Knowledge

To what practical use can you put product knowledge? Here are a few suggestions:

> *To help sell services.* With sound product knowledge you are in a better position to fill a person's or a business's financial needs through the use of the services offered by your financial institution. Information about how to sell services appears in Part Five.
>
> *To help the customer with a problem.* Don't expect customers to have the knowledge of banking that you do. Many customers don't even know that some basic services exist. Often, with a solid grounding in product knowledge, you can give the customer with a problem an easy answer.
>
> *To enrich your own job.* People who know what they are doing as part of the overall picture do a better job and they enjoy their work more. Knowing how services and functions mesh together in your institution can make you more effective and can enhance your career potential.

Not every teller needs to become an expert on every phase of banking, of course. What is required is that every teller knows what services the institution offers and who *can* give expert advice. Thus, you can be a liaison between customers and other personnel who can be of service.

A Vast Range of Services

Just stop for a moment and consider the vast range of services your institution offers. A southern institution once printed a list of its services . . . and found that there were 150 ways that it could help people and businesses in the communities it served. Although the list included auto loans, boat loans, appliance loans, home improvement loans, and many other such categories that could all be considered *installment loans*, the institution that published the list had a good point—although the bookkeeping is similar on all installment loans, the *purpose* of each loan is different. And that's what concerns the public. People don't really care about financial institution procedures, but they do care whether or not it will lend them money to buy cars or appliances or to fix up their homes.

How many ways does your institution serve the people and businesses in your community? This chapter considers some of the basic retail services that most financial institutions offer.

CHECKING ACCOUNTS

Types of Checking Accounts

Checking accounts are called *demand* deposits. The depositor, or anyone he or she designates, can present a check that must be paid on demand if the check is properly made out and if there are sufficient collected funds.

There are two basic types of checking accounts, the regular and the special. The *special account* is designed for the person who writes only a few checks a month. It usually requires no minimum balance and charges are based on per-check fees. A monthly fee is also often charged. This type of account is restricted to use by individuals or persons qualifying for joint-account status.

Regular accounts provide the bulk of checking volume. They are used by individuals, businesses of every kind, organizations, governments, and even other financial institutions. To offer maximum benefits to all of the possible users and to offer legal protection to the institution and its depositors, different types of regular checking accounts are used. Some of the more common types are described in the following paragraphs:

Individual account. The individual account, as its name implies, is for use by one person. The only document necessary to open this type of account is a signature card that is properly signed.

Joint account. A joint account is one in which two persons hold their money in common; that is, the financial institution will pay a check signed by either one. This type of account is usually held by a married couple or by a parent and child. The account usually includes "rights of survivorship," which means that if one of the people dies, the other can still claim all of the money remaining in the account.

Business accounts. Business accounts include all types of businesses: proprietorships, corporations, and partnerships. In each case, proper papers must be filed to open the account or to change the signing requirements. An officer familiar with the type of account should specify what papers are necessary. When cashing a check drawn on a business account, you should be sure that it is properly signed. Often two signatures are required, or signature requirements may change with the amount of the check.

Guardianship accounts. Guardianship accounts are used in cases in which a guardian has been appointed by the courts to look out for the interests of someone who cannot take care of himself or herself. This includes children, mentally disabled persons, senile individuals, and so forth. In addition to the signature card, the financial institution should have a copy of the court appointment. Here again, you should check signing requirements when cashing checks drawn on these accounts.

Estate accounts. Estate accounts are used to safeguard the funds of a deceased person while his or her executors are settling the person's affairs. In addition to signature cards, the financial institution should have a copy of the death certificate or a brief version of it commonly called a "short" certificate. Items for deposit should be checked for proper endorsement, and signing requirements should be checked when cashing checks. They can vary widely.

NOW Accounts

Many years ago, before the Banking Act of 1933, it was traditional for financial institutions to attract demand deposits by paying interest on checking deposits. This included deposits kept by one financial institution in another institution for purposes of establishing a correspondent relationship. Many institutions had such correspondent accounts with institutions in New York to help their customers in stock market dealings. And, when the collapse came in 1929, many people felt it was magnified in its effect by the fact that those deposits were attracted by the payment of interest.

The Banking Act of 1933 amended the Federal Reserve Act to read, "No member bank shall, directly or indirectly, by any device whatsoever, pay any interest on any deposit which is payable on demand. . ."

That was in 1933. And it related strictly to checking accounts. Savings accounts could and did earn interest. Then, in 1969, Ron Haselton, president of the Consumers Savings Bank, Worcester, Massachusetts, reasoned that if statement savings were legal, which they had been in Massachusetts since 1961, and if computers had made possible the computation of daily interest, then a daily-interest no-passbook savings account was, in fact, a demand account, because no wait for posting and no notice of intent to withdraw were required. If the depositor's money was payable on demand, why not with a negotiable instrument as well as with a withdrawal slip?

The Consumers Savings Bank opened accounts called NOW accounts, short for Negotiable Order of Withdrawal. The original NOWs looked like checks, except that they bore the word NOW and the name of the institution through which they were payable. Soon, this practice was stopped, and a NOW account draft looked and worked exactly like any check—except that the balance in the account earned interest.

At first, interest-paying NOW accounts were offered by both savings institutions and commercial banks in New England and New York, while credit unions in many states offered interest-paying share-draft accounts, which are essentially the same thing. In addition, financial institutions in many states offered automatic transfer accounts, a complicated technique for creating a means of paying interest on demand deposits.

Then, late in 1980, it became legal for all financial institutions to offer NOW accounts. The problems most of them faced involved these issues:

- Was it necessary to require a minimum balance, and if so, how much?
- Should a monthly service charge be made?
- Should a per-check charge be made?

Many questions regarding potential profitability have caused wide variations among financial institutions in pricing structures; and the costs of money, processing expenses, and changing economic conditions are bound to create many differentials in interest-paying accounts among different institutions and regions of the country. These differentials relate to the amount of interest paid, the minimum balance required to forestall service charges, whether or not other accounts at the same institution are counted toward the required minimum balance, and monthly maintenance fees and/or per-check charges for accounts that fall below the minimum balance. For this reason, you should check with your supervisor to learn the details of any plan your institution may offer if you aren't sure of the details. And, equally important, you should learn how your institution's plans differ from those of other institutions in your area.

Overdraft Checking

An overdraft checking account enables the customer to overdraw his or her account by incurring a loan, which, depending on the financial institution, may be for a pre-specified amount or the amount of the overdraft. In this way, the customer's checks are in no danger of being returned for insufficient funds. The service costs nothing unless the account is overdrawn, in which case the institution charges interest on the loan. Again depending on the institution, repayment may be credited from the customer's next deposit, or a portion of the amount of the loan may be deducted from the account on a monthly basis. The customer must apply for an overdraft account just as he or she would for a credit card or a personal loan.

Sweep Accounts

A "sweep" checking account gives the business or professional customer an opportunity to have all balances above a specified amount transferred, or "swept," automatically each day from the company's checking account into investments where it can earn interest. A monthly fee is required, and federal deposit insurance does not cover the amount in this portion of the account. If the balance in the checking account drops below the specified amount, part of the investment is returned to the account.

Buyer-Protection Checking

In order to attract customers, some financial institutions offer special protection to their checking account customers for purchases paid for by check. Certain items may not be eligible, such as services, motorized vehicles, consumable or perishable items, animals or living plants, additions to real estate, and traveler's checks, tickets, or other negotiable instruments. A yearly maximum coverage per account holder may apply.

Late in 1989, First West Virginia Bank was the first financial institution to offer buyer protection, doubling the warranty on certain purchases bought with checks by members of its VIP 50 club. Early in 1990, Valley National Bank of Arizona became the first major institution in the country to offer the program under which manufacturers' U.S. warranties were doubled by up to one year and items were insured against loss, fire, theft, and damage for up to 90 days from the date of purchase.

The Numbers on Checks

You've seen them. They look like large fractions in the upper-right-hand corners of checks. You know that each financial institution has its own number, and you know what your institution's number is. But do you know what they mean and how they came into being?

These numbers look like fractions because they consist of two separate sets. The top set is the American Bankers Association (ABA) transit number. The bottom number is the Federal Reserve routing symbol.

Transit, which refers to the important process of sending checks to the financial institutions on which they are drawn for payment, is a complicated process that takes a great deal of time in every institution. The numerical transit system, adopted by the ABA in 1911, was designed to make this awesome task easier. The fact that the same numerical system is still in use is a tribute to those who designed it.

The system works as follows. The top figures consist of two parts—3-1, for example. The first number in the example, 3, is called a *prefix* number. The rules for prefix numbers are:

- Numbers 1 through 49 are assigned to cities.
- Numbers 50 through 58 are eastern states.
- Number 59 is Hawaii.
- Numbers 60 through 69 are southeastern states.
- Numbers 70 through 79 are central states.
- Numbers 80 through 88 are southwestern states.
- Number 89 is Alaska.
- Numbers 90 through 99 are western states.
- Number 101 is for various territories, American Samoa, the Caroline Islands, Guam, Mariana Island, Marshall Islands, Midway, Puerto Rico, Virgin Islands, and Wake Island.

Thus, in the example, the prefix number 3 applies to a city. Specifically, it is the number for Philadelphia. The second number, the 1, is the number that was assigned to a specific financial institution in Philadelphia. The transit number 3-1 refers to CoreStates Bank, N.A.

Consider another example, the transit number 70-138. The 70 refers to the state of Illinois. The number 138 was assigned to a bank in Belleville, Illinois. Thus, 70-138 is the transit number for Magna Bank of Illinois.

The *routing symbol* is the bottom part of the "fraction." This figure has three parts, although it appears to be written as one number. The first digit in a three-digit number or the first two digits in a four-digit number refer to the Federal Reserve district. The next digit describes the Federal Reserve Bank or branch serving the area where the financial institution on which the check is drawn is located. The last digit has two purposes. It further locates the institution geographically, and it also indicates which checks are receivable for immediate credit and which are receivable for deferred credit when they reach the Fed in that area.

For example, below CoreStates Bank's 3-1, the number 310 appears. It is written like this: $\frac{3-1}{310}$. The bottom number means the following: 3 is the Federal Reserve Bank of Philadelphia, 1 is the main office of that FRB (it has no branches), 0 means checks are presented in Philadelphia for immediate credit.

In the other example, the number 810 appears below the 70-138. The 8 refers to the Federal Reserve Bank of St. Louis. The 1 refers to the fact that checks clear through the main office of that Fed. The 0 tells you that checks are presented in St. Louis for immediate credit.

Here are the routing numbers:

Federal Reserve District	Bank Number	Savings Institution or Credit Union Number
Boston	01	21
New York City	02	22
Philadelphia	03	23
Cleveland	04	24
Richmond, VA	05	25
Atlanta	06	26
Chicago	07	27
St. Louis	08	28
Minneapolis	09	29
Kansas City, MO	10	30
Dallas	11	31
San Francisco	12	32

You can find an institution's routing symbol in any complete financial institution directory. These symbols and numbers were conceived and assigned long before the use of high-speed computers for check clearing was considered, but they make such clearing much easier.

Magnetic ink character recognition (MICR), developed by the ABA and put into use in 1959, is a common language that financial institutions use in processing checks. MICR numbers are printed across the bottom of almost all checks. The special numerals from zero to nine were designed to enable electronic sorter-readers to quickly and accurately read the figures and sort the checks. As pointed out in Chapter 18, MICR numbers that appear on checks do not reflect light as normal printing does. Thus, shiny MICR numbers may indicate that a check is counterfeit.

Before checks are distributed to customers for their use, the MICR numbers that have been printed on them include the routing number, the financial institution number, the customer's account number, and the number of the check. After the check has been written, the MICR dollar amount is imprinted on the check by the first institution that processes it.

Truncation

No discussion of checking accounts would be complete without a mention of "truncation." Truncation means to shorten by cutting off, and financial institutions use the word to mean storing checks instead of returning them to depositors, thus "shortening" the checking account service. Customers seem more willing to accept nonreturn of canceled checks when their institutions put heavy advertising emphasis on free check storage along with the assurance that should a customer need a check, it can be quickly located, photocopied, and sent to him or her.

Why does truncation appeal to financial institutions? Here are some of the reasons:

- Each year, many billions of checks are processed in America by financial institutions. This costs a great deal in time and money.
- Truncation reduces time spent in stuffing statements with canceled checks.
- Truncation reduces equipment costs for storage and filing devices.
- Primarily, truncation reduces growing postage costs because statements require only minimum postage without the bulk of enclosed canceled checks.

With truncation, every check is numbered, in sequence, as most checks already are. The financial institution prints out a statement showing what checks have been paid, which also indicates, by number, what checks in the numbered sequence have not yet cleared. Using the check register, the customer can then reconcile his or her statement.

Some financial institutions are also replacing traditional checking account statements with abbreviated statements produced by imaging systems.

With "image statements," customers receive miniature copies of the checks that they write each month. Institutions that use this type of system report that they have been able to streamline their operations, cut postage costs, and increase their fee income.

SAVINGS ACCOUNTS

Savings accounts had already been in existence for 600 years when Moses led his people out of Egypt. Clay tablets that date back to 2000 B.C. show entries regarding the deposit of gold and silver by Babylonians in a depository temple. Ancient Roman bankers started the payment of interest on savings. Savings accounts have been around for a very long time.

Time Deposits

Savings accounts are called *time* deposits. Customers may have to give notice of intent to withdraw funds and allow a certain time to elapse before receiving the funds. Under the Federal Reserve regulation, this time is set at not less than 30 days. Financial institutions have not actually used this privilege of delay with regular savings accounts for many years, but in the event of bad economic times, it would be a safeguard since it would allow the institutions to liquidate investments in time and make payments.

Savings accounts are not the only kind of time deposits. Certificates of deposit and special-notice accounts of many types are also time deposits. In each case, either notice of withdrawal or a specific maturity date is required.

Why People Save

Anything as ancient as the practice of saving money that has survived and is still flourishing must be doing so for good reasons. Four thousand years ago, or today, people saved or are saving in financial institutions for two important reasons: to accumulate a money reserve against future possible needs and to provide for the safety of their funds. People could accomplish the first goal by keeping their money under a mattress or in a sugar bowl. Indeed, many have tried it, and some have succeeded. But why risk losing carefully saved money to fire or theft? When savings are kept in a financial institution, they are safe.

Savings accounts have a real value in our society today. Specifically, they:

- Provide a safe place for anyone to accumulate money.
- Stabilize our economy by teaching thrift.

- Help people to save for their future plans.
- Allow financial institutions to lend needed funds to various businesses.
- Help fight inflation.

This last point is important. Savings do offset inflation for individuals. Some people say, "If the rate of inflation is higher than the interest on my savings account, I'm losing money." Theoretically, that may be true, but it is poor logic. How much will the person lose if he or she saves nothing at all? In five years, how much will such a person have compared to the person who saves regularly? Theoretically, you can beat inflation with shrewd investing, but bad choices may cause you to lose everything. The wise person will save to prepare for what an uncertain future may bring.

Savings Do Grow

Financial institutions pay interest on savings because they are, in effect, *borrowing* money from the depositor. True, they do ensure his or her safety of funds, but at the same time, they reserve the right to invest those funds for profit and to pay the depositor a part of that profit as interest. This payment of interest is an incentive to deposit money in a savings account.

In the past, Federal Reserve Regulation Q set the maximum legal interest rate on regular savings accounts, but under the Depository Institutions Deregulation Act of 1980 as passed by Congress, this regulation was phased out by March 31, 1986, after which rates became competitive.

Many people look at interest rates as short-term factors that have little influence on their savings. They may ask, "Even if the interest rate were as high as 10 percent, how much could that add to my savings? On $100 that means only $10." However, this figure does not take *compounding* into consideration. For example, each dollar saved today will grow, with daily compounding of interest, to $1.75 in 10 years at 5.5 percent. The saver should also consider the benefit of compounding on regular deposits. One dollar saved each year for 10 years, with monthly compounding and interest of 5.5 percent, will grow to $13.69.

To illustrate the benefits of compound interest, explain to savers and potential savers the Rule of 72, which states that the effect of compounding on a one-time deposit may be estimated by dividing 72 by the interest rate. The result shows approximately how many years it takes for the money to double by compounding. For example, at 5.5 percent interest, a deposit will double in 13 years. In order to maximize the effect of compounding, people should begin saving as early as possible and should continue to save on a regular basis. Here is a brief chart to illustrate the Rule of 72:

Rate	Years to Double
3%	24
4	18
4.5	16
5	14.4
6	12
7	10.3
8	9

Truth-in-Savings

The Truth-in-Savings Act is a regulation that became effective in mid-1993. Its purpose is to enable depositors to determine more easily what their interest-bearing deposit accounts yield and to compare their earnings with what other financial institutions are paying. Included in the law are the requirements that financial institutions:

- Calculate interest on a daily basis on the full amount in the account.
- Disclose a uniformly computed "annual percentage yield" (APY) on each account, the period covered, the minimum balance required to achieve that yield, and the minimum balance needed to open the account. The APY is the interest earned on $100 for a 365-day period, expressed as a percentage and rounded to the nearest two decimal points. For example, an APY of 4.5 percent would earn $4.50 for each $100 that is on deposit.
- Disclose any fees that may have an effect on the yield and any penalties charged for early withdrawals.
- Include information on statements about the yield earned, the amount of interest paid, fees that must be paid, and the length of the reporting period.

In addition, financial institutions will not be allowed to advertise that accounts are free for which they require a minimum balance, charge transaction fees, or allow only a limited number of transactions.

Consumer advocates are pleased with the law because it allows people to comparison shop among financial institutions for the best deal.

Types of Savings Accounts

Savings accounts are many and varied, but they can generally be categorized as follows:

Regular savings accounts. Designed for individuals, these accounts are the most common. Deposits and withdrawals, which can be made at any time for any amount, are posted in the customer's passbook each time a transaction is made. Many financial institutions offer no-passbook accounts and send out periodic statements to their customers showing the deposits, withdrawals, and interest paid during the period.

Certificates of deposit (CDs). A CD is a receipt issued in the name of the customer attesting to the fact that he or she has a certain amount of money on deposit that the person agrees to leave in the financial institution for a stipulated period of time. At the end of this period, the certificate matures and may be cashed in. Penalties of lost interest are charged for early withdrawal. The period of time required varies from 30 days up to eight or more years. Interest rates are based on the law of supply and demand and vary frequently, with the longer-term and/or higher-denomination CDs commanding the highest rates.

Money market deposit accounts (MMDAs). In order to compete with money market mutual funds, financial institutions are authorized to offer MMDAs, which are insured, unlike money market mutual funds, which are not. They are available to all types of depositors. A minimum opening deposit and a minimum average daily balance for each calendar month—often $1,000—is required, with some institutions paying higher interest rates for accounts with higher balances. Although there are no restrictions on the number or size of in-person withdrawals that a customer may make, only three third-party checks may be written per month, often for a specified minimum amount. Depending on the institution, interest rates may change daily or may be established for as long as a month, and a fee may or may not be charged for account maintenance.

Club accounts. Christmas or Hanukkah club and vacation club accounts are a form of forced savings by which customers can save for holiday or vacation expenses. Using a coupon system, club account customers place periodic deposits of specified amounts in their accounts. Withdrawals are not permitted; instead, a check for the entire amount deposited is mailed to the customer at the end of the savings period. This is the traditional club account; however, some financial institutions offer passbook club accounts of various types that earn regular savings interest and that can be continued from year to year. These special-purpose accounts are essentially regular savings accounts.

Nondeposit Investment Products

Annuities are a form of savings that are not insured against loss. They have been described as "insurance in reverse." Usually, the buyer, or the annuitant, pays in a lump sum, then on maturity receives the amount that has accumulated in a lump sum or in regular payments on a lifetime basis or for some other guaranteed period of time. Earnings grow tax-free until payout begins. Since many annuities are purchased for retirement, the annuitant is usually in a lower tax bracket by the time those payments are received. There is no limit on the size of the contributions that can be made.

Because of their tax-deferred earnings and because they satisfy a need for future additional income and are sound savings and investment vehicles, annuities appeal to the 50-plus market. They can provide lifetime income pay-outs that help to ensure that the customer will always receive a monthly check and will never outlive his or her income.

Many financial institutions offer their customers mutual funds as well as annuities. However, under guidelines from the Office of the Comptroller of the Currency and the Federal Deposit Insurance Corporation, financial institution employees who accept deposits are barred from selling investment products. But they can make referrals to authorized, licensed sales representatives. In fact, many of the institutions that offer these products provide referral training for their tellers.

Financial institutions are required to tell their customers who invest in mutual funds that the money is not insured by the FDIC, and many of them ask their customers to sign a statement acknowledging this fact. These customers should also understand that the investments can fluctuate in principal and yield. The FDIC also requires that the sales representatives refrain from recommending investment products until they've learned that a prospective investor's financial condition and objectives are appropriate.

In addition, national institutions that are located in towns with fewer than 5,000 people are permitted to sell insurance. This is an advantage for those that do so because they have access to a large number of prospects among their customers. Some of the types of insurance that financial institutions offer are life, health, and disability; auto and homeowner's; and commercial property and casualty insurance.

IRAs and Keogh Accounts

IRAs, or Individual Retirement Accounts, are for all employed persons and their non-wage-earning spouses. Keogh accounts are for self-employed people who pay self-employment tax and earn income for work performed. Most employees of these self-employed people must also be covered under Keogh. In both cases, savers are permitted to begin withdrawing money at age $59\frac{1}{2}$ and must begin to do so by age $70\frac{1}{2}$.

If money is withdrawn before age 59 1/2, a 10 percent penalty tax is due. However, starting in 1997, no penalty is charged for IRA withdrawals that are used to pay medical expenses that exceed 7.5 percent of a taxpayer's adjusted gross income or that are used by certain unemployed people to pay medical insurance premiums. If a person wishes to begin making withdrawals from an IRA before age 59 1/2 without having to pay the penalty tax, he or she is permitted to do so if the money is withdrawn in "substantially equal periodic payments" during that person's life expectancy and if such withdrawals are made for five years or until age 59 1/2, whichever is longer.

A qualified person may deposit up to 100 percent of his or her earned income or $2,000, whichever is less, in an IRA each year. In addition, starting in 1997, two-income couples as well as single-income couples may contribute up to $4,000 per year. In the past, a single-income couple could not contribute more than $2,250 to an IRA.

Interest that is earned in an IRA can accumulate on a tax-deferred basis until the funds are withdrawn. Prior to the change in the law in 1986, all those who contributed to an IRA could deduct the entire contribution from their taxable income. Since 1987, however, some IRA contributors are permitted to deduct the full amount contributed, some can only deduct a portion of that amount, and some are not allowed to deduct any of it. The rules are as follows:

1. Those who do not have employee retirement plan coverage—and, for those filing jointly whose spouse also has no coverage—still may make a fully deductible contribution to an IRA, regardless of income. A married person who files singly may deduct his or her entire contribution if he or she has no retirement plan coverage, regardless of whether or not the employed spouse is covered.

2. Those who do have employee retirement plan coverage must follow deductibility rules that depend on their adjusted gross income, as shown here:

Adjusted Gross Income of Those		Contribution
Filing Jointly	Filing Singly	Deductibility
$40,000 or less	$25,000 or less	Fully deductible
$40,000–$50,000	$25,000–$35,000	Partially deductible
Above $50,000	Above $35,000	Not deductible

The amount that may be contributed to a Keogh depends on which of three variations the self-employed person chooses. In a "money-purchase" Keogh, the individual must contribute a fixed percentage of earnings each year, up to a maximum of 20 percent of net income or $30,000, whichever is less. Under a "profit-sharing" Keogh, he or she may or may not contribute each year, up to a maximum of 13.04 percent of net income or $30,000, whichever is less. The third option involves a combination of the two plans. The entire amount of the contribution is tax deductible, and earnings grow on a tax-deferred basis.

The person who contributes to a Keogh plan can accumulate tax-deductible savings during high-earning years and pay taxes on them at a later date, when lowered earnings plus additional exemptions for age will result in substantial tax savings. This is also true for IRA contributors whose contributions are deductible. Even for those who may not deduct contributions, IRA deposits as well as Keogh deposits have the advantage of growing on a tax-deferred basis, accentuating the multiplier effect of compound interest.

In spite of their obvious advantages, these plans have not been taken advantage of by everyone who is eligible. One reason is that some people intend to make annual deposits but at the last minute find they haven't put any money aside. Retirement-plan customers would be wise to save in a variable-rate IRA that will accept weekly or periodic deposits. In this way, taxes do not have to be paid on the interest that is earned as would be required for a regular savings account.

LOANS

Tellers are so accustomed to seeing money come in in the form of deposits and seeing it go out in the form of withdrawals or cashed checks that they often forget the many dollars that go "out" of the financial institution to make loans. Loan dollars are important. It is the interest paid on loans that makes up the major portion of income for most institutions and provides the money for meeting its expenses—including tellers' salaries.

Commercial Loans

Commercial loans are made by financial institutions to business enterprises to finance the production, distribution, or manufacture of goods or services.

These loans are usually short-term; that is, they are payable at a specified time ranging from 30 days to six months or payable on demand. Typically, commercial loans are arranged for periods of either 30, 60, or 90 days.

Commercial loans may be *secured* or *unsecured*. For example, an institution may require a relatively inexperienced business or one with a less-than-excellent financial statement to put up collateral for the loan, such as equipment or inventory. This is an example of a *secured* loan. Most commercial loans, however, are made by financial institutions based on their analysis of the customer's ability to repay. Such a loan is *unsecured*.

Though terminology may differ slightly from one institution to another, commercial loans are usually not installment-type loans. Commercial loans are due to be paid in full on the day the note comes due. In certain cases, the institution may agree in advance to accept a partial payment and then reset the loan for the balance due, but this creates a new loan and is not an installment payment.

Consider the following case:

Jones Distributors Company sells toys, both retail and wholesale. Christmas time imposes a terrific strain on its facilities. It is necessary that the company ship toys to retailers starting in September and that it keep an extra large inventory on hand until late December to meet retail and wholesale requirements. To do this, the company arranges a commercial loan for 90 days for $100,000 in mid-August. In mid-November, as previously arranged, it uses a portion of the money it has so far received in sales to pay back $50,000 and makes a new loan for the balance. In mid-February, it will pay the balance. In the meantime, Jones Distributors has had the use of a great deal of extra working capital on which it can earn a profit.

In this typical type of commercial loan, the financial institution benefited from the payment of interest. The borrower had extra money to put to work, which not only earned greater profits for it, but created jobs in the community, added to the tax income of the various governments, and indirectly helped all of the other retailers that Jones Company supplied.

Commercial loans are vitally important in our economy. Directly or indirectly, they affect every aspect of the production and distribution of goods and services in our country.

Installment Loans

A personal installment loan is one in which an agreement is made that the borrower will repay the money lent, plus the interest charged, over a period of time in a series of regular payments, usually monthly. Most installment loans are made to finance automobiles, but other common purposes for which money is borrowed include home modernization, educational expenses, seasonal bills, medical expenses, purchase of appliances, and payment of taxes. Any good reason for needing money, such as those just listed, is a good reason for an installment loan.

State laws and the policies of financial institutions vary, but generally anyone may get a personal loan who:

1. Is of legal age and able to make a contract;
2. Has a good credit history, which would include having borrowed before with a good record of repayments; and
3. Has a good job with a steady income.

In addition, it helps if the person owns his or her own home, since the financial institution could go against the equity in it if the loan should become delinquent. In the case of someone with a marginal credit rating, the institution may still be willing to make the loan if another person with acceptable qualifications is willing to guarantee it. Most financial institutions find that over 90 percent of their loan applicants get exactly what they request. There is one type of loan that most institutions refuse to make, however, because it is simply too costly. That type of loan is one for a very small amount. This is because it would cost an institution more to do a credit check and set up the necessary bookkeeping on such a loan than it would earn in interest.

Mortgage Loans

Many people can afford to pay cash when they buy a new washer, dryer, or other major appliance. Some can even sit down and write a check when they buy a new car. But there are very few people who don't have to borrow when they buy a home. Only a very small percentage of home buyers can produce the large amount of cash that this investment requires.

The most common way to finance a home is with a mortgage loan. Many people erroneously think that the word "mortgage" means "loan," but it doesn't. A mortgage is a legal document that pledges property as security *for* a loan. Should the borrower fail to repay the loan as promised, the mortgage gives the lender (or mortgagee) the right to take the property to satisfy the loan. Obviously, any financial institution holding a mortgage would only foreclose—that is, take the property—as a last resort. Financial institutions do not want to be in the real estate business, nor do they like to see people lose their homes.

For this reason, mortgage lenders exercise a great deal of caution when considering a mortgage application. Most importantly, they must be satisfied that the applicant has the capacity to repay the loan satisfactorily. To encourage lenders to make certain loans, two government agencies, the Federal Housing Administration and the Veterans Administration, guarantee a certain percentage of the amount of a mortgage loan made to qualified borrowers. With lower down payments and interest rates, these loans, commonly called FHA and GI loans respectively, along with the traditional "conventional" mortgage, make up the bulk of home mortgage loans.

Almost all home mortgage loans have certain features in common. The borrower is required to make a certain down payment based on a percentage of the sale price of the property. And the borrower repays a portion of the principal along with any interest due so that the loan is self-amortizing. Thus, the loan is paid in full at the end of the term.

Unfortunately, rising real estate prices have made home ownership increasingly difficult for many families. In addition, financial institutions are becoming increasingly reluctant to make a commitment of 20 to 30 years for a mortgage at a fixed rate. Some loans put on the books years before at very low rates have cost institutions money during times when savings interest has been considerably higher.

Thus, the banking industry has responded with alternatives. For example, many offer *adjustable rate mortgages* (ARMs). Under this type of mortgage plan, the lender usually offers a lower initial interest rate than is being charged for fixed-rate mortgage loans. The rate is then adjusted periodically, typically every six months, every year, or every three years, with the mortgagor's monthly payment changing accordingly. The rate adjustment is based on an index of money market changes. Financial institutions like ARMs because they offer long-term protection against inflationary interest trends. A kind of hybrid mortgage loan that combines adjustable and fixed rates in a single loan is also available through some lenders.

Likewise, *graduated payment mortgages*, or GPMs, are being made by some institutions. Here, the payments start low and increase gradually for a period of several years, finally leveling off for the balance of the term.

Prospective mortgage customers should realize that the sale price of a home isn't the only cost involved in purchasing it. There may be any or all of the following costs in addition: an appraisal fee, survey, title search, title insurance, tax stamps, recording fees, notary fee, attorney's fees, processing charges, credit surveys, property taxes, insurance premiums, as well as "points" charged by the lending institution. The term "points" refers to the number of percentage points charged against the value of the mortgage, in which case the full amount of the mortgage must be repaid even though less money is actually available because of the deduction. In other cases, the points might be payable in cash at the time of closing. For example, if a lender charges a new mortgage customer 3 points on a $100,000 mortgage, $3,000 would either be charged immediately or the cash available under the mortgage would be reduced to $97,000.

All of these additional costs mean that people who are contemplating buying a home shouldn't play it too closely when figuring their finances. If they barely have enough for a down payment or, as some people do, if they borrow the down payment, they're taking a real risk of running out of money. This is especially true considering the fact that most houses, even new ones, need some alterations or repairs almost at once; buyers must be ready to meet at least some of these expenses out of their own pockets.

Few people can afford a home without substantial financial assistance, and that's where mortgage loans come in. Even if your institution doesn't make mortgage loans directly, chances are it is still involved in helping to provide housing in the community. Some institutions that do not make mortgage loans to individuals do make construction loans to builders and then help arrange for individual mortgage money from another source when the properties are built.

No discussion of mortgages would be complete without a mention of *reverse mortgages*. Designed to provide cash for older homeowners who want to keep their homes but can't qualify for home equity loans, reverse mortgages provide monthly checks, a lump sum, or a line of credit to those whose property is completely paid off or nearly so. Depending on the homeowner's age and life expectancy, the reverse mortgage can amount to 30 percent to 80 percent of the equity in the home. The loan is repaid by selling the house after the homeowner dies or moves. At the beginning of 1996, the Federal National Mortgage Association (Fannie Mae) entered the reverse mortgage market, which greatly expanded the availability of these loans.

Home Equity Loans

As the tax-deductibility of interest expense was gradually reduced under federal tax laws, an innovative type of loan became more and more popular all across the country. Because the interest deductibility phase-out, completed by 1991, does not apply to mortgage loans, financial institutions began offering credit that is backed by mortgages on private residences. Called the home equity credit line, this type of loan includes the following features:

- A homeowner generally may borrow up to 90 percent of the appraised market value of his or her home, minus the amount due on the first mortgage. Thus, if a couple owns a home worth $100,000 and the balance due on their first mortgage is $20,000, they may be able to establish a home equity credit line of $72,000.
- Once the credit line is established, withdrawals, the minimum requirement for which vary from one institution to another, may be made via checks or, at some institutions, via debit cards. Amounts needed, up to the credit maximum, may be spent for any purpose.
- The accounts typically have a life of 10 to 15 years, and monthly payments usually must include a percentage of the principal, although some financial institutions allow interest-only payments.
- Interest rates, which are generally lower than those charged for home improvement loans, are usually based on the prime lending rate plus one or two percentage points. Closing costs and origination fees vary from one institution to another.
- Interest is tax-deductible on loans of up to $100,000 or the appraised market value of the house, whichever is less.

Although financial institution personnel are concerned about the possibility that some people may overspend and risk losing their homes, the nationwide heavy promotion of these tax-advantaged loans is bound to make them even more popular with consumers who find them to be a convenient, low-cost way to borrow money. In fact, under the 1988 Home Equity Consumer Protection Act, consumers must be given a Federal Reserve pamphlet that explains the risks, as well as information regarding a loan's terms and conditions. As a teller, you should learn the details about home equity loans offered by your institution and by others in your community.

Credit Ratings

Credit regulations ban denial of credit to anyone on the basis of age, religion, race, national origin, sex, marital status, or welfare status. They also require a potential lender to tell the would-be borrower why credit is refused. *However*, this doesn't mean, of course, that anyone can just automatically get a loan. People must still meet the criteria that financial institutions and other lenders traditionally have imposed—the ability and intent to repay the loan.

Although credit ratings are not of direct concern to you, as a teller, some of your customers who have questions may prefer to ask your advice rather than talk to a loan officer. Naturally, if the customer has a complicated problem, you should refer him or her to someone with definitive answers, but the data presented here can help you to answer some of the questions you will get.

The following is a checklist used by some financial institutions in rating applicants for installment credit. It illustrates what a loan officer looks for when considering an application and just how important the various factors are.

- How many years has the person owned a home?
  - ☐ Ten years or more (6 points).
  - ☐ Six to 10 years (4 points).
  - ☐ One to five years (2 points).
- Does he or she rent?
  - ☐ Same residence five years or longer (2 points).
  - ☐ Same residence two to five years (1 point).
- How long has the person held his or her present job?
  - ☐ Over 10 years (5 points).
  - ☐ Four to 10 years (3 points).
  - ☐ One to three years (2 points).
- What are his or her present obligations, excluding rent or mortgage?
  - ☐ Monthly obligations 25 percent or less of monthly income (5 points).
  - ☐ Monthly obligations 30 percent of monthly income (3 points).
  - ☐ Monthly obligations over 30 percent of monthly income (deduct 2 points).
- What are the person's credit references?
  - ☐ Satisfactory rating from a financial institution or loan company (2 points).
  - ☐ Satisfactory rating from a charge account or other installment credit over $100 (2 points).
- Extra considerations:
  - ☐ A satisfactory loan, open or closed, with this institution (2 points).
  - ☐ A checking account with this institution (1 point).
  - ☐ A savings account with this institution (1 point).

TOTAL POINTS _____

In general, a passing score would be 12 points. Obviously, a recent graduate would have trouble obtaining this score; but often the financial institution will stretch a point to help newcomers, newlyweds, and recent graduates if their overall credit background isn't impaired and if they show signs of a stable future. On the other hand, a person could get a high score and be turned down if he or she had a terrible credit reference from a recent loan that went bad. This checklist is just a guide to the probable credit rating of average people applying for an installment loan.

Prime Rate

The prime rate is the interest rate charged to first-class *commercial* borrowers. It is usually the lowest rate available to anyone, and it varies from one financial institution to another.

The prime rate goes up when there is a greater demand for loans than there is money available. This means that all sorts of institutions that make loans are hard pressed to meet the demand. As a matter of fact, financial institutions try to keep the prime rate down as much as possible but must respond to an increasing cost of doing business.

A high prime rate doesn't just mean that people and businesses are paying more for the money they borrow. It also means that money is harder to get or "tight." This means that many institutions will do much stricter credit analyses of the applications and statements of individuals and firms, will reject more marginal credit risks, and will look for deposit accounts from would-be borrowers. In general, loan availability is closely tied to deposits. When deposits are up and financial institutions have plenty of money, loans are easier to get and cost less.

The Community Reinvestment Act

The purpose of the Community Reinvestment Act (CRA), a law that was put into effect in 1977, is to make certain that financial institutions extend credit, especially for housing, to low- and moderate-income communities from which they get deposits. In 1989, changes in the CRA law were made under the Financial Institutions Reform, Recovery, and Enforcement Act (FIRREA) that require institutions' compliance ratings to be made available to the public 30 days after they receive an evaluation from the regulatory agency that conducts an examination.

Ratings are termed "outstanding," "satisfactory," "needs to improve," and "substantial noncompliance." Financial institutions' records are taken into consideration when they make application to open or relocate a branch or to merge with or acquire another institution. They must also prepare a CRA statement about each community they serve, establish a public comment file about their performance, and post a CRA notice in the lobby of each of their offices.

As a teller, you probably receive training in the basics of the Community Reinvestment Act. This is because it is important for you to be familiar with it and to know how to respond to requests for information and for copies of your institution's CRA statement and public comment file. It is also important for you to handle such requests in a friendly, polite manner and to learn all you can about how your institution is responding to the specific needs of the communities in which it operates.

SAFE DEPOSIT SERVICE

Every year, America's variety and discount stores sell thousands of small metal boxes with little pressed metal locks and keys. Trusting but unthinking people fill them with valuable papers, family jewelry, mementos, and sometimes with a supply of "rainy-day" cash. In addition, most people who use such boxes hide them from possible burglars by putting them under their beds. And, just to make sure they won't lose the key, they attach it right to the handle of the box.

Even if they hide the key, a burglar isn't going to worry about it. The thief will simply thank them for putting valuables so neatly in one place, take the box, and open it later with a screwdriver. Should a fire break out, the thin metal of the box will concentrate the heat just as an oven does and guarantee the destruction of the contents.

The alternative to this protection system is a safe deposit box at a financial institution. Every family has valuables even if it isn't rich. (Did you ever try to replace a lost government document?) This means anyone with valuable papers needs a safe deposit box.

Basic Facts About Safe Deposit Service

Suppose you could say to a customer, "How would you like to have your own private little vault at our institution, to which no one could have access but you, which would be safe from burglars, fire, prying eyes, and even your own carelessness—and for which we would charge you only pennies a day?" Many financial institutions make just this offer in the form of safe deposit service.

Putting gold, silver, or jewels on deposit for safekeeping at religious temples was one of the earliest forerunners of modern banking. Today, this service has become highly complex, with various rules, both state and federal, under which financial institutions operate. Here are the basic facts that you should know about the service:

Financial institutions make very little profit from safe deposit service.
It is offered for two reasons: to make complete financial service available, and to encourage the customer to maintain a more lasting relationship with the institution.

Financial institutions do not have any master or extra key that they can use to get into a box. No one has access to a box but the customer. If he or she loses the keys or fails to pay the rental and cannot be reached, a locksmith must drill the old lock out of the box and install a new one.

The institution is responsible for the contents of the box if it allows an unauthorized person to have access. Because the contents are not deposits in the institution, they are *not* insured. However, the renter may have some coverage on the contents under his or her homeowner's insurance policy. It is very important to keep in mind that the institution is responsible if, in fact, it allows unauthorized access. This is the reason for all of the strict precautions in regard to admission to a box and the control of keys to unrented boxes.

No single employee of the institution should have control of keys to a safe deposit box before it is rented. The reason is obvious. If someone later claims something is missing, it could become a case of whether or not the employee could have made a duplicate key and might involve a my-word-against-his situation. Proof of dual control protects the financial institution and the employees.

No employee of the institution should keep a key for a customer after a box is rented. Employees are often asked to do this. The customer may say, "I trust you, and I'm sure to lose my key. Please keep it for me." It's hard to say, "no," especially to a friend, but a firm "no" is the only correct answer. Friendship fades when a customer thinks that something is missing, and the person who kept the key may find himself or herself accused.

It is important that an access slip be signed each time a person gets his or her box. The signature should match the one on file. Many problems can be avoided if access records are strictly kept.

If an employee handles either the customer's key or box, he or she should never do so out of sight of the customer. NEVER seat the customer comfortably in a safe deposit booth, take his or her key, and go into the vault to get the box by yourself! That may seem like courteous service, but it's poor security. The customer should have possession of his or her key at all times, except when it is used to open the box, and that should be done in his or her full view. Then the customer should be handed the box at once. Do not leave the person's key in the lock while he or she goes into a booth. Relock the receptacle door and return the key as you hand him or her the box. Take the key back with the box and reopen the receptacle door to replace the box while the customer watches. And be sure to inspect the booth when the customer is ready to leave to see that nothing from the box has been left behind.

When a box is surrendered, thoroughly check, in the presence of the customer, to be sure that nothing has been left inside. When a renter gives up a box, have him or her turn over the keys and sign a release attesting to its surrender and the fact that all of its contents have been removed. A box should also be inspected to make sure that it is empty when it is about to be rented.

A safe deposit box is the best bargain in security a customer can get. Because you do follow security procedures and because burglars and fire can't get at the contents of a box, customers should use safe deposit service to protect their valuables and important papers. If income-producing papers are kept in the box, such as stock certificates or savings bonds, the rental fee is tax deductible on Schedule A, Form 1040.

What Should Be Kept in a Safe Deposit Box?

Safe deposit service is not intended simply for providing security for priceless jewelry, valuable stock certificates, or expensive coin or stamp collections. Everyone accumulates irreplaceable documents that can be safeguarded in no better place than a safe deposit box. Included should be copies of government or court-issued documents—marriage certificates, birth certificates, deeds, divorce papers, military discharge papers, auto titles, and adoption and citizenship papers. Irreplaceable items, such as baby and childhood pictures, can also be protected in this way.

Everyone should periodically update the contents of his or her box and personal records in general. Discarding useless or outdated things adds to efficiency. More important is adding copies of valuable new records that a person should protect.

The rule is simple. Any paper that would be difficult or impossible to replace or that could cause problems with the government or financial loss if it were missing should be included in a safe deposit box.

What Shouldn't Be Kept in a Safe Deposit Box?

Customers should also know which things to avoid keeping in their safe deposits boxes. Here's a list:

Cash. Some people think that keeping cash in a safe deposit box will avoid inheritance taxes. It won't. A state inventory of box contents is common, and the money will be taxed anyway. Extra cash should be kept in a savings account where it can earn interest.

Life insurance policies. It may take some time after a person dies to get the legal papers to open his or her box. In the meantime, the insurance claim cannot be filed. Insurance papers are not difficult to replace if lost or destroyed, so they don't need the protection of a box.

Wills. A copy of a will may be kept in a box, but it is also important that a member of the family or a friend or attorney also have one in case of delay in getting the box opened after death. Thus, keeping the only copy of a will in a safe deposit box could delay settlement of the estate.

"Now that we've got a sitter for the kids, where would you like to shop?"

Cemetery plot deeds. Again, time may pass before the box can be opened, and the deed to a plot is needed at once. The same is true for burial instructions.

Because safe deposit boxes in some states are sealed on the death of a renter, even when in joint name, many financial institutions recommend not only that replaceable papers that may be needed when the renter dies be kept elsewhere, but that a husband and wife have boxes in each individual name with important documents on the other person in their respective depositories. And their personal items should be kept in their own boxes to avoid paying estate taxes on such items that are kept in joint boxes. A person who is a principal in a closely held corporation, and this includes many doctors, lawyers, shop owners, and small businesspersons, can avoid having his or her box sealed on death by putting the safe deposit in the name of the corporation.

Safe Deposit Procedures

Financial institutions require positive identification of anyone renting a box. After establishing the identity of a would-be renter, the institution has him or her sign signature cards. A box may be rented in much the same way that a checking account is opened. In other words, it may be individual, joint, partnership, corporate, or organizational. In the latter three cases, a resolution or certificate of authority must be filed in addition to the signature cards.

After the box is rented, no one except the renter may open it, and that person may not do so until he or she has filled in an identification slip that includes his or her signature, the date and time of entry and exit, and the initials of the employee who gives the renter access.

The vault attendant will then trip the first of a dual locking system with the institution's *guard key*, and the customer will complete the procedure by opening the box with his or her key. Neither the financial institution nor the customer can open the box without the key of the other. If a locksmith must drill the box open for some reason, it is usually done in the presence of competent witnesses, and the contents are inventoried and verified.

Safe deposit service is vitally important to your customers, yet many of them don't know about it or understand it. If your institution provides this service, make sure you know the rental fees for the more popular size boxes; then let your customers know that for a very small fee they can get *real* safekeeping for their important papers and valuables.

TRUST SERVICES

Many financial institutions offer trust services. Whether or not yours is among them, it is important for you to know what these services are and who might use them.

Settling Estates

This is the most common trust service. When a person dies, someone must act as *executor* or *administrator* to see that the wishes of the deceased are carried out regarding the disposition of his or her property. For this reason, many people will name the trust department of a financial institution as executor in their wills. There are many advantages to this. First, it costs nothing until the estate is actually being administered, and then the fees charged by the institution are set by law at the same low rate any executor may charge. Second, a financial institution, unlike an individual who may be named, never dies or gets ill. Third, the institution can use its expert knowledge of taxes and investments on behalf of the beneficiaries of the estate.

Trust Administration and Guardianships

A trust exists when one person administers property and another person is entitled to the benefits received from the property. Various legal documents and proceedings create different types of trusts, but the important thing is that a person may authorize the financial institution to administer property that he or she owns for the benefit of others. An employer might do this by having an institution administer investments to benefit a profit-sharing plan for its employees. A trust might be established under a will whereby the person leaves property to be administered by the institution for the benefit of another person. There are many types of trusts.

A financial institution may also be named to act as guardian of the property of a minor or of a person who cannot care for his or her own interests. Guardians are appointed by a court that has jurisdiction in such matters.

Estate Planning

There are many other trust services not mentioned here, but an important one that must be listed is estate planning. Here, the financial institution, in conjunction with a person's attorney, will help develop a plan whereby his or her estate will function in accordance with that person's wishes with a minimum of expense, including taxes.

Although you will have little to do with trusts directly, you should know something about them. They are an interesting part of the banking business, and your customers may have questions about them.

SAVINGS BONDS

United States savings bonds were originally issued by the Treasury Department on May 1, 1941. Called "war bonds" when they were sold during World War II, the lowest denomination sold for $18.75, which the purchaser could redeem for $25 after maturity 10 years later. Savings stamps, sold during the war years, could be bought for as little as a dime apiece and for as much as $5. The stamps could be redeemed for a bond when the buyer had saved the amount of the purchase price. In the meantime, the stamps did not earn interest.

Savings bonds changed the savings habits of the nation. Based on patriotic duty, but paying rewards in cold cash, they offered an incentive to save. Thus, the "payroll savings plan," with payroll deductions, and the "bond-a-month plan," with automatic transfers from an account at a financial institution, came into being and helped many individuals and families to save and build a secure financial base.

Types of Bonds

Two types of savings bonds are currently offered for sale:

Series EE bonds. Formerly Series E bonds, this type is bought at a discount from the face amount and redeemed after maturity for the full face value. The difference is the interest earned by the buyer.

Series HH bonds. Formerly Series H bonds, this type is purchased for the face value, and the U.S. Treasury pays interest by check semiannually. They are available only by exchange of Series EE and older bonds.

U.S. Treasury Series EE bonds are sold in denominations of $50, $75, $100, $200, $500, $1,000, $5,000, and $10,000. The cost is half the face value. Thus, a $50 bond sells for $25. Series EE bonds may not be cashed in for the first six months after they are purchased. Under regulations that took effect in 1995, Series EE bonds issued *before* May 1, 1995, are guaranteed a fixed rate of interest if they are held for at least five years. Those held for more than five years earn the higher of 85 percent of the average yield of five-year Treasury notes or a guaranteed minimum that is retroactively calculated to the date they were purchased. The interest is credited either monthly or semiannually depending on the date the bonds were issued.

Series EE bonds issued *on or after* May 1, 1995, earn 85 percent of the average yield of six-month Treasury bills. Those held for more than five years, up to 17 years, earn 85 percent of the average yield of five-year Treasury notes. Bonds held longer than 17 years earn the rate that is in effect for the extended maturity period. The interest is credited twice a year, with the rates announced on May 1 and November 1. People who redeem bonds before a six-month period has elapsed lose that period's earnings.

Series EE bonds issued *on or after* May 1, 1997, earn 90 percent of the average yield of five-year Treasury notes during the preceding six months. The interest accrues monthly rather than twice a year. A three-month interest penalty is charged for those that are redeemed within five years.

Your institution should have U.S. Savings Bond Redemption Tables available so that you can determine your customers' bond values.

Series HH bonds are available in denominations of $500, $1,000, $5,000, and $10,000. Often used for retirement income, these bonds pay interest twice a year via direct deposit into the owner's account and federal taxes must be paid on that interest in the year it is received; however, federal income tax on the accrued interest from the EE bonds exchanged for the HH bonds can be deferred until the HH bonds are redeemed or mature.

The advantages U.S. savings bonds offer include the following:

- Interest rates, tied to the rates paid on other government securities, have become more competitive. The bonds don't cost anything to buy; no service charges or commissions are required.
- No state or local taxes are charged on the interest that has accrued. Owners can wait to pay federal taxes until the bonds are redeemed, or they can elect to treat the yearly increase in value as annual income.
- Bonds are backed by the U.S. government, and if they're lost, destroyed, or stolen, they can be replaced.
- Under the provisions of the Technical and Miscellaneous Revenue Act of 1988, the interest on Series EE bonds is totally exempt from federal taxes if the bonds were bought after December 31, 1989, and are used to pay for educational expenses in the year the bonds are redeemed. The money may be used to pay for tuition and fees for a bond owner's dependent child's higher education or for his or her own. Money spent for room, board, and books is not tax-exempt. Qualified technical schools as well as colleges and universities are in-

F I G U R E 24-1

Order Form for Series EE U.S. Savings Bonds (front side)

PD F 5263 Department of the Treasury Bureau of the Public Debt (Revised August 1993)	**ORDER FOR SERIES EE U.S. SAVINGS BONDS** OMB No. 1535-0084

PLEASE FOLLOW THE INSTRUCTIONS ON THE BACK WHEN COMPLETING THIS PURCHASE ORDER.

1. **OWNER OR FIRST-NAMED COOWNER (Bonds registered to)**

    Name

    Soc. Sec. No.

2. **BONDS TO BE DELIVERED "CARE OF"** (Do not complete this section unless name is different from the owner or first-named coowner in section 1 above.)

    Mail to:

3. **ADDRESS WHERE BONDS ARE TO BE DELIVERED**

    (NUMBER AND STREET OR RURAL ROUTE)

    (CITY OR TOWN)   (STATE)   (ZIP CODE)

4. **COOWNER OR BENEFICIARY** Coownership will be assumed if neither or if both blocks are checked (See #4 on back).
    The following person is to be named as   coowner   beneficiary

    Name

5. **BONDS ORDERED**

Denom.	Quantity	Issue Price	Total Issue Price	FOR AGENT USE ONLY
$ 50		X $ 25.00 = $		
$ 75		X $ 37.50 = $		
$ 100		X $ 50.00 = $		
$ 200		X $ 100.00 = $		
$ 500		X $ 250.00 = $		
$ 1,000		X $ 500.00 = $		
$ 5,000		X $ 2,500.00 = $		
$ 10,000		X $ 5,000.00 = $		
TOTAL ISSUE PRICE OF PURCHASE		$		AFFIXED AGENT STAMP CERTIFIES THAT TOTAL AMOUNT OF PURCHASE IS CORRECT

6. **DATE PURCHASE ORDER AND PAYMENT PRESENTED TO AGENT**

                                                                              (MO.)   (DAY)   (YR.)

7. **SIGNATURE**

    IF YOU NEED A GIFT CERTIFICATE, PLEASE ASK THE PERSON ACCEPTING THIS FORM TO PROVIDE ONE TO YOU.

    PURCHASER'S SIGNATURE

    (   )

    PURCHASER'S NAME, IF OTHER THAN OWNER OR FIRST-NAMED COOWNER. (Please print)   DAYTIME TELEPHONE NUMBER

    STREET ADDRESS (If not shown above)   CITY   STATE   ZIP CODE

    SEE INSTRUCTIONS FOR PRIVACY ACT AND PAPERWORK REDUCTION ACT NOTICE   FRB COPY

Series EE U.S. savings bonds, which are purchased through the Federal Reserve, can be bought at Federal Reserve banks or branches or ordered through financial institutions or company payroll savings plans.

F I G U R E 24–1

Order Form for Series EE U.S. Savings Bonds (back side)

INSTRUCTIONS FOR COMPLETING THE PURCHASE ORDER

1. **OWNER OR FIRST-NAMED COOWNER** (Bonds registered to). Clearly PRINT in-block letters the full name and social security account number of the owner or first-named coowner. If this is a gift bond purchase, use the owner's name and social security number (if available). If the owner's social security number is unavailable, use the purchaser's S.S.N. See example below.

Name J O H N T S M I T H

Soc. Sec. No. 1 2 3 — 4 5 — 6 7 8 9

Generally, only residents of the United States, its territories and possessions may be named on Series EE savings bonds. Bonds may be registered as follows:

   (a) Individuals in their own right - The bonds may be issued in the names of individuals (whether adults or minors) in single ownership, coownership, or beneficiary (P.O.D.) forms of registration.
   (b) Others - Bonds are also available in other forms of registration. Trust forms of registration must be submitted on Form PD F 5263-1.

---

2. **BONDS TO BE DELIVERED "CARE OF".** After "Mail to:" print the name to whom the bonds are to be delivered if different from the owner or first-named coowner shown in 1. above. If the same as in 1. above, leave blank.
   NOTE: This information will appear on the bond, but does not establish any ownership rights.

---

3. **ADDRESS WHERE BONDS ARE TO BE DELIVERED.** In all cases, print the address where the bonds are to be delivered.
   NOTE: This information will appear on the bond.

---

4. **COOWNER OR BENEFICIARY:** If you wish to name a coowner or beneficiary on the bonds, check the appropriate box to indicate the form of registration desired and print the person's name.

   If you name a coowner: The bonds may be cashed by either coowner. The name of a living coowner cannot be eliminated without the written consent of that coowner.

   If you name a beneficiary: The bonds may not be cashed by the beneficiary during the lifetime of the owner. The name of a beneficiary can be eliminated without the beneficiary's consent.

---

5. **BONDS ORDERED.** Indicate next to the appropriate denomination the number of bonds being purchased; the total price involved for each denomination (no. of bonds X issue price); and the total amount of purchase. If you fail to indicate the denomination preferred, issue will be made with the fewest number of pieces which equal the total amount of purchase.

---

6. **DATE PURCHASE ORDER AND PAYMENT PRESENTED TO AGENT.** Indicate the date on which the purchase order and payment is presented (received) and accepted by the bank or other financial institution authorized to act as an agent of the Treasury Department.

---

7. **SIGNATURE.** Please sign this purchase order and print your name and address if it does not appear in the registration of the bonds. In order to promptly resolve any problems connected with this purchase order, also please provide a telephone number where you ordinarily may be reached Monday through Friday, from 9 a.m. to 5 p.m.

NOTE: Upon completion, submit purchase order and total amount of purchase to a financial institution authorized to receive savings bond orders. ALLOW ABOUT THREE WEEKS FOR PROCESSING.

NOTICE UNDER THE PRIVACY AND PAPERWORK REDUCTION ACTS

The collection of the information you are requested to provide on this form is authorized by 31 U.S.C. Ch. 31 relating to the public debt of the United States. The furnishing of a social security number, if requested, is also required by Section 6109 of the Internal Revenue Code (26 U.S.C. 6109).

The purpose for requesting the information is to enable the Bureau of the Public Debt and its agents to issue securities, process transactions, make payments, identify owners and their accounts, and provide reports to the Internal Revenue Service. Furnishing the information is voluntary; however, without the information Public Debt may be unable to process transactions.

Information concerning securities holdings and transactions is considered confidential under Treasury regulations (31 CFR, Part 323) and the Privacy Act. This information may be disclosed to a law enforcement agency for investigation purposes; courts and counsel for litigation purposes; others entitled to distribution or payment; agents and contractors to administer the public debt; agencies or entities for debt collection or to obtain current addresses for payment; agencies through approved computer matches; Congressional offices in response to an inquiry by the individual to whom the record pertains; as otherwise authorized by law or regulation.

We estimate that it will take you about 10 minutes to complete this form. This includes the time it will take to read the instructions, gather the necessary facts and fill out the form. If you have comments or suggestions regarding the above estimate or ways to simplify this form, forward correspondence to Bureau of the Public Debt, Forms Management Officer, Parkersburg, WV 26106-1328 and the Office of Management and Budget, Paperwork Reduction Project 1535-0084, Washington, DC 20503. **DO NOT SEND completed form to either of the above addresses; instead, send to the correct address shown in the instructions on this form.**

cluded. At the time of purchase, buyers must be 24 years of age or older, and the bonds must be bought in the buyer's name. This benefit gradually phases out for people who are in higher-income brackets. The allowable ceiling is increased for inflation on a yearly basis.

Savings plans at financial institutions usually offer more benefits to most people, but for those with special needs, savings bonds are worth considering.

DIRECT DEPOSIT SERVICE

Because it is much less costly for the government to utilize a direct-deposit system for issuing payments compared to sending individual checks to each recipient, and because problems created by missing or stolen checks are thus greatly reduced, direct deposit, having been strongly encouraged, has become increasingly popular. As pointed out in Chapter 16, those who signed up to receive Social Security benefits after August 1, 1996, are required to use direct deposit, and, beginning in 1998, all recipients who have an account at a financial institution will receive their payments that way.

Some Social Security check recipients, however, would rather not have their checks deposited directly because they look forward to the trip to their financial institution as a break in their routine. They don't realize that direct deposit via electronic funds transfer can mean:

1. Virtual elimination of checks stolen from mailboxes—a common occurrence.
2. A decreased chance of robbery or mugging after they leave the financial institution with a cashed check.
3. Elimination of lost or misplaced checks before they are cashed or deposited.
4. No need to delay trips or vacations while waiting for checks to arrive.
5. No need to go out in inclement weather to cash or deposit checks.
6. Elimination of red tape formerly caused by changing addresses.
7. For those who still keep their money hidden at home, direct deposit means the safety of money in a financial institution.
8. Immediate access to their funds on the day they are deposited.

This much security and convenience can be very beneficial for older customers. So when a person comes to your window to cash or deposit one of these checks, suggest that he or she sign a completed Direct Deposit Authorization Form. Stress their personal safety and that of their money. Explain that problems with any individual account are unlikely and that direct deposit is a valuable customer service that is here to stay.

The government has had a great degree of success in getting other recipients, such as those in active employment or in the military, to accept direct deposit. While it has been leading the way in the direct deposit of checks, many companies are also making direct deposit of employees' paychecks—sometimes with one master check or even an authorized transfer. Some financial institutions even pay their employees with a direct credit to their employees' accounts.

Direct deposit makes sense because it reduces check volume and the cost of operations. In the years ahead, it is a service that is bound to grow even more.

STEPS TOWARD EFTS

Computers have changed the routine systems of banking and business in general. They perform high-speed mathematical or logical computations. In addition, they may store, correlate, and process into useful terms information that has been fed into them.

Computers have opened two avenues to financial institutions. First, by using computers properly, they are able to perform the bookkeeping and record-keeping functions necessary to their business more quickly, accurately, and efficiently than before. Second, by utilizing the unique capabilities of computers, they are able to offer their customers new and expanded services.

Automation in banking is definitely necessary! A banking expert once predicted that unless automation replaced a large portion of the volume of checks written in this country, within a few years, well *over 40 percent of the total labor force* would be required for check processing alone. Checks, of course, have made our prosperous society possible. The government couldn't possibly print, nor could people carry, the amount of money that would be needed to replace all checks. Yet, if we are to reduce the enormous flood of paperwork that checks create, they must be cut in number.

Electronic funds transfer systems, or EFTS, are part of the answer. And computers have made EFTS possible. The direct deposit of government payment and company paychecks discussed in the foregoing section is a good example of the effective use of EFTS.

Another use of EFTS is the electronic verification of personal checks in retail stores. Although the writing of a check is still involved, the number of returned checks is dramatically reduced in stores where these machines are available to customers who wish to pay for their purchases by check.

Also available in some stores are point-of-sale terminals that allow a customer to pay for purchases with the use of a debit card, which automatically debits his or her account at a financial institution and credits the account of the merchant.

The electronic payment of bills is another effective use of EFTS. A customer who uses this service authorizes the financial institution to make an automatic transfer of funds from his or her account to that of a payee for such things as rent, mortgage payments, and other fixed monthly expenses. Many people, however, object to the idea of having their bills paid automatically through EFTS. What happens when a person wants to hold a bill for a while? To take advantage of a grace period, for instance? Or while a claim for defective merchandise is settled? Or until payday rolls around? How can a computer be programmed to have the flexibility and control that a person enjoys when he or she writes his or her own checks to pay bills? In practice, therefore, a substantial volume of checks is likely to be around for a long time.

Electronic cash cards are also growing in use. As mentioned in the Introduction to this book, plastic smart cards, sometimes called stored-value cards, are available in various denominations, usually $10, $20, $50, and $100 amounts. When a card is used to make a purchase, a terminal deducts the amount spent and the remaining value is re-encoded onto the card. When the card's total value has been spent, it may be thrown away, or the card may be capable of being reloaded with additional cash value. Prepaid telephone calling cards are also available, which allow consumers to pay in advance for future telephone calls.

Automated Tellers

One of the most useful machines involved in banking automation is the automated teller machine, or ATM. ATMs are usually set in the outside wall of a financial institution, though in many areas institutions operate them at off-premises locations, such as supermarkets, shopping centers, and airports. By pushing buttons, a customer can perform some or all of the following operations, depending on the institution's computer setup and the services it offers:

1. Checking or savings withdrawals;
2. Checking or savings deposits;
3. Transfer of funds from one account to another;
4. Credit card loans;
5. Getting up-to-date balances on checking or savings accounts;
6. Payment of mortgages, loans, or other bills due the institution.

In addition, other services are also being offered, including:

1. Drive-up service so that customers can use the machines from their cars;
2. The dispensing of movie tickets, postage stamps, and transit tickets;
3. The sale of gift certificates;
4. The printing of account statements;
5. Multilingual access to serve non-English-speaking customers.

Here's the way the machine works:

- The customer is issued a plastic card with a magnetic strip across the back. If he or she is to have loan privileges, it will probably be a charge card, such as MasterCard or Visa. The card may also be useful as a debit card for making purchases.
- The customer is also given a code, known only to that person, with which he or she can activate the machine. Some financial institutions issue the code, or personal identification number (PIN), and send it to the customer separate from the card. Or customers may be able to choose their own letter or number sequence that will be easy for them to remember.
- To use the machine, the customer inserts the card in the proper slot, punches in his or her PIN, indicates the type of transaction he or she wishes to make by pushing the appropriate buttons, and either puts money in the proper slot or removes it from another, depending on what is being done.

Usually, withdrawals can be made in rounded amounts, like $20 or $50 with many financial institutions setting a limit, such as $100 per day per account, as a security measure. However, more recently introduced ATMs have the capacity to instantly cash checks for odd amounts that are within predefined limits. They are able to scan a check and read the MICR numbers that identify the financial institution on which a check is drawn and the customer's account and check numbers. Machine users are even able to cash part of a check and deposit the rest and to buy certificates of deposit.

ATMs have real value in high-traffic areas where teller lines are long and personnel are overworked. A substantial percentage of the transactions performed on some machines involves getting balances—a real time-saver for busy tellers. In addition, while the machines were originally intended primarily for after-hours use, more and more customers are using them during regular banking hours for check-cashing, simple deposits, and other basic transactions. In some cases, the machines are profitable to the financial institutions, especially where a good loan volume is involved. But most important, they offer a service to customers that many find useful—basic banking functions available at any hour of the day or night, every day of the year.

Many financial institutions charge fees for the use of ATMs. Some charge their customers for making cash withdrawals on their own machines, and most charge for cash withdrawals made via ATMs owned by another institution. Fees vary depending on the service provided.

Guiding Your ATM Customers

In spite of the fact that automated teller machines have become commonplace, some customers still don't understand exactly what they're for or how to operate them. If your financial institution makes one or more available for your customers to use, here are some tips that can help to avoid problems and to promote the use of ATMs:

- Teach your customers how to operate your ATM. Learn exactly what transactions can be made on the machine and how to operate it to perform each one. Then, if a customer needs help, be ready to teach him or her just what to do.
- Instruct customers on security as well as machine operation. Review the section titled "ATM Card Security" in Chapter 21. Especially, advise them to keep their PINs confidential and to avoid writing them on or near their cards. And suggest that they exercise caution when using the machine late at night when few people are around. Many financial institutions are trying to avoid ATM crimes by improving lighting, relocating machines away from concealed areas, distributing warnings to their customers, and installing surveillance equipment.
- Sell the idea that using an ATM means greater convenience for your customers. Stress that ATMs can be used 24 hours a day, not just after hours.
- Tell your customers where the machines at your other offices are located so that if your ATM happens to be down and they need to use one after banking hours, they'll have alternatives.
- Be friendly and sympathetic to your customers if your ATM fails to operate. Problems can happen. The card slot can become jammed, the machine may snatch an outdated card, or a card may fail to work because the magnetic strip is damaged.

Automated teller machines won't replace live tellers in the foreseeable future. When it comes to money matters, people like to deal with other people.

But if a machine can do some of the routine parts of a teller's job and leave him or her free for more important areas of customer service, it is very useful.

The Effects of EFTS on Tellers

Tellers will be affected by EFTS only to the degree that they will be relieved of the rush and crush of nonprofitable detail work that now takes time away from important duties. And even though checks won't be completely replaced, most of the routine functions that involve huge volumes of checks will be eliminated, such as paycheck cashing, handling of huge business deposits made up largely of checks, and handling of night-deposit transactions.

The teller of the future will be more and more a "customer service representative." As stated in the Introduction, his or her duties will stress:

- The handling of money, which will continue to be the basic medium of exchange.
- Handling the complicated transactions with which only a human being with common sense can cope.
- Maintaining the all-important personal contact with the customers of the financial institution.
- Problem-solving; a computer can add figures with lightning speed, but it can't spot specialized needs that customers may have.
- Selling services; more and more, marketing on a direct and personal basis will be important to financial institutions. And tellers will be important in this effort.

EFTS actually helps tellers in their work, because all teller's machines are "on line" with the computer. And the changed functions, by eliminating routine mechanical ones, will upgrade the teller's job.

AGENCIES THAT SERVE FINANCIAL INSTITUTIONS

To understand ways in which your financial institution serves others, it is important that you also know about those agencies that back it up in its service role. These include agencies that offer direct service support, such as the Federal Reserve Banks, the Federal Deposit Insurance Corporation, the National Credit Union Administration, the National Credit Union Share Insurance Fund, and, for many institutions, the local clearinghouse association.

In addition, there are numerous associations that provide education facilities, method expertise, legislative backup, and, in general, a forum for the banking industry to share ideas and techniques for better service. These include, to name just a few, the American Bankers Association (and under it, the American Institute of Banking, to which many tellers belong), the Bank Administration Institute, America's Community Bankers, the Credit Union National Association, Financial Women International, the Bank Marketing Association, and numerous independent state and local associations.

The Comptroller of the Currency

The Office of the Comptroller of the Currency is a semiautonomous part of the Treasury Department. Appointed by the president for a five-year term, the comptroller is responsible for overseeing the charter, examination, and regulation of all national banks. The Office of the Comptroller conducts annual examinations of these banks, copies of which are given to the Federal Reserve. Along with the Federal Reserve and the FDIC, the Office of the Comptroller is also responsible for granting charters to all new national banks.

The Federal Reserve

Under the Federal Reserve Act, the Federal Reserve is allowed to issue its own currency with backing and limitations prescribed by law. This allows for a somewhat flexible supply of money to better serve the needs of the nation. More important, the act states that the legal reserves of member financial institutions are to be held locally in the reserve city within their own district. All national institutions are required to be members, and state institutions meeting the qualifications are also welcomed.

The Federal Reserve Banks are not government owned. They are owned by their member institutions, which also hold stock in them. The government *does* see that the public interest is represented by presidential appointment of a Board of Governors in Washington, which in turn appoints three of the nine directors of each Fed, the remaining six being elected by the members.

Functions of the Fed include providing checking accounts for financial institutions, supplying them with money, clearing checks, transferring funds, and lending them money. In addition, the Fed acts as a bank for the government, audits members, and controls the nation's money supply.

Insuring Agencies

In recent years, although there has been an increase in the failure rate of financial institutions, most people still trust them, and with good reason.

Some people may remember "Black Friday"—October 31, 1929—when the stock market fell and dragged the whole economy with it. By 1933, 25 percent of the labor force was unemployed, and breadlines were common. From 1930 until the end of 1933, 9,106 financial institutions were suspended. There were long lines of people waiting at their doors to take their money out; although many of the institutions were perfectly safe, they still suffered.

Steps were taken to help meet this and future crises. The powers of the Federal Reserve Banks were increased. The gold standard was abandoned. Ceilings were set on deposit interest. Banking regulations became tighter. Under the Banking Act of 1933, the Federal Deposit Insurance Corporation (FDIC) was created. And in 1934, the Federal Savings and Loan Insurance Corporation (FSLIC) was formed. These agencies bolstered public confidence by guaranteeing deposits in member institutions up to a substantial legal limit.

Then, in August of 1989, because of the difficulties experienced by the savings and loan industry, the Financial Institutions Reform, Recovery, and Enforcement Act (FIRREA) was signed into law. This legislation restructured the regulatory system for savings and loans and provided for the resolution of insolvent thrifts. One of its key provisions stipulates that deposit insurance coverage for both banks and savings and loans is to be directed and administered by the FDIC in two separate funds:

- The Savings Association Insurance Fund (SAIF) replaced the FSLIC and is now under FDIC jurisdiction.
- The Bank Insurance Fund (BIF) backs the deposits of banks previously insured by the FDIC, which still directs and administers the fund.

If possible, the FDIC will "fix" a bank or association that is having troubles. It may do this by lending the institution money, buying its assets, or giving it deposits. Usually, it will help by arranging a merger with a stronger institution. If these measures can't work, the agency will close the bank or S&L, sell the assets, and pay the depositors up to $100,000 for each separately owned account, or, in certain situations, up to the legal limits arrived at by the agreement of attorneys representing the institution and the agency or by a ruling in a court of law.

The FDIC also has other functions, which include:

- Conducting examinations. Technically, the FDIC may examine any insured financial institution, but usually it limits examinations only to certain insured institutions that are not members of the Federal Reserve.

- Issuing regulations similar to Federal Reserve regulations to insured, nonmember institutions.
- Giving approval for insured, nonmember institutions to offer trust services.
- Working in cooperation with the Federal Reserve and the Comptroller of the Currency in the supervision of financial institutions.

Deposits in federal credit unions are insured by the National Credit Union Share Insurance Fund (NCUSIF). All federal credit unions must be insured, and most state-chartered credit unions are also required to have coverage, either through NCUSIF or private cooperatively-funded insurance. In fact, at the beginning of 1996, only three state-chartered credit unions were uninsured. The coverage is substantially the same as that offered by the FDIC.

Even beyond the coverage of the FDIC and NCUSIF, Congress has pledged the "full faith and credit of the United States" to help in any situation should the insuring agencies be unable to help insured institutions.

Insurance Coverage

Over the years, deposit insurance coverage has gradually increased to its present limit of $100,000. This coverage is the same for the SAIF, the BIF, and the NCUSIF. Here is a brief synopsis of the deposit insurance rules:

Individual accounts. Many people assume that each one of a person's single-ownership accounts in the same financial institution is insured for up to $100,000. This is not so. All such accounts in a single institution are added together and insured in the aggregate for a maximum of $100,000, including principal and interest. This includes checking accounts, savings accounts, certificates of deposit, money market accounts, and so forth.

Joint accounts. It is possible to establish coverage well beyond $100,000 in the same institution with the right mixture of individual, joint, and trust accounts. Like individual accounts, joint accounts held by the same people in the same institution are considered in the aggregate. However, individual accounts for the parties involved are insured separately from their joint accounts. Thus, a husband and wife would be insured for a total of $100,000 in their joint accounts; in addition, each one's single-ownership accounts would be insured for the maximum amount.

Joint accounts held by either person with other depositors can also increase the coverage. However, one person cannot be covered for more than

$100,000 in his or her joint accounts. Suppose, for example, that John and Mary Smith have $100,000 in a joint account at the same institution where Mary has $100,000 in a joint account with their son and another $100,000 in a joint account with their daughter. In this case, Mary, who holds $150,000 in her share of the joint accounts, would have $50,000 that is not covered. If one of the children's accounts were joint with John instead, the whole $300,000 would be insured.

> *Trust accounts.* Testamentary accounts, or revocable trust accounts, are insured up to $100,000 for each beneficiary and each owner if the trust is established for the benefit of a spouse, a child, or a grandchild (adopted children and stepchildren are included). If the beneficiary is someone else, the value of the account is combined with the account owner's individual accounts and the aggregate is insured for a maximum of $100,000. In addition, if a husband and wife set up a single revocable trust account, naming themselves as the only beneficiaries, the account is insured as a joint account, not as a testamentary account. Irrevocable trusts are insured separately from both the grantor's and the beneficiary's other accounts.
>
> *Retirement accounts.* Previously, an individual could have up to $100,000 of insurance coverage for each type of retirement account that he or she had at one financial institution. However, the FDIC insurance rules were changed in 1993 so that all of the retirement accounts under one name must be combined for a total of $100,000 coverage.

Another change in FDIC insurance coverage affects pension plans. In the past, each person in a pension plan was insured for up to $100,000, even though the funds were deposited in one account, a practice that is referred to as pass-through insurance. However, pension plans at certain financial institutions may now only be insured for $100,000 per plan instead of per person. Institutions affected are those whose capital ratios fall below a specified level, which means that this particular requirement applies to only a small percentage of institutions.

The Clearinghouse

A clearinghouse is simply a group of local financial institutions that meet at a specified time and place to exchange checks drawn on each other. Each institution tallies up the total of checks it has distributed against the total it has received. Payment of the difference is made to or received from the clearinghouse. In this way, a few simple bookkeeping transactions replace many that would be necessary if each institution dealt with the other on an individual basis.

The clearinghouse illustrates how members of the banking industry, even though they are competitors, work together to give prompt, accurate financial service to the community. In addition, modern clearinghouses illustrate how financial institutions use the latest technologies to gain efficiency. As new computers and automation techniques are developed, they are quickly added to clearinghouse procedures, thus reducing handling time and costs for the millions of checks that they process. In fact, many thousands of financial institutions now participate in regional automated clearinghouses (ACHs).

Customers Are Important

Just as it's important to know and understand your financial institution's services and how beneficial they are to the community, it is also important to know and understand your customers and how much they mean to you and your institution. Without customers, your institution would not exist. It is their needs that it fills and their transactions you handle as a teller. The deposit customer, in effect, lends money to your institution, which it is then free to invest. In return for this, the customer receives compensation in the form of interest, checking convenience, and safety of funds.

The most common investment that financial institutions make is loans. The money deposited by some people is carefully lent to others who pay for its use. This loan interest provides the savings interest paid to the depositor, if any, and covers the expenses of the financial institution—including tellers' salaries. Customers are important, and it's necessary to let them know it by serving them with courtesy as well as efficiency.

CUSTOMER COURTESY THAT COUNTS

What do you do when a clerk in a store is rude to you? If it happens once, you may overlook it. If it happens twice, you'll probably take action. Chances are, the action you'll take is simply to shop somewhere else. Customers who are insulted usually go to the competition.

Courtesy is defensive selling at its most basic. It keeps customers coming back. A sarcastic financial institution employee can chase customers away in droves.

What Is Courtesy?

Let's start with what courtesy is *not*. Courtesy is not simpering or groveling. Courtesy is not backslapping. Courtesy is not handing out "customer appreciation" flyers once a year to say what your actions should have been saying all year.

Instead, courtesy is:

Being pleasant. Smiling. Having a friendly attitude.

Being helpful. Being willing to do what the customer wants if it's possible.

Being appreciative. Using the customer's name. Saying "thank you" and "please."

Courtesy is a good habit to develop and, once developed, it helps the individual who practices it. On the job or off, everyone likes courteous people.

Courtesy should apply to everyone. Any teller will tell you that some customers are great, such as Mr. Brown, the businessman, or Mrs. Smith, who has two cute little kids, or Jane, who is working her way through college as a cashier at the local market. And some customers are a pain, including Mr. Jones, who always brings in a large deposit that is extremely messy and filled with errors, or Mr. White, who has a child who isn't cute at all because he takes the office apart, or Sally, the waitress, who comes in and spreads malicious gossip while doing her banking. If this sounds familiar, it's because customers are average people. Some are nice, some aren't, and many fall somewhere in between.

It's easy to be pleasant and helpful to nice customers and just as easy to be abrupt with those who aren't. But even though Mr. Jones's deposit is messy and often in error, it is one the institution wants; and he may have other needs that could develop while he is being given the courteous service he deserves. In addition, the teller doesn't have to live with Mr. White's unruly son or repeat Sally's gossip. Both need only be tolerated briefly. All customers, regardless of their personalities, deserve good service, a smile, a "thank you."

Remember the Tact in Contact

Success in human relations often depends on a little word with a big meaning—tact. *The Random House Dictionary* defines it as "a keen sense of the right thing to say or do in dealing with people or situations."

All customer dealings require some degree of tact. Remember these points as you serve customers:

- A tactful teller never allows a confidential conversation to be overheard.
- A tactful teller intuitively knows what subjects to avoid and when to be circumspect in handling others.
- A tactful teller is positive, not negative in his or her dealings with others.

Sometimes the change of a single word makes an enormous difference in a person's reaction. For example, tell a man he's *stingy* and you've made an enemy; say that he's *economical* and he'll probably feel complimented. Call a woman *extravagant* and she'll be furious; say that she's *generous* and she'll think you're a very discerning person.

So the moral is, watch out for words that antagonize. They will be remembered longer than anything else you say. Tact is an important part of courtesy.

First and Lasting Impressions

As a teller, you have an excellent opportunity to put a positive attitude towards others into practice because you deal with the public all day, every day. Think of each time a customer comes to your window as another chance to be positive and courteous.

Make your first impression a good one. When a customer approaches you, stop what you are doing as quickly as possible, look him or her in the eye, smile, and say hello. Be sincere. If you actually want to be friendly, the other person is more likely to be responsive. Here are a few important basics to remember:

- Your main objective should be to put your customers at ease. A financial institution can be an intimidating place. Some customers may be confused by the way your institution handles their financial affairs. They may be afraid of making a mistake and being embarrassed. You can overcome this if you act friendly. Impatience or a stilted businesslike manner makes people more uncomfortable. Unfamiliar terms only make them nervous.
- A good way to put a customer at ease right from the start is to greet him or her by name. This sets that individual apart from everyone else. When you use a customer's name, you are identifying him or her as an individual and showing your respect. He or she is no longer just a long account number; now the person has identity.

- Just as a friendly attitude is contagious, so is a rude one. If you get out on the wrong side of the bed and show it, your customers will react negatively toward you. On the other hand, the greatest test of *your* ability to deal with other people is to remain courteous and friendly when you're faced with a grouch. If a customer is angry and upset with your institution for some reason, realize that everyone makes mistakes from time to time and that it's possible the customer is justified in his or her feelings. Probably the best thing you can do in this case is to turn such a person over to the office manager if you cannot solve the problem.

- Speed in finishing transactions may be important during rush hours, but when there is obviously no need for it, hurrying an individual along will only make the customer feel you want to get rid of him or her. Instead, be friendly to the person and try to give extra service. Daily consideration of others soon becomes a habit. It's the little extras that always make the big impressions.

Remember, your customers are doing your institution a favor by banking there. *You are not doing them a favor by handling their transactions*—they can always take their business down the street to one of your competitors. Show them that you appreciate their coming to you.

SAY IT WITH A SMILE

When was the last time a customer saw you smile? The big responsibility of a cash drawer and the pressure of lines at the window make it easy to forget to smile. It's a good thing to do, though, because when you smile:

- You *instantly* establish a friendly basis for the exchange. Even if the customer was coming in to complain, you've probably softened him or her.

- You have complimented the other person. You've shown the customer that he or she deserves a nice smile.

- You have made yourself better looking. Really! Just watch the people on TV. Don't they look better when they're smiling? So do you.

Make Your Smile Sincere

Make your smile a sincere one by really feeling like smiling. The best way to do that is to develop the habit until your sincere smile becomes a part of you.

Try smiling at yourself in the mirror. When you see what a real smile looks like, it'll make you feel like smiling at everyone.

The nicest thing about smiles is that they are contagious. Some tellers never seem to get grumpy customers at their windows; maybe it's because they cured the grumpiness with smiles before a word was ever said. Try this test. Next time you're shopping on a really miserable day, try giving each salesclerk a big smile. Watch the change. You'll be amazed! And you'll get better service.

Use Names

To really start off right with a customer, match that sincere smile to the person's name. Like this: (Smile) "Good morning, Mr. Jones." You have just told Mr. Jones that you respect him enough to use his *name*. And you did it with a smile that said, "I like you." And, since you represent your institution to your customers, when you smile and greet them by name, thereby showing friendly respect, your institution is showing friendly respect. And you stand out as an individual because of your attitude.

If you don't know a person's name, look for it. It may be on an endorsement or a passbook or on a check or account book. Don't be cautious about it; look for it and use it. The customer will be flattered that you did. Incidentally, each time you use the name, it will make it easier for you to remember it the next time.

Say "Thank You"

Another thing to say with a smile is "thank you." The word "thank" means to express gratitude, appreciation, or acknowledgement. You may not feel grateful for a transaction, but you may well appreciate it. After all, handling transactions is what creates a job for you, and you must at least acknowledge it. Say "thank you" with a smile, and you have ended the transaction on the same happy note with which it began.

Of course, this presupposes that the "thank you" will be said properly and not in a singsong manner or not snapped at the customer. Nor should it be mumbled absently as you turn away to another interest. The best way to say it is to look at the customer, smile sincerely, and say "thank you" as though you mean it.

Smiling, using the customer's name, and saying "thank you" help both you and your financial institution. It helps to give your institution a reputation for being a nice place with which to do business, and it gives you a reputation for being a nice person.

PLAY DOWN NUMBERS

"Hello. This is Teller Number 24 at Branch Number 7 of Financial Institution Number 3-7. Is this Customer Number 206-77-9103? Your check, number 507, which you cashed with me today . . ." Silly? Sure it is. But customers can get to feel that all they are is a series of digits. The average person has a Social Security number, motor vehicle registration number, checking account number, savings account number, and telephone number complete with area code, all of which he or she may need to know in everyday transactions. Of course, everyone has dozens of other numbers they rarely need, such as those for insurance policies and various customer identification numbers.

"Hello. This is Miss Jones from the Main Street branch of First National Bank. Is this Mrs. Roberts? I wanted to ask you a question about the $50 check you cashed at my window this morning . . ." Better, isn't it? The customer is a person again, with feelings, instead of an impersonal, unfeeling series of figures designed to set off a certain electronic reaction in a computer.

So play down the number side of customer record-keeping as much as possible and make an extra effort to treat your customers as individuals. Banking is still people serving people.

HOW TO REMEMBER NAMES AND FACES

As the foregoing sections indicate, customers expect tellers to remember them. There is a good psychological reason for this—tellers handle the customers' most important asset, their money. Therefore, as they should, customers attach great importance to their banking transactions. In their thinking, it is not unreasonable to expect the tellers to attach similar importance to their dealings, hence to themselves. So after a few times at your window, customers expect you to cash their checks without asking, "Do you have an account here?"

This may seem unreasonable to you. The same customers may shop at a supermarket week after week, even use the same checkout clerk, and never expect the clerk to remember them. But the fact is, people expect more of those who work at their financial institutions than they do of their grocers. So it is part of your job to remember the names and faces of your customers, both for their psychological gratification and to expedite your work, especially as it involves security.

Look at People

The biggest reason most people don't remember faces is because they don't look at people—really look at them. Each time they meet someone new, they just give the person a cursory glance that simply doesn't register in their minds. This doesn't mean that as a teller you should stare at someone as though he were a possible armed robber, but it does mean that you should look him squarely in the eye and try to consciously imprint his picture in your mind.

This is easier to do with some people than with others. An especially attractive person of the opposite sex tends to register more quickly. And everyone tends to remember the friendly, extroverted customer who smiles and introduces himself or herself to a teller at their first transaction. It is also easy to remember someone with an unusual physical trait. The trick is to remember the average person who's not overly attractive or outgoing or physically distinctive.

Look at the customer. It may take two or three times at your window for that person to really register, but he or she will eventually. And, as you get more practice, you will improve your mind's ability to recall what your eyes have seen.

Remembering

Repetition of another person's name will help you to remember it. To properly use a person's name, of course, be sure you get it right. It's next to impossible to remember a name you're not sure of in the first place.

If the customer introduces himself or herself or if someone else makes the introduction, and you don't understand, *ask.* "I'm sorry, your name is . . . ?" Said with a smile, it's bound to get results. It if doesn't, if you still can't understand, ask again. If the name is in writing and you can't read it, ask. The other person won't get aggravated because you are talking about his or her favorite words.

Once you're sure you have the name right, use it at once. "Yes, Mrs. Brown. Would you like small bills or large? Of course, Mrs. Brown. Thank you, Mrs. Brown." Sound repetitive? It won't to the customer, and it will help you to remember the name.

At later meetings, if you can't recall the person's name right away, take a peek at his or her check or deposit ticket. But do be sure the name is that of the person at the window. And avoid trying the trick one teller used when she said, "You have a most unusual name. How do you spell it?" To which the customer indignantly replied, "S-M-I-T-H!"

If you still have trouble remembering a name, try to associate it with an outstanding facial or physical characteristic. Then make up a jingle about it. Try to use humor; it will help your memory. For example, think to yourself, "Mrs. Rose has a small nose," or "Connie Blair has bleached blond hair." This isn't always easy, of course. What if the customer is named Carson or Walters? First, try to associate the name with someone famous. The names Carson and Walters could be associated with the well-known TV personalities. And if the name is still too tough, try to make a word association. Thus, Miss Murray may be associated with the word "Christmas."

Above all, *want* to remember names, and you'll soon acquire a habit that really pays off.

Using a Customer's First Name

It's important to make your customers feel special and to create an air of warmth and friendly service that will keep them coming back to your financial institution. Sometimes this can be achieved by addressing the person by his or her first name. But be certain that this will not offend the customer.

Here are some commonsense rules:

- Don't use a first name unless you get to know the customer well enough to be sure it will be welcomed.
- Don't use a first name if you are much younger than the customer or if the customer is elderly or otherwise deserving of the respect of a courtesy title.
- Unless your institution's policy states otherwise, do use a first name when you have a good rapport with the customer. Otherwise, address the person as Mrs. Jones or Mr. Smith; using the customer's name is always preferable to calling the person "ma'am" or "sir."

Knowing how to handle one-on-one customer relationships is a part of your job. Being able to decide when to use a first name and when to use a courtesy title is an important part of that knowledge.

PLEASE SAY "PLEASE"

Your window is closed because you are helping to make up a payroll. A customer approaches. You look up and say, "I'm sorry, you'll have to go to another window." The fact is, the customer doesn't *have* to go to another window at all. If that person wants to, he or she can go to another financial institution!

The word "please" reflects good manners. But the best reasons for saying "please" are the good side effects it produces. For example:

- It is easy to smile when you use the word, and this creates a friendly atmosphere.

- As stated before, when you smile, you're better looking.
- It's very hard to say "have to" or "must" or "can't" when you're saying "please." Thus, the sentence in the example will come out: "Please go to the next window. Ms. Jones will be glad to help you."

Saying "please" is an easy habit to develop. Every time you have to ask or tell anyone to do something, start the sentence with "please." In that way, an order becomes a request and a request becomes a friendly asking for cooperation. Wouldn't you like it if everyone said "please" to you? Why not set the example? Please?

YOUR WINDOW IS A MIRROR

For security reasons, each teller has a defined workstation. This area is referred to in personal terms as Mary's or John's "window." What do people see when they look at yours? Actually, they are looking at a reflection of you and your financial institution. If the area is messy, they assume that you do messy work; and since your institution handles their money, that's not good. The physical image your window presents to the public is important.

What Can Happen

When you see a place day in and day out, it's not easy to spot all of the things that contribute to making it look messy. Your office's counters may need straightening up; old posters and decals may need to be scrapped. Or all of the tellers' workstations may need a general tidying.

For example, Mary's station may be festooned with flower stickons. John's may reflect his hobby of fishing by being decorated with pinups of trout, bass, and pickerel. If Jane likes jokes, the area around her window may be decorated with cartoons. And, to prove that this type of habit is universal, a few favorite cartoons, as well as a loan chart, might be found under the glass on the branch manager's desk.

There's nothing wrong with this kind of personalization if it doesn't get out of hand, which it easily can. Seeing it every day, Mary may not realize that what began as a blossom or two has become a veritable greenhouse. And John may not realize that his trout have spawned into an aquarium, while Jane is surrounded by a cartoon festival. At this point, it looks messy, so the teller may subconsciously think, if the area looks messy, why not let it *be* messy? Paper clips and rubber bands begin to litter the counter. Advertising literature, deposit tickets, withdrawal slips, and other papers become shuffled. Soon the whole office is a mess.

Cluttering a personal work area is so common, it's often overlooked. So take a good look at your window from the customer's point of view. Then, if it's needed, start a general cleanup and create a neat and efficient looking reflection of yourself and your office.

GIVE EXTRA SERVICE

Whatever your goals in life, realize that it's the "extras" that can make them happen. This doesn't include just the occasional extra that your supervisor is sure to notice, but day-in, day-out consideration for others until the actions become habit. Often your willingness to provide extra help will be recognized and your rewards will be real.

Giving extra service means going beyond accuracy and courtesy to suggest helpful ideas. Here are some specific "extras" that you can do for your customers:

Represent your customers with your financial institution. If your customers have a complaint, see that they get satisfaction, and fast. Don't just refer them to someone else—represent them.

Be available. Yes, long lines can make this impossible, but whenever you can, be ready to listen to your customers and to give them any help you can.

Put your banking contacts to work for them. You'd be amazed at what and who you know that your customers don't. You can help meet their banking needs just by giving them a name or introducing them to someone who can assist them.

Point out opportunities. If a customer is self-employed, tell him or her about Keoghs or Individual Retirement Accounts, for example. Or suggest higher-interest certificates if the person has had a windfall.

Help them with their problems. Never make the mistake of assuming that customers know as much about banking as you do. What may be obvious to you may be a godsend to them. Suggest ways in which your institution can help.

Be honest. Be honest in handling customers' transactions, of course. But beyond that, be honest in stating problems and possible solutions. No one likes to expect something and be disappointed later.

Be dependable. If you promise to do something, do it, and do it on time.

Keep your customers informed. When policies change, when new services are available, when any changes that will affect customers are about to take place, be sure they know how they will be affected.

Passing the Buck

Another effective way to give extra service is merely to avoid buck passing. The customer, especially when on the telephone, wants an answer, not to be shifted from person to person. If a situation arises in which you don't know an answer, admit it, but promise to get it and call back. Then take the trouble to get the right answer and *do* call back or have the person with the right answer return the call.

Suppose, for example, that a regular customer comes in for a loan and the loan officer is out. This happened at a midwestern financial institution, and the receptionist suggested that the customer return later when the loan officer would be back from vacation. Unfortunately, the customer was in a hurry, so he went to another institution that gave him his loan and got his deposit accounts as well. The loan officer should have arranged for someone else to handle his customers' needs during his absence. In addition, the receptionist should have suggested a better alternative than just coming back later.

As a teller, you have certain regular customers. Be sure they get to know others in the office so that they won't feel slighted during your absence. If a customer asks to see an officer who isn't there, don't just suggest that he or she come back another time. Make sure the person has the chance to see someone else.

Be alert for the chance to give extra service and take advantage of the opportunities to do so until this becomes second nature. In the final analysis, the biggest difference between your financial institution and the one down the block is *you* and the others on your staff. If you make an extra effort to serve your customers, not only do they benefit, but your institution benefits by being the best in town. It will be so good, in fact, that your customers would never think of changing and might even bring in their friends. How could they feel differently considering the extra service you give?

COURTESY AT THE DRIVE-IN

A good title for this section might be "How to Stay Human Through Glass, Steel, and Wire," for that's exactly the problem tellers face when assigned to work drive-in or walk-up windows. In some cases, even physical distance is added as a problem when customers are far off in remote-controlled locations where visual communication depends on closed-circuit television.

The idea behind mechanized banking devices, including drive-in and walk-up banking, is to offer customers faster and more convenient service. It is hoped that the availability of such service will entice them to deal with that financial institution. Whenever you handle transactions for drive-in customers, remember:

- They are just as important as the customers who walk into your institution.

- Some people become very self-conscious when talking into microphones or similar devices. For example, many people hang up when an automatic telephone-answering device asks them to record a message. Many are also nervous about talking to a teller through a drive-in mike, fearing their words will be broadcast throughout the office behind the teller.

- The things that turn customers off and make them nervous can work the same way with the teller. Put the teller who is warm and friendly on a face-to-face basis in the glass/steel/wire barrier of a drive-in, and he or she may become just another part of the machinery. Therefore, an *extra* effort to be friendly becomes necessary.

- Even though customers may be in a hurry or there may be a line of cars waiting, it takes no more time for you to be courteous and friendly than it does to be brusque and impersonal.

Techniques That Help

The following techniques are sure to improve the impression you make on each of your drive-in customers:

1. Greet each one with a big smile. And keep smiling—it shows in your voice as well as on your face.

2. Make a special effort to respond quickly to a customer's arrival at the window.

3. Be careful not to "abandon" customers by leaving the window without a brief explanation, even if it's only, "I'll be back in a moment." From outside, the customer can't see that you've only gone a few feet away to answer a phone or look in a file.

4. Keep the line moving as quickly as possible without sacrificing accuracy, of course. If a customer is late for an appointment because the teller spent 10 minutes chatting about trivia with the person in the car ahead, the friendly smile and warm hello when it's his or her turn aren't going to mean very much. So keep conversation to a minimum.

5. Have all supplies fingertip ready. Having to look for basic things while the customer waits can be maddening.

6. Use the customer's name as often as reasonably possible. This will go a long way toward removing an impersonal feeling.

7. Use communication aids such as microphones properly. Speak clearly and in your normal voice.

8. When cashing checks or completing cash-back split deposits, always place the money in a small envelope. This helps to prevent loose bills and/or receipts from being blown away. More important, it shows customers you're concerned about them and the service they rightfully expect to receive.

9. When customers ask for their balance, write the amount, without any identifying information, on a piece of paper so it won't be overheard by someone on the street or in the lobby. Maintaining privacy and confidentiality is an important part of a teller's job.

10. Always resupply your drive-in customers with deposit and savings withdrawal slips so that, when they come the next time, their transactions will be completely made up and your line of cars can move along smoothly.

11. End with a smile and a "thank you."

Someday when you have a few free minutes, go outside and take a look at your drive-in from the customer's viewpoint. Then, taking turns with a co-worker, practice being both a teller and a drive-in customer. This can help you to know what techniques are the most effective for your particular office. Remember when working the drive-in to be extra security conscious. Crooks know that drive-ins are fast-transaction windows and capitalize on this by passing bad checks to the busy drive-in teller. At some financial institutions, a high percentage of the forgeries come in at the drive-in.

The drive-in window is a great convenience for your customers but it can be depersonalizing. It's up to the teller who works it to keep up the human side of banking. Courtesy there, as well as inside the office, can win friends and customers for you and your institution.

DEALING WITH SPECIAL TYPES OF CUSTOMERS

Handling Children

Parents frequently take children along with them when they go to do their banking. Every doting father or mother is delighted when someone pays attention to his or her little boy or girl. It's easy when the child is well-behaved, but how about having to be nice to the not-so-darling little monster who is noisily taking apart the office? What should you do when mommy or daddy beams as little Tommy kicks an important business customer in the shins or as little Suzy creates a deposit-ticket snowstorm?

"Let's see . . . you've got your balloons, lollipops, calendar, potholder, and dog discuit. Uh . . . would you like to make a transaction too?"

Unfortunately, some people are oblivious to the faults of their youngsters and expect everyone else to react with the same indulgent attitude. And most people, being polite, will control themselves and tolerate the obstreperous child for long periods of time. However, as a teller, you owe it to your other customers to end the ordeal as quickly as possible. Politely but firmly suggest serving such a customer at once. "Excuse me, Mrs. Brown, but may I serve Mrs. Jones ahead of you? Little Tommy seems to be tired." Little Tommy, of course, is ready to wrestle a gorilla, but your approach has been tactful because you have suggested a benefit, not a criticism, to the child and his mother.

Fortunately, most children who come into the office will be well-behaved and deserve to be treated with respect. Probably the biggest offense adults make against children is to push them aside in line. Granted, the child's time probably isn't as important as the average adult's, but you should treat children with the same courtesy that you treat adults. Polite children may not talk back when they are treated unfairly by an adult, and they do deserve to be helped in their turn when they are conducting real business.

To deal effectively with child customers (and perhaps develop more profitable future adult customers), teach them the proper way to do things. Probably the most common service used by children is the savings account. In this case, it means teaching them how to fill in a deposit or withdrawal slip, to bring in the passbook for the entry of interest when needed, to safeguard the passbook, and to save regularly. Although children hate to be patronized, they love to be able to do adult things.

A noncustomer child who is visiting the office with his or her parents is a good prospect for a savings account. While your financial institution probably won't get rich on the account, the child will learn thrift and become a better customer when he or she gets older. And saving money has a great appeal for young children. If your institution has coin folders or coin banks, suggest one to the parents. Even a few penny wrappers can help. Then mention that the child can have his or her own savings account to watch those pennies add up.

Most children won't tear up your office, and few will be customers unaccompanied by their parents. The average child accompanies his or her mother or father, behaves fairly well if the parent doesn't take too long, and gets impatient if he or she stops to chat with a friend. This child will respond very well to:

> *A smile and a hello.* Most children will beam and their parents will bask in the rays of a smile directed to their offspring. There is nothing demeaning about being polite to a child. Children emulate those they respect, so if you say "please" and "thank you," they probably will, too.
>
> *A lollipop.* Many financial institutions make these inexpensive giveaways available to tellers to distribute to youngsters. If yours does, use the candy to best advantage, that is, to occupy the child. Ask the parent if the child may have the lollipop, then hand it to him or her at the beginning, not at the end of the transaction. Or if the child is starting to squirm while the parent is still in line, give him or her the candy then and hope it will act as a pacifier while they are waiting.
>
> *Being treated his or her age.* Many people fawn over infants and toddlers and ignore older children in the preteen and early teen years. These boys and girls appreciate a warm, cheerful, "Hi, John. How are things in the sixth grade?" or some other comment relevant to their activities.

It's good customer relations to be nice to children. Be friendly to them and their parents whenever the opportunity arises.

Dealing with the Elderly

Sometimes dealing with senior citizens can be a challenge for a busy teller. When a long line of impatient people builds up as an elderly woman takes interminably long to complete a simple transaction or when an aged man just can't understand some of the complications caused by modern technology, a teller needs extra sharp customer relations skills. When you deal with older people, you should tactfully try to:

Guard the elderly against themselves. Few older people can afford to lose their money, so an alert teller should take steps to protect them against such loss by putting money in envelopes and by suggesting that they carry it in a secure place.

Guard the elderly against others. Elderly people are often the targets of con men and women. Therefore, you should be on the lookout for suspiciously large withdrawals made by elderly people and tactfully try to find out what's going on. Don't hesitate to call a supervisor if necessary.

Watch for those who prey on the elderly. For example, since an alarming number of checks disappear from mailboxes every month, you should be suspicious if a teenager wants to cash a Social Security check. Refer such people to your supervisor. Be tactful, but be watchful, too.

Be patient. Some older people have diminished alertness. Others just welcome the chance to chat with you. Of course, this can be very annoying to people who are behind them in line.

Here are some tips that can help you to deal effectively with the senior citizens who come into your office:

1. If a person has real trouble understanding how to do something, do it for him or her, if possible. If it is a recurring situation, suggest that the person come in at a specific time when you know things won't be busy. Then, set aside a few minutes to really show the customer what to do and explain why it is done that way.

2. If a person wants to chat interminably while a line builds up, be polite but firmly end the conversation. For example, say "Mr. Johnson, it's always nice to chat with you, but now I must help Mrs. Green."

3. Some older people are against anything new. They complain about MICR numbers, computers, and automated teller machines. Let them. Don't argue; just be polite and finish the transaction as best you can.

4. Don't be condescending. Not all elderly people are senile or hard of hearing. Start with the assumption that the elderly person at your window is alert, competent, and intelligent. You'll find that he or she usually is.

5. Be alert during bad weather. Floors often become slippery in bad weather, and older people may have stiff joints that can precipitate a

bone-breaking fall. If a particularly shaky elderly person is at your window or coming into your office, don't be shy about offering a helping hand.

Positive customer relations requires taking extra steps to deal effectively with certain people, such as children and the elderly, who may need your special attention.

Customers with Hearing Problems

People with hearing problems require special consideration from tellers for obvious reasons. In the first place, understanding is essential to the satisfactory completion of any banking transaction. Second, confidentiality and security can both be violated if care is not taken.

Here are some specific tips, from the National Association of the Deaf, for dealing with any of your customers who have a hearing problem:

1. Remember that being deaf or hard-of-hearing involves *physical*, not mental, impairments. Don't insult the intelligence of the person who has a hearing problem.

2. Don't immediately reach for a pencil and paper. First try rephrasing any statement that was not easily understood. Some sounds are harder to interpret than others, so making the same point while using words with completely different sounds may enable you to be understood. For example, "Would you please go to the next window?" could be restated as "She (pointing to the next teller) will take care of you."

3. Assume that the person with a hearing problem relies to some degree on lip reading. However, don't ask, "Can you read my lips?" The question may be offensive. Just try it. Face the person directly and speak distinctly and in a normal voice. Some words are difficult to lip read—those with "f" or "v" sounds, for example. And, because they look alike, you should be careful that "fifty" isn't misinterpreted as "fifteen" or "nineteen" isn't mistaken for "ninety."

4. Repeat difficult words if necessary and if rephrasing is impossible. But don't mouth or exaggerate them. In many cases, that makes them harder to lip-read.

5. When confidentiality or security is involved, use a pencil and paper. Above all, don't shout.

6. If you have difficulty in understanding the speech of a deaf person, you may need someone who is skilled at interpreting to help.

Some financial institutions take special care to serve customers who have hearing problems by airing TV ads that feature a person using sign language or by marketing devices that allow such customers to do their banking from home by communicating through the telephone line and using a TV screen as a monitor.

Customers with Visual Problems

According to the Massachusetts Commission for the Blind, two issues underlie the problems experienced by blind persons when it comes to their banking transactions—privacy and independence. When they are using regular printed checks, passbooks, statements, and the like, blind persons must rely on someone else to read personal financial information to them or to actually conduct their transactions. Some are involved in joint accounts that may not serve their best interests but are more convenient in practical terms. To counteract these problems, some financial institutions provide large-print or raised-line checks, taped statement information, instructions in Braille for using ATMs, and other accommodations for blind customers.

Even in the absence of these special services, financial institutions can make many efforts to serve blind customers appropriately. Here are some tips that you can follow when such a person comes to your window:

1. Don't shout. Many sighted people tend to speak to those who are blind in a loud voice as if volume somehow compensates for the person's inability to see.

2. As with the deaf or hard-of-hearing, realize that a visual problem is physical and not mental and that blind people have perfectly normal intelligence.

3. Offer to fill in any needed forms and provide other assistance if it is requested or clearly needed. However, avoid being overly "helpful" and drawing attention to the situation inappropriately.

4. If the blind person is accompanied by a sighted person, don't avoid talking to the blind person. All too often, people tend to ignore the blind and to converse indirectly through an intermediary.

5. When a blind person makes a withdrawal or cashes a check, return the cash by stating the number and denominations of the bills. Blind people generally fold their bills in different ways to distinguish denominations, so you should help in that process if your assistance is requested. Here is one method of doing so: Leave all $1 bills unfolded and flat as most sighted people do with all of their currency.

Fold $5 bills crosswise once and insert in the billfold fold side up. Fold $10 bills lengthwise and insert fold side up. Fold $20 bills once lengthwise and then again crosswise and insert folded side up. If the customer you are dealing with uses a different method, however, don't confuse him or her by suggesting this one.

6. For security reasons, do your best to maintain privacy for your blind customer. Explain the transaction and amount involved in as unobtrusive a way as possible. And, if the nature of the person's business warrants it, deal with the customer away from the window where no one can overhear your conversation.

With a little awareness and sensitivity and the same courtesy you extend to all of your customers, you should be able to serve those with both hearing and visual problems with little difficulty.

Customers Who Use Wheelchairs

The National Easter Seal Society offers advice on the best way to extend courtesy to people with a variety of disabilities. It includes the following tips for dealing with people who use wheelchairs:

1. Treat adults in a manner befitting adults. Use a person's first name only when extending that familiarity to others who are present. Never patronize people in wheelchairs by patting them on the head.

2. Leaning against or hanging onto a person's wheelchair is similar to leaning against or hanging onto a person and is generally considered annoying and unacceptable behavior.

3. When talking to a person in a wheelchair for more than few minutes, place yourself at the wheelchair user's eye level to spare both of you a stiff neck.

4. When giving directions to a person in a wheelchair, consider distance, weather conditions, and physical obstacles.

5. Allow a person who transfers out of a wheelchair to keep it within reach.

A Law for the Disabled

In 1990, Congress enacted the Americans With Disabilities Act (ADA), which took effect in mid-1992. Besides its effects on employment practices, the law requires changes in financial institution services, forms, and physical facilities to accommodate customers with disabilities. Some of the changes may include physically altering ATMs to make them more accessible, lowering check-writing counters, offering application forms in braille, equipping customer service numbers with telecommunications devices for the deaf (TDDs), and reevaluating the forms of identification required for cashing checks.

HOW TO TREAT CUSTOMERS AT BUSY TIMES

Holiday crowds or rush hours make banking difficult. As lines grow long, tempers tend to grow short. Often the same people who cheerfully wait in line for 20 or 30 minutes at a discount store or supermarket become snappish and impatient if they must wait even five minutes at their financial institution. And lunchtime and other rush hours at any season of the year can make your work hectic.

Be Efficient and Look Efficient

People never get quite as irritated when they have to wait in line at a financial institution if they are convinced of two things—that the teller is not wasting time and that he or she is doing something important. It pays to let your customers know that you are doing your best to serve them as efficiently as possible. Therefore, actually be as efficient as you can. Don't waste steps, motions, or minutes. This will help you to look efficient. Finally, tell the customer that what you are doing is important: "Just one moment, Ms. Jackson, I must take a few seconds to count this cash and put it away." Counting money and putting it safely away is something Ms. Jackson will realize is important—and efficient—and she won't mind waiting as much.

Be Extra Courteous

The extra pressures of busy times call for extra courtesy to compensate. Don't forget that a real part of customer courtesy is seeking to be of more service. Seasonal expenses may mean personal loans are needed. Shopping convenience may call for a credit card. A Christmas Club, to make *next* year-end easier to cope with, is in order for that season of the year. Bill paying requires the convenience and safety of a checking account. Be especially watchful for your customers' needs and, if at all possible, take a few minutes to suggest how an additional service could help them.

Here are some tips that can help when you're faced with a long line of waiting customers:

1. Be sure to use each customer's name and to greet him or her with a smile. Especially at holiday time, personal service after impersonal treatment elsewhere is comforting.

2. Look down the line between each transaction and smile and nod to the waiting customers. This says, "I know you're there, and I'll be glad to help you in just a few minutes."

3. Don't close your window on a line of people. If your lunchtime is coming up, guess ahead at how many people you can handle, and then have others get in another line. Tell them that you must close your window in a few minutes.

4. Be extra careful not to be taken in by con artists when you're in a hurry. Take the few moments required to be sure whenever you have a question about a transaction.

5. End each transaction with a "thank you" and if it's holiday time, the appropriate holiday greeting.

Customer courtesy is always important, because whatever time of year or whatever time of day it is, customers are always important. They are the reason your financial institution exists.

TELLER PERFORMANCE RATINGS

A financial institution's level of service may be the primary element that differentiates one institution from another within a particular trading area. Therefore, rating the quality of service provided by tellers and other public-contact personnel and applying standards to measure their performance is one of the ways financial institutions are attempting to deliver first-rate customer service.

"Shoppers"

Have you ever heard of a financial institution being "shopped"? Here's the way it works:

- A firm of professional "shoppers" gets a contract from an institution to rate its public-contact employees.
- The shoppers come to the institution's offices and, while using actual services, score new-accounts clerks, tellers, and others on their effectiveness as public-contact people. Qualities that are rated may include promptness of service, friendliness, helpfulness, and sales ef-

forts. Measurements of teller productivity can also be used in making decisions regarding office staffing and hours of operation.

- Each office and, in some cases, each employee is given a score. The employee may be told by the shopper that he or she has just been rated, or the employee may be told later by a supervisor.

Under one financial institution's program, for example, a shopper from an outside organization visits tellers three times each quarter. He or she enters an office of the institution, goes to a window, and conducts a transaction, looking for certain behavior. The shopper then leaves the branch, grades the teller, and sends back the information so that the institution and the teller can see how well or how poorly he or she rated.

Ten is a perfect score, based on 10 specific things a teller must do during each customer transaction, some of which include such basics as smiling, thanking the customer, and using the person's name. A negative evaluation can result in a teller being removed from contact with customers and being given additional service training. He or she is then given three or four chances to improve over a 12-month period.

Ratings by Customers

Some financial institutions use electronic devices that ask real customers to rate the quality of service they receive. Such devices consist of small black boxes with a plastic sign that asks a question. The customer pushes one button for a "yes" answer and another button for a "no" answer. Responses are automatically recorded and can be monitored with a hand-held remote control.

One particular institution used the machines as part of a successful customer-service program that also involved individual customer surveys and an ongoing quality-service guarantee program. As part of the latter, tellers were supplied with brand new $5 bills, one of which was given to any customer who had to wait for service for more than three minutes.

Whether your institution employs a formal rating system or not, you'll always do well if you remember to:

- Give prompt service;
- Act friendly and helpful; and
- Try to sell services that can save your customers time or money.

If you do, you're certain to rate high with the institution and your customers wherever you work.

YOU AS A BANK CUSTOMER

Banking where you work as a teller is like shopping in a store where you're an employee—it couldn't be more convenient and it's profitable for the financial institution or store. Thus, to encourage employees to use their services, many institutions go out of their way to provide benefits that aren't offered to regular customers. For example, employees may be offered the following:

- Loans with interest rates that are less than nonemployees pay.
- Mortgages for fewer points than nonemployees pay.
- Direct deposit of the employee's salary into a checking account that provides unlimited free check-writing and ATM access.
- A reduction in the rate charged for overdraft privileges.
- Credit cards for those who qualify.
- Free traveler's checks.

A Special Program

One particular financial institution that employs between 5,000 and 6,000 people is among the growing number of institutions that provide special services for employee customers. Among other things, the full-time employees who work in this special unit are committed to getting answers for staff members on simple consumer loans within 24 hours. Those who take out loans get a 10 percent discount from the base interest rate paid by regular customers, with no loan fees; and all application information is kept strictly confidential. The institution also gives employees a 50 percent discount on safe-deposit rentals, has waived setup fees on home equity loans, and allows employees to take out construction loans.

Perhaps the most unique aspect of this institution's employee banking program is a designated employee teller window in the main office. Located in a low-traffic section of the branch banking area and used only by employees, it opens 30 minutes earlier and closes 30 minutes later than other teller windows. Another employee window is open at the institution's service center.

If your financial institution offers a similar program, it is in your best interest to take advantage of it if you're not already doing so. Institutions that focus on good customer service realize that employees make good customers, too.

26 CHAPTER

Dealing with Difficult Situations

THE CUSTOMER ISN'T ALWAYS RIGHT

To be successful, a teller must have a special attitude about his or her relations with the public because the public has a special attitude toward the teller. The services financial institutions offer are unique in that they deal with people's money; and people take their money very seriously. Therefore, they expect those who handle their financial affairs to be above average.

People in other businesses who deal with the public can usually govern their behavior with one easy rule—"the customer is always right." But a financial institution employee can't take that attitude. He or she must consider *all* customers, not just the one being dealt with at the moment. So the customer *isn't* always right. Sometimes he or she just can't have a check cashed. Sometimes a person is lax with a loan payment and must pay a late charge.

How does this affect you? If you are able to work within the framework of these customer-protecting policies and, at the same time, build the goodwill of each individual customer, you have a skill that will enhance your entire life! People who can deal with others in a positive way make friends in all phases of their lives.

Five Rules for Success

The following goodwill-building rules will enable you to develop successful public relations:

1. Have *confidence* in your financial institution.
2. Let others know you *like* them.
3. Take a positive *interest* in others.
4. Have *confidence* in yourself.
5. *Know* your job and do it well.

To remember these rules, take the first letter from the key word in each and put them together. They spell CLICK—and that's just what you'll do with everyone as you practice them.

Confidence

Confidence is so important that it is the key word in two of the rules. Without it you can't succeed, and with it it's hard to fail.

Confidence in your financial institution is important. If you truly believe that your institution is a strong pillar in the financial lives of the people in your community, you will reflect this fact in your dealings with them. Have confidence in your institution, not just because of its many dollars of assets, but because of the people who work together to staff it, one of whom is you.

Confidence in yourself is important, too. It means you have self-respect and that you're not afraid to let people know it. And you build that self-confidence when you know your job and do it well. Nothing gives a person more confidence than knowing what he or she is doing and doing it well. One good way to be sure you know your job is to always dig a little deeper into things. This doesn't mean you should drive your supervisor crazy with foolish questions, but it does mean you should ask why. Go beyond the daily routine of your job. Ask questions. Read about things. Perhaps even take advantage of some of the fine educational opportunities the banking industry offers. Get to know your job better and always do it to the best of your ability.

Other People

No one can get along in life without other people. So two of the rules deal with them. Win them over by having a positive interest in them and by letting them know that you like them. Give that "little extra" service with each transaction. Watch out for their interests, as well as your institution's. And let your customers know that you like them and that you appreciate their business.

When the Customer Isn't Right

If you sincerely practice the five rules for successful public relations, you'll avoid most sticky situations. Customers who want the unreasonable will understand why it is unreasonable when the employee who knows his or her job explains things properly. They will respect the teller who has confidence in the financial institution and in his or her own ability. Finally, they will respond in a positive way to the teller who has a positive interest in them and shows that he or she likes them.

HOW TO SAY "NO"

Everyone likes to say "yes." "Yes" is a positive, friendly word. But the very nature of banking often forces you to say "no." For this reason, some people wrongly associate a "Scrooge" image with financial institutions. You can help prevent this impression, at least as far as your institution is concerned.

When someone asks you to do something that requires a refusal because of your institution's policy, consider this: Often the person is not really asking you to do something wrong, he or she is just asking for help. The thing you were asked to do was only his or her idea of what that help should be. Often you can say "yes" even though you may not be able to do the specific thing requested. You very well may be able to offer just what the person really needs—help, something people always appreciate.

Cashing Checks for Strangers

Perhaps the most common (and often most difficult) request is made by the stranger who wants to cash a check. No one needs to cash a check, just as no one needs to go to the drug store. A person may need medicine, which usually will involve a trip to the druggist; but the trip is not the need, it is only an action instrumental in filling the need. By the same token, your stranger doesn't really need to cash a check. What he or she does need is either cash or simply to get rid of the check. In any case, first determine the real need. If a stranger simply wants to convert the check into something more tangible, you can easily help this person by having him or her use the check to open a new account. If the need is really for immediate cash, perhaps you can still help. Is there someone known to your financial institution who can endorse the check? Would the appropriate officer approve a split deposit with a minimal amount of cash until the check has cleared?

The "customer" of today who wants to cash a check may be a real customer tomorrow who deposits money, makes loans, or uses other services on which your institution earns income. So, using tact and courtesy, try the following:

1. Be polite when you refuse to cash the check.
2. Carefully explain your institution's policy without making any implication that you distrust the "customer." People who know they are honest may get uptight at any inference, stated or implied, that they might not be.
3. Offer an alternative suggestion to cashing the check.
4. If necessary, refer the "customer" to a supervisor.

Other Requests

Every teller gets impossible requests from customers or from people off the street who consider themselves to be customers. Besides being asked to cash checks for strangers, you may be asked to do the following:

- Cash checks for customers, then hold the checks from processing for a few days.
- Accept improperly endorsed checks because the payee wasn't available to sign them or for other reasons.
- Backdate loan payments received at the window.
- Give out balances on another depositor's account.
- Put a hold on another person's account.
- Cash checks for a depositor who has insufficient funds but who promises to make a deposit before the checks clear.
- Do all sorts of things that are against your institution's policy and usually common sense as well.

Faced with such requests, you would have to refuse, of course. But sometimes this can be difficult to do. Here are some tips that can help:

1. Don't let a soft heart overrule common sense. This may sound a bit like Scrooge after all, but it's good advice. If you stick your neck out and then get in trouble, you'll often find that the person you helped doesn't even appreciate it. Find out where local people can legitimately go to get help. Then refer them there in cases of real need.

2. Never let a customer talk you into doing anything illegal, such as holding checks until they are made good.

3. Never backdate a loan payment or other document. You can get into a real legal hassle on this if someone dies or if other reasons to contest property come up.

4. *Follow your institution's policies in all matters.* And when you think an exception should be considered, refer the matter to an officer.

5. Say "no" as politely as you can, even to the most outrageous request. Give the person the benefit of the doubt; perhaps he or she didn't know any better. Then politely explain why you must refuse and, if possible, suggest other courses of action to the person.

6. Make sure you are interpreting policies in the same way as other tellers in your office. If you're not, find out why and try to set up uniform procedures. Customers will resent different rules from different tellers.

7. Be sure to apply policies consistently. Don't make exceptions. People will be more willing to accept procedures and rules they know to be routine. They'll get angry if they think you're discriminating against them.

8. Be especially careful to be discreet. This means using a soft voice when explaining your institution's policies to the customer.

In any case, remember that a pleasant feeling toward your financial institution means future good accounts. Never just say "no." Instead offer whatever help your institution's policy will allow.

CLEAR UP WRONG IDEAS

Financial institution employees' hours are from nine to three...everyone knows that! And all of them are cold and unfriendly! Far too often, the public believes these things. Financial institutions spend a great deal of money and effort to overcome the latter idea, especially.

Many people actually believe the following statements. Watch for these and other wrong ideas and help to clear them up whenever you can:

- A financial institution has a master key that will open any safe deposit box.
- Examinations are solely to prevent defalcations.

- Financial institutions make service charges to increase income.
- Financial institutions make exorbitant profits.
- Anyone with good character is entitled to a loan from a financial institution.
- Anyone who works in a financial institution can take care of any banking service.
- Tellers must pay shortages out of their own pockets.
- Financial institutions ought to cash any check without question.
- Financial institutions are paid for selling savings bonds.
- Financial institutions do not welcome small checking accounts.

You are in a position to hear many common misconceptions that the public has about the banking industry. Correct them if you can and try to prevent them by explaining your institution's policies and services properly and in a friendly way.

Customer Misunderstandings

When it comes to customers' misunderstandings, the best time to clear them up is right at the beginning. When customers open an account, make a first deposit or withdrawal, make a first loan payment, or whatever, is the time to make sure they know what they're doing.

Don't ask customers, "Do you know how a checking account works?" They'll say, "Sure," even if they don't. In the first place, they don't want to seem stupid. In the second place, they may really think they do know. After all, they've seen people in line at the market making out checks, so what else do they need to know?

Instead, say to customers, "Let me take a minute to explain how our checking accounts work." This gives them a face-saving out. You've suggested it, and you've implied that your checking accounts may have a feature or two different from those with which they're "familiar." Or with a first deposit or withdrawal, say, "May I take a moment to explain our forms to you?" This approach can avoid future trouble.

But what do you do when a person gives you a check on the same account to cover an overdraft? Or when someone insists he or she can't be overdrawn because some checks are still left in his or her checkbook? It's not as easy as nipping problems in the bud, because you have to teach the customer something without hurting his or her feelings or implying that the person is less than bright. Lines like these may help:

- "Yes, that is confusing, but let me explain the way our financial institution does it."
- "Perhaps when we opened your account, we didn't make it clear. Let me tell you about uncollected funds."
- "If you have a minute, perhaps I can give you a few tips on keeping an accurate balance."

Next time you're faced with a customer who doesn't understand, remember there are some in every financial institution in the country. Be polite, explain things courteously—and keep smiling!

HANDLING CUSTOMER COMPLAINTS

Even the best-managed office in the banking industry gets a complaint from a customer occasionally. When this happens, it fits into one of three categories: the complaint may be completely unreasonable; it may be legitimate and involve only your office; or it may be legitimate and involve a staff member or a department that is outside your office.

Unreasonable complaints are often the most annoying but easiest type with which to deal. While a few people may complain because they enjoy stirring up trouble, many do so because they simply don't understand a service or procedure. To avoid offending such a person and possibly losing his or her business, listen to the customer and show that you're concerned, but don't feel compelled to admit that there is a basis for the complaint if it isn't warranted. Hear the person out without interrupting, then say, "I understand, but...," and give a polite explanation of the true situation.

Within Your Office

When a legitimate complaint is made that involves your office, it's usually best to handle it there and end it there. If the complaint concerns an operating error, this shouldn't be difficult. Everyone makes mistakes from time to time, and your customer will be satisfied if you simply acknowledge the error, do what you can to have it corrected, and thank him or her for calling it to your attention. If the complaint involves a problem that should be resolved by someone else, take a moment to introduce the customer to that person.

A problem can arise, however, when the complaint is of a personal nature, such as, "Your drive-in teller was rude to me!" or "You kept me waiting too long!" When this type of complaint is made, following these steps can help:

1. Don't act resentful. Instead, try to see things from the customer's viewpoint and act friendly and sympathetic.

2. Listen to the complaint carefully and fully. Don't build up the situation, but ask questions and even take notes if necessary. Be sure you understand why the customer is upset and show that you care.

3. A great deal of tact is required when a legitimate complaint involves an office co-worker. In this case, tell the customer you're sorry about the situation and assure him or her that you'll pass the word along to the proper person so that it won't be repeated. Then, depending on the nature of the complaint, quietly and confidentially relate what the customer said to the employee who is involved or to your supervisor. While you don't want to create resentment on the part of a co-worker or seem to be a tattletale, the complaint shouldn't be ignored.

4. If you're the object of the complaint, apologize, explain why the situation occurred, and assure the customer that you'll do your best to see that it doesn't happen again. If it involves something over which you have no control, such as having kept the customer waiting in line because your office was understaffed at the time, discuss the matter with your supervisor.

Outside Your Office

Some complaints may involve offices or departments other than your own. Here again, simple operating errors aren't hard to deal with and will usually only require that you tell the customer you regret the error and that you'll notify the person in order to get things corrected.

Complaints of a personal nature against individuals from other offices or departments are more difficult to handle. If a complaint is against an employee, don't try to deal with it yourself. Hear the customer out, then pass along the information to your supervisor and let him or her take it from there.

The most difficult complaint to handle is one that involves a member of your management. In this case, listen to the customer and determine whether there seems to be a real cause for the complaint. If it sounds as though there is, assure him or her that you'll mention it to your supervisor, who is sure to handle it tactfully. Then privately explain the nature of the complaint to your supervisor in a noncritical, objective manner.

Failing to follow the chain of command and going over someone's head to report a complaint is not a good idea. An alternative, especially when the same complaint is made more than once, might be to discuss it with the proper individual in your institution's human resources or personnel department. Such a person should be able to deal with touchy situations fairly and confidentially.

RUDE AND GROUCHY PEOPLE

Everyone has had the unpleasant experience of coping with an unreasonable, rude grouch. Sometimes this can be so frustrating that you find yourself becoming cranky. Grouchiness, it seems, can be contagious; but as a teller, it is a disease you simply cannot afford to catch. How, though, can you prevent it?

First, you can try to be sympathetic toward people who act this way. Grouchiness and rudeness are the outward symptoms of personal problems. And you are in a position to give these unhappy individuals a strong, helpful dose of medicine.

The effectiveness of a smile and using a name often will stop grouchy people in their tracks because it gives them a reason to like themselves a little better. But how about the hard-core bear who snarls through your friendly smile?

Psychological experiments have shown repeatedly that it is extremely difficult for anyone to be angry without raising his or her voice. Further, it is human nature for a person's voice to assume the loudness and tone of the person to whom he or she is speaking. Understanding this fact puts you in the driver's seat whenever you must deal with someone who is grouchy or belligerent. It takes great self-control on your part, but keeping your voice low and pleasant eventually will force the other person to lower his or her voice and sweeten his or her temper. Interestingly enough, this technique works just as well on the telephone as it does in person.

One word of caution. While you are using this low, pleasant tone, be careful not to give the impression that you are timidly cowering from this growling bear. Like any wild creature, he or she delights in making the terrified rabbit quake, but shrinks from the confident, self-assured person. Remember these four "Cs" for dealing with the difficult: Keep Cool, Calm, Collected, and Courteous.

A Sense of Humor Helps

Here they come to your window—Mr. and Mrs. Johnson with Junior. This pair of parents doesn't believe in correcting their child no matter what he does. They feel it will warp his personality if anyone ever says "no" to him. On their way across the lobby, Junior kicks a customer, sticks out his tongue at your office manager, and smiles as he dumps the trash can under the new account clerk's desk. No one can touch him—he's invincible under the protection of his indulgent parents.

Or here comes the complainer. Last week she squawked because she wrote a check that took five days to clear. Yesterday she yelled because she wrote a check that cleared immediately, resulting in an overdraft, when she was counting on a few days to make her deposit. Now here she comes to your window. What will she complain about today? Today, it seems, she doesn't like the fact that you're not open on Tuesday nights until 10 o'clock. She's never been in on a Tuesday and never past 2 P.M., but she feels sorry for the shift workers who get off at 9 on Tuesday evenings.

What do you do when people try their best to make your day a little less pleasant? Don't let them! Find something in the situation to laugh at, and the hassle might become a joke. For example, get mental revenge on those permissive parents by visualizing what Junior has probably done to their best china. Or think about some of the funny situations that must arise in the home life of the complainer.

It's a shame that there are those who must make hassles a part of their lives. But don't let them upset you. Learn to fend them off with a good sense of humor.

THE IRRATIONAL CUSTOMER

Picture this scene. The office is quiet. Tellers are busy handling lines of customers. Your manager is on the phone with a customer. Suddenly a man's agitated voice yells, "I don't want to talk to the manager. You cheated me and I'm talking to you!" At this point, every customer focuses on the trouble spot. Every employee holds his or her breath. And the situation is in your hands.

Realize that this person has problems. A normal person wouldn't act this way, even if he were right and the teller was in error. So start by putting down the impulse to yell back because that's just what he wants. He'd love to start a shouting match.

Instead, answer him calmly. "I think we should discuss this quietly. Would you please step into our conference room? Let me get Miss Brown, our manager, to join us. Then we can straighten things out." *Don't* give him a chance to argue about this. *Do* make him come with you by walking toward the conference room and showing him the way. He has to follow because his argument is leaving him. Miss Brown can be called or signaled after you reach the privacy of the conference room or as you pass her office. It's a good idea to get her in on things at this point.

Then hear the customer out. Remain pleasant and polite. Even a really sick person can't continue yelling at someone who is calm, pleasant, and sympathetic. There are two possibilities—either the customer is right or he is wrong. If he's right, admit it, apologize, correct the mistake, and forget it. Quietly get him to leave. If he's wrong, allow the customer to save face if possible. Don't bawl him out; do appeal to his ego. Naturally, you can't admit to an error you or your institution didn't make, but you can try to save a customer within reasonable limits. Most important, keep calm. You owe it to yourself, your fellow employees, and your rational customers.

There are two important things to remember when you are faced with someone who acts irrationally or who, for example, may be drunk and is either a potential annoyance to others or may cause damage or injury:

1. *Don't panic.* There are very few situations in life that call for instant reactions; so rather than blurt out or do something you may regret, take a few seconds to think things over. It may seem like an eternity to you, but the other person won't even notice such a brief delay.

2. *Get help if you need it.* If personal or property damage ever occurs, if a belligerent drunk is annoying the customers, if someone gets sick, or if any really difficult situation develops, get help fast. Call your supervisor or the office manager. If that person isn't around, get help from another teller. It's no reflection on you, just good sense to realize that two heads are better than one.

In any case, when you're dealing with an improbable situation that sometimes can confront a teller, keep cool and use your common sense. Try to do the right thing, and chances are you will.

RESPECT YOUR CUSTOMERS' PRIVACY

Because doctors get accustomed to dealing with sick and injured people, they sometimes tend not to take a very minor ailment as seriously as their patients might. People who work in financial institutions are the same way. Dealing with money every day, they tend to take financial matters somewhat for granted. But consider this interesting fact: People will discuss religion, sex, controversial politics—almost anything—with far more openness than they will their financial affairs. Ask average people the most intimate questions, and you're more likely to get an answer than if you ask them what their salary is, if they have an outstanding loan, or if you inquire about their savings account balance.

This gives you an idea of just how seriously people take their financial privacy. Therefore, as a teller, with access to highly confidential information, it's an important part of your job to see that privacy is respected. You have the moral obligation to protect the financial privacy of your customers just as much as a lawyer must safeguard his clients' rights, a doctor his patients' health problems, or a clergyman the secrets he learns through counseling or confession.

Reread the section on handling confidential information that appears in Chapter 7, "After Working Hours." Those rules apply whether you are on the job or off. Then consider the following special situations.

When a Customer Is Overdrawn

Some tellers, especially the inexperienced, tend to view a customer who has an overdraft or a return as a potential deadbeat. It isn't necessarily so. The very affluent often operate with minimum cash balances.

Most people are terribly embarrassed when they have a check returned or overdraw an account. They may have made an unintentional error or they may have been trying to race the check to their financial institution with a deposit. Either way, a teller must not embarrass them by violating their confidence. If you must discuss an overdraft or returned item with a customer, do it very quietly. If necessary, go to a conference room for a few minutes.

Customers' Paychecks and Balances

Tellers are in a unique position. They accept for deposit or cash the paychecks of people in every local business. So they know the take-home pay of many specific individuals. In addition, they have a pretty good idea of the earnings of a person in a particular company at a certain job level.

Frankly, it sometimes makes tellers a bit jealous when someone with whom they went to school cashes a paycheck for substantially more than he or she makes. This is one source of paycheck problems.

Another problem occurs when the subject of salaries comes up. It may be tempting for a teller to say, "Joe isn't doing so hot. I cash his check," or "Sue is really making it. I cash a lot of checks for people at her company, and, at her level, the pay is about so-and-so." Don't say it. Most people are very secretive about their income and would resent it highly if you told anyone—family, friends, relatives, or even your co-workers—what their salaries are. Balances are confidential, too. If a teller gets and divulges or hints at a balance, every listener immediately loses respect for him or her.

On the other hand, however, balances can be accidentally divulged. Giving a customer an up-to-date balance in a voice that can be overheard, for example. Or letting a passbook be seen by someone else in line. Write down requested balances on a piece of paper, omitting the customer's name and account number. And keep passbooks from being seen. Letting a customer's balance be known isn't just a breach of confidence, it may also be setting him or her up for a ripoff.

Late Loan Payments

Like overdrafts, late loan payments are not a definitive sign of impending bankruptcy. And you should not mention them to the customer. Many people try to make loan payments on the last due date and occasionally miss. They are risking an occasional late charge to get maximum interest on their funds. Others with perfectly adequate incomes sometimes have, as the old saying goes, "too much month left at the end of their money," and let a payment go late on purpose.

In any case, the rule is *courtesy* and *confidentiality*. If there is any cause to suspect that something is wrong, don't comment on the late payment or confront the customer. Tell an officer right away and let him or her take action.

If, on the other hand, a customer ever mentions that he or she is short of funds and can't make a payment, ask that person to contact a loan officer immediately. Unfortunately, many people are either embarrassed or frightened of this situation and try to avoid the person who can help them the most. A loan officer is always willing to help the person with a legitimate problem. He or she may do anything from making arrangements for payment at a later date to resetting the loan if necessary. In any case, the customer will sleep easier knowing that the problem has been dealt with and that he or she won't be getting late notices or collection phone calls.

Some Additional Rules

You may take financial situations more and more for granted as time goes by, which might create some carelessness. To avoid indiscretions, be sure to observe these rules:

1. Talk about confidential matters to customers in a low voice that can't be overheard.

2. When you call bookkeeping for a check verification or to phone in a hold, keep your voice down. Don't be overheard.

3. Make it a point to see only confidential information that you need to know. Don't even look at loan applications, for example, unless you must have the information for business purposes. A loan application covers everything—income, net worth, outstanding obligations. You probably don't take applications, but you may have access to credit files. But if you don't look at them, no one can expect you to divulge information you don't have.

4. If you are asked to violate confidences, refuse, no matter how other people tease and wheedle. You will only gain stature in their eyes— but if you do tell, they'll never trust you again.

Handling sticky situations is part of your job as a teller. And keeping financial information absolutely confidential is a vital part of it. If you make respecting the privacy of others second nature, you can't go wrong. It's the sign of a true professional.

WHEN AN ACCOUNT IS CLOSING

Many financial institution accounts close each year. This means that just to stay even, an institution must replace a certain percentage of its accounts annually. This figure involves the number of accounts, not the amounts on deposit. Actually, when it comes to dollars, the accounts that close are often small. But this doesn't mean they aren't important. To the contrary, a declining balance may indicate that a customer has already switched to another institution and is just waiting for all of his or her checks to clear and the balance to drop before writing a final check to close. Or in the case of a savings account, the customer may be making deposits in another financial institution and withdrawals from the one he or she intends to leave.

Why do accounts close? The most common reasons involve death, moving out of town, the need for immediate cash, no further need for the account, enticement by a competitor, or dissatisfaction with an institution's service.

As a teller, you are often the first person who is in a position to talk to a customer who is planning to close an account. True, a bookkeeper may spot a declining balance and should report this to the proper person in the office the depositor uses. But usually the first clue will be given right at your window. Consider the following situations.

The Person Who Is Moving

People make two kinds of moves. One is to a new home nearby, the other, to a home out of town. People who move to a new residence in a location near an office of your financial institution can be retained as customers. Often, they simply don't realize that your institution has an office near the new house. All it takes is telling them about it and offering to ask the manager of that office to expect them.

Retaining accounts of customers who are moving out of town is difficult, if not impossible. But, in many cases, people who are transferred out of town by an employer may be back in a few years as part of the company's cycle. So be sure to let such customers know you'll be ready to be of service again should they return.

The Angry Person

When a customer is angry with the financial institution, it is for one of two reasons. Either the institution did something offensive and was in the wrong, or it did something—or failed to do something—that the customer misunderstood. In either case, there is a possibility that the account can be saved.

If necessary, get the help of your supervisor in this situation. If your institution is wrong, admit it, apologize, and take corrective action. On the other hand, real tact is required if the institution isn't in the wrong but the customer thinks it is. In this case, don't get uptight. Don't argue or lecture. Point out that the customer has misunderstood, and offer to take any corrective action allowed within the framework of your institution's policy.

Money Needs

Sometimes people will close a savings account because they need cash and need it now. Unfortunately, these customers usually don't replace the money later when they can. Suggest that such people talk to a loan officer, and offer to introduce them.

Other people have changes in lifestyle, such as retirement, and no longer need a certain account. In such cases, suggest a service that *will* fill their needs.

WHEN THE LOBBY LINES ARE LONG

In Chapter 25, under the heading "How to Treat Customers at Busy Times," this subject was discussed from the standpoint of a teller's looking efficient and being extra courteous. Now consider some ways to handle those difficult long lines in order to expedite your customers' business.

Work Routines

Here are some tips for you to try when the lines at your office get really long and you feel pushed:

- Work at your normal speed. Trying to rush can produce errors, which will delay things now and keep you from settling later. Remember that accuracy in handling money is your first obligation.
- Don't skip your break. A quick snack, a chance to wash up, a break, however brief, can refresh you and give you the capacity to go back and meet the challenge. Just make sure to take your breaks so that a maximum of windows are covered. And, of course, don't linger beyond the allotted time.
- Allow new, inexperienced people to help only with routine jobs. When you have a logjam of customers, it's not a good time to expect a new teller to handle things. His or her questions may delay you and could cause errors.
- Make sure your workstation is neat. Finish each transaction by putting everything where it belongs. Having a backlogged mess of paperwork can cause real headaches. You often don't remember what you think you can. So write things down and be neat and efficient.
- Avoid trying new techniques. If you have a time-saving idea, fine. But don't try it out when you're rushed. Remember it and try it out later when the lobby isn't as crowded.

Expediting Service

Here are some steps you and your co-workers might consider in order to speed things up when lobby lines are long:

- Set up an express line for customers with one transaction.
- Set up a "fast-cash" system with precounted bills in packets of $10, $25, $50, and $100. Use slack times to prepare the packets.
- Stagger tellers' lunch hours so that every window is covered at expected peak hours.

- Encourage customers to use an ATM for very routine transactions. Automated teller machines aren't just after-hours devices; they're also time savers.
- Set up a "take-a-number" system.
- Establish a single line that feeds to all windows with the next customer to be served simply going to the next open window.

The latter two suggestions, of course, tend to make customers feel less important and take away the option of going to the tellers they favor.

If your customers believe that you're doing your best to serve them as efficiently as possible and if they feel you're giving them personal service in spite of the crowds, they won't mind waiting in line nearly as much.

MERGERS AND THE TELLER'S JOB

If your financial institution has been involved in a merger or if it may be in the future, there are some important things that you, as a teller, should keep in mind.

Your Customers

When a merger is announced, the customers involved are primarily concerned about three things: the safety of their money, whether or not local branches will remain open, and whether or not tellers whom they know and like will remain on the job. You can help calm their fears by answering their basic questions, by directing more complicated ones to an office spokesperson, and by giving them any available explanatory literature.

Here are some other things that might change after a merger takes place:

- Customers may be given new account numbers, especially if any duplicates result because of the merger.
- When a new name for the merged institution is to be used, customers will receive new checks, new ATM cards along with a new PIN, and new credit cards.
- Interest rates may change, although they will probably stay the same for existing loans and for CDs that haven't yet matured.
- Deposit insurance may be affected. If a customer has funds on deposit in both institutions for a total that exceeds the $100,000 limit, protection is normally provided during the first six months after a merger and, for CDs, until the first maturity date after the end of

those six months. After that, a customer will probably transfer some of the money to another financial institution.

Your Staff

Mergers can be difficult for the staffs of both financial institutions. For one thing, they often involve a lot of change all at once. On top of that, stress can be created by the fact that not all jobs may survive.

Here is some advice for tellers from a regional manager of an institution that was involved in a merger:

- Do the best job you can. Don't allow anxiety to affect your attendance. Don't complain. Keep a positive attitude and put on a good customer-service face. Be helpful toward your fellow employees, lending them a hand when needed.
- Maintain effective communications. Don't pass on rumors and gossip about what's happening. This only upsets and demoralizes other employees and doesn't accomplish anything.
- Learn the new techniques and policies of the combined institution and follow them to the best of your ability. But don't complain about any changes.
- If your office is not to be consolidated with another, tell concerned customers in a friendly way, "This office will stay open, and I expect to continue working here. Of course, we'll be sure to tell you about any changes that are planned." Then give them whatever written information your institution has provided.

Surviving a merger is a matter of attitude. The necessary changes can be unsettling, but if the employees of the combined institution really want to make it work, it will. Change, after all, isn't always for the worse; it's often for the better.

27

CHAPTER

Financial Tips for Customers

Two simple rules for giving financial advice to people in social situations during off-duty hours are discussed in Chapter 7. Two simple rules also apply when it comes to giving on-the-job advice to your customers:

1. This rule is the same in both situations: *Know what you're talking about.* If a customer requests your advice and you're not really sure what the answer should be, introduce him or her to someone else at your institution who is more knowledgeable in that subject. No one expects you to be an expert in all phases of banking. And the customer who asks for guidance will appreciate getting accurate, up-to-date information from anyone who can supply it.

2. *Don't overstep your authority.* When you are working at your window, you are considered to be a spokesperson for your institution. Therefore, it could create a problem if, for example, you promised a loan to a customer who had yet to apply for one and was later turned down, or if you offered a higher interest rate on a savings certificate than your institution was prepared to pay. When matters come up for which you do not have authority, simply introduce the customer to the appropriate person who does have the authority to speak officially under those circumstances.

However, as a teller, you are in a unique position to spot customers' needs or areas of confusion and to answer their questions. The following sections relate to some of those subjects for which you can offer helpful financial tips.

THINGS YOUR CUSTOMERS SHOULD UNDERSTAND

Here are three of the most common errors some of your customers may make in their banking techniques. When you spot them, be tactful, be polite, and offer to take a minute to explain the proper procedures.

Endorsements

Most people today are aware that carrying around a check they have received is potentially dangerous. What they don't realize is that endorsing it in blank—that is, simply signing it on the back—literally converts it from a negotiable item to a bearer item, which means that anyone can cash or deposit it just by endorsing it again with a real or fictitious name.

The safest procedure of all is for a person to endorse a check as soon as it is received, but to use a restrictive endorsement, such as "For Deposit Only, John Doe." Or, even safer, "Pay to XYZ Institution for deposit to the account of John Doe." No one can steal or find such a check and then cash it.

Obviously, it also means that the customer can't get cash immediately because the check must be deposited, but the protection is well worth the short delay.

Reconciliations

Unfortunately, too many people don't know how to reconcile a checking account statement. Here are the instructions given on the back of many statements:

1. Enter the current balance as shown on the statement.
2. Enter all deposits made but not shown on the statement.
3. Total items 1 and 2.
4. Enter the total amount of outstanding checks.
5. Subtract item 4 from item 3. This figure should agree with the balance in the checkbook, minus any charges made by the financial institution.

If a customer has kept an accurate record of the checks he or she has written, reconciling the account should be a simple enough procedure. Advise any checking customer who mentions problems to be sure to write down every check written, keep an accurate running balance in the checkbook, and reconcile the statement as soon as possible after it is received. If the customer has trouble with the reconciliation, suggest that he or she take the following steps:

1. Make sure all of the checks returned with the statement are placed in numerical order, checking off in the register those that have cleared and noting on the reconciliation form those that have not cleared.
2. Compare the actual check amounts with the amounts written in the checkbook register.
3. Make sure all deposits are accounted for, either checking them off in the register if they appear on the statement or noting them on the reconciliation form if they don't.
4. Make sure any financial institution charges that appear on the statement have been subtracted from the checkbook balance and, if the account earns interest, that the amount paid has been added in.

If the customer still has trouble balancing the checkbook against the statement, he or she should:

1. Recheck all of the math.
2. Make sure all outstanding checks are accounted for, including any from previous statements.
3. Make sure the amounts of any counterchecks he or she may have written have been subtracted, as well as ATM withdrawals and deductions resulting from the use of a debit card.
4. Compare the amounts of the checks that have cleared against the amounts on the statement.
5. Check the financial institution's math.

If all else fails, suggest that the customer bring his or her checkbook and statement to the office to get some in-person assistance from the appropriate individual. It would be best if the person called first to set up a mutually convenient time to work on the account.

Uncollected Funds

Uncollected funds probably cause more confusion for customers of financial institutions than any other subject. All the customer knows is that, when you won't cash his check drawn against a balance just created by the deposit of his Aunt Mabel's check for a period of several days, you are either (a) being arbitrary and unreasonable; (b) impugning the honesty of his kindly aunt; or (c) helping your institution to rip him off.

When confronted with a check drawn on uncollected funds, smile and follow your institution's policy. When you must refuse to cash a check drawn on uncollected funds, explain simply that, while your institution has the check that was deposited, it does not have the money that check represents. Go on to explain that it will take X number of days for that money to reach your institution and your customer's account from the institution on which the deposited check was drawn and that, until your institution has the money, you are not allowed to cash the check because doing so would, in effect, be giving the person a loan on which he or she has not paid interest. Keep smiling. Never say, "I can't cash your check until that deposit clears because we don't know if the check is good or not." And if the customer gets testy, refer him or her to an officer—with a smile.

Hopefully, someday, schools everywhere will require basic training in financial dealings. But until then, as a teller, you are occasionally expected to be a teacher. Be prepared to explain your "subject" with courtesy and tact.

As noted in Chapter 21, under the provisions of the Expedited Funds Availability Act, Regulation CC requires that financial institutions clear local checks after two business days and nonlocal checks after five business days. In order to facilitate the processing of checks, signatures and financial institution stamps must be placed in certain specified areas on the back of each check:

1. Endorsements must be within an inch and a half of the trailing, or left-hand, edge of the check.
2. The three-inch space on the leading, or right-hand, edge is for subsequent collecting institution stamps, with routing information.
   Thus, checks can be returned to their point of origin without being rerouted through Federal Reserve clearinghouses.
3. The remaining space in the middle is for the depository institution stamp.

Since September 1988, these areas have been clearly printed on all checks. If any of your customers should make a mistake about the placement of an endorsement or object to the space restriction, politely explain that federal regulations, not your institution's, require signatures to be written in the same place on all checks. Then point out the positive fact that these regulations are for the benefit of customers in order to make their deposits available for withdrawal more quickly.

TAX ADVANTAGES FOR AVERAGE CUSTOMERS

Wealthy people can and do hire tax lawyers and accountants to figure ways to legally avoid paying unnecessary taxes. However, many people fail to realize that persons of average means can also take legal steps to reduce their tax liability. And some of those means are available through services offered by your financial institution. Pass these tips along to your customers when it is appropriate.

Custodial Accounts

Under the law, during his or her lifetime, a person may give up to $10,000 and a married couple may give up to $20,000 a year to each of any number of beneficiaries, and have these gifts be free of federal gift tax. Congress may change the limits, so people should check before making a commitment. But the principle is this: The gift tax exclusion allows a person to put some money aside for his or her beneficiaries and not have it subject to taxes. Here's the way it works:

- The money must be a gift. That means it must go into the ownership of the beneficiary. A savings account for such purposes should be designated a "custodial" account, and the person making the gift has no right to use the money for his or her own benefit. It can be used only by or for the benefit of the beneficiary.

- Gifts that are to be used for the recipient's medical or educational expenses, and that are paid directly to the medical or educational facility that is involved, are not counted toward the annual $10,000 gift tax exclusion.

- Under the Uniform Gifts to Minors Act (UGMA), the first $650 of interest earned in 1997 on savings given to a child who is under age 14 is tax-free. The second $650 is taxed at the child's rate. For amounts over $1,300, the interest is taxed at the parent's rate. After the child reaches age 14, the income is taxed at his or her own rate. An adult is designated as custodian and has control of the assets until the child reaches legal age, which is 18 in many states. At that point, the young person may use the funds for any purpose he or she wishes. In the meantime, the tax advantage does not apply if a parent is the custodian and the money in the account is used to pay for any of the child's basic necessities, such as food, clothing, or shelter. This is because such expenditures are considered to be the parent's obligation.

Keogh and IRA

As outlined in Chapter 24, "Know Your Services," Keogh plans are those that allow a self-employed person to put money aside for retirement and not have to pay federal income taxes on that money until it is withdrawn for retirement use—thus making it taxable at a lower rate. In Individual Retirement Accounts (IRAs), which are for employed persons and their non-wage-earning spouses, interest is allowed to accumulate on a tax-deferred basis until the funds are withdrawn. Some people may also deduct all or a portion of the amount contributed from their taxable income. See Chapter 24 for details.

Again, here is a way many "average" people of modest means can utilize your financial institution to effect a real tax saving.

Loan Interest

Starting in 1991, personal interest charges were no longer tax-deductible. This includes interest paid on credit card charges, personal loans, auto loans, and finance charges from stores and other companies that allow customers to pay their bills in installments. Mortgage interest is tax-deductible, however. And for families just starting on the road to home ownership, this can amount to a huge deduction. In addition, interest paid on home equity loans, backed by mortgages on private residences, is also deductible. The features of this type of loan are outlined in Chapter 24.

Safe Deposit Rental

If a safe deposit box is used to store only personal items or tax-exempt bonds, the rental fees are not tax-deductible. But if any papers are included that relate to income-producing activities, such as stocks or savings bonds, the fees are deductible. And it goes without saying that anyone who owns stocks or bonds should keep them in a safe deposit box.

U.S. Savings Bonds

U.S. savings bonds offer possible tax advantages for the average person, which are described in the section about savings bonds in Chapter 24.

Tax advantages are not just for the wealthy. The average person can and should use them. They can save a taxpayer many dollars each year in ways that are not only legal, but that are encouraged by the government. You and your financial institution can help your customers by suggesting these services to them, and your local IRS office can give expert advice on the details.

SPECIAL TIPS FOR WOMEN

Chances are good that women make up a large proportion of the customers you serve at your window. In some cases, the financial problems these women face differ from those your male customers face. The reasons for these differences may be *legal*—although legal differences are fast disappearing—they may be *traditional*, or they may be *real*. As a teller, you should be aware of some of the more common special problems of women and be prepared either to help your customers solve them or to refer them to other people who can help.

Credit Problems

In the past, many credit problems of women were caused by legal differences, but with the Equal Credit Opportunity Act, most of them have been overcome.

Of special importance is the fact that every married woman should take steps to establish a credit record in her own name. It makes sense for a married woman with an income of her own to have some loan accounts separate from those of her husband. Then, should she become widowed or divorced, she will find getting credit is easier. Yes, under the law, joint accounts are carried in the names of both spouses—and that helps—but separate accounts may make more sense.

Refer any woman with this problem to an officer for advice—*before* she needs credit. Taking the steps now can avoid future problems.

Joint Accounts

Joint accounts have been called "poor man's wills," the implication being that they are an easy way to transfer ownership of property in the event of the death of one person. Unfortunately, this is an oversimplification. In some states, a joint deposit account can be tied up for some time in probate, and if it's all the money a couple has, a woman with no regular source of income can have problems. So, although joint deposit accounts are great, it often makes sense for a wife to have an account in her own name as well.

Joint ownership of real estate may actually increase the tax liability of an estate. When it comes to joint property and estate taxes, suggest that a couple see an attorney or an estate planning officer for advice.

Wills

People used to think that wills were something husbands or wealthy widows should have. But nowadays we know better—wives should have them, too. And so should unmarried persons with any property.

It's a good rule to avoid do-it-yourself wills. Often, they are simply not acceptable for probate. It costs so little and makes so much sense to have a lawyer do the job properly. Again, refer people with questions on this to an estate planning officer if your institution has one. If you have a trust department, it may be a good idea to have your institution named as executor. It can often save an estate real problems—and money.

Life Insurance

"I believe in life insurance, not wife insurance!" Shades of the 1890s! Do you know what it would cost a family in dollars to replace a woman who is earning a living? Or even what it would cost to replace a housewife and mother? A woman should have adequate life insurance so that her death will not mean the financial ruin of the family. In some states, savings banks sell low-cost life insurance over the counter, offering protection to both men and women without charging commissions.

Widow's Benefits

Widows—and they are all too common—are entitled to various benefits, including those from Social Security and the Veteran's Administration. There may be company benefits as well. Suggest that every woman customer know what she is entitled to *before* she needs to claim it. It may save her a lot of problems at a time when she doesn't need any more of them.

TIPS FOR CHECKING ACCOUNT CUSTOMERS

There's an old saying in financial institution advertising circles to the effect that a checkbook enables a customer to "write his or her own money." And it's true. Nothing else offers the safety of funds and convenience of a checking account. From the standpoint of security, however, that same convenient account does offer crooks the opportunity to rip off the financial institution or its customers.

When you open a new checking account or when you see a customer doing something questionable with an existing account, review the following points with the customer. You could save the person, your institution, or both a great deal of grief.

1. *Never write a check in pencil or with an erasable pen.* It's amazing how many otherwise intelligent people will write a check in pencil, rationalizing that it's "only for a small amount," not realizing that an eraser and a few added lines can make it a sizable amount.

2. *Fill up checks completely.* Spaces shouldn't be left where words or figures could be altered or inserted. The amount in figures should be started snug up to the printed dollar sign, and the amount in words should be started as far to the left as possible. Then a line should be drawn or typed to the printed word "dollars."

3. *Keep checks and checkbooks in a safe place.* Many stolen checks are taken from a desk top or unlocked drawer.

4. *Destroy old checkbooks and checks.* Many people will get a new checkbook because they have switched financial institutions, gotten married, or whatever—then they'll keep the old checkbook lying around carelessly or just toss it intact into the trash can. Forgers love such people!

5. *Don't presign checks.* Although it's hard to believe, this happens all the time. A person gives a friend a presigned check to go shopping. Or an "efficient" person presigns several checks in advance, then leaves the checkbook on his or her desk. In an actual case, a blind man presigned a stack of checks and entrusted them to a "friend" to pay his bills. Guess who turned out not to be a friend at all?

6. *Don't leave a checkbook in the glove compartment of your car.* Thieves love this. Sometimes they get the car plus the checks to pay to run it.

7. *Don't keep identification in your checkbook.* This is a favorite for those women who hate to fumble through a messy purse for a driver's license. They tuck it into the flap of their checkbook so it will be handy when they need it. The crooks find it handy, too. Checkbook and ID should not even be kept in the same purse. Men present less of a problem since their ID is usually in a trouser-pocket wallet while their checkbook is in a shirt or jacket pocket.

8. *Don't endorse checks before going to the financial institution,* unless they are "for deposit only," as outlined in the section of this chapter, "Things Your Customers Should Understand."

9. *Keep the financial institution informed.* Checking customers who have a change of address should tell the financial institution or statements and canceled checks could go bouncing through the mails for some time. Of course, if checks are lost or stolen, the institution should be notified immediately.

10. *Check your statement promptly.* This should include examining all checks to be sure they are yours and that they don't include any from another account or any forged items.

The foregoing rules are nothing more than common sense, yet many people violate them every day. Having a checkbook is the ultimate in financial convenience and safety; but, like all privileges, it entails responsibility.

FINANCIAL SELF-PROTECTION

Inflation occurs when the purchasing power of the dollar goes down in relation to the face value of money. In economic terms, it takes place when demand exceeds supply. In practical terms, it means that people on fixed incomes, such as retired persons, or those on relatively stable incomes must suffer real hardship. What can you advise your customers to do to protect themselves financially?

Prepare a Financial Statement

Each customer should begin by knowing where he or she stands. On a sheet of paper, the person should list the current value of:

- All accounts at financial institutions
- Cash on hand
- House (the fair market value)
- Car(s) (again, the fair market value)
- Personal property
- Investments
- Pension rights vested
- Insurance cash value
- Other assets

Then deduct:

- The outstanding home mortgage
- Balance due on auto loans

- Balance due on other loans
- Unpaid bills
- Unpaid taxes
- Other debts

The remainder is the person's *net worth*. If a person has been working for a few years and bought a home several years or more ago, he or she may be surprised to learn just how much this net worth is. On the other hand, those just starting out may be disappointed.

Personal net worth is many things. It is what the person stands to lose if something should go seriously wrong, such as a major illness or a lawsuit. And it is what he or she can call on should there be a need to borrow.

Update Insurance

Everyone should update the insurance on his or her home every year or two in light of inflation. Enough insurance 10 years ago isn't nearly enough today. Insurance should be based on the total *replacement* cost of the property, not the market value. A competent agent can help with this.

Health insurance should also be updated, especially to be sure that a catastrophic illness won't wipe out that net worth the person has calculated.

Auto insurance should also be updated. The minimums so often carried are simply not sufficient in a major accident. And those extra amounts cost very little. It's the basic policy that costs a lot.

Finally, don't forget life insurance. The customer's own "replacement value" also increases as time goes by. Term insurance is inexpensive and effective.

Establish a Savings Plan

Those who have sums of money can invest in mutual funds, the stock market, collectibles, jewels, precious metals, commodities, or even in the money market. But there are two big risks here, and the *untrained* person should be wary. For one thing, none of these investments are guaranteed, so that even the principal amount can be lost or reduced. The second risk is that, even if the value of such an investment should rise, it too may fail to meet the rate of inflation. A safer alternative is investing in certificates of deposit.

Those who have no money, on the other hand, often say, "Why should I save? I should spend, even if I have to borrow, which means I'll have goods with today's value and will pay for them with tomorrow's inflated dollars." This sounds pretty smart, but it's really just an excuse for nonsavers to continue doing what they've been doing all along—failing to save. The fact is, the person who buys a consumer item at today's prices and pays for it with tomorrow's inflated dollars will probably end up in several years with an almost worthless asset, will have paid interest at a rate that even beats inflation, and, worst of all, will have no savings at all.

This is not to condemn borrowing. It is to point out that wise consumers borrow when it is prudent and save as well. Thus, they will continue to put their money in regular savings accounts and to transfer accumulated large sums to CDs.

Cut Costs

When people cut costs, they add dollars to their pockets that can eventually end up in savings and increased net worth. There are a number of areas in which this can be done. For example, people might:

- Practice simple auto maintenance.
- Grow their own vegetables.
- Do their own household repairs.
- Set up cooperatives for such things as transporting the children, buying food in quantity, or sharing expensive, seldom used appliances.

As a teller, you aren't expected to be a financial advisor. But you should be prepared to give your customers a few basic guidelines. It's a wonderful way to increase your "bankability"!

"BANKABILITY" PLUS!—THE TELLER AS A SELLER

A good definition of the term "marketing" is, "All of the activities directed toward and resulting in the flow of service from the financial institution to the customers." This means marketing includes *advertising, public relations, customer relations, employee training, staff relations, merchandising, and selling.*

Chances are, your institution has an officer or a department charged with the marketing function. You may use a different word, but the responsibility is the same. In very large institutions, the marketing responsibility may be broken up and shared by different departments. In any case, someone approves the advertising, prepares publicity releases, supervises employee training, arranges for lobby displays, and so forth. But, by definition, marketing isn't the job of any one person or department. Marketing is *all* of the activities that bring in new customers and keep old customers coming back. This means that marketing is *everyone's* job. Bookkeeping is strictly operations, or is it? Preparing neat and accurate statements certainly has a positive effect on customer satisfaction. Think of the various jobs in your institution. Loan officer. Customer service representative. Vault attendant. Computer operator. Each and every one of them has a direct or indirect marketing function.

Then consider yourself. As a teller, you are part of the first string on the marketing team. Without your help, the best advertising program will fail; and with your help, even a mediocre program can succeed. When you smile, your institution is friendly. When you give that important "little extra" service, your institution is helpful. Marketing is a part of your job because it *has* to be. It is not an extra duty. When you are face to face with a customer, no one else can smile at him or her and handle the transaction in a friendly way. No one else can tell that person that your financial institution appreciates the business by saying "thank you." At that moment, you *are* the institution to that customer.

Marketing is an important function in modern banking. It is a function shared by every officer and employee. Including you. And selling is an important function of marketing.

Why is selling necessary? Consider these facts:

- Financial institutions spend a lot of money on advertising to bring in new customers. But bringing them in isn't enough; they have to be sold.

- The typical customer uses only *one* service. Because people need more services than they use, the answer is selling.

- In most institutions, many accounts close each year through normal attrition—customers move, die, or have a change in their lifestyle that negates their need for a service.

- To get new business from prospects brought in by advertising, or to sell additional services to present customers, each financial institution must rely on public-contact personnel. For the most part, that means tellers. A teller sees many more people each day than a loan officer, a platform officer, or a branch manager does. And the teller also gets to know his or her customers better than anyone else in the office.

28 CHAPTER

Selling Is Part of Your Job

WHAT IF YOU HATE THE IDEA?

"I'm a teller. My institution entrusts me with a very large amount of cash. I'm expected to handle it honestly and efficiently. I'm expected to settle my work accurately every day. I'm expected to be at my station promptly every day. And now my institution tells me that I'm expected to sell services, too. Is this fair?"

This is a question that may be in your mind, and it's a good one. The answer is, "Yes, your institution is perfectly fair to expect you to sell its services. Selling is as much a part of your job as settling accurately."

Analyzing what selling really is will help to explain:

- Selling starts with a *positive attitude* toward your customers. If you have a choice of two stores in which to shop, both with similar merchandise and prices, you'll choose the one with the more helpful, friendly employees. These employees have a positive customer attitude, and you show your appreciation by preferring to do business with them. This means that your attitude plays an important role in your selling job at your financial institution. The nicest thing about a positive attitude is that having one makes you a more popular person, both in and out of your job—and it doesn't cost you any time or money to develop one. A positive attitude is more than half of your selling job because with it you sell *yourself*; and you must sell yourself before you can sell your institution's services.

- The next part of selling is simply to *know your job* and do your work cheerfully and efficiently. People rely on those who know what they're doing, and they make their judgment on present performance. This is selling by example. When you do your job in a friendly, efficient way, people will automatically think of your institution when they need additional service.

- Selling services is a natural extension of your operational functions. No one expects you to be a high-powered salesperson like some of the people who sell life insurance or encyclopedias. All that selling services really means is to *spot financial needs and then suggest helpful ways to fill those needs.*

- The last part of your selling job, after you have kept your eyes open for a person's financial need and know a way that your institution can help, is to *ask for the business.* Not in a high-pressure way, but by making suggestions. Mrs. Wilson mentions that she needs a new car? *Suggest* an auto loan. Mr. Doe received an inheritance and doesn't know what to do with it? *Suggest* a savings certificate. The Bensons are going to Mexico? *Suggest* traveler's checks for the trip and a safe deposit box for valuables left at home. Sometimes, of course, more than just a suggestion may be required. You may need to refer a customer to a person who is trained in a certain service, such as a Keogh or an IRA. Or you may need to follow up personally.

Selling is everyone's job. It helps your institution to grow and helps you to grow along with it. And it's not hard. All it takes is a positive attitude, knowing your job, looking for financial needs, and asking for the business. It's fair for your institution to expect you to be part of its sales efforts because all it's really asking is that you do your job—which is to be of service—cheerfully and well.

So what do you do if selling really turns you off? What if you decide to approach a prospect and find that you just can't be effective? Professional salespeople have a name for this. They refer to it as "call reluctance." It sometimes gets so bad that they will drive to an appointment and then be unable to go in to meet with the prospect.

Examine your attitude. If you have trouble selling or dislike the idea, start by finding out why.

- Do you think selling isn't respectable? Some people associate it with the obnoxious foot-in-the-door types everyone has encountered.

- Do you hesitate to sell because you're afraid of being rejected?
- Do you think that people may dislike you if you attempt to sell them a service?

Selling *is* respectable and is not demeaning in any way. And people who say "no" are not rejecting you. They just don't feel they need the service you have suggested. And they certainly won't dislike you for asking if you have a sincere interest in them, if you suggest services with a smile and in an attempt to be helpful, and if you never push them into something they don't want.

Selling can be a pleasant job. But if the word bothers you, you may prefer not to call it selling at all. Just call it helping others.

USE YOUR INSTITUTION'S ADVERTISING

Financial institutions advertise because they want their names to become known so that they will be familiar to the public. In addition, they also advertise for other reasons:

To create a public image. This desired image may vary from institution to institution and may include such hopes as being known as one that is easy to deal with, a safe institution, one that is conservative with the depositors' money, a very modern space-age financial institution, or a convenient institution in the community. The image may be projected by word usage, ad layout, even by media or ad location. For example, a "modern" ad may appear on the entertainment pages of the newspaper while a "conservative" ad may appear on the financial pages.

To explain the benefits of banking service. It's amazing, but many people still don't know, for example, how convenient a checking account is.

To ask people to come in and do business.

These are the main reasons for advertising. And the end result, it is hoped, is to develop new business.

How does your institution advertise? On TV? On radio? In newspapers? On roadside billboards? In local magazines? These are the traditional mass media that financial institutions use.

Your job of selling will be made more effective if you carefully read your advertising or listen to it on radio or TV. Advertising helps to make people receptive to the idea of using a new service. It tells the prospect that your institution is there, that it offers services, and that it wants his or her business. It may even list the benefits of the service. All that remains is for you to ask for the business along with a smile of welcome. Familiarize yourself with your institution's advertising so that you and the customer will be on the same wavelength.

Advertising in Your Lobby

Your lobby contains several selling tools that you can use. To attract customers to use additional services and to develop goodwill toward your institution, the following items may be provided:

Posters. Posters and point-of-sale displays at your window are a means of getting a message across quickly. Checking accounts are convenient. Regular savings grow rapidly. Safe deposit boxes protect against fire and theft. They can also remind you to sell a particular service. Look at the posters in your office. Then watch for opportunities to sell the services they advertise. In this way, your efforts will be reinforced by the poster message.

Advertising folders. Advertising folders are a good potential sales tool that can be used in these ways:

1. As a source of information. Study each folder to learn the details of the services offered and the ways in which they benefit the customer.

2. As a reinforcement for a sales approach. After broaching a subject to a prospect, giving him or her a printed piece to take along can serve as a good reminder to get the person to take action.

3. Instead of a direct sales approach. At those times when you're just too busy to sell services verbally, you may find it helpful to include an advertising folder along with the cash or receipt that you give the customer.

4. As information for new customers. If available, a general service folder that lists all of your institution's retail services along with all of its locations and hours should be given to each new customer. In addition, these folders should be given to people with a significant change of status that might indicate a change in banking needs, including those in new jobs or businesses, newlyweds, new homeowners, recent graduates, and so forth.

Newspaper ads. You can turn your institution's newspaper ads into displays by clipping them neatly, mounting them on cardboard, and placing them at the window or even taping them to a glass divider. Or use the ads like advertising folders, saying, "Did you see this ad that describes the service we're talking about? Let me show it to you . . ." Then you can use the ad to make your sales talk. It would even be a simple matter to clip useful newspaper ads and paste them into a scrapbook.

Statements of condition. Statements of condition tell the discerning person a lot about a financial institution. They reflect the rate of growth, describe the investments, reflect the care of management. Keep a supply of your current statements at your window and be ready to use this information to answer any questions a customer might have. Read your institution's statement. Ask about any parts you don't understand. It's information you should have. Reread the section titled "Your Statement of Condition" in Chapter 9.

LOBBY DISPLAYS

Your office lobby is prime marketing space. It may be made available as a community service or it may be used to sell your services. And, because the lobby is also your work area, you may have to cope with some inconvenience that the displays can cause.

Sales Displays

Displays that market services may take the form of such things as new cars, which indirectly sell auto loans, or they may be used to make a direct merchandising appeal, such as a display of safe deposit boxes.

In any case, you are the person customers are most likely to query about the service being touted through the display. Ideally, the person who sets it up should go over the various aspects of the service involved with all staff members, giving them the answers to any questions that might be raised. But the display may be set up without any answers provided. So be prepared on your own. When such a display is placed in your lobby, ask questions, have literature on hand if it is available, and, in general, be ready to sell the service when the display generates questions.

Community Displays

Providing lobby space as a community service is a form of corporate courtesy and a way to share in meaningful endeavors. It might take the form of anything from a lobby full of artwork to a group of Swiss bell-ringers to a display of puppies from the SPCA.

Even if such displays cause you some inconvenience, realize that supporting such activities is part of your institution's involvement in the community and try to learn to live with them. Many tellers find they provide an interesting break in routine and create a friendly atmosphere in which person-to-person courtesy becomes a little easier, especially when it comes to shy or grumpy customers. You can even enjoy them. It's surprising how much you can learn by looking at them yourself and by asking questions of the people involved.

Maintenance

Whether a civic or a service display is set up in your lobby, someone should be responsible for its maintenance. If your workstation is nearby, here are a few things you can do to help with this:

1. Try to keep the display area safe. Check to see that it is neat and pick up any loose items that might cause people to trip.
2. Help it to work. In the case of a service display, keep literature neat and available if it is part of the exhibit. Keep posters visible.
3. Maintain security. Don't let part of a display create a barrier behind which a robber could hide.

If your institution uses lobby displays, your cooperation in their use can be a big help, and the displays can help to make your selling job easier.

YOUR COMPETITION

Banking is one of the most competitive businesses in the country. Considering this, where do you stand in the midst of this competitive spirit? What kind of attitude should you have?

First of all, be realistic in your approach to competitors. Accept the fact that the other financial institutions in your community are also reputable and are staffed by nice, friendly people much like yourself who serve their customers honestly and well. So, while you should be competitive, you should never, ever "knock" the competition. It probably wouldn't be fair, and it's certainly not good manners.

Even though banking is competitive, those who are employed by financial institutions are friendly in their dealings with each other, and it's a good tradition to uphold. They share vital credit information, cooperate in check clearings, participate in large loans, and otherwise do business together. And they often share in projects for the good of the community. The competition may be keen, but it's honest and in the spirit of fair play. Besides, putting down the competition always makes a poor impression on others. Keep this in mind when you deal with your customers.

Selling against the Competition

When ads or news stories contain headlines that tell about a competitive advantage offered by the institution down the street, how should you handle it? Try the following:

1. *Have a positive outlook.* Keep in mind that your best prospects are your present customers. They are convenient to your office and they know and trust you and your co-workers. What the competition has to offer is not likely to make them change financial institutions if they are satisfied with your service.

2. *Keep selling.* Stress the positive points about your institution and its services. Even though you may expect sales to drop off somewhat during a competitive crisis, they won't stop altogether if you and the other tellers keep trying.

3. *Play fair.* If a customer asks a question about your competition, answer it as honestly as you can. If you use deception to get a prospect to come to you and he or she later finds out the facts, that person will be very angry. At the same time, be sure to state the true advantages that your own institution offers, of course.

Here are some specific examples of how to cope with the competition:

The premium offer. Although premiums are not offered as frequently as they were in the past, good premiums can attract new customers. If you are competing with an institution that is using one, remember that, no matter how good the premium may be, it will not appeal to everyone. Premiums may be offered for savings accounts, so, if necessary, put your sales emphasis on other services for a time. Follow up every prospect, and you'll find some people who would rather have your service than the other institution's premium.

Higher savings rates. Many financial institution employees feel that the most difficult of all sales situations occurs when the competition offers higher savings rates. However, if the difference is small, it won't mean much to the average saver. And perhaps your own rates will be going up. Find out. If they are, use this information to keep your present accounts and to sell new ones. And stress your institution's advantages for savers, such as free official checks, free traveler's checks, and the like.

Lower loan rates. Surprisingly, lower loan rates won't interest many people as much as these advantages that your institution may offer: ease of application with confidential, friendly service; quick availability of money; being treated with respect. If people who borrow are given this kind of service, they won't fight about a small interest differential.

Selling against stiff competition isn't always easy, but it can be done. As a teller with many sales opportunities, you have the best chance of anyone in your institution to prove it.

SELL BENEFITS

"Mrs. Jones, our prices are about the same as any other supermarket in town, sometimes higher. Our service is average. But we'd like your business. Will you do your shopping here?" Sounds ridiculous? Of course. What Mrs. Jones wants to hear is, "Our prices are usually lower than any place else in town, our food is as good or better, and our clerks will give you cheerful, efficient service. We can save you time and money. Will you shop with us?" Now they're talking her language! Save *her* time. Save *her* money. They're telling her how *she* benefits.

The same idea holds true when it comes to selling the services of your financial institution. People care about how it can help them. As a teller, you're in a unique position to tell them. And it's easy. First, look for the prospective customer's need, figure out which service can satisfy that need, then tell him or her the benefits of that service.

Here are the most important things prospective customers want:

Earnings. Everyone is interested in making more money. And with the wide variety of checking accounts and savings plans that are available today, people are more conscious of interest rates than ever before. Knowing what your institution pays is important.

Economy. Financial institution services, like all services, cost money. And when an account is unprofitable, the customer will be assessed a reasonable charge. Know how your customers can make their accounts profitable and save this cost—usually by increasing balances or reducing activity. Another aspect of economy is realizing that your services can save your customers money. Paying bills by mail with checks, for example, is far less costly than using precious time and gas to drive all over town.

Convenience. If your institution offers better hours, more parking spaces, a drive-in or walk-up window, automated teller machines, or any other things that can add to a customer's convenience, you have a benefit to talk about. Convenience saves the customer time and/or trouble, and that is something everyone likes.

Efficiency. Prospective customers worked hard for their money, so when they entrust it to a financial institution, they'll want to know that it's being treated in a businesslike manner. They demand honesty as a minimum. Efficiency is a businesslike benefit.

Safety of funds. Prospective customers want to be sure their money is safe. They know that deposit insurance protects them, but they also want to know that their money won't be misplaced or mishandled. They need to believe in the integrity of the institution and its people.

Understanding. Everyone has occasional money troubles. Prospective customers, however, sometimes think that people who work in financial institutions are personally perfect in this respect. This often makes them reluctant to discuss problems with these employees. Just showing understanding and not being critical is a big benefit that you can offer.

Problem solving. Some people need to borrow money. Some need a safe place to deposit it. Some people aren't even sure what their problem is. This is where you can help. People will tell you things. "I'm going to buy a new car." "My wife is going to have a baby." "My son is going to start college next month." When people tell you things, listen carefully. Then ask yourself, "How can our institution help in this situation?" Sometimes the answer will be that it can't; in that case, forget it. But often it can help. Then it's up to you to tell your prospective customer how your service can *benefit* him or her. "Mrs. White, why don't you let me have our manager talk to you about an auto loan? There's no obligation, and I'm sure *we can save you money*." "Mr. Collins, that's swell! Congratulations! How about starting an education account now, before the baby is even born? *It will be a convenient way for you* to handle any money gifts the baby gets as time goes on. And, of course, *you'll earn generous interest*." "College? That's great! Why not let us help you with a checking account to handle your son's allowance? *It's more convenient for you* than sending it to him, and *it's a safer way for him* to handle his money."

These few illustrations show how to solve prospective customers' problems by selling benefits. Try it with the people who come to your window and you'll sell your institution's services.

29

CHAPTER

Cross-Selling

THE HOW AND WHY OF CROSS-SELLING

Cross-selling, which simply means adding new accounts by building on the existing customer base, makes sense because you are utilizing a relationship of mutual trust that already exists and are reaching people who are known to be convenient to your institution. Thus, the technique of cross-selling can best be summed up as being alert for obvious opportunities for your financial institution to be of further service to present customers.

This does not imply using old-fashioned high-pressure sales techniques. Nor does it imply taking unfair advantage of a customer's trust. It does mean being responsive to your customers' needs as expressed in their words and actions. Thus, when Mr. Ryan says, "I'm going to have to scratch to get the money for Johnny's tuition next month," instead of sympathetically saying, "Oh, yes, aren't prices terrible?" you could say, "Perhaps we can help. Let me introduce you to our loan officer, Mr. Smith." And when Mrs. Black says, "We're planning to go away for the summer," don't just wish her a good time. Be sure to add, "How can we help you enjoy yourself more?" and then make suggestions.

Why should you do your best to cross-sell your institution's services? Here are some excellent reasons:

- Even though the typical institution offers a great many retail services, most customers use only one.
- A study conducted some years ago revealed the following statistics:

1. A customer with just a checking account has a 50-50 chance of closing it.
2. A customer with just a savings account has a 2-to-1 chance of staying with the institution.
3. When a person has both a checking and a savings account, the chances that he or she will stay with the institution jump to 10 to 1.
4. When a person has an installment loan in addition to checking and savings, the odds are 18 to 1 that he or she will stay with the institution.
5. When you top off the checking, savings, loan combination with a safe deposit box, the customer's chances of remaining with the institution soar to 100 to 1!

So to sum up the *whys* of cross-selling:

- Most people need more banking services than they now have.
- When customers have more than one service, their relationship with the institution is strengthened.

CROSS-SELLING OPPORTUNITIES

In trying to sell more services to your present customers, it helps to realize that most of them are normal, everyday people who tend to suffer from inertia when it comes to taking action, even if using more services will benefit them greatly and cost them little or nothing. With that in mind, consider some techniques used by successful sales professionals that will help you to do well in this phase of your work.

Talk to a lot of people. No matter how skillful you become, you can never hope to sell a service to every person you approach. Making a sale depends on several factors, including how well you choose the person with whom you talk, your sales ability, personal factors involving the prospect, timing, and even luck. For example, you may suggest an additional service to someone the very day he or she receives an inheritance—or the day the individual loses his or her job. Although you couldn't have known about it, such things will influence your success.

Know your prospects' needs. If a person desperately wants an apple and you keep trying to sell him or her an orange, you'll lose the sale and alienate the prospect. Thus, it's important to be able to determine a person's banking needs. There are two ways to do so:

1. Ask what the needs are. This doesn't mean actually saying, "What services do you need?" Chances are the person doesn't know exactly how a service can help or even that it exists. But the prospect will know about a *financial* need. Then it's up to you to choose a service that will fill it.

2. Anticipate needs. This usually involves applying the needs of others in similar circumstances and assuming that your prospect has the same ones. Thus, young parents probably need a savings account, and a high school graduate who is going away to college probably needs a checking account.

The important thing to remember is that if you zero in on a particular prospect's real need, you'll get an attentive response. And that means you're more likely to make a sale.

A True Story

Years ago, a man applied for a personal loan at the main office of a financial institution in a large northeastern city. "Have you ever borrowed here before?" asked the platform officer. "Yes," replied the man, "quite a few times." Calling for his file, the officer found that the customer was applying for his *thirty-first* personal loan in just over 20 years!

While filling in the loan application, the platform officer asked, "Do you have a checking account?" "Yes." "Where?" "At First National across the street." "Savings account?" "Yes." "Where?" "At First National across the street." At this point, the puzzled officer said, "Mr. Jones, we'll give you your loan, of course. You're an excellent customer. But may I ask why you borrow here and have your checking and savings accounts across the street?" "I don't know," said the customer, "I guess it's because no one ever asked me to open them here." He had borrowed from that financial institution 30 times without anyone ever trying to cross-sell another service.

Clues to Additional Needs

Here is a synopsis of just some of the cross-selling opportunities that may come to your attention and should not be ignored. You should be alert for many more.

- Customers who deposit a paycheck in your institution but save at another one, or don't save at all, should be cross-sold savings.

- People who just regularly cash a paycheck may not be customers in your eyes, but they are in their own. Suggest a checking account.
- Sell a package of services to vacationers. A personal loan for expenses, a credit card, a checking account to pay bills, traveler's checks, a safe deposit box for valuables that shouldn't be left in the house—even a vacation club for next year—are all possibilities for these people.
- Suggest that loan customers who are making a final payment open a savings account and start to pay themselves the amount they've been paying your institution.
- Suggest safe deposit boxes to all depositors. With the current crime situation, this pennies-a-day protection is something everyone should have.
- Suggest checking accounts to any loan customers who make payments with money orders, cash, or checks drawn on another institution.
- Suggest that customers cashing a Christmas Club check use part of it to start a regular savings account. Many people do and go right on saving this way.
- When a couple is buying a new house with a mortgage loan from your institution, they may need a home improvement loan.
- Suggest an education loan for college tuition to the customer who mentions a son or daughter who is about to graduate from high school.

Obvious opportunities. Additional service. Present customers. That's all cross-selling is. But it is extremely important.

HOW TO SELL CHECKING ACCOUNTS

Keep these special advantages of checking accounts in mind in order to succeed in selling them to prospective customers:

Easy bill-paying. This is an important aspect of convenience and economy. With bills due, often hundreds of miles away, a checking account is essential.

Safety of funds. Not only are funds safe because deposits are insured, but, more important, they are safe because checking account customers won't lose their cash. They write money as they need it, actually making "withdrawals" at any time of the day or night simply by signing a paper and giving it to the person to whom they wish to pay money, while the cash itself is secure in the financial institution.

Easy record-keeping. A checking account offers customers a simple but effective and businesslike method of bookkeeping. And, at tax time, each canceled check is a legal receipt of payment, whether it has been returned with a customer's monthly statement or photocopied later by the institution at the customer's request.

Help in budgeting. When dollars are tight, budget-wise people know they must start by knowing where their money goes. A checkbook is the easiest way to keep track of expenses.

Privacy. What people do with their money is their business, and a checking account keeps it that way.

Help in building a credit standing. Getting to know the institution through a properly handled checking account is a good basic start to a good credit rating. This goes for stores, too. Paying bills by checks that always clear promptly makes merchants appreciate the person's business and be more willing to extend credit.

Service from the financial institution. The institution accepts deposits to checking accounts in the form of checks as well as cash, collects them for customers, and credits them to their accounts, no matter on which institution they are drawn. Then the customers are sent periodic statements as proof of their records.

Effortless banking using the mail. As much as your institution likes its customers to come in, when they can't, a checking account makes it easy for them to do business via the mail.

Possible earnings. Certain personal checking accounts offer all of the advantages listed plus the opportunity to earn interest.

These are just some of the benefits of a checking account. Every teller who puts his or her mind to it could probably think of even more. Checking accounts were once for businesses and rich people, but today they are a modern necessity for every family.

Prospects

Almost everyone needs a checking account except children and some of the elderly who need assistance with their affairs. This is because everyone needs safety of funds, convenience, efficient record-keeping, and the other benefits checking accounts provide. Obvious prospects include:

Check cashers. In most financial institutions, the number-one prospects for checking accounts are check cashers. They include people who cash paychecks or other checks drawn on your institution and those who cash government checks. As previously mentioned, some of these people may not have an account with you. Nevertheless, they consider themselves customers because they cash a check at your institution from time to time. This gives you a real advantage in making sales—it means you're not selling to strangers, you're cross-selling to "customers." While you can't normally cash checks drawn on other institutions for strangers, when such a check is presented to you, you do have the chance to suggest that it be used to open a checking account.

Loan payers. When people make a loan payment of any kind at your window— installment, commercial, mortgage—notice how the transaction is made. Do they pay by check? Is that check drawn on your institution? If not, suggest a checking account. By money order? Explain the benefits of a checking account. In cash? Point out that checks are safe and provide bookkeeping records and legal receipts. If your institution is convenient for borrowing, it's also convenient for checking.

New borrowers. Many new loan customers borrow money to spend. And there's no better, more efficient way to spend it than with a checking account. The home improvement loan borrower, for example, can write checks to pay contractors, workers, and suppliers. The person who borrows to buy a car can arrange a loan in advance, have the money in a checking account, and thereby make a deal from a cash-in-hand position. The person who makes a personal or bill-payer loan can pay bills and make purchases while keeping good records of expenses. When you refer a would-be borrower to a loan officer, suggest a checking account as well.

People who withdraw savings. People often save money to accumulate enough to buy something special. When a saver makes a withdrawal at your window, suggest that he or she use the funds to open a checking account. Explain that, if the person carries a large amount of cash, it could be lost or stolen. A checking account offers complete protection of funds. If the person has an official check made out for the withdrawal, he or she may find when making a purchase that a little more money is required or that some expenses weren't anticipated. A checking account with some extra money on deposit would allow the customer to write a check for the exact amount.

New businesses. With the complexity of tax laws and the other confusions new businesses face, a checking account is a must for even the smallest store or other business. Some businesses, however, operate with too few checking accounts. Many use only one account for general purposes, payroll, and so on. Watch for these potential checking needs among your business customers:

1. A separate payroll account. This can make control of this large expense much more accurate and efficient.
2. Escrow accounts to separate the funds of certain clients or customers. These are especially useful for real estate agents, lawyers, and those who receive the funds of others for temporary safekeeping.
3. A travel account for the businessperson who travels frequently. This helps to avoid confusion in the main books at the office.
4. A separate account to pay suppliers. This can aid in inventory control.

Suggest that your business customers ask their bookkeeper or accountant which additional checking accounts can help them. Their cost will be small compared to their benefits.

Newlyweds. People starting out in marriage can best get their financial affairs off on the right foot by controlling their spending through the use of a checking account.

Graduates. Recent graduates are usually cutting some of the ties to their parents and are getting started in a job or profession. This means they now have their own funds to handle. A checking account is an important part of that responsibility.

Newcomers. It really makes things easier for the new family in town when they establish a checking account at the local financial institution. Merchants look at the check and know they belong. It's a good way to "send down roots."

How to Sell Them

First, find the prospects. Watch for those to cross-sell in your office and for others in the neighborhood that your institution serves. Then explain the benefits of checking accounts as they apply to each prospective customer.

Nine major benefits were listed at the beginning of this section. Remember them and try to think of more. When you spot a prospect, let him or her know in a friendly way that your institution can help and that it would like the opportunity to do so. That's all there is to selling what many feel is the most important deposit service ever offered. Whom do *you* know that should have a checking account?

HOW TO SELL SAVINGS ACCOUNTS

When present customers' or other prospects' activities or conversations reveal that they need a savings account, remember to explain the benefits that will appeal to them. They include the following:

- Money deposited in a savings account is safe. The funds are carefully invested and are insured.
- When customers have money in your financial institution, they are in a cash-buying position. They can save on finance charges and take advantage of bargains.
- Money in a savings account earns interest.
- Money in a regular savings account is always available when customers need it for emergencies.
- Customers with money in your institution can enjoy luxuries and can make dreams a reality without going into debt.
- Money in a savings account can help make retirement a pleasure instead of a struggle.
- Money in a savings account makes parenthood easier.
- A savings account can help make it possible to pay for college.
- It is convenient to save by mail.

All of these benefits are related to the individual. For example, perhaps John's savings account means a vacation trip; Bill will use his savings for retirement; Sue and Bob are saving for a down payment on a house; Peter, age 10, is saving for a bicycle; Ellen is saving simply because it makes her happy to see the dollars mount up and to know that whenever she needs them, for any purpose, they'll be there.

Watch for people who should be saving. When John talks of going on a trip, Bill his retirement, and so on, mention savings accounts to them.

The Hard Part of Saving

Money in a savings account is something that can help a person or family weather a period of rising costs. But people might say, "Oh, come now. If I have trouble making ends meet, how can I possibly save money?" It's not easy, that's true. But it is possible. Here are a few tips you can pass along to savings prospects who ask you to suggest ways that will enable them to save:

- Cut down expenses and put the money you save into a savings account. Quit smoking or having cocktails out or eat meat less frequently. Whatever you decide, put aside the money saved in a savings account to keep it from getting mixed in with "spending" money.
- Set up a "withholding" tax for yourself. Take a few deposit slips and date them several paydays ahead. Fill in a reasonable amount in the appropriate space, and put the slips where you keep your bills. Then when payday comes, you can pay yourself first.
- Save all or part of gifts. If your aunt sends $20 every birthday and $50 at Christmas, add it to the regular amounts you save yourself.
- Get a coin bank and use it. When you have a lot of change, put some of it in the coin bank. And if payday rolls around and there are still a few dollars left, put them in the little bank, too. When it's full, add the contents to your savings account and start filling the coin bank again.
- Plan to set aside a portion of any windfall *before* it happens. This would include such items as bonuses, inheritances, winnings, or any sort of unexpected income.
- Get the family into the act. Have the children put aside in their own savings 10 percent of allowances or earnings. And get your spouse to contribute on a regular basis to the "main" fund and to the coin bank, too.
- Finally, keep your goals reasonable. At the end of the year, tally up. Chances are, you'll be a "thousandaire" by this time. And you'll find the saving was relatively painless. Best of all, during a time of rising costs, you'll have something not everyone has—money in a savings account and the sense of security that goes with it.

Savings Prospects

Everyone is a savings prospect, although not everyone knows it. As a teller, many people come to your window who ought to save. Included are the paycheck casher, the safe deposit renter who has securities, new parents, someone who is cashing a tax refund, the person with a raise in pay, someone who earns tips, someone who inherits money, the customer who keeps an extra-large checking account balance, the employee with a new job, and anyone with a dream that savings can help to make a reality.

These are the kinds of people you meet every day. Just listen at your window, and they'll tell you their needs. Then you can tell them how savings can benefit them. For example:

Comment: My daughter just started high school . . .

Your reply: Have you considered saving for her college education? There's still time, and it will save you money in the long run.

Comment: I've been with the company a year and just got a raise.

Your reply: That's great! You've gotten along without spending that extra money until now, so why not put it aside each month in a savings account where it can earn interest for you?

If you tell people how saving regularly will benefit them, you'll sell savings accounts.

Keogh and IRA Prospects

With all the publicity, you'd think that every eligible person must know about Keoghs and Individual Retirement Accounts. But, as pointed out in Chapter 24, "Know Your Services," many people don't and, of those who do, many have failed to act.

When the opportunity presents itself, mention these excellent plans to the following types of people:

- Doctors in private practice. These professional people are high-income earners and are usually in a high tax bracket. A Keogh account would enable them to deduct a substantial amount from their before-tax earnings and would allow them to pay the taxes on both principal and interest after retirement when their tax bracket will be considerably lower.
- Lawyers. Remember the story of the shoemaker who went barefoot? Many lawyers may know a great deal about Keoghs and IRAs, but they haven't gotten around to doing anything about retirement even though they know they should.
- Architects, accountants, storeowners, writers, plumbers, self-employed teachers, and any others who work for themselves are prospects.
- Don't forget salespeople, part-time employees, or older employees who are excluded from a company pension plan as prospects for an

IRA. Many people who work for others don't have any retirement program other than Social Security.

- Also, the person who is qualified for a Keogh account but who does not wish to include his or her employees may open an IRA. This could be a real benefit to many small businesspersons who simply could not afford the employee contributions Keoghs require.

Selling savings is a pleasure when there are as many customer benefits involved as there are in Keogh accounts and IRAs. If you haven't already been trying to sell them, now is the time. Your customers will be grateful.

Business Customers

Business people have a tendency to put extra dollars back into their businesses. This is understandable, but they should also consider a savings account. A savings account is a great place to accumulate money for really important capital needs. Instead of adding a few dollars at a time to the business, a large sum can be accumulated that will accomplish something important.

And even businesspeople should accumulate some funds for personal pleasure or specific personal goals. Therefore, business customers should be cross-sold the other way, too—into any personal accounts that they can use.

HOW TO SELL LOAN SERVICES

Your institution's loan services are highly specialized; therefore, so are the responsibilities of the appropriate officers and departments. Ultimate approvals, thus final sales, must come from them. But it is the responsibility of everyone in your institution to be on the lookout for good prospects for these services and to nurture these prospects into a potential sale.

This means that everyone in the institution should know the *benefits* of the various types of loans that are available in order to be able to arouse the interest of the prospect, even if the final closing requires the cooperation of someone else.

Telling the Loan Story

The loan sales talk, like the sales talk for any service, stresses benefits. But one important difference must be kept in mind when creating or telling the loan story. Everyone is proud to have a deposit account. Safe deposit box renters are pleased with themselves for their prudence. Buyers of traveler's checks know that they are wise in the ways of the world. But many people, unfortunately, are a little ashamed of having a loan. This is foolish, of course, but it's true. Even proud new home buyers don't like the details of their home financing discussed publicly. So when you talk about loans, talk quietly and privately. Customers' confidence mustn't be violated.

Here are some of the ways that people benefit by making loans at your institution:

It's easy to borrow. Red tape is a thing of the past when borrowing from a financial institution. Applications are simple to complete.

Service is fast. Financial institutions are geared to approve applications quickly and to make cash available promptly.

Service is confidential. The institution learns some private things about borrowers, but it keeps these things as secret as they should be.

Each type of loan that your institution makes has its own individual benefits in addition to those listed above. For example, consider this popular loan service. Some of the advantages of a home improvement loan are:

- Immediate enjoyment of better living.
- Increased value of property.
- Minor home repairs now avoid more costly repairs later.
- Monthly payments can be tailored to the family budget.

In a sales talk, these benefits and those that apply to all loans might be used to good effect:

"Mr. Doe, when your brother was here yesterday, he mentioned that you and Mrs. Doe are thinking of making some improvements to your home. What are you planning to do?"

"Well, Jane has been after me for some time to put in a new kitchen; and while we're torn up, I thought I might just go ahead and add the den I've been wanting."

"That sounds very nice. You know, home improvement loans are a specialty of our institution. They make it easy to enjoy the improvements you want right away, and you can make convenient monthly payments from future income."

"That sounds good, but I don't like to pay those high interest rates."

"Then you're at the right place, because our interest rates are low, and not just hidden in long-term payments."

"How long would I have to wait to get the money?"

"Not long at all. Sometimes we can process an application within 24 hours. Let me have Mrs. Foster talk to you and take your application. She'll be glad to give you any more information you may want . . ."

And that's how a casual comment—in this case from the prospect's brother—can become an important new account for your institution.

Selling Auto Loans

Getting the cash for a car in advance has two advantages: With the money already in hand, the buyer is less likely to allow a dealer to talk him or her into buying a higher-priced vehicle. The buyer also has a greater chance of getting a rebate from the seller, which might not be forthcoming if the car were dealer-financed. In fact, with a rebate, a regular auto loan from your institution may actually cost less than a dealer-financed loan that appears to be less expensive.

Because many people have a tendency to make all of their arrangements in one place, they may plan to finance their cars through the dealer without ever thinking of your institution for this purpose. This is where you can help. Look for these clues:

People who withdraw funds from savings accounts. When you notice a large withdrawal, it's possible that the money is intended for the down payment on a car. Although you can't ask what the money is for, the customer may tell you about it. Or, if you can get him or her talking about cars, the customer may mention that the withdrawal is for the purchase of a new one.

People who buy large money orders or ask for large official checks. This may or may not tie in with a large withdrawal. In any case, such a person may be making a down payment on a car.

Customers using the drive-in may mention the fact that they intend to buy a car. The fact that the customer is in an older car while talking to you might lead him or her to chat about buying a new one.

Customers at your window may want to discuss buying a car. People like to talk to their tellers and get advice on financial dealings. And buying a car may be included.

Train yourself to be alert for these prospects, then try to sell them a loan from your financial institution. Doing so won't be difficult if you keep a few basics in mind:

Know what your institution offers. What rate does it charge for a new-car loan, a used-car loan, and even for a home equity loan, which may be used to purchase a car? For what terms can these loans be made? How much money can a customer save by borrowing from your institution compared to financing through a local dealer?

Know the loan interviewer to whom prospects should be referred. Then, when you get a prospect interested, take the trouble to personally introduce him or her to the loan officer. If you can't leave your window, do it by phone. It will make the prospect feel more comfortable.

Use any sales aids you have available. This includes pertinent literature and copies of your institution's ads, posters, and displays.

Explain benefits. Tell the prospect that a rebate is more likely if he or she has the money in advance. Explain that interest rates at your institution may actually save the person money; that it has fast, confidential service; that repayment schedules can often be arranged to suit his or her budget; and that your institution welcomes loan applications from good customers.

When you sell auto loans, you help your customers, you help your institution to develop profitable new business, and you help yourself by getting credit for important sales and by sharpening your techniques in dealing with others.

Selling Other Services to Your Loan Customers

Your institution's loan customers are prospects for other services. For example, an auto loan customer may need a safe deposit box for important papers, starting with the auto title and insurance policy; a customer who has an education loan for an older child should be saving for a younger one; a vacation loan borrower should have a checking account and traveler's checks; a person who would like to borrow a small amount just until payday to make a purchase is a prospect for your institution's credit card.

Here are three major types of prospects to consider:

Perpetual borrowers. Although these people always have a loan, you shouldn't make the mistake of putting them down. Constant borrowers make their payments on time and are profitable business for your institution. However, for their own good and for the institution's, they should be savers as well as borrowers. You can spot these prospects because they come to your window to make loan payments or may mention their loans when they make other transactions. While being careful not to offend them, you can suggest that saving is just like making small regular payments, but this time the benefits go to them. Having a good credit rating is a plus, but not as good as having money in a savings account.

On-them check users. These borrowers, who make loan payments in person or by mail using postal money orders or checks drawn on other financial institutions, could use a checking account at yours. When they come to your window to make a loan payment, ask for the business right on the spot. Make note of the names and addresses of those who pay by mail from their payment slips or checks and watch for them the next time they come in. Turn over the names of those you won't see to someone who can follow up with a letter.

Paid-up loan customers. What a wonderful day it is for borrowers when they hand over the last coupon with the money to pay off a loan. But now what will they do with the money they're in the habit of paying out? As mentioned previously, why not save part of it? After all, if they're not used to having the money, putting some away should be fairly painless. Watch for customers whose loans you know are being paid down. Then, when they're at your window, ask for the business or make a note to do so the next time you see them. These people are happy and pleased with themselves. Be pleased with them and suggest that they make a small immediate deposit to get started.

CROSS-SELLING TO THE "MATURE MARKET"

People who are aged 50 and older are often referred to at financial institutions as the "mature market." And they are a particularly important group of prospects for banking services. Besides their growing numbers, these people are apt to be financially stable, have children who are grown, mortgages that are paid off in many cases, and are at the peak of their earnings potential. In fact, it has been reported that over 75 percent of the assets in the United States are held by households headed by people aged 50 and older. This makes them important prospects for financial institutions to attract and to please.

Because of their affluence and growing numbers, financial institutions are endeavoring to attract members of the mature market by offering them special financial services. These may include free checking accounts and traveler's checks, higher savings rates, credit cards with no annual fee, reduced loan rates, and lower safe deposit box fees.

Of course, financial institutions place special emphasis on how well these people are treated by public-contact personnel. As a teller, keep the following

points in mind whenever you try to cross-sell services to these important customers:

- Don't treat people aged 50 and above as though they are elderly.
  Many of them do not consider themselves to be old and dislike being
  termed "senior citizens" or "golden agers." Nowadays, mature consumers often feel 10 or 15 years younger than they really are. They
  tend to be active and healthy and are living longer than any prior
  group of people their age.
- Respect mature adults' intelligence and longer experience. Older consumers have been found to be more likely to do their homework than
  their younger counterparts when it comes to making financial decisions. This means, in order to sell them your institution's services,
  it's important for you to be knowledgeable about those services yourself.

Try to keep these tips in mind and act friendly and understanding whenever you make an effort to cross-sell your institution's services to your mature
customers, no matter what their age.

30

CHAPTER

Your Sales Talk

FINDING NEW CUSTOMERS

In addition to its present customers, your institution has several other good sources of prospects for your services. First, consider the basic factors that qualify someone as a prospect. Someone who can't possibly use a service is not a prospect. Neither is someone who must travel many miles past competing financial institutions that offer similar services. This leaves those people who have a financial need that your institution can fill and who are located in a spot that is convenient for taking advantage of that service. For the typical financial institution, this includes thousands of people, some of whom you know. Ask yourself:

- Where do I eat lunch? Has anyone who works there or eats there regularly ever indicated a need for service?
- Where do I shop? Has anyone at any of the stores ever said something that would show a need?
- Where do I go to relax? To buy gas and oil? To follow my hobby? Is someone a prospect in any of these places?

Think about friends, neighbors, and even family members who might be in need of banking services. Don't be timid about the idea of selling them. No one will ever resent a sincere interest on your part to improve their financial status.

A smaller but important group that is often overlooked includes people who are convenient to your other offices. Since the idea is for your whole institution to grow through new business, these prospects should also be encouraged to use your services.

Four Groups of Prospects

There are four basic groups of people who are not customers of your institution but perhaps should be. They include: new residents; new businesses; people whose situation has created a need, such as recent graduates, newlyweds, and those who are newly employed; and people who have a need but don't know it, such as those who frequently buy money orders or who accumulate money that they keep at home.

How do you find these potential customers? Here are two suggestions:

Ask others. This is especially helpful in finding new residents or businesses. Ask Mrs. Jones, "Has anyone moved into the house next door to you yet?" Or ask Mr. Smith, "Who's going to replace Mr. Doe at your office?" Or ask the real estate agent, the postman, or the policeman who checks your office for leads on newcomers and new businesses.

Keep your eyes open. What route do you use to get to work? Why not take a slightly different one occasionally? See if there are any "Sold" signs in front of houses. See if there are any new businesses opening. Learn to be aware of what's happening in your institution's area.

People Who Walk In

Noncustomers who come into your office for various reasons are also good prospects for your services. Consider the following people:

The check-casher. Tellers are often faced with a person who is unknown to them who wants to cash a check. "After all," the person reasons, "financial institutions are where you cash checks, and this is a financial institution, so why not?" You can't, of course, cash a check for a stranger that is drawn on an out-of-town institution. But to send him or her away without suggesting an alternative would be a mistake, too. Therefore, a simple "no" isn't the right answer. Perhaps this person would be willing to use the check to open an account. Or he or she may be a newcomer who is planning to take a job with a local firm that would be willing to endorse it. In any case, the check-casher is a prospect and should be treated as such.

The information-seeker. "Where can I find a real estate office?" "Can you direct me to the XYZ Company?" Whatever he or she wants, the person who seeks information may be a potential customer. A few questions will provide the answer. "Are you new in town?" said with a friendly smile will never be resented. "Oh, I'm just passing through," disqualifies the person as a prospect. But if the answer is "yes," chances are he or she is looking for friends as well as for the XYZ Company, and that includes employees at a friendly financial institution. Most people who relocate come with a good supply of cash and may wait days or even weeks before they go into a financial institution to talk business. In such a case, helping the person by providing information can open the door to a future relationship. After giving him or her the information, it's a good idea to add, "As soon as you're settled and have a few minutes, drop in and let us help you with your banking needs." Most newcomers will open an account with the first convenient financial institution that asks them to, so it pays to be alert for them.

The new account opener. A third group of prospects who come into your office are strangers who enter specifically to open a new account. They may be newcomers to the community as well. If they are, you should take the opportunity to make them welcome. Opening a new account at a financial institution where you're unknown and where you're eyed suspiciously can be very unpleasant. Actually, of course, this may be in the customers' imagination; but it could leave a bad taste that would eventually get them to do their banking elsewhere after they know the community better. Walk-in noncustomers who become new customers are, of course, good prospects for additional services. Welcome them as customers, try to learn what their needs are, and suggest ways that your institution can fill them.

HOW TO GIVE YOUR SALES TALK

Every successful sales talk has four basic elements:

1. **Brevity.** The successful salesperson gets to the point with as few words as possible.
2. **Interest.** If a brief talk is interesting, the listener will pay attention.

3. Clarity. If the prospect doesn't understand the salesperson, the game is lost from the beginning. If he or she does, the sale is on its way to being made.

4. Motivation. A good sales talk gets a prospect to take action—now. Not because the person is pressured, but because he or she wants to.

Keep these points in mind whenever you try to sell one of your institution's services. Then follow these steps for making a sale:

- Start by knowing about the service you want to sell. You don't have to be an expert in every phase of banking, but you should know what the service is, who can use it, how it works, how it helps people, what procedures are necessary to use it, and how much it costs or earns.

- When you're face-to-face with the prospect, say what you want to say in simple English. Avoid using technical banking terms and complicated explanations.

- Be natural. Use your own words, your own expressions. Be yourself. Don't become a machine the minute you start a sales talk.

- Follow a logical, step-by-step sequence. If you try to sell a particular service several times, this will happen almost automatically. You'll discover which phrases work, which words spark interest, the best order to cover points, and when to wrap up.

- Include real experiences. This makes a sales talk interesting and believable. Of course, don't violate customer confidences or dominate with your own experiences and opinions. But say things such as:

  "I have a customer who's deposited just $5 to his savings account every week for over 10 years. With interest, he now has over $3,000. He never really misses such a small amount and always pays himself first."

  "I have a customer who found he saved several hundred dollars by financing his car here . . ."

- As stated before, sell benefits. This ties in with relating real experiences. Most people are primarily interested in themselves—in what will help them. "We'd love to have your account," some tellers might say, to which the prospective customer is likely to think, "Who cares?"

- Ask for the business. No matter how you interest people or how you motivate them with the ways in which a service can benefit them, most people still need help in making a decision. This is discussed in more detail below.

- Finally, don't oversell. When a prospective customer agrees to open an account, apply for a loan, or take whatever action you've been suggesting, stop right there. Listing the benefits of the service that are not of interest to the prospect might get the person to change his or her mind.

If you use the foregoing techniques for giving a sales talk, you're certain to bring in valuable new business for your financial institution.

ASKING FOR THE BUSINESS

Suppose you spot a prospect, explain the benefits of the service to him or her, and nothing happens. What more can you do? This is a good question. After all, as stated before, you're not a high-powered commission salesperson; and your institution isn't in the business of pressuring its customers. But there is one thing that you can and should do: *Ask for the business.*

A psychological factor involved here that anyone who is going to be successful at selling must understand is this: Most people need help in making a decision. Making decisions is hard work, and people avoid making even small ones. For example:

Teller: . . . so you can see, Mrs. Jones, having a safe deposit box makes good sense. The cost is so little, yet you know all of those important papers will be safe.

Mrs. Jones: Of course, you're right. I just never much thought about it before.

The teller now has two choices. He or she can say nothing further and leave Mrs. Jones in an embarrassing silence, which she will probably end by saying goodbye and going about her business; or another line can be added to the dialogue . . .

Teller: Why don't you let me have our manager get you a signature card so that you can start using a box right away?

Now Mrs. Jones has two choices. She can say "yes" or she can say "no." The chance of her saying "yes" is much improved because the teller has suggested a course of action that makes it easier for her to make a decision. Now she knows what the next step in renting a box is and doesn't have to feel foolish by asking.

More Examples of What to Say

The example of the teller and Mrs. Jones is a good one to illustrate the kind of situation in which the customer can act on the spot. Here are a few more ideas about what to say when asking for the business:

Auto loans . . . "Mr. Smith, when you decide for sure that you're going to buy a car, please let me know. I'm sure we can save you a lot of money in finance charges."

Checking accounts . . . "Let me get you a signature card to take home. Just talk it over with your wife and if you decide to open an account, both of you sign it. Then we can get you started right away." Or . . . "It would only take a few minutes to open an account for you. May I get you a signature card?"

Savings accounts . . . "Why not let us open an account for you now? It won't cost you a cent; and if you should decide later to buy stocks with the money, it will be here waiting for you."

Credit cards . . . "Take this application. If you'd like to apply now, I'll introduce you to our manager. If you'd like to take it home and think it over, just mail it to us after you've filled it in."

Problems in Completing a Sale

Even if you have a real knack for spotting prospects' needs and a thorough knowledge of your institution's services, you may still find yourself at a loss when it comes to completing a sale. This is a common situation that may be caused by one or more of the following problems:

A lack of skill in closing a sale. In this case, two factors may be involved. The first is inexperience in selling; the second is having the disturbing feeling that closing a sale is somehow a less-than-honorable thing to do.

Overcoming these factors requires learning to give a positive sales presentation. Telling your customer how the service will benefit him or her, explaining its cost, if any, and its profitability, if any, is certainly an honorable approach. While you're talking, keep the word "positive" in mind. The so-called positive approach used by high-pressure salespeople often involves asking a prospect a series of questions that require "yes" responses, thereby hoping to force a successful close. However, you needn't learn to develop this technique because you shouldn't use it. Financial institutions can't afford to alienate prospects with high-pressure techniques or they'll ruin the chance for later sales opportunities. So when it's time to close a sale, just ask for the business in a straightforward way: "If you'd like to have a checking account, we can help you right away. Would you like to open one now?"

> *Embarrassment.* Some tellers are embarrassed to complete a sales presentation by actually suggesting action. As a result, as discussed previously, situations develop in which the prospect is given a detailed description of the benefits of a service and then is left hanging. Presumably, he or she is then supposed to ask, "Well, what do I do next? How do I open an account?" But that person may also be embarrassed to seem pushy, so the sale goes unmade.

Don't be embarrassed to ask for the business. The prospect knows that making a sale won't earn you a commission. And it's better to get a "no" than to keep yourself and your prospect tied up in an indefinite sales situation. After getting a "no," you can direct your attention to someone else.

> *Fear of answering objections.* In this case, a teller may simply be uncomfortable about continuing to try to make a sale after the prospect objects or even asks a question. If you feel this way, realize that many so-called objections are really just questions that an overly sensitive salesperson takes as a put-off. So begin by listening to the prospect and analyzing what he or she is saying. For example, if someone concludes, "I'd like to think about this," your answer should be, "Fine. And if we can help, please let me know." You don't need that sale today, but you may need that prospect tomorrow. However, if the person says, "My Aunt Mary says that keeping a checking account is a waste of time," that's an objection you can readily answer.

The secret of closing a sale is simply to ask for the business without using any tricks or gimmicks. And when the prospect does say "yes," stop talking—no more sales points and no more closing.

WHEN YOU CAN'T SEEM TO SELL SERVICES

Is the Customer the Problem?

Flat tires, sick children, leaky washing machines, overdue or large bills, and scores of other unexpected factors can make prospects for your services touchy and make your selling efforts difficult. However, this kind of problem isn't as insurmountable as it seems. It will help if you keep these points in mind:

- Realize that for every prospect for your services who has had a bad morning there is another who has had a great morning. The trick is to find that person.
- Balancing problem situations with ideal situations can best be done by creating *more* situations. The prospect who is in a great frame of mind can be found if more prospects in general are found. This means talking about services to many people.

Are You the Problem?

At times it may seem that no matter what you say to a prospect in trying to sell one of your services, he or she will say "yes" immediately. Yet at other times, no matter how hard you try, you just can't seem to make a sale. Therefore, you may wonder if it's possible for you to be consistently good at this part of your job.

The answer is simple. As a teller, you can't always be at a peak because you're human and subject to the ups and downs that everyone has. But there is one thing you can do—keep a positive attitude so that the downs won't seem as bad. While you wouldn't want to change those wonderful days when everything goes great, you can soften the days when things tend to go wrong.

To help make your selling lows become gentle valleys instead of deep canyons, realize what's right about the good days and what's wrong about the bad days. Next time you have a really good day, take a few minutes to ask yourself:

- How do I feel in relation to average or below-average days? Do I feel better physically? Do I feel better mentally?
- Am I in an unusually optimistic mood today?
- Is the world around me better than average today? How's the weather, for example?
- Did anything special happen to lift my spirits today?
- Am I making sales because I expect to make them?

Now cross-check by rephrasing the questions when you have a bad day:

- How do I feel in relation to average or above-average days? Do I feel worse physically? Do I feel worse mentally?
- Am I in an unusually pessimistic mood today?
- Is the world around me below average today?
- Did anything special happen to turn me off today?
- Am I losing sales because I expect to lose them?

The answers to these questions will often be quite obvious. On exceptionally good days, people usually *feel* exceptionally good—and vice versa. Optimism usually accompanies and contributes to above-average days, and pessimism accompanies and contributes to low days.

In addition, everyone is affected by those around them. For example, a grumpy, bickering staff can touch off a bad day. And some people are affected by the weather, finding that they have difficulty selling on rainy days or when the barometer is dropping sharply. When this happens, it would be better if they'd use those days for other purposes and really push during the bright, cheerful ones.

Finally, the greatest contributor to good or bad selling days is the person's attitude about expected sales. Our feelings can determine our actions, and our actions determine whether we succeed or fail.

You can help yourself to avoid bad days by recognizing their symptoms. Recall the analysis you did and try to offset negative trends by actually seeking out things characteristic of good days. If, for example, a surly bus driver got your day off to a bad start, try to offset it by exchanging a few cheerful words with your friendliest co-worker.

Keep in mind the fact that sales are what build your financial institution . . . and your worth as an employee.

SELLING THROUGH TEAMWORK

Teamwork means sharing responsibilities with other employees, backing each other up, and building and maintaining a spirit of pride in your financial institution. This makes it a more pleasant place in which to work and a more enticing place for customers to do business. It also makes selling easier and more effective and gets sales results more often.

Team Members

Your institution's sales team includes the following:

Tellers. Because you have the most contact with customers, you and your fellow tellers are the key people in your institution's sales efforts. You have the first, and often the only, chance to spot possible needs for banking services. And you have the best chance to ask for the business at the psychologically right moment—when the prospect is first talking about his or her needs.

Marketing department personnel. These staff members provide the cover of advertising under which sales efforts can be most effective.

Usually, they're also responsible for directing the institution's sales training as well as its public relations and business development activities.

Branch managers and platform officers. These are the people who can take care of special situations involving tricky accounts . . . or who can make that loan you solicit. Customer-contact officers can work together with tellers to produce outstanding sales results.

Loan interviewers. In small financial institutions or in branches, this function is often filled by platform officers or branch managers. In institutions where loan interviewers are separate individuals who handle routine installment loans, they are key members of the sales team.

New accounts clerks. Along with tellers, these employees have a first-class opportunity to sell. They have the chance to cross-sell customers additional services when they open their accounts. Often, they are the people to whom busy tellers refer prospects.

Operations personnel. These employees maintain the accurate and neat records that keep customers satisfied and coming back. In addition, they can provide information for tellers and other contact personnel to pursue.

Management. It's a mistake to overlook senior officers as part of the sales team. Yes, the president or executive vice-president brings in business, but back up a teller or branch manager in his or her effort? Why not? If the prospective account is really a good one, it pays to get some top-level involvement in the solicitation.

Teamwork Techniques

The people listed above aren't the only members of your institution's team. Guards, vault attendants, telephone operators, receptionists, and secretaries are also important when it comes to selling your services. How can all of you work together? Here are a few ways:

Through referrals. Suppose you spot a prospect for a personal loan. Even though you can't make loans because that isn't your job, it would be a good idea to refer such a prospect *in person* to the team member who can handle his or her needs. Often, the best way to do this is to signal or phone the proper person and have him or her come to your window to meet the customer. Next best is to phone the team member while the prospect listens as you explain that you're sending the customer to his or her desk. In cases in which the customer doesn't want to see the other person just then, perhaps because of a time situation, at least give the prospect the name of the other team member in writing. This may be on a piece of appropriate literature, or it might be suitable for this purpose to have a supply of the employee's business cards.

As a teller, you can also *receive* referrals from others. You're in a position to watch for and solicit your regular customers for additional accounts after a bookkeeper, loan officer, or other team member passes on a possible need to you. Let other members of the team know you'll follow up any leads they give you.

Some financial institutions find that small, printed referral forms are helpful. On each form, they list the names of the originator and the person receiving the referral, the prospect's name, the type of account involved, and a brief statement of how the account might be successfully solicited.

> *Through joint action.* In this case, you would ask another person to help make the sale because he or she has more expertise in a particular subject than you do. Without alarming the customer by "ganging up" on him or her, you might, for example, have a vault attendant explain the costs and sizes of your safe deposit boxes. Or you might ask a loan interviewer to quote rates. This is teamwork selling at its best.

> *Through help with officer's calls.* Many financial institutions ask their managers and other officers to make outside calls. As a teller, you can help support this activity by reporting changes in the status of accounts to the interested officer, by passing on tips on new businesses opening in the area, by informing the officer of unusually large withdrawals or account activity, and by passing on the names of any new people involved in an account. If you can give the officer a clue as to the needs a commercial customer may have, he or she will have a better chance of making a sale.

Fairness is an essential ingredient of successful teamwork. So if you find a prospect or make a sale, you should get recognition for it. At the same time, you should give credit to anyone who helped you make the sale, being sure that your own efforts are also recognized. When you sell a new account, write your supervisor a brief note about it, carefully sharing the credit if you had help.

Conclusion

Selling the services of your financial institution doesn't require the high-pressure sales approach of the used car salesman. He'll probably never see his customer again, but you will. You'll have lots of chances to sell the same person because you have so many services to offer. That's why, in the examples in this section, there was no pressure put on the customer. When you find a prospect for your services, explain the benefits. Then help him or her to make a decision by tactfully asking for the business. Selling your services is as easy as that.

On the other hand, if all of the following statements apply to your institution, you can forget about this important part of your job. THERE'S NO NEED FOR YOU TO SELL SERVICES IF:

- Every present customer of your institution knows about all of your services.
- Every prospective customer knows about your institution and how it could benefit him or her.
- There are no young people in your area growing into banking needs, no people getting married, having babies, sending kids to school, no newcomers moving in, no new businesses starting up.
- Your institution has no competition.
- Your institution has all the business it wants or can handle.

But if none of these statements apply to your financial institution, then the tips in this section and throughout this whole book can help you do a more effective job of selling your services and building your "bankability" plus.

GLOSSARY

ABA number: The number assigned to a financial institution by the American Bankers Association for purposes of identification.

Account analysis: The practice in some financial institutions of computing the cost of maintaining a checking account, usually based on collected balance versus activity. Any excess cost over profit on the balance is passed on to the customer as a service charge.

Advice: A written notice of specific account activity. Credit advice and debit advice refer to forms sent to advise customers of credits to or charges against their accounts.

Altered check: A check on which the payee, endorsement, amount in figures or words, or date have been changed, usually for fraudulent purposes.

Annual percentage rate (APR): The amount, expressed as a percentage, of the yearly cost of credit. By law, this figure is stipulated by all lenders in a uniform way so that customers can make comparisons.

Asset: A thing of value owned by a person or business. Money in a savings account is an asset to the saver.

Audit: An investigation into the safe and honest operation of a financial institution. An audit is conducted by the institution's own auditors or a firm hired by them. *See* Examination.

Auditor: A financial institution officer, answerable directly to the board of directors, who is responsible for regular and careful examination of the books and accounts of the institution.

Automated teller machine (ATM): A computer-controlled terminal through which financial institution customers can transact routine business at any time of day or night with the use of an access card and a secret code number called a personal identification number or PIN.

Automatic overdraft account: A checking account that, when overdrawn, automatically creates a loan that pays the overdraft, subject to a prearranged credit agreement between the financial institution and the depositor.

Average daily balance: The balance in a deposit account that can be computed in many ways, but usually by adding together the closing balance each day for a month and dividing by the number of business days in the month. *See* Balance.

Bait money: Banded bills kept by tellers to include with any money taken during a hold-up. The denominations, serial numbers, issuing Federal Reserve Banks, and series dates of the bills are recorded by the financial institution to aid law enforcement officers in apprehending and prosecuting the criminals.

Balance: The total in an account. Also called the ledger balance. The average daily balance is the numerical average of balances added together and divided by the number of additions. The most important figure is the collected balance, which is the amount actually cleared into deposit in a customer's account.

Balancing: See Settling.

Balloon payment loan: A loan that terminates with a large single payment.

Bank draft: A check drawn by a financial institution against an account it maintains in another financial institution.

Bank holding company: A corporation that owns one or more banks, formed for legal purposes to allow the bank and/or the corporation to have broader powers.

Bank Insurance Fund (BIF): The insurance fund, under the direction and administration of the Federal Deposit Insurance Corporation, that backs the deposits of banks. This fund is separate from the fund that backs the deposits of savings and loan associations.

Bank Secrecy Act: The law that is designed to help the federal government in the investigation of organized crime and other criminal matters. It requires the maintenance and preservation of records of financial transactions for possible use in criminal, tax, or regulatory proceedings; and it attempts to identify those who try to further their illegal activities by conducting their transactions in currency and certificates of deposit, by using foreign financial facilities, or by the international transportation of currency or bearer instruments.

Bearer: The person actually holding a legal instrument, such as a check, payable to "bearer" or endorsed in blank.

Blank endorsement: The endorser's signature on the reverse of an instrument. This legally makes the instrument a bearer instrument that anyone can then negotiate.

Blanket bond: An insurance, uniquely for financial institutions, that insures against loss from robbery, fraud, embezzlement, forgery, and other security hazards.

Board of directors: A group of people from the business and private sectors of the community who oversee the affairs of the financial institution. They elect the president and other officers and choose replacements for their own members whose terms have expired.

Bond: A certificate of debt, usually issued by a government or corporation, that entitles the owner to interest.

Bookkeeper: In a financial institution, that person who keeps records of the transactions of depositors, specifically checking depositors.

Branch: A financial institution office that operates separate from, but under the direction of, the institution's main office.

Bulk cash: Bagged or rolled coin or banded currency.

Call report: A certified statement, issued by demand of regulatory authorities, that describes a financial institution's condition as of a specified date.

Cash drawer: The compartment in which a teller keeps his or her working cash. It should be locked when not in use by the teller to whom it was assigned.

Cashier's check: An official check drawn by a national financial institution on itself; thus, it is as good as cash. *See* Treasurer's check.

Cash-in ticket: A paper filled in by a teller when cash is received, which is forwarded to the proof department in place of the cash for settlement.

Cash item: A check or other obligation payable on demand; an item good for immediate credit to a depositor's account.

Cash letter: A transmittal letter that accompanies cash items from one financial institution to another and describes the items sent.

Cash-out ticket: A paper filled in by a teller when cash is paid out in a split or cash-back deposit that accompanies the cashed check to the proof department for settlement.

Certificate of deposit (CD): A receipt for funds in a special deposit with a financial institution. CDs vary widely in amount and term, and the rate of interest depends on both of these factors.

Certified check: A check drawn by a depositor on his or her account that has been certified by a financial institution officer, thus withdrawing the funds from the depositor's account and holding them in a special fund until the check is paid. A certified check is a guarantee of payment if it is properly presented and endorsed.

Charter: The legal authority for a financial institution to do business as certified in a document issued by a government or federal authority.

Chattel mortgage: A legal document pledging personal property for a loan. *See* Mortgage.

Check: A negotiable instrument containing a date, signed by a maker, ordering a financial institution to pay a certain sum on deposit with the institution to a designated person or to the bearer.

Check digit: A suffix number, which is part of the MICR number, that can test the validity of an account number by activating a computer programmed to do this. *See* Magnetic ink character recognition.

Checking account: A demand deposit account against which checks may be drawn by the owner.

Christmas Club: A type of forced savings plan, usually with coupons or preprinted deposit slips, with payout, if any, at or near holiday time.

Civil Rights Act of 1968: Among other things, this law, as it relates to financial institutions, prohibits discrimination against prospective homebuyers or mortgage loan applicants on the basis of race, color, national origin, or sex.

Clearing: The process by which checks are forwarded for collection to the financial institution on which they are drawn.

Clearinghouse: A place where representatives of financial institutions serving a specified locality meet to exchange checks for clearing and to settle their accounts with each other. Modern clearinghouses use the latest automation technology to aid in their operation.

Coin: Metallic money, minted by government authority, which is legal tender. "Coin" is a collective noun, just as "currency" is. The word "coins," as used in financial institutions, refers to more than one piece of metallic money in a given transaction. Thus, "The teller received her vault *coin*," or "I gave him four *coins* in change."

Collateral: Property pledged by a borrower as security for repayment of a loan.

Collection item: An item accepted by a financial institution for which actual payment must be received before proceeds will be credited to the depositor's account. Such items include notes, acceptances, bond coupons, and nonpar checks.

Commercial bank: A bank that handles all types of banking business, including business loans and business checking accounts. Some commercial banks also offer trust services.

Commercial loan: A short-term loan made to a business, usually repayable in a lump sum, which includes interest due.

Community Reinvestment Act (CRA): A law, the purpose of which is to ensure that financial institutions extend credit, especially for housing, to people in low- and moderate-income neighborhoods from which they get deposits. Compliance ratings are made available to the public and are taken into consideration when an institution makes application to open or relocate a branch or to merge with or acquire another institution.

Compounding: The practice of paying interest on the principal and the accumulated unpaid interest that is earned by savers. This results in the payment of a rate that is higher than the annual simple interest rate.

Comptroller of the Currency: Pronounced *controller*. An official of the U.S. Treasury Department who is responsible for chartering and supervising national banks.

Conditional endorsement: An endorsement that makes transfer of a negotiable instrument subject to a specific condition.

Consumer credit: Loans, usually installment loans, extended to individuals, repayable in monthly installments that include amortized interest.

Cooperative bank: A state-chartered savings and loan association in some New England states.

Correspondent: A financial institution that maintains an account relationship or exchanges services with another financial institution. Correspondents frequently clear checks for each other or participate in large loans, thus sharing the risk.

Co-signer: A person who guarantees the payment of a loan for another person.

Counterfeit: Originally, spurious money, but increasingly, phony checks or bonds as well.

Coupon: A small promissory note attached to a bond that can be detached at maturity and deposited for collection.

Credit: In banking, a term that usually relates to loans. Thus, "credit (or loan) department," or "check credit account" (automatic overdraft). Also, "credit" is an accounting term meaning to increase liabilities or income.

Credit card: A card used to borrow money or buy goods on credit.

Credit rating: A person's or business's credit history, along with present and future financial status, used as a measure of ability and intent to repay obligations.

Credit union (CU): A financial institution that performs consumer banking functions for members of a specific group as defined by its charter. CUs may be federally or state chartered.

Creditworthy: The description of an individual's or a company's ability to repay a debt if incurred.

Cross-selling: The act of selling an additional service to a present customer. Tellers have a unique opportunity to cross-sell because they are in direct contact with customers more than anyone else who works in their financial institutions.

Currency: In banking, paper money. In economics, all media of exchange, including coin.

Currency Transaction Report (CTR): Under the Bank Secrecy Act, the form that financial institutions use to report currency transactions of over $10,000 to the Internal Revenue Service. This is required in order to help to prevent money laundering.

Custodial account: An account set up under the Uniform Gifts to Minors Act (UGMA).

Debit: An accounting term meaning to increase assets.

Debit card: A card used to make banking transactions at automated teller machines or point-of-sale terminals.

Decedent: A person who has died. Decedent's estate refers to the total assets owned by a person at the time of death.

Deed: A legal document that transfers real estate from a seller to a buyer.

Demand deposit: A deposit payable on demand to the depositor or to his or her order. Funds in checking accounts are demand deposits.

Deposit: Funds left with a financial institution for safekeeping or to earn interest. Also, currency or checks given to a teller by a customer to be added to the customer's account.

Depositor: A customer of a financial institution who deposits funds.

Deposit receipt: A receipt for cash or checks deposited given to the customer by the teller.

Deposit slip: An itemization of cash and/or checks included in a specific deposit.

Difference: The sum by which a teller is out of balance when settlement is made. *See* Overs and shorts.

Discount rate: The rate, expressed as a percentage, that is charged by the Federal Reserve for loans made to financial institutions.

Dishonor: To refuse to pay a check on presentation because of a deficiency caused by the maker, such as insufficient funds in an account.

Dormant account: *See* Inactive account.

Draft: A signed written order, which is addressed by one person, the maker, to the drawee, to pay a sum of money to a third person, the payee. A check is the most common type of draft, with a financial institution being the drawee.

Drawee: The financial institution on which a check is drawn.

Dual control: A security system common in financial institutions whereby two persons must simultaneously release control over certain assets.

Due and unpaid: A loan payment that is overdue.

Electronic funds transfer systems (EFTS): A catchall phrase for the developing uses of computer technology in banking.

Endorsement: A signature plus any other writing in which the holder of an instrument transfers his or her rights to that instrument to someone else.

Endorser: A person who makes an endorsement.

Equal Credit Opportunity Act: A law that prohibits discrimination because of race, color, religion, national origin, sex, marital status, or age (except for minors under the legal age to sign a contract), or receipt of public assistance.

Escheat: The transfer of funds in an inactive account to the state after a period of time specified by law has passed since the last activity and after attempts to locate the owner of the funds have failed.

Estate planning: A common trust department function that consists of planning the management of a person's assets to maximize investment earnings and reduce costs and taxes to a minimum consistent with good safety practices.

Examination: An investigation to determine whether a financial institution is operating safely and in conformity with banking laws. Examinations are conducted by state and federal regulatory agencies. *See* Audit.

Executor: A person named in a will to administer the proceeds of an estate. A person who dies without a will has a court-appointed administrator to perform this function; but, in this case, there is much less chance that the decedent's wishes will be followed.

Expedited Funds Availability Act: The law under Regulation CC that requires financial institutions, beginning in September of 1990, to clear local checks after two business days and out-of-town checks after five business days.

Fair Credit Billing Act: A law that requires prompt correction of billing errors on credit or charge accounts.

Fair Credit Reporting Act: A law that requires procedures for keeping credit information accurate, relevant, and confidential.

Federal Deposit Insurance Corporation (FDIC): The regulatory agency, established in 1933, that insures depositors' accounts at most banks. It also conducts examinations of and issues regulations to insured banks that are not members of the Federal Reserve and works in cooperation with the Federal Reserve and the Comptroller of the Currency in bank supervision.

Federal Reserve Banks: The 12 institutions, one of which is in each Federal Reserve district, that regulate credit and the money supply through dealings with financial institutions.

Federal Reserve Notes: Currency that comprises today's most common paper money, which is based on the assets of the Federal Reserve Banks.

Federal Reserve System: The central banking system in the United States, established in 1913, that issues money and performs services on behalf of financial institutions and the federal government. The system includes the Federal Reserve Banks and their branches.

Federal Savings and Loan Insurance Corporation (FSLIC): The federal agency that once insured depositors' funds at those savings and loan associations included under the organization's coverage.

Fiduciary: One who holds property in trust under the terms of a trust agreement.

Finance charge: The total amount in dollars that is paid to get credit.

Financial Institutions Reform, Recovery, and Enforcement Act (FIRREA): Legislation signed into law in 1989 to restructure the regulatory system for savings and loans and provide for the resolution of insolvent thrifts.

Financial Women International: Formerly National Association of Bank Women (NABW). A national organization of women in the financial services industry, headquartered in Chicago, whose purpose is to empower women in that field to achieve their personal, professional, and economic goals while influencing the future shape of the industry. Membership includes officers and managers.

Float: That part of the customer's ledger balance for which the funds are uncollected. Thus, while the total balance includes the float, this is not the amount the depositor's financial institution has actually received from other institutions.

Forgery: The making or alteration of a document or instrument with the intent to defraud.

General ledger: A financial institution's books of its own accounts, as opposed to the accounts of its customers, which are kept by the bookkeeping department.

Guardian: An individual appointed by a court to administer the affairs of another person, usually a child or someone who is mentally incompetent.

Guard key: also called a passkey. The financial institution key that, with the customer's key, allows access to a safe deposit box. It is important to know that both must be used. Thus, the guard key keeps any unauthorized person from opening the box, and the customer's key keeps the financial institution from opening the box.

Hold: A restriction on all or part of a customer's balance, usually placed by a teller until a cashed check has cleared.

Holder in due course: A person who accepts an endorsed negotiable instrument—most commonly a check—in good faith, for value, and without notice that it is overdue, has been dishonored, or has any claim against it.

Inactive account: An account that has had no deposit or withdrawal activity for some time.

Individual account: An account in the name of one person, as opposed to a joint account, a partnership account, or a corporate account.

Informal check: A check on which the amount written in figures and the amount written in words (or by a checkwriter) do not agree. In such cases, the legally valid amount is the amount written in words.

Interest: The amount paid for the use of money. Thus, financial institutions pay savings depositors interest for the use of the funds on deposit, and borrowers pay financial institutions interest for the use of the money advanced to them.

Joint account: An account in the names of two or more people. The "right of survivorship" may be included if this is part of the agreement.

Kiting: A scheme to defraud financial institutions by falsely inflating the balances in two or more accounts.

Kitty: An unauthorized fund set up by some tellers in which small cash overages are collected and from which small cash shortages are made up. Kitties are unauthorized in all financial institutions and are a violation of good banking practice.

Ledger: The final record in which accounts are kept. Savings accounts are detailed in the savings ledger; checking accounts are detailed in the checking ledger. Most ledgers today are kept by computer.

Legal tender: Money, which, by law, must be accepted in payment of "all debts, public and private." *See* Money.

Liability: An obligation. The money in a savings account is a liability to the financial institution because it owes it to the saver.

Line of credit: An agreement by a financial institution to extend credit to a customer up to a predetermined limit. The institution can modify the agreement or withdraw from it if the borrower has a change in financial status.

Loan: A contract whereby a lender agrees to lend money to a borrower. Usually the borrower signs a promissory note, agreeing to pay back the funds at a certain date and with a certain amount of interest.

Magnetic ink character recognition (MICR): The name of the standardized program developed by the American Bankers Association for encoding checks for automatic handling.

Maker: The person who signs a check or note; the person who promises to pay an obligation when due.

Mature market: A term often referred to at financial institutions for people who are aged 50 and older.

Maturity: The date when a note or other obligation becomes due and payable.

Money: Currency or coin that is issued by a government as legal tender and that is accepted as a medium of exchange.

Money laundering: The practice used by criminals to pass money from the sale of drugs and other illegal activities through financial institutions in order to hide its true ownership.

Money market deposit account (MMDA): An insured account offered by financial institutions that competes with money market mutual funds, which are not insured.

Money order: A type of official check sold by financial institutions so that people can make guaranteed payments. Money orders are also issued by the postal service and by retail outlets that are often located in poorer neighborhoods. Money orders sold in stores are usually more expensive.

Mortgage: A legal document pledging property, usually real estate, as security for a loan. The mortgage is only a document; the loan itself is a mortgage loan, though in common usage, the word "mortgage" often refers to the loan.

Mutual savings bank: A financial institution that is owned by its depositors and accepts savings deposits. In modern operation, they offer personal checking accounts as well as savings accounts; and many make personal loans and home mortgage loans. They may also offer services to businesses.

National bank: A commercial bank with a federal charter.

National Credit Union Share Insurance Fund (NCUSIF): The agency that insures depositors' funds in federal credit unions and covered state-chartered CUs.

Negotiable instrument: An unconditional written order or promise to pay money, which can be transferred from one person to another. A check is the most common form of negotiable instrument.

Negotiable Order of Withdrawal account (NOW account): An interest-paying checking-type account for personal use.

Net worth: The excess of assets over liabilities, less capital investment. Thus, an individual's net worth is the total value of what the person owns minus the total amount of what he or she owes.

Night depository: A service offered to business customers whereby they can place money in a secure place until banking hours when it can be proved and deposited.

Nonpar items: Checks for which the drawee financial institution charges a fee before remitting to the institution presenting the checks for collection. This is rare; nonpar checks are not accepted for collection through the Federal Reserve. Nonpar institutions are usually small, rural ones that are state chartered.

No-passbook savings: Also called statement savings. Savings accounts that are similar to regular savings accounts except that a monthly, quarterly, or other periodic statement is issued to the depositor and for which a passbook is not included.

Not sufficient funds (NSF): The term used to describe a depositor's funds when there is not enough money in an account to cover a check when it is presented for payment to the drawee financial institution.

NOW account: *See* Negotiable Order of Withdrawal account.

Numismatics: The study or collection of coins or medals. A person involved in this activity is called a "numismatist."

Official check: A check drawn by a financial institution on its own cash. *See* Cashier's check, Treasurer's check.

On-us: The term used to describe a check drawn on an employee's own financial institution. Thus, a teller who cashes a check drawn on the institution where he or she works is cashing an on-us check.

Overdraft: The amount by which a check or draft presented against a checking or NOW account exceeds the amount in the account. Thus, if a check for $25 is presented against an account with a balance of $10 and if the check is approved for payment, an overdraft of $15 exists.

Overs and shorts: Common names for tellers' differences; also, in some cases, the general ledger account to which differences are charged.

Par items: Checks paid by the drawee financial institution at full face value.

Passbook: A small book supplied by a financial institution to a customer in which is kept a record of the dates and amounts of savings transactions and a running balance of the account.

Passkey: *See* Guard key.

Payee: The person or organization to whom a check or other obligation is payable.

Person: As used in legal matters, a person is an individual as well as a corporation, which, by law, enjoys many of the privileges of a "natural person." And, loosely, the term includes any individual, company, or organization doing banking business.

Point: An extra one percent of an amount borrowed that is charged as a fee for making the loan. This fee is commonly charged with mortgage loans.

Point-of-sale terminal (POS terminal): A computer terminal that enables a customer of a financial institution to make specific transactions right at the place a sale is made, usually a supermarket or retail store. *See* Remote service unit.

Postdated check: A check dated with a future date. The check is not acceptable for processing until that date has been reached.

Presenting: Forwarding a check to the drawee financial institution for payment. The presenting institution is the one that does the forwarding.

Prime rate: The rate, expressed as a percentage, that is charged for loans made to those larger business borrowers that have the highest credit ratings. Hence, it is the best rate available.

Promissory note: Also referred to as a note. A written promise made by one person to pay another person a certain sum of money on demand or at a future specific or determinable date.

Proof: Generally, the comparison of the total of a batch of items with another total arrived at by a different person or a different method. When the totals agree, the items are said to prove out or to be in balance.

Proof department: In many financial institutions, the name of the department that sorts and proves items coming into the institution either from tellers, from other institutions, or from clearinghouses.

Qualified endorsement: A check endorsement with the words "without recourse" or some other limiting phrase. A check of this type would not be acceptable by a teller except with an officer's approval.

Raised check: A check on which the amount has been increased with the intent to defraud.

Reconciliation: The calculations that are performed by a checking-account customer after receiving the monthly statement from the financial institution to determine whether the figures and the balance in the customer's check register agree with those shown on the statement.

Remote service unit: A point-of-sale terminal or an automated teller machine that is located at a spot other than that of the financial institution.

Restrictive endorsement: A check endorsement that restricts the transfer of the item in some manner. The most common is "for deposit only."

Return item: A check that is returned unpaid by the drawee financial institution. Common reasons for this include not sufficient funds, uncollected funds, account closed, and missing or incomplete endorsement.

Right of survivorship: A legal agreement between the persons on a joint account that stipulates that the survivor or survivors are the sole owners of the funds on deposit in the event of the death of the other owner or owners. This is a feature of many joint accounts.

Routing symbol: The number below the line in the fraction-like figures on every check that designates the Federal Reserve district of the drawee, the Federal Reserve office through which the item may clear, and whether the check is payable for immediate or deferred credit.

Safe deposit box: A small locked box within the financial institution vault, rented by a customer for the storage of valuables and documents. An annual fee is charged, and no one has access to the box except the customer after he or she signs an access card or register.

Safekeeping: Rental of space in a vault that is available to customers for the storage of valuable items that are too large to fit in a safe deposit box.

Savings account: A time-deposit account, with or without a passbook. Those without a passbook are commonly called "no-passbook" or "statement savings" accounts.

Savings and loan association (S&L): A financial institution that performs most consumer banking functions, and that specializes in all types of savings accounts and home mortgage loans. S&Ls may be mutual, that is, owned by their depositors, or they may be owned by stockholders. They may be state or federally chartered. *See* Cooperative bank.

Savings Association Insurance Fund (SAIF): The insurance fund, under the direction and administration of the Federal Deposit Insurance Corporation, that backs the deposits of savings and loan associations. It replaces the Federal Savings and Loan Insurance Corporation (FSLIC).

Savings Bank Life Insurance (SBLI): Low-cost life insurance that is sold over the counter at most mutual savings banks in Massachusetts, New York, and Connecticut.

Savings bond, U.S.: An interest-bearing debt certificate that is issued by the U.S. government. Common types are Series EE bonds, which pay a face amount including compounded interest on maturity, and Series HH bonds, on which purchasers receive interest monthly by check.

Savings certificate: *See* Certificate of deposit.

Secured loan: A loan secured with collateral. Such loans are often made at lower rates of interest than unsecured loans.

Security officer: The officer charged with the responsibility for security of the financial institution as defined by the Bank Protection Act of 1958.

Service charge: A fee for service. In banking, this is usually the charge applied against a customer's account for maintaining a checking account. *See* Account analysis.

Settlement sheet: The printed form on which a teller makes settlement at the end of each day.

Settling: The procedure whereby the teller's cash is proved against the day's transactions. Also referred to as making settlement or balancing.

Share draft account: A checking account offered by a credit union.

Shoppers: People from outside organizations hired by financial institutions to evaluate the service performance of tellers and other public-contact personnel. The shoppers use actual services, and the employees are not aware at the time that they are being rated.

Signature card: A card signed by a financial institution customer that provides the institution with a specimen signature for verification purposes. Signature cards also usually contain information about any account signing requirements or restrictions.

Silver certificates: Paper money issued from 1878 to 1963. Until June 24, 1968, a silver certificate could be redeemed on demand by the bearer for a dollar in silver. These bills were replaced by Federal Reserve Notes.

Slide: A form of transposition that is caused when the operator of a computer, calculator, or adding machine fails to add the zeros when entering figures that should include them.

Smurfing: The practice used by criminals under which they hire people to buy official checks, traveler's checks, or money orders in order to avoid the over-$10,000 reporting requirements of the Bank Secrecy Act.

Sorter-readers: Also called document handlers. Machines that sort checks by their routing codes. When teamed with a computer, many proof operations can be handled by sorter-readers.

Special endorsement: An endorsement that names the person to whom the check is being transferred, for example, "Pay to the order of Mary Smith, /s/ John Brown."

Split deposit: A deposit in which a portion is credited to the depositor's account and the balance is taken in cash. Split deposits should be avoided whenever possible because they are a cause of errors and are hard to trace when looking back differences. The customer should deposit the whole amount, then cash his or her check. These deposits are commonly called splits or may be referred to as cash-back deposits.

Stale check: A check with a date that has passed long enough before to be considered unreasonable for payment without verification. Financial institutions differ on what they consider stale; 30, 60, or 90 days are common periods.

Statement: A written summary of all banking transactions in an account during a certain period of time, usually one month, that is prepared by a financial institution for the customer. Originally this term referred to a customer's statement of a checking account, but recent computer advances have made it feasible to provide statements for savings accounts as well and, in many cases, for all banking transactions, including loans and credit cards.

Statement of condition: A detailed listing of a financial institution's assets, liabilities, capital, and net worth as of a specific date. The major statement that is issued is the year-end statement.

Stop payment: An order, given by a checking or NOW account customer, to not pay a specific check or draft that has been issued. A charge is made by the financial institution for processing a stop payment.

Suspicious Activity Report (SAR): Under the Bank Secrecy Act, the form that financial institutions use to report transactions of $5,000 or more when illegal activities are suspected. Financial institution employees who are under suspicion are subject to being reported regardless of the amount of money that is involved.

Sweep account: A type of checking account that allows business or professional customers to have balances above a specified amount automatically transferred from the company's checking account into interest-earning investments.

Teller's stamp: The rubber identification stamp used by a teller. This item is of great importance; it can be used for illegal or fraudulent purposes and should be kept locked up when not in use by the person to whom it was issued.

Thrift institution: In banking parlance, thrifts include savings and loan associations, mutual savings banks, and cooperative banks.

Time deposit: A deposit for which notice to withdraw funds technically may be required. Savings accounts are time deposits, though notice is seldom required on regular accounts. Certificates of deposit specify a maturity date and a penalty is charged for early withdrawal.

Transaction: An individual business dealing between a financial institution and a customer.

Transit department: In many financial institutions, the department that routes checks to other institutions for payment; it is often an adjunct to the proof department.

Transit number: The ABA number that appears as the top number of the fraction-like figures on every check. It identifies the specific financial institution.

Transposition: An interchanging of digits resulting in a difference that is divisible by nine.

Traveler's check: Special checks sold to travelers with an insurance feature that protects the buyer against loss if the checks are lost, stolen, or destroyed.

Treasurer's check: An official check drawn by a state financial institution on itself; thus, it is as good as cash. *See* Cashier's check.

Truncation: The growing practice of storing checks at the financial institution rather than returning them to the customer. Should the customer need a copy of a check at any time, the institution provides him or her with a photocopy. Truncation saves sorting and filing time as well as postage costs.

Trust: A trust exists when one person holds property for the benefit of another person. Thus, a financial institution, as a corporation (or "person" under the law), may administer property for its customers when authorized to do so. Trusts are usually created under wills, by court orders, or by agreement.

Trust company: A state-chartered commercial bank whose functions include trust services. All trust companies offer trust services, as do many financial institutions whose names do not include the words "trust company."

Trust department: The department charged with the administration and development of a financial institution's trust services.

Truth-in-Lending Law (TiL): The law that requires disclosures of the terms of consumer loans so that borrowers can make informed credit decisions.

Truth-in-Savings Act: The law that requires uniform disclosure of the yield and conditions related to interest-bearing deposit accounts so that savers can make informed investment decisions.

Uncollected funds: That part of the customer's balance for which checks deposited have not cleared for payment. *See* Balance, Float.

Uniform Commercial Code (UCC): The law accepted by all 50 state legislatures that governs basic business transactions.

Uniform Gifts to Minors Act (UGMA): The regulations that govern custodial accounts under which an adult is designated as custodian and has control of the assets until the beneficiary reaches legal age. A specified amount of income from these irrevocable gifts is taxed to the minor instead of the donor.

United States Notes: Also called greenbacks. Bills that have a red Treasury seal and were most recently issued in $100 denominations. These bills were originally intended to finance the Civil War and are no longer being issued.

Unsecured loan: A loan unsecured by collateral, made on the signature and based on the credit rating of the borrower.

Uttering: Knowingly offering a forged or counterfeit check or counterfeit money to a person with intent to defraud.

Vacation club: A savings plan that is similar to Christmas Club, the ostensible purpose of which is to accumulate funds for vacation expenses.

Vault cash: Cash kept in the vault as a reserve, under the control of a head teller or supervisor, from which tellers can draw when they run low on cash at their windows.

Will: A legal document whereby a person gives specific instructions on the disposition of his or her property to be made after death.

Withdrawal: An order, signed by a customer, to take a sum of money from his or her account in the form of cash or an official check.

Zero-out proof: A method for settlement whereby a figure is put into the proof machine and items are then charged against it. A zero balance indicates settlement has been reached.

INDEX

ABOUT THE AUTHOR

Joan German-Grapes has been an author in the field of banking since the 1960s. Besides designing bank training programs, her other work for the industry includes co-authorship with the late Donald R. German of the first three editions of this book as well as the *Bank Employee's Security Handbook*, two collections of successful bank promotions, *Tested Techniques in Bank Marketing, Volumes I and II*, and the *Bank Employee's Marketing Handbook*. She is also the author of *The Bank Employee's Fraud & Security Handbook*, a 1994 BankLine publication.

In addition, since its inception in 1969, Joan has been the author/editor of the popular monthly newsletter, the *Bank Teller's Report*, published by Warren, Gorham & Lamont. And, for many years, she served as the editor of the *Branch Banker's Report* and as a contributing editor to the *Bank Marketing Report* for that publisher.

Joan has written articles for many magazines, including *Bankers Magazine, Consumers Digest, Cosmopolitan, Modern Maturity, Money Maker,* and *Woman's Day*, among others. She has also written several children's books and is the author or co-author of eight nonfiction books for adults, most of which are in the field of consumer finance. The most recent of these is *Ninety Days to Financial Fitness*, published by Macmillan Publishing Company.

Joan is a member of the American Society of Journalists & Authors, the Authors Guild, and the Boston Authors Club.

EMERGENCY TELEPHONE NUMBERS

Your Name_____Office _____

	Name of Individual (if known)	**Telephone Number**
Local Police	_____	_____
State Police	_____	_____
FBI	_____	_____
Fire Department	_____	_____
Rescue Squad	_____	_____
Doctor	_____	_____
Backup Doctor	_____	_____
Ambulance	_____	_____
Hospital	_____	_____
Garage	_____	_____
Our Security Officer	_____	_____
Other financial institution officials to notify in case of emergency	_____	_____
	_____	_____
	_____	_____
	_____	_____
	_____	_____
	_____	_____
	_____	_____
	_____	_____
	_____	_____

15353097R00236